Microsoft®

Programming Microsoft® Web Forms

Douglas J. Reilly

PUBLISHED BY
Microsoft Press
A Division of Microsoft Corporation
One Microsoft Way
Redmond, Washington 98052-6399

Library of Congress Control Number 2005934092

Printed and bound in the United States of America.

1 2 3 4 5 6 7 8 9 QWT 8 7 6 5

Distributed in Canada by H.B. Fenn and Company Ltd.

A CIP catalogue record for this book is available from the British Library.

Microsoft Press books are available through booksellers and distributors worldwide. For further information about international editions, contact your local Microsoft Corporation office or contact Microsoft Press International directly at fax (425) 936-7329. Visit our Web site at www.microsoft.com/learning. Send comments to *mspinput@microsoft.com.*

Acquisitions Editor: Ben Ryan
Project Editor: Kristine Haugseth
Copy Editor: Crystal Thomas
Technical Editor: Kenn Scribner
Indexer: Brenda Miller

Body Part No. X11-50072

For Dr. Hans Gerdes and Dr. Yuman Fong of Memorial Sloan-Kettering Cancer Center, and for clinicians everywhere working to cure cancer one patient at a time

Contents at a Glance

Table of Contents

Acknowledgments

It is not an exaggeration to say that without Dr. Hans Gerdes, I might not be here. I have a genetic predisposition to a number of cancers that have kept me working with Dr. Gerdes for many years. Like all doctors at major cancer centers such as Memorial Sloan-Kettering, Dr. Gerdes has access to all sorts of technology that is useful when treating a difficult case such as mine. The technology is useful, but not sufficient. Dr. Gerdes listens to me, understanding my feelings and needs, and helps me to interpret the findings that the technology provides. On two occasions, Dr. Gerdes has referred me to Dr. Yuman Fong, who is a surgeon. I am happy to say that after two surgeries, I not only trust, but genuinely like, Dr. Fong. To both of these fine doctors, "thanks" seems inadequate.

Writing a book is really a team project, even when only one author's name is on the cover. On this project, I have been really fortunate to work with project editor Kristine Haugseth, copy editor Crystal Thomas, and technical editor Kenn Scribner. Kenn especially has taught me quite a bit about how to craft a great technical book. On more than one occasion, these folks saved me from myself. On a number of other occasions they tried, but I insisted on having things my way. Thus, where the book succeeds, it is almost certainly because of Kristine, Crystal, and Kenn. Where it fails, it is clearly due to me alone.

My family–Erin, Tim, and my wife, Jean–tell me I have been a little cranky while working on this book. I find that hard to believe, but I will take it from them. They have allowed me the freedom on many occasions to follow my dreams, and they continue to do so, even when it hurts. Special thanks to Jean. There is little doubt that when I married her, I married up!

Introduction

When I first heard about Microsoft ASP.NET 2.0, I knew that creating ASP.NET 2.0 applications would be a very different sort of experience from development in previous generations of ASP.NET. Scott Guthrie, Microsoft product unit manager in Web Platforms and Tools, introduced ASP.NET 2.0 by stating that the primary goal was a 70 percent reduction in the amount of code developers must produce. I am not certain that a 70 percent code reduction is possible in all cases, but for most Web Forms applications, the amount of code is certainly reduced by at least 50 percent.

It is with that in mind that this book was written. As I worked with early versions of ASP.NET 2.0, I was impressed by how much could be done with very little code. Especially noteworthy is the reduction in code possible for handling database access. Also, database access is more flexible than it was in previous versions of Microsoft Visual Studio, even with the reduced need for code. Just as ASP.NET 1.*x* allowed developers to conveniently describe text boxes and validation rules declaratively, ASP.NET 2.0 allows developers to perform most database-related tasks by using declarative syntax inside ASP.NET 2.0 markup files.

As with previous versions of ASP.NET, nothing prevents you from creating ASP.NET 2.0 applications with any standard text editor. However, I expect that because of improvements to Visual Studio 2005, most developers will use it for Web Forms development with ASP.NET 2.0. This book uses Visual Studio 2005 for all examples.

Who Is This Book For?

As I wrote this book, I had in mind two groups of developers. In the first group are new developers who are just starting out with ASP.NET Web Forms development. For these developers, I have included information on how to take full advantage of the tools offered by Visual Studio 2005 to develop Web Forms applications.

The second group consists of experienced developers who are moving to Web Forms applications after having developed Windows applications or services. Even developers experienced in other areas can find themselves at a loss when confronted with new tools and technologies. These developers have many of the same needs as completely new developers when it comes to using the new tools offered by Visual Studio 2005, although they might find much of the code easier to understand.

Although the book is not a complete introduction to HTML and cascading style sheets, I have included sections on both of these Web technologies. Developers in either group who have experience with these technologies can skip these sections.

Organization of This Book

The book is organized so that each chapter builds on what you learned in the previous chapters. Chapter 1, "The Web Forms Environment," is an overview of the Web Forms environment. Web Forms applications are different from Windows Forms applications, and several of the differences are important for Web Forms developers to understand.

Chapter 2, "A Multitude of Controls," introduces you to many of the controls that you can use to create Web Forms applications that do an amazing amount with a minimum of code. In many cases, several controls might do the job, but one particular control is the best choice. After you have read Chapter 2, I hope you will be able to choose the most appropriate control each time.

Chapter 3, "Web Form Layout," introduces several Web technologies, including ASP.NET-specific technologies such as Master Pages and Wizard controls, as well as technologies not specific to ASP.NET, such as HTML and cascading style sheets. Taken together, these technologies allow you to create attractive, compatible, and efficient Web Forms.

One of the neatest additions to ASP.NET 2.0 is Web Parts. "Working with Web Parts" is the title of Chapter 4, and that is exactly what that chapter will show you how to do. Web Parts are little bits of Web Forms functionality that the end user can customize. For example, imagine that you have a company portal: some users will want the general news at the top of the page, while other users will want the company stock price as the leading item. Web Parts allow users to control the layout and look of such a page.

Data binding is a critical part of most Web Forms applications. One of the great things about ASP.NET is that it allows developers to create dynamic Web Forms applications. The new data source controls included with ASP.NET 2.0 allow developers to declaratively access data on Web Forms. Chapter 5, "Data Binding," covers this topic.

The ASP.NET controls included with the framework are great, and they do almost everything that most developers will ever need. Notice that I said "almost everything." When you encounter a situation in which the standard controls are not adequate, the techniques covered in Chapter 6, "Custom Controls," will come in handy.

Many Web Forms applications require the ability to restrict who is using the application, as well as who has rights to perform certain actions. Chapter 7, "Web Forms User Security and Administration," covers the new features of ASP.NET 2.0 that make administering user security much easier than in earlier versions of ASP.NET.

Finally, not every application is a Web Forms application. But even Windows Forms applications can benefit from access to Web Forms. Windows Forms in Visual Studio 2005 have a new control, the *WebBrowser* control, that allows Windows Forms developers to integrate Web Forms into their applications. Chapter 8, "Integrating with Windows Forms Applications," gives a brief introduction to this control. One example shows how to create a cool tabbed Web browser, and another demonstrates how your Windows Forms code can interact with Web Forms.

Appendix A, "Creating and Deploying Applications in IIS," shows you how to get your application off the development machine and onto a live Web server.

System Requirements

You'll need the following hardware and software to build and run the code samples for this book:

- Microsoft Windows XP with Service Pack 2, Windows Server 2003 with Service Pack 1, or Windows 2000 with Service Pack 4
- Visual Studio 2005 Standard Edition or Professional Edition
- Microsoft SQL Server 2005 Express Edition (included with Visual Studio 2005) or SQL Server 2005
- 600-MHz Pentium or compatible processor (1-GHz Pentium processor recommended)
- 192 MB RAM (256 MB or more recommended)
- Video (800 x 600 or higher resolution) monitor with at least 256 colors (1024 x 768 High Color 16-bit recommended)
- CD-ROM or DVD-ROM drive
- Microsoft Mouse or compatible pointing device

Configuring SQL Server 2005 Express Edition

Chapters 5–7 of this book require that you have access to SQL Server 2005 Express Edition (or SQL Server 2005) to create and use the BikeBlog database, which is included with the source code for this book. If you are using SQL Server 2005 Express Edition, log in as Administrator on your computer, and follow these steps to grant access to the user account that you will use to perform the exercises in these chapters:

1. On the Windows **Start** menu, point to **All Programs**, point to **Accessories**, and then click **Command Prompt** to open a command prompt window.
2. In the command prompt window, type the following command:

   ```
   sqlcmd -S YourServer\SQLExpress -E
   ```

   Replace *YourServer* with the name of your computer.

   You can find the name of your computer by running the *hostname* command in the command prompt window, before running the *sqlcmd* command.

3. At the 1> prompt, type the following command, including the square brackets, and then press **Enter**:

   ```
   sp_grantlogin [YourServer\UserName]
   ```

   Replace *YourServer* with the name of your computer, and replace *UserName* with the name of the user account that you will be using.

4. At the 2> prompt, type the following command, and then press **Enter**:

   ```
   go
   ```

   If you see an error message, make sure that you typed the `sp_grantlogin` command correctly, including the square brackets.

5. At the 1> prompt, type the following command, including the square brackets, and then press **Enter**:

   ```
   sp_addsrvrolemember [YourServer\UserName], dbcreator
   ```

6. At the 2> prompt, type the following command, and then press **Enter**:

   ```
   go
   ```

   If you see an error message, make sure that you typed the `sp_addsrvrolemember` command correctly, including the square brackets.

7. At the 1> prompt, type the following command, and then press **Enter**:

   ```
   exit
   ```

8. Close the command prompt window.

Prerelease Software

This book was reviewed and tested against the August 2005 Community Technical Preview (CTP) of Visual Studio 2005. The August CTP was the last preview before the final release of Visual Studio 2005. This book is expected to be fully compatible with the final release of Visual Studio 2005. If there are any changes or corrections for this book, they will be collected and added to a Microsoft Knowledge Base article. See the "Support for this Book" section in this Introduction for more information.

Technology Updates

As technologies related to this book are updated, links to additional information will be added to the Microsoft Press Technology Updates Web page. Visit this page periodically for updates on Visual Studio 2005 and other technologies.

http://www.microsoft.com/mspress/updates/

Code Samples

All of the code samples discussed in this book can be downloaded from the book's companion content page at the following address:

http://www.microsoft.com/mspress/companion/0-7356-2179-9/

Support for This Book

Every effort has been made to ensure the accuracy of this book and the companion content. As corrections or changes are collected, they will be added to a Microsoft Knowledge Base article. To view the list of known corrections for this book, visit the following article:

http://support.microsoft.com/kb/905046

Microsoft Press provides support for books and companion content at the following Web site:

http://www.microsoft.com/learning/support/books/

Questions and Comments

If you have comments, questions, or ideas regarding the book or the companion content, or questions that are not answered by visiting the sites mentioned previously, please send them to Microsoft Press via e-mail to

mspinput@microsoft.com

Or via postal mail to

Microsoft Press

Attn: *Programming Microsoft Web Forms* Editor

One Microsoft Way

Redmond, WA 98052-6399

Please note that Microsoft software product support is not offered through these addresses.

Chapter 1

The Web Forms Environment

In this chapter:

To say that the Internet has changed the software development landscape is a tremendous understatement. Prior to Web application development there was generally a single type of platform on which applications were developed. For instance, when I first began developing software, I wrote software for glass teletype environments, initially on the Atari 800, but eventually on the IBM PC under MS-DOS. Although the programming languages and the system calls required on the two machines were very different, the overall paradigm was exactly the same. When Microsoft Windows took over for MS-DOS in the microcomputer operating system market early in the 1990s, I found that Windows software development was very different from glass teletype development. I now had to deal with multiple windows and threads, an event-driven program management loop, and a great many more system calls.

However, having worked with one windowing environment, I saw that working in any other windowing environment was still not a great leap in understanding. Although Windows desktop applications are still very popular, today we know that the Web application environment is tremendously important to businesses large and small. But Web applications also come with differences in how we develop and deploy software, as well as significant differences in how we view the application's programming model. The differences are significant: stateful vs. stateless, hosted environments, and a myriad of target client environments. Web Forms applications might need to run on the PC, the Macintosh, or even Windows Mobile-based Pocket PCs and Smartphones, which all run very different browsers. And so, developers must program Web applications differently than they did for traditional desktop applications.

What Is a Web Form?

In the early days of the Internet, most Web pages were not interactive, with the exception of hyperlinks that allowed users to quickly navigate from one page to another. (This in itself was an amazingly useful innovation.) Eventually, though, these static pages containing links began to incorporate increasingly complex, dynamic content. In addition to hyperlinks, Web pages began to include forms that could be filled out by the user to allow real applications to run on the Web. The user interface offered by Web Forms is nowhere near as rich as the user interface in a windowing environment; in many cases, however, it is good enough. Perhaps even more important, although Web Forms user interfaces are not always as appropriate as other environments, they are used every day by users of all sorts, and so may be more familiar.

Developers who author Web Forms applications continue to find those applications challenging, especially those developers who do not have a Web background. For developers writing applications for Microsoft technologies, the answer for many years has been Active Server Pages (or ASP) and, more recently, Microsoft ASP.NET. ASP (also sometimes referred to as Classic ASP) commonly used Microsoft Visual Basic Scripting Edition (VBScript) as the scripting language, and it offered only modest designer support. Sure, Microsoft Visual InterDev was a passable HTML designer, but it provided little support to server-side developers. There were no controls, like those that Visual Basic developers were accustomed to, but rather HTML widgets with no server-side support.

However, ASP.NET authoring challenges have gradually decreased with each new version. The first version, ASP.NET 1.0, was released with the .NET environment. The most notable addition in ASP.NET 1.0 was the inclusion of an event model, similar to what Visual Basic developers were used to. To support this event model, ASP.NET 1.0 added Web server controls to allow developers to more easily respond to events raised in the browser. ASP.NET 1.1 primarily cleaned up some minor issues with ASP.NET 1.0. ASP.NET 2.0 (the focus of this book) adds some noteworthy features, all designed to greatly reduce the number of lines of code that developers must write to create a Web Forms application. These new features include several new controls, provider support for member management and security, and the new data source controls that free the developer from a great deal of code previously required to retrieve data from a database.

Why Create Web Forms Applications?

As I have mentioned, and as I will continue to emphasize in this chapter, developers who want to create great Web Forms applications face real challenges. So a reasonable question might be, why bother?

Web Forms Can Run Anywhere, on Any Device

A Web Forms application can be reached from anywhere, on virtually any device. I often use my Pocket PC Phone Edition to check the Web from wherever I am. For instance, I was recently at a minor league baseball game where I saw a friend wearing a blue wristband. I am familiar with yellow wristbands (LIVESTRONG–cancer survivorship) and pink wristbands (breast cancer awareness), but I was unfamiliar with the meaning of a blue wristband. I was able to quickly check the Web and determine that a blue wristband represents autism awareness.

Web Forms Can Run Without Installation

When you are creating an application for a small number of users, how the application is deployed is not a major concern. When you are creating an application for use by dozens or even hundreds of users, how the application is deployed becomes a much greater concern. The last major non-Web application I developed was a document management system for a major health care system. The application had to be deployed on a couple of machines on every nursing unit in one of the hospitals. It was a very difficult deployment because the PCs in the hospital system were not entirely standard. Each machine installation presented new and different challenges; changes to any PC, such as installing service packs or other applications, could cause problems for the application.

On the other hand, I also created a Web Forms application that was used by three hospitals in the same hospital system. Initially, the application was used by a dozen or so users at each hospital. During an emergency, the application had to be used by over 50 users at one of the facilities. The "deployment" of the Web Forms application was as simple as e-mailing a link to the application to the additional users who needed access.

Web Forms Are Familiar

Web Forms applications look like the Web pages that most of your users are already familiar with. If your users can use eBay and Amazon.com, they can probably use your application with minimal training.

Web Forms Applications Scale Well

The load placed, per user, on server resources for Web Forms applications is generally less than the load placed on a traditional client-server application. A client-server application generally keeps the client and server connected for the life of the application. A Web Forms application connects with the client computer only when the user submits a form. Also, the power of the client computer accessing a Web Forms application is not as important as it is in a client-server application scenario. The client PC needs only to run the browser; virtually all the code runs on the Web server. Client-side JavaScript is the one exception, and generally that code does not involve a great deal of processing.

How Do You Create a Web Form?

Creating a full-fledged Web Forms application requires a reasonable amount of work, but creating a single form is quite simple. ASP.NET Web Forms applications can be created by using any text editor; however, Microsoft Visual Studio 2005 is generally the easiest tool to use.

To create an ASP.NET Web Forms application in Visual Studio 2005, click New on the File menu, and then click Web Site (rather than Project), as shown in Figure 1-1.

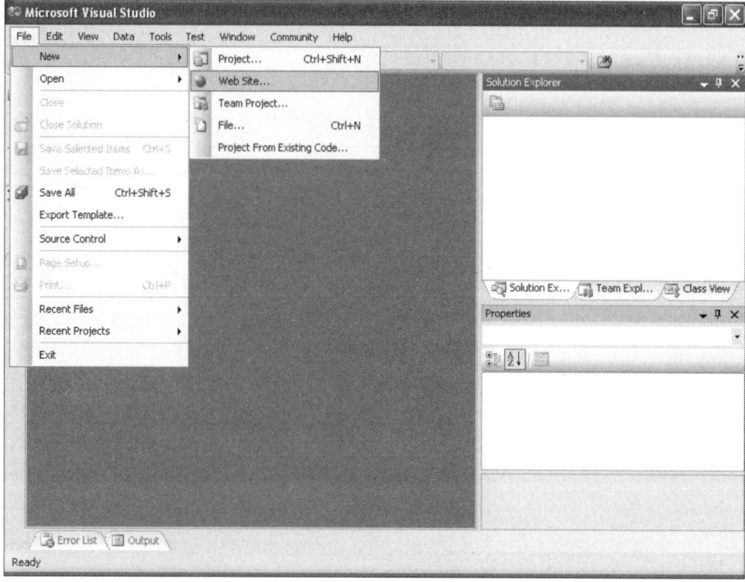

Figure 1-1 Creating a new Web site in Visual Studio 2005

The next dialog box allows you to further specify the exact type of Web site you want to create, as shown in Figure 1-2.

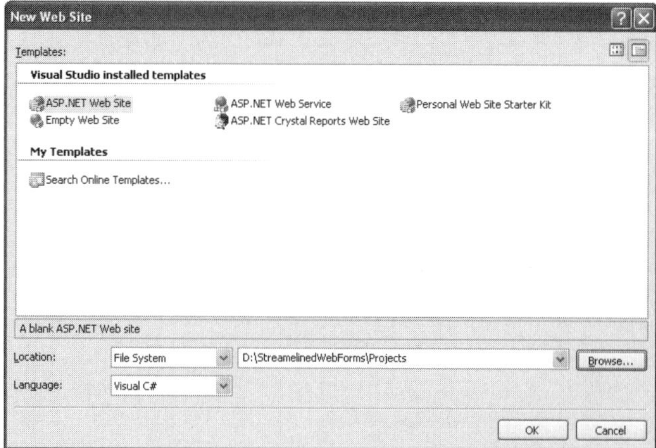

Figure 1-2 The New Web Site dialog box in Visual Studio 2005

This dialog box lists several installed templates. The templates listed when you create a new Web site will likely be different from the ones shown here. For this example, select the ASP.NET Web Site template. You can also specify a location (there is, however, more to this than just selecting a folder–I will discuss this later in this chapter). In this example, I specified a file location different from the default location. If multiple programming languages are installed, you can also specify the language to use for the Web site. On my machine, running the Enterprise Architect version of Visual Studio 2005, I can create a Web site using Visual Basic .NET, C#, or J#. For the examples in this book, I will use C#. Click OK, and you will see a screen similar to the one shown in Figure 1-3.

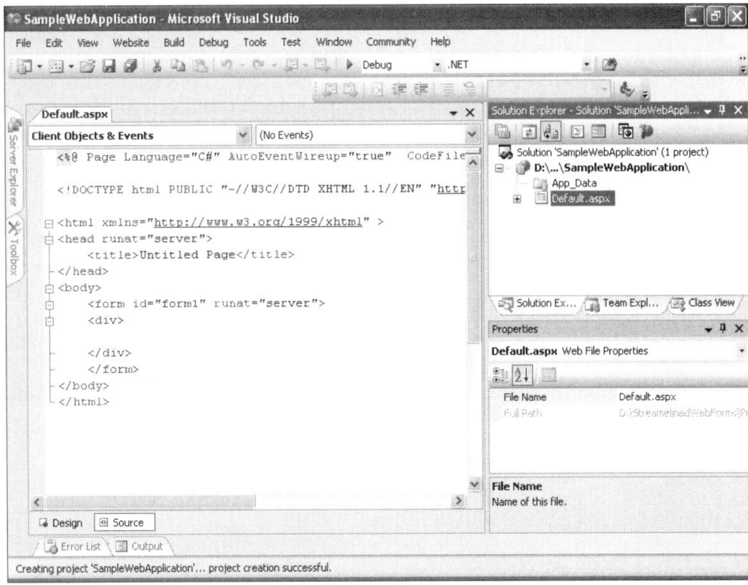

Figure 1-3 A new Web Form in Visual Studio 2005 in Source view

If you click the Design tab at the bottom, the form design surface appears, as shown in Figure 1-4. (Source view, shown previously, will be described later in this chapter.)

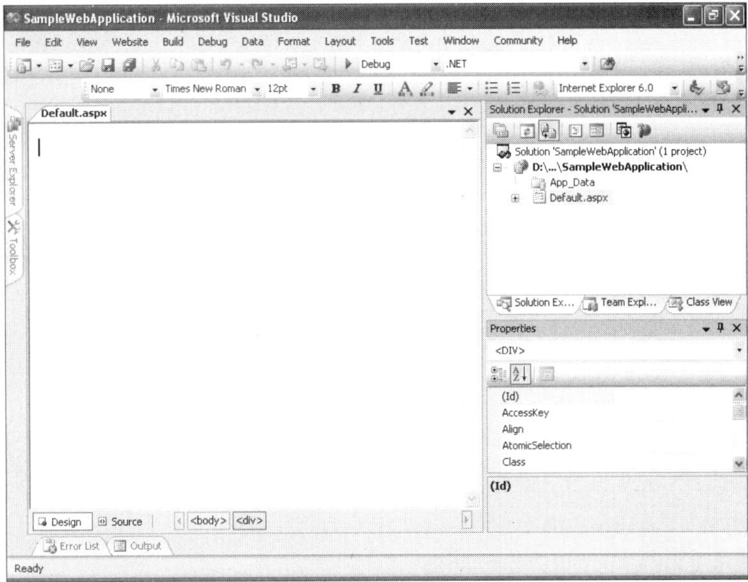

Figure 1-4 A new Web Form in Design view

Note The Web page created by Visual Studio when you create a Web site is named Default.aspx. By default, when you create code for the page, Visual Studio creates a file with the same name as the Web page, with .cs (or .vb for Visual Basic .NET pages) as the extension. Thus, the file with code for Default.aspx is named Default.aspx.cs. Note that this is not a requirement, just a convenient convention.

Another thing to note is that nothing in ASP.NET requires you to place the code in another file (commonly called a *codebehind* file). Visual Studio .NET 2003 and earlier versions essentially required you to use codebehind files. Visual Studio 2005, however, gives you the option to include all the code in the .aspx file. Unlike earlier versions, Visual Studio 2005 even allows the use of IntelliSense technology when working with code inside the .aspx page. When you create a new Web Form, clear the Place Code In A Separate File check box to have all code in the .aspx file.

In Design view, you can drag and drop controls onto the form. Note, though, that unlike Windows Forms, there is no convenient grid to help you align controls. For example, if you drag a label, text box, and button onto a Web Form, the controls (by default) do not stay exactly where you drop them. They move to the upper left of the screen.

Note Visual Studio .NET 2003 and earlier versions allowed you to set a page up for grid layout. When a Web Form was set for grid layout, controls dropped onto a Web Form stayed exactly where they were put. Visual Studio 2005 eliminates this option. Grid layout may sound like a great idea if you are used to Windows Forms development. In reality, it is a terrible way to lay out a Web Form. When grid layout is used, each control contains a style element that hard-codes the location of the control. Given the extremely different screen geometry of the various Web browsers, using this exact positioning, rather than more HTML-friendly ways (such as tables and cascading style sheets), allows you to create forms that do not travel well. For instance, a form laid out with a rigid format that looks great on your desktop PC will look terrible on a mobile device's browser. Chapter 3 will cover Web Form layout in detail.

The result of dropping the three controls onto a Web Form in Visual Studio 2005 is shown in Figure 1-5.

Obviously, this is not an ideal layout for a form. To solve this problem in Design view, you can click to the right of the button, press the Left Arrow key so that the cursor appears between the button and the text box, and then press Enter to move the button to a second line (aligned with the left margin). You can do the same to move the text box down onto its own line. The screen should look something like Figure 1-6.

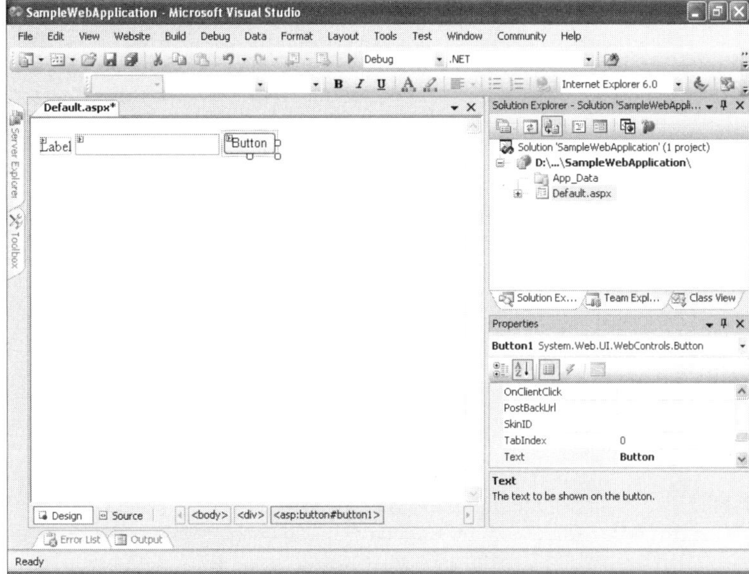

Figure 1-5 A Web Form with a label, text box, and button

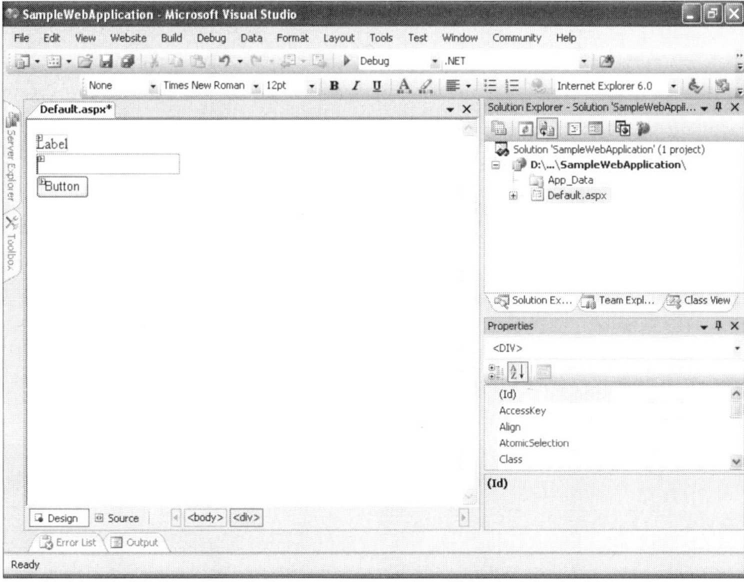

Figure 1-6 A Web Form with a label, text box, and button aligned on the left

This is better, but of course not as good as it can get. It is, however, worth looking at the Web Form in Source view, by clicking the Source tab, as shown in Figure 1-7.

Auto Hide Mode

The following screens show the Solution Explorer window and the Properties window. In Auto Hide mode, a window is represented by a tab on one side of the screen. To enable Auto Hide mode, do the following:

1. Rest the mouse pointer on the Auto Hide button (with the push-pin icon) in the title bar of the Solution Explorer window. See the arrow shown here.

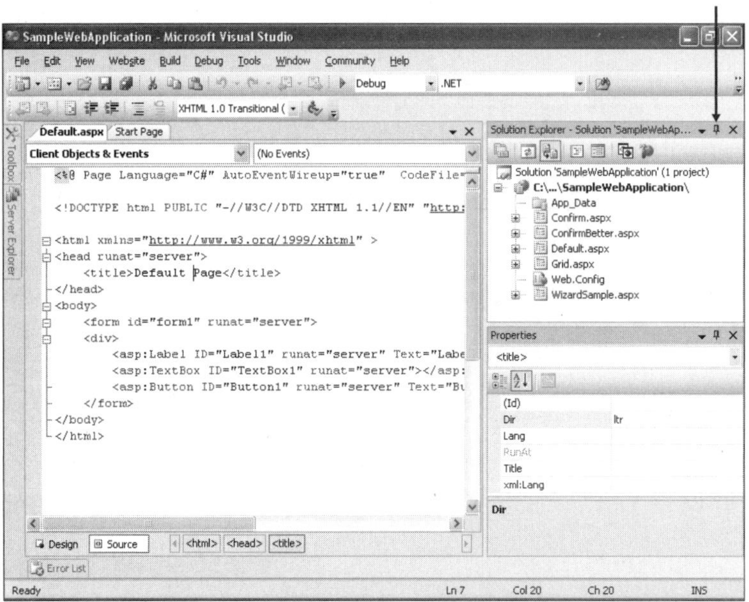

2. Click the Auto Hide button, and the Solution Explorer window appears as a tab in the right margin, as shown here. (Note that the Properties window now fills the right pane.)

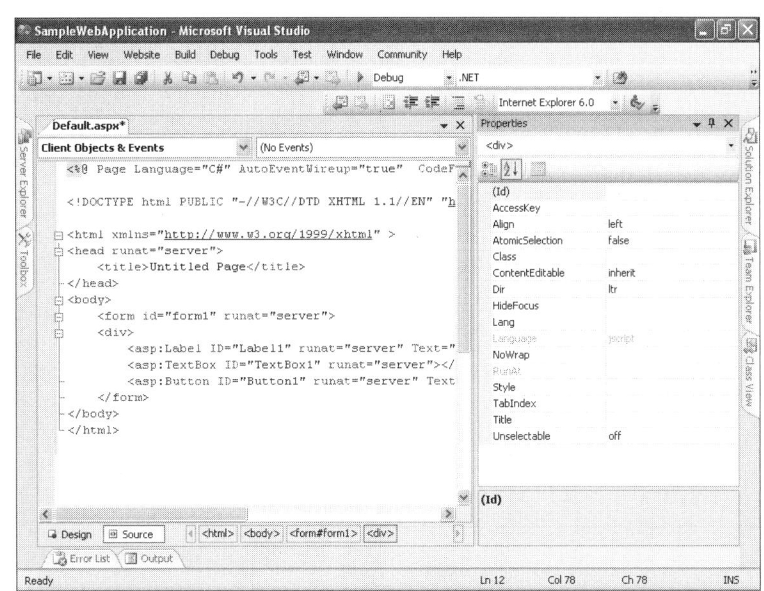

3. Repeat the process for the Properties window (locate and click the Auto Hide button).

Using the Auto Hide feature to show or hide these two windows might be helpful to you, depending on the screen resolution of your development machine.

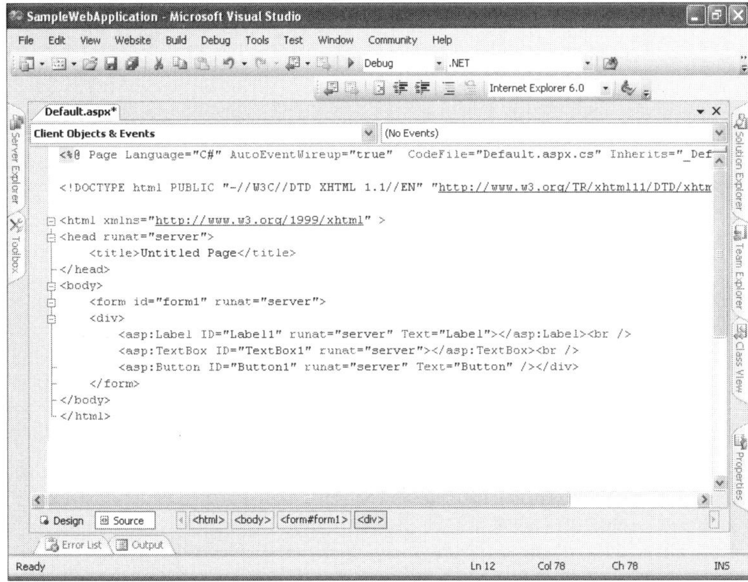

Figure 1-7 The Web Form in Source view

If you had looked at the Source view of the Web page before you aligned the three controls, you would have seen a single difference. Although each of the controls (identified by a tag beginning with *<asp:*) was already on a separate line, the *
* tags would not have been there. The *
* tags were added by Visual Studio when the Enter key was pressed in Design view. The fact that a literal carriage return had no effect on the display in Design view and the *
* tags did illustrates a very important characteristic of Web Forms. A Web Form is persisted using a markup language.

Much of the markup in Default.aspx shown in Figure 1-7 was placed there by Visual Studio. An important bit of markup is in the first line of the source.

```
<%@ Page Language="C#" AutoEventWireup="true"
    CodeFile="Default.aspx.cs" Inherits="_Default" %>
```

This type of line in ASP.NET is called a *directive*, and this line specifically is called an *@ Page* directive. The following table describes the common attributes of the *@ Page* directive.

Table 1-1 Common @ *Page* Directive Attributes

Attribute	Description
AspCompat	Indicates whether the page must be executed in a single-threaded apartment, which allows COM components created by tools such as Visual Basic 6.0 to run on your page. Running single-threaded apartment COM components in an ASP.NET page is a very bad idea, because it can seriously degrade the performance of your page.
AutoEventWireup	Indicates whether the events on the page are automatically assigned based on the names of the events. The default value is *true*.
CodeFile	Indicates the name of the file that contains the code for the page.
Debug	Indicates whether the page should be compiled with debug symbols. The value can be *true* or *false*.
ErrorPage	Defines a target URL to redirect to when an unhandled error occurs.
Language	Specifies the language used to compile code blocks associated with the page.
SmartNavigation	Indicates whether the page supports the smart navigation feature of Microsoft Internet Explorer. The value can be *true* or *false*. Although this feature, which returns users to the same place on a page after a post-back, can sometimes be useful, it can be a less-than-perfect solution in practice.
ValidateRequest	Indicates whether request validation should occur. The value can be *true* or *false*. The default is *true*. If *ValidateRequest* is *true*, and a user enters any HTML markup (that is, as text containing <, >, and so on) into a text box, an exception is thrown. The exception is thrown because text containing those characters could be used for cross-site scripting attacks. You must set the value to *false* if the user is expected to enter markup in a text box.

Source View and HTML

The source code that describes a Web Form is, in various forms, easily visible to both the developer and the end user of the application. For Windows Forms applications, any textual representation of the form layout is not generally directly manipulated by the end user, and only with great difficulty is it manipulated by the developer.

The fact that Visual Studio considers the underlying text representation important enough to make it one of the two views, Source view and Design view, tells you something about the importance of the text representation of forms. Although Design view has improved greatly in the latest version of Visual Studio, some things are still easier in Source view. For instance, creating complex HTML table layouts (which will be described in Chapter 3) can be much easier to do in Source view than in Design view.

It is significant that in earlier versions of Visual Studio, the view now known as Source view was called HTML view. HTML stands for Hypertext Markup Language. To fully understand HTML, it is important to understand what a markup language is. A markup language consists of a set of labels that are embedded within text to identify portions of the text for identification or display purposes. The labels are often referred to as *tags*, and in many markup languages, these tags are identified by enclosure between less than (<) and greater than (>) characters. HTML generally uses tags to identify portions of text for different display features, such as bold, italic, and underline. HTML also contains tags that allow you to format blocks of text, such as the paragraph (*<p>*) tag and the break tag (*
*).

Note Most markup languages follow a very precise structure, with no variation allowed. They are considered unparsable if not well formed. *Well formed* can mean several things, but important among the features of a well-formed document is that each element has a beginning tag and an end tag. This requirement can be met in two ways. Often, it is met by two completely separate tags. For example, text can be marked as bold in HTML by being placed within an opening *<b>* tag and a closing *</b>* tag. Alternately, tags can be self closing. The break tag (used to cause text to break to the next line) can be well formed by using a self-closing tag (*
*). Many Web pages and even HTML references use the break tag (and a variety of other tags) that contain only an opening tag (a break tag would be *
*). Although most browsers accept this sort of broken markup, it is not, strictly speaking, correct.

HTML grew up around some other real browser implementations, many of which allowed or even encouraged sloppiness. For instance, the Microsoft Internet Explorer 3.x browser would properly handle a Web page that contained an opening tag for a table but no closing tag. Other browsers (notably Netscape) did not. Developers who tested only on Internet Explorer often created pages that did not work correctly in other browsers, even when the "broken" browser was expecting the document to be in the correct format. My intention in this book is to create markup in which all opening tags are closed (or are self closing) and all tags are nested correctly. Please let me know if you see any place where I have fallen short!

Although text in Source view looks like HTML, it is not completely normal HTML. A few items that are not standard HTML appear in the source text of the Web page, but for now I will focus on the controls I added to the page: the label, text box, and button. Any tag in an ASP.NET page that begins with *<asp:* is an ASP.NET Web control. In the tag, *asp* represents the *namespace* the control resides in. Namespaces are used in many areas to allow an object to be uniquely identified. For example, if multiple developers created controls named *textbox*, as long as the controls existed in different namespaces, they could be referenced on the same page without any ambiguity. Later in this book, namespaces will be used in code so that the code can be uniquely identified.

If the source code shown in Source view is not proper HTML, how can the page be viewed in a browser? Rather than guess, the best way to determine what will happen is to run the application. When you click Start Debugging on the Debug menu (or simply press F5), you see a dialog box like the one shown in Figure 1-8.

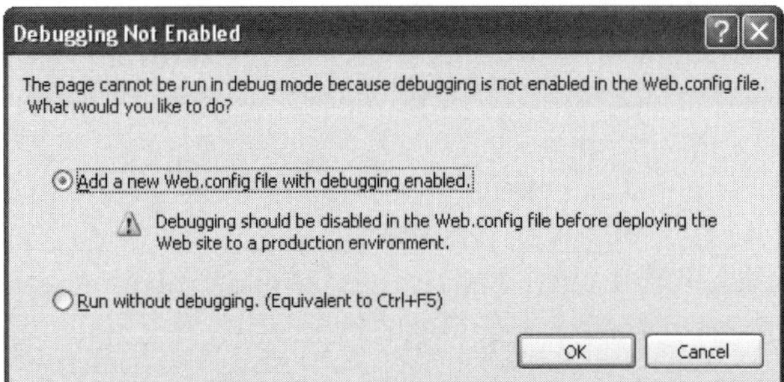

Figure 1-8 The dialog box prompting you to create a Web.config file before debugging in Visual Studio

This message appears because Visual Studio 2005 does not create a default Web.config file when the Web site is created. The Web.config file can be used to configure many aspects of the Web site's performance. Visual Studio 2005 prompts you to create the Web.config file only when needed. Click OK to allow Visual Studio to create a Web.config file that will allow the program to run and be debugged.

> **Note** Another significant difference between Visual Studio 2005 and earlier versions is the way in which Web sites are managed. In Visual Studio .NET 2003, a project file (with a .prj extension) was created along with a new Web site. The project file contained several settings, as well as a list of files to be included when the Web site was compiled. Visual Studio 2005 uses a "projectless" model. There is no project file, and rather than the entire project being compiled in advance into a single dynamic link library (.dll) file, individual page files, as well as other code files, are compiled into individual .dll files. The individual .dll files are not stored or saved (like the single .dll file in Visual Studio .NET 2003 that was stored in the bin folder).
>
> There are other implications of this change. In earlier versions, you could exclude files from the project in Solution Explorer. In Visual Studio 2005, when you exclude a file, an .exclude file extension is added. ASP.NET will not try to compile a file with the extension .exclude.

When you run the application, a browser appears as shown in Figure 1-9.

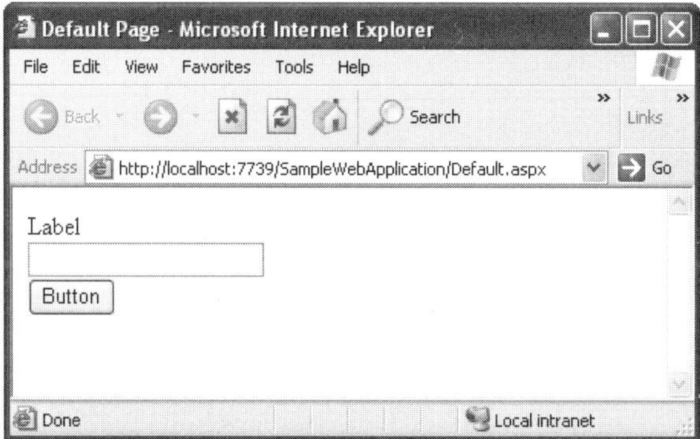

Figure 1-9 The sample Web application running in Internet Explorer

The resulting Web Form shows a label, text box, and button, just as we would expect. One of the beauties of Web development is that whenever we want to see how something works, all we need to do is look at the HTML source in the browser. By clicking Source on the View menu in Internet Explorer, you can see that the source for the resulting Web page looks like the following.

```
<!DOCTYPE html PUBLIC "-//W3C//DTD XHTML 1.1//EN"
"http://www.w3.org/TR/xhtml11/DTD/xhtml11.dtd">

<html xmlns="http://www.w3.org/1999/xhtml" >
<head><title>
    Default Page
</title></head>
<body>
    <form method="post" action="Default.aspx" id="form1">
<div>
<input type="hidden" name="__VIEWSTATE" id="__VIEWSTATE"
    value="/wEPDwUKMTIxNDIyOTM0MmRk9bZa8LK8gUtQIOUvnFGr1uITvLw=" />
</div>

    <div>
        <span id="Label1">Label</span><br />
        <input name="TextBox1" type="text" id="TextBox1" /><br />
        <input type="submit" name="Button1"
           value="Button" id="Button1" /></div>
    </form>
</body>
</html>
```

Although this source looks similar to the code in Figure 1-7, the Web controls (identified by the *<asp:* in the beginning of their tags) have been replaced by standard HTML tags.

This transition, from the ASP.NET markup on the server to proper HTML on the client, is the key to understanding how ASP.NET works. A Web Form is requested by a client (generally using a browser). The server responds to the request, converting the ASP.NET markup on the server to HTML markup that is sent to the client.

Note Only HTML (and possibly JavaScript) actually runs on the client when an ASP.NET application runs. An important implication of this is that the Microsoft.NET Framework need not be on the client machine. Also, both the Web server and the browser are often running on the same machine when a Web Forms application is being created. I will have more to say on this subject later in this chapter.

A Web application communicates between client and server (again, even if both are running on the same machine) using Hypertext Transfer Protocol (HTTP). HTTP is a stateless protocol. This means that, rather than the client browser and Web server establishing a connection when the user first enters a site and dropping the connection only when the user leaves the site, each and every request for a page establishes a connection, transfers information, and closes the connection. Although this is great for performance and scalability of a Web site, it is inconvenient for many applications.

Although HTTP is a stateless protocol, ASP.NET does a good job of hiding that fact. When a client first connects to a Web application, ASP.NET establishes a session. A session can contain information that is added by the Web Forms and then retrieved later. There are limits to what can and should be stored in session state. Most importantly, session state can be a significant drag on server resources if the number of sessions is quite large or if session state for individual clients is quite large.

In addition to session state, ASP.NET maintains another important type of state for the developer, which is view state. This type of state maintains the form's control values between postings. Let's look back at the sample Web application shown in Figure 1-9. If you enter some text in the text box and click the button, the text you entered is still in the text box when the page is redisplayed. Given what I have said about each request being a new request to the server, and given that we have not added any code to persist the text entered into the text box, how does the text get repopulated? The answer is in the HTML code shown previously. The significant bit of source code is this line.

```
<input type="hidden" name="__VIEWSTATE" id="__VIEWSTATE"
    value="/wEPDwUKMTIxNDIyOTM0MmRk9bZa8LK8gUtQIOUvnFGr1uITvLw=" />
```

This is a standard HTML tag declaring an *input* element, with type *hidden*, meaning that it is not visible when the page is rendered in the browser. The *value* attribute of this tag contains encoded text that is the key to persisting values between postbacks. This is a tag used by ASP.NET to remember state information between postbacks. This special *__VIEWSTATE* HTML control is used to maintain page-level information between postbacks. The information maintained in this way is called view state. Rather than maintaining state on the server, view state is maintained inside the page and sent from the server to the client and back again.

View state is useful for maintaining values on a single page, and it will be covered in more detail later in this chapter.

> **Note** A *postback* is what we call it when a Web Form is posted back to itself. When a screen is first presented to the user, this *is not* a postback. When the user clicks a submit button and the server-side code is executed, this *is* a postback.

Understanding Where Code Is Run

I spend a great deal of time supporting Web Forms developers, especially new ones, on *www.asp.net*. The aspect of Web Forms development that causes the greatest confusion for new Web developers is not understanding where ASP.NET code actually executes.

A common scenario is this: A new Web developer has developed his first Web Form, and among the seemingly trivial things that he attempts is to display some feedback using the *MessageBox.Show* method. *MessageBox.Show* is a method used in Windows Forms applications to display a very simple message box. Depending on the developer, either of the following problems could occur:

- The code does not compile, with the complaint that the name *MessageBox* does not exist in the current context.
- The developer added a *using* line to the code and a reference to the Web site so that the *System.Windows.Forms* namespace (where *MessageBox* is located) is recognized and the code compiles, but it does not show a message box.

This example uses the *MessageBox.Show* method, but any number of other methods commonly used in Windows Forms applications just do not make sense in a Web Forms application. The following sidebar titled "What's Done Where?" addresses the underlying reason why a message box cannot be implemented directly in ASP.NET code.

What's Done Where?

The actions taking place–and where those actions are taking place–when a Web page is requested are shown in the following table.

Step	Action on the Server	Action on the Client
User requests page	Nothing	User types URL
ASP.NET builds HTML	C# code is executed and page is parsed	Nothing
User sees content	Nothing	Browser displays content

The important part of this sequence of events is that when the C# code is executed, it is executed on the server. Although the client and server can in some cases be the same machine, that is not normally the case. The new Web Forms developer who manages to get a Web Forms application that calls the *MessageBox.Show* method to compile might get a message box to appear, but it will not appear where the developer wants it to, on the client.

If the changes required for the page to run are made, and the page compiles, why would the message box not appear on the server where the code is executing? To understand the answer, you need to know a little about the way that Windows commonly runs services.

When you are developing an ASP.NET page, you will almost certainly be sitting right at the server as the page runs. However, when a real Web application is running, it is very likely that no one will be sitting at the server when the application is accessed. Often the machine running a Web page is at a remote site, often a site where a server or a portion of a server is rented with good, public Internet access. In these situations, having the Web server running and displaying messages is more than just not helpful, it can actually be detrimental to the function of the application. For instance, imagine that our Web Form with the call to the *MessageBox.Show* method actually did run and display a message box on the server. If no one is there to see it, what should happen to the application? *MessageBox.Show* is a *blocking* call. That means that it will wait, or *block*, in this case waiting for user input. Blocking is not good when you are running a Web server. However, more important than what would happen if the message box were to appear on the server is the fact that the message box will *not* appear on the server.

Why is this so? If our Web application is able to display a message box while server-side code is running, the message box is displayed on a virtual console that will not be visible, even to a user who might be sitting in front of the server. Windows services should not try to show any user interface; even if they do, any user interface will be "displayed" in an invisible virtual display rather than on the monitor at the server.

There are other implications of how Windows services run. For instance, every process running on a Windows-based machine runs under some user context. On the machine I am using to write this book, I am logged in as the user "XEON\Doug," which means that I am user Doug on a machine named XEON. When I do anything on the machine, Windows checks to ensure that XEON\Doug has rights to perform the task that I'm attempting.

Controlling Windows Services

So, how does it work when a Windows service wants to perform some operation on a file or other resource protected by Windows? To control Windows services, you can select Administrative Tools from the Control Panel, and then open Services. In the list of services, you can scroll down to the bottom of the list and double-click the World Wide Web service, which opens a dialog box with four tabs. On the Log On tab, you will see something like this.

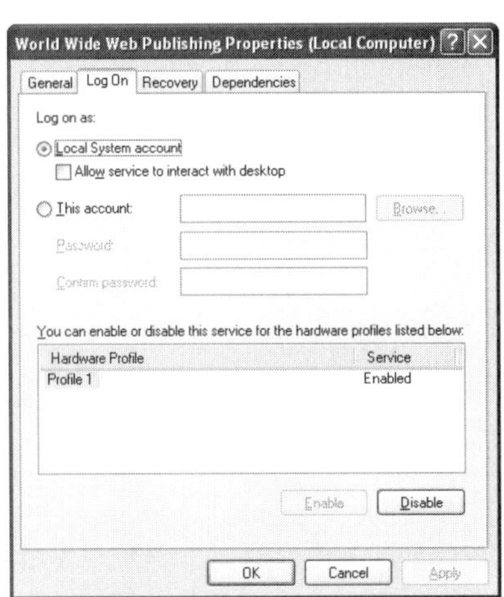

A Windows service can either log on using the special Local System account (as my World Wide Web service does), or it can log on as a specific user. The specific user can be a user on the machine or a domain account. In any event, the user you specify here will be the user whose context the World Wide Web service will operate as.

In addition to allowing you to specify the user that the World Wide Web service will operate as, the Log On tab also allows you, if the service is running as the Local System account, to interact with the desktop. Allowing a Windows service to interact with the desktop is almost never a good idea, and in any case the service must be written in a special way to allow such interaction. Services almost never interact with the desktop, and the World Wide Web service is no exception. Leave this check box cleared.

While talking about the World Wide Web service and the ways in which it works, it is important to revisit the New Web Site dialog box last seen in Figure 1-2. When you create a Web site using the File System location, the Web site is not actually created and run using the World Wide Web service. Rather than using a service, Web sites created using this method run in a Web server that runs as a regular user process. Although now bundled into Visual Studio 2005, this Web server was previously distributed as the Cassini Web server. This regular user process does not run the Web page on TCP/IP port 80 (the port Web applications normally use), but instead uses a random port, and the sites created this way are accessible only on the machine where you are debugging the code.

It's important to note that a Web application running in the Visual Studio Web server can access any resources that the user running the application has access to. This can be convenient, but it often leads to applications that work properly when you are developing and debugging the application in Visual Studio, but fail with some security-related problem when they're moved to a "real" Web server.

You can elect to create a Web site in Visual Studio using the Web server. Rather than leaving the Location combo box set to File System, you can change it to HTTP. When you do this, you are prompted to enter a full HTTP path for the Web site (rather than the full file path), as shown in Figure 1-10.

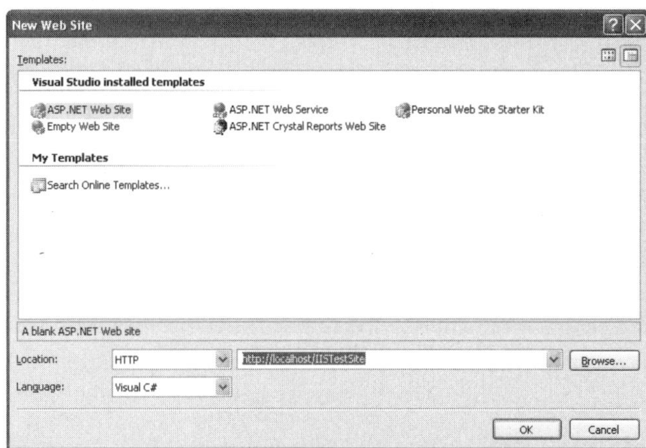

Figure 1-10 The New Web Site dialog box for an HTTP site

When you create a new Web site using an HTTP location, Visual Studio automatically creates the Internet Information Services (IIS) application for you. When you need to deploy the application on a Web server without Visual Studio installed, you will have to manually create the application in IIS. Appendix A, "Creating and Deploying Applications in IIS," explains exactly how to do this.

The ability to create Web sites in Visual Studio in so many ways can lead to some confusion, but this flexibility is necessary. Many corporations will not allow developers to run IIS (which uses the World Wide Web service), and so the easy availability of an alternative way to develop Web sites is important. None of the applications in this book will be affected by the location used for new Web sites.

> **Note** Displaying a message box is just one of the things that you cannot do using server code. There are a variety of other things that you might be used to doing in a Windows Forms application that you cannot do directly in a Web Forms application. For instance, in a Windows Forms application, you might drop a timer on the form and use the *OnTimer* event to perform some task (such as updating a grid). Timers that operate on the server will not work as you expect them to. There are alternatives, discussed in the following section.

Mixing Client and Server Code

Now we know that we cannot just call the *MessageBox.Show* method on the server in our .NET code. How can we do things like show a message box on the machine where the user is browsing (the client machine)? The answer lies in executing code on the client. Ideally, we could use the same programming environment and language to develop client and server code. Sadly, that is not an option.

To run on the client machine, code must operate in the browser. Currently, the only language supported by virtually all major browsers is JavaScript (the Microsoft implementation is known as JScript). Support runs all the way from Internet Explorer on my desktop machine down to Pocket Internet Explorer on my Pocket PC Phone Edition.

Unfortunately, using JavaScript on a Web Form is not as straightforward as using C# in Visual Basic .NET on the server. The client code must be placed appropriately in the HTML, and it cannot be called directly by server code. For example, a button click event can be captured in an HTML form by using code like this.

```
<input type="submit" id="btn" OnClick="HandleClick()">
```

The HTML *input* tag can represent several different widgets on the screen. When the *type* is "submit", the browser renders the tag as a button, and when the button is clicked the form is submitted.

The *OnClick* attribute of the *input* tag calls the JavaScript function *HandleClick*. JavaScript is a very large language, one that has been the subject of numerous books. One of the most common functions in JavaScript is *alert*, which displays a simple message box. The *alert* function accepts a single argument, a string that is displayed in a message box. The exact look of the message box is dependent on the operating system on which the browser is running.

On the HTML side, the client event handler is identified by the *OnClick* attribute in the *Input* tag. Unfortunately, in the ASP.NET markup, the *OnClick* attribute on the ASP.NET Web controls is already used to identify the server-side event handler. To accommodate this, when you assign a client-side *OnClick* event handler, you must identify it with the *OnClientClick* attribute.

You can see how the *alert* function is used in Listing 1-1, which presents the markup for a page (Confirm.aspx) that displays a screen showing the text that the user entered.

Listing 1-1 HTML Source from Confirm.aspx

```
<%@ Page Language="C#" AutoEventWireup="true" CodeFile="Confirm.aspx.cs"
Inherits="Confirm" %>

<!DOCTYPE html PUBLIC "-//W3C//DTD XHTML 1.1//EN"
"http://www.w3.org/TR/xhtml11/DTD/xhtml11.dtd">
```

```
<html xmlns="http://www.w3.org/1999/xhtml" >
<head id="Head1" runat="server">
    <title>Confirm</title>
<script language=javascript>
<!--
function Test(what)
{
    if ( what.TextBox1.value=='' )
    {
        alert('You Entered: NOTHING!');
    }
    else
    {
        alert('You Entered: ' + what.TextBox1.value);
    }
}
//--></script>
</head>
<body>
    <form id="form1" runat="server">
    <div>
        <asp:Label ID="Label1" runat="server" Text="Label"></asp:Label>
        <br />
        <asp:TextBox ID="TextBox1" runat="server"></asp:TextBox><br />
        <asp:Button ID="Button1" runat="server" Text="Button"
            OnClientClick="Test(this.form)" OnClick="Button1_Click"/></div>
    </form>
</body>
</html>
```

A few elements of this page require some explanation. First, the *<head>* section of the page contains a script block. The script block contains a function (named *Test* in this case) that accepts a single parameter, which it expects to be a form—although JavaScript is not strongly typed and will allow you to pass any value. The function verifies whether anything has been entered and echoes the entered text or, if nothing is entered, displays a message box that says, "You Entered: NOTHING!" The *<!--* and *//-->* at the beginning and end of the script block are there to ensure that the page is parsed correctly.

This is a very simple page, but ASP.NET pages can be much more complex. Rather than using just text boxes and buttons, some ASP.NET pages use very complex controls that can actually contain other controls. The Wizard control will be covered completely in Chapter 3; for now, you only need to know that it is a container control for additional controls.

When you add a Wizard control to a page, and then add a text box to one of the steps of the wizard, you end up with a Web Form that looks like the one shown in Figure 1-11.

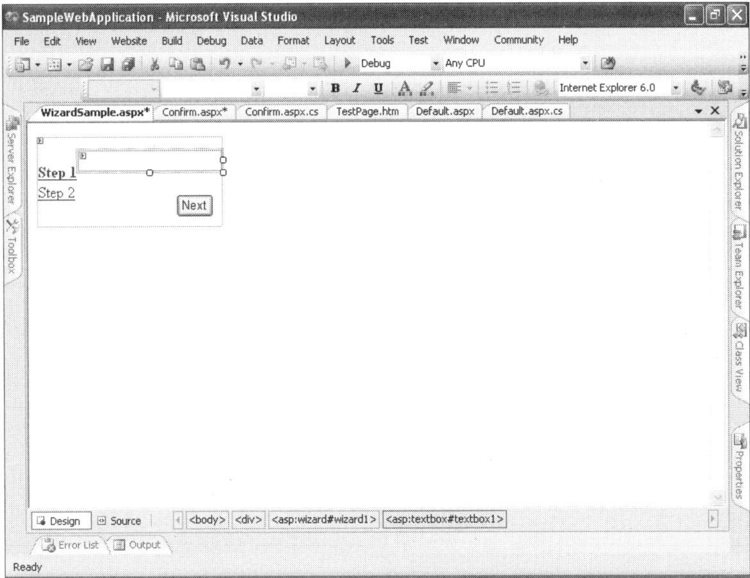

Figure 1-11 A Web Form with a wizard that includes a text box

When you run the Web Form shown in Figure 1-11, the source for the page (which can be viewed in Internet Explorer) is as shown in Listing 1-2.

Listing 1-2 HTML Source from WizardSample.aspx

```
<!DOCTYPE html PUBLIC "-//W3C//DTD XHTML 1.1//EN"
"http://www.w3.org/TR/xhtml11/DTD/xhtml11.dtd">

<html xmlns="http://www.w3.org/1999/xhtml" >
<head><title>
    Untitled Page
</title></head>
<body>
<form method="post" action="WizardSample.aspx" id="form1">
<div>
<input type="hidden" name="__EVENTTARGET" id="__EVENTTARGET" value="" />
<input type="hidden" name="__EVENTARGUMENT" id="__EVENTARGUMENT" value="" />
<input type="hidden" name="__VIEWSTATE" id="__VIEWSTATE"
value="/wEPDwULLTE4ODY2MTUxNzZkGAQFHl9fQ29udHJvbHNSZXF1aXJlUG9zdEJhY2tLZXlfXxYIBT9XaX
phcmQxJFN0YXJ0TmF2aWdhdGlvblRlbXBsYXRlQ29udGFpbmVySUQkU3RhcnROZXh0SW1hZ2VCdXR0b24FPFdpem
FyZDEkU3RhcnROYXZpZ2F0aW9uVGVtcGxhdGVDb250YWluZXJJRCRDYW5jZWxJbWFnZUJ1dHRvbgVFV2l6YXJkMS
RGaW5pc2hOYXZpZ2F0aW9uVGVtcGxhdGVDb250YWluZXJJRCRGaW5pc2hQcmV2aW91c0ltYWdlQnV0dG9uBT1XaX
phcmQxJEZpbmlzaE5hdmlnYXRpb25UZW1wbGF0ZUNvbnRhaW5lcklEJEZpbmlzaEltYWdlQnV0dG9uBT1XaXphcm
QxJEZpbmlzaE5hdmlnYXRpb25UZW1wbGF0ZUNvbnRhaW5lcklEJENhbmNlbEltYWdlQnV0dG9uBUFXaXphcmQxJF
N0ZXBOYXZpZ2F0aW9uVGVtcGxhdGVDb250YWluZXJJRCRTdGVwUHJldmlvdXNJbWFnZUJ1dHRvbgU9V2l6YXJkMS
RTdGVwTmF2aWdhdGlvblRlbXBsYXRlQ29udGFpbmVySUQkU3RlcE5leHRJbWFnZUJ1dHRvbgU7V2l6YXJkMSRTdG
VwTmF2aWdhdGlvblRlbXBsYXRlQ29udGFpbmVySUQkQ2FuY2VsSW1hZ2VCdXR0b24FB1dpemFyZDEPEGQUKwABZm
ZkBRdXaXphcmQxJFdpemFyZE11bHRpVmlldw8PZGZkBSRXaXphcmQxJFNpZGVCYXJDb250YWluZXIkU2lkZUJhck
```

```
xpc3QPEGRkZmQLciREcHz1hDO82HgrQZUD6P3FOw==" />
</div>

<script type="text/javascript">
<!--
var theForm = document.forms['form1'];
if (!theForm) {
    theForm = document.form1;
}
function __doPostBack(eventTarget, eventArgument) {
    if (!theForm.onsubmit || (theForm.onsubmit() != false)) {
        theForm.__EVENTTARGET.value = eventTarget;
        theForm.__EVENTARGUMENT.value = eventArgument;
        theForm.submit();
    }
}
// -->
</script>


<div>
<table cellspacing="0" cellpadding="0" border="0" id="Wizard1"
    style="border-collapse:collapse;">
    <tr>
    <td style="height:100%;"><a href="#Wizard1_SkipLink"><img alt="Skip
    Navigation Links." height="0" width="0" src="/SampleWebApplication/
    WebResource.axd?d=2DwIkOCGwqRaTpfx8kmSBQ2&amp;t=632519130927750990"
    style="border-width:0px;" /></a>
        <table id="Wizard1_SideBarContainer_SideBarList" cellspacing="0"
        border="0" style="border-collapse:collapse;">
        <tr>
        <td style="font-weight:bold;">
        <a id="Wizard1_SideBarContainer_SideBarList_ctl00_SideBarButton"
        href="javascript:__doPostBack
        ('Wizard1$SideBarContainer$SideBarList$ctl00$SideBarButton','')">
        Step 1</a></td></tr>
        <tr>
        <td><a id="Wizard1_SideBarContainer_SideBarList_ctl01_SideBarButton"
        href="javascript:__doPostBack
        ('Wizard1$SideBarContainer$SideBarList$ctl01$SideBarButton','')">
        Step 2</a></td></tr>
        </table>
        <a id="Wizard1_SkipLink"></a>
        </td>
        <td style="height:100%;">
        <table cellspacing="0" cellpadding="0" border="0"
        style="height:100%;width:100%;border-collapse:collapse;">
        <tr style="height:100%;">
        <td>
        <input name="Wizard1$TextBox1" type="text" id="Wizard1_TextBox1" />
         </td></tr>
         <tr>
         <td align="right">
            <table cellspacing="5" cellpadding="5" border="0">
```

```
<tr>
            <td align="right"><input type="submit"
            name="Wizard1$StartNavigationTemplateContainerID$StartNextButton"
            value="Next"
            id="Wizard1_StartNavigationTemplateContainerID_StartNextButton" />
             </td></tr>
             </table>
        </td></tr>
        </table>
    </td></tr>
</table>

</div>
</form>
</body>
</html>
```

Because this is a more complex form, the resulting HTML is much more complex. An interesting aspect of the HTML source is the size of the view state, stored in the hidden HTML input tag named *__VIEWSTATE*. It's huge! Recall that this is a Web Form with a single Wizard control, and that one step of the Wizard control contains a single text box. Some other controls make even greater use of view state. The size of view state can become a limiting factor for some applications. The content of the *__VIEWSTATE* input tag must be encoded on the server, transmitted to the client, resubmitted to the server, and decoded there. Between the load on the server and the burden on the network connection (which for many Internet sites includes several dial-up users) minimizing view state is an important goal.

Another interesting aspect of the page is the JavaScript toward the top. The function *__doPostBack* is included with any page that can cause a postback in a way other than a standard submit button, which includes just about any ASP.NET Web Form. Just above the *__doPostBack* function is an interesting bit of code that requires some explanation.

```
var theForm = document.forms['form1'];
if (!theForm) {
    theForm = document.form1;
}
```

The *__doPostBack* function needs the variable named *theForm*, and this code sets it. Then, if the variable has not been set properly, the code sets it in another way that will work for browsers that do not understand the first way. The Internet has a history of both standards and lack of standards. Although HTML is standardized, the internal object models inside browsers are not. The preceding code should allow the variable *theForm* to be set properly for most modern browsers.

One more interesting aspect of this page (and the reason I am showing it) is the way in which the name of the text box appears in the resulting HTML. The control is clearly named *TextBox1* in the .aspx page, but it appears as follows in the resulting HTML.

```
<input name="Wizard1$TextBox1" type="text" id="Wizard1_TextBox1" />
```

Note that the name of the control in the HTML is *Wizard1$TextBox1*, and the ID is *Wizard1_TextBox1*. Why does ASP.NET change the ID you specified in the ASP.NET markup, *TextBox1*, to *Wizard1_TextBox1*? Imagine not a Wizard control, but rather a user control (a control that you can create yourself, which will be covered in Chapter 6, "Custom Controls"). Suppose that you placed multiple copies of that user control on a single form. If ASP.NET did not create a unique client ID, the page would not work in the browser. Adding the prefix *Wizard1* plus another special character (depending on whether the name or the ID is being modified) is called *fully qualifying* the identifier. If the JavaScript for the *Test* function from Listing 1-1 were used here, it would not work, because the name of the text box is fully qualified.

Fortunately, there is a way to get the ID rendered on the client for any Web control. All Web controls expose a property named *ClientID*. Whenever you create JavaScript for use on a Web Form, it is critical that you use the *ClientID* property when accessing specific controls, rather than the ID you assign to the Web control on your .aspx page.

Configuring IIS

Internet Information Services (IIS) is a real, full-featured Web server. IIS is "real" by comparison to the Visual Studio Web server used for development because:

- You can access the Web pages served by IIS from any machine connected to the Web server running IIS. The Visual Studio Web server can be accessed only on the machine on which it is running.
- IIS virtually always runs on the standard HTTP and HTTPS ports, whereas the Visual Studio Web server always runs on a randomly assigned port.

IIS can be installed on Windows 2000 Professional, Windows 2000 Server, Windows XP Professional, and Windows Server 2003. IIS cannot be installed on any home edition of Windows. Windows 2000 (all editions) installs IIS by default, which has created many machines with a running Web server and no one looking at the security implications of doing so. IIS is not installed by default on any operating system later than Windows 2000.

IIS can be installed from the Control Panel by opening Add Or Remove Programs. In the Add Or Remove Programs dialog box, click Add/Remove Windows Components. In the Windows Components Wizard dialog box, you can select Internet Information Services (IIS) and simply click Next. Or, if you want to view details of the IIS components being installed, you can click Details and select the specific portions of IIS that you want to install. To deploy an ASP.NET application, you must ensure that the World Wide Web service is installed, because this is the portion of IIS required for ASP.NET applications.

Appendix A contains more details on moving your Web Forms application to IIS.

Conclusion

In this chapter, you learned what Web Forms are and why they are important. You also learned about where Web Form code is executed, and how to mix the server code provided by ASP.NET with client code that can enhance the user experience.

Next, in Chapter 2, I will give an introduction to ASP.NET Web controls. The Microsoft ASP.NET 2.0 team wanted a 70 percent reduction in the code required to create many common Web applications. There may be some dispute as to whether they completely met this goal; however, the team's effort did lead to the creation of a new set of controls and enhancements to existing controls that allow for more *declarative* programming. Rather than using so much code, by placing controls on the page and setting properties, you can *declare* how a Web Form should function.

Chapter 2

A Multitude of Controls

In this chapter:

When developers first began to create Web Forms applications, the process was very different than it is in the Microsoft ASP.NET 2.0 development environment. A major element missing from the mix, for example, was the ability to drag and drop controls onto a Web Form. Controls provide encapsulated functionality, and developers can quickly create applications in ASP.NET 2.0 by combining controls. Controls may have fallen short of the ideal of using components to wire together complete applications, but they do offer the ability to reduce the amount of code for common tasks.

Controls can be visual or non-visual. Most controls expose some user interface. For example, labels and text boxes are visual controls. When you place one of these controls on a form, you expect that the resulting form will have, respectively, a label or text box. On the other hand, a control such as a *SqlDataSource* control is non-visual and can be placed on a control in Microsoft Visual Studio Design view. Although a non-visual control might be used by a visual control such as *GridView* or *DropDownList*, non-visual controls do not appear on the form, because they are strictly server-side controls.

Controls fall into two broad categories. The first, and easiest to create, is a user control. A user control is a control that you create just like you would create a Web Form. A user control allows you to drag and drop other controls (and even other user controls) onto the user control design surface, and then create event handlers on the events exposed by the user controls, as well as the controls on the user control. The other category of controls is known generically as server controls. Although it is possible to create new server controls, developers commonly use server controls created by other developers. Chapter 6, "Custom Controls," will cover creation of both user controls and custom server controls.

The *System.Web.UI.WebControls* Namespace

The *System.Web.UI.WebControls* namespace contains a collection of classes that allow you to create Web server controls on a Web page. You can programmatically control the Web server controls because they run on the server.

> **Note** In addition to Web server controls, there is a mostly parallel hierarchy of controls in the *System.Web.UI.HtmlControls* namespace. The controls in the *HtmlControls* namespace provide a very thin layer on top of the native HTML controls. The *HtmlControls* namespace hierarchy is a little more lightweight than the *WebControls* namespace that I will describe here. However, the object model for the controls in the *WebControls* namespace is more consistent than it is for the controls in the *HtmlControls* namespace. The *HtmlControls* namespace very closely matches the underlying HTML controls, and the lack of consistency in the namespace is a result of the lack of consistency in the underlying HTML controls. Controls in the *HtmlControls* namespace have their place when no server-side postback updates are required. I have found no compelling reason to use any of the controls in the *HtmlControls* namespace in this book.

To fully explain the controls in the *WebControls* namespace in a reasonable amount of time, it is best to first describe the base classes used for the controls in the *WebControls* namespace. A few simple controls inherit directly from *System.Web.UI.Control*, but the bulk of the controls inherit from a class that descends from *System.Web.UI.Control* named *System.Web.UI.WebControls*. First, let's look at *System.Web.UI.Control*.

The *System.Web.UI.Control* Class

System.Web.UI.Control is the base class for several simpler controls, such as *Literal*, *Placeholder*, *Repeater*, and *Xml*.

The declaration for the *System.Web.UI.Control* class is as follows:

```
public class Control : IComponent, IDisposable, IParserAccessor,
    IUrlResolutionService, IDataBindingsAccessor, IControlBuilderAccessor,
    IControlDesignerAccessor, IExpressionsAccessor
```

This declaration says that the *Control* class implements eight *interfaces* (the names following the colon that begin with *I*). An interface is similar to a class, in that it declares properties, methods, and events. Unlike a class, however, an interface does not provide any implementation of the properties, methods, and events. An interface identifies operations that an object supports. When a class implements an interface (in C#, by providing the name of the interface after a colon following the class name), the class must provide implementation for every member of the interface. Interface implementation establishes a contract in which the class (and the Microsoft .NET Framework, in this case) ensures that the members of the interface are implemented in the class. If a new member is added to an interface, it should be added to a copy of the interface with a different name, and the existing interface must remain the same.

This rule is not enforced by the .NET Framework; however, changing an interface will result in compile-time or run-time errors.

> **Note** Commonly, interface names begin with *I*. This is a standard convention rather than a requirement, but it makes sense to follow it.

Of the eight interfaces implemented, a few are primarily for use in the Visual Studio Design view. Unrelated to these, the *IDisposable* interface is a common interface that provides a standardized way to ensure that any unmanaged resources are cleaned up without needing to wait for garbage collection to take place. Another interface, *IComponent*, is one that all components must implement to be used.

The most important members of the *Control* class (first properties, and then methods) are outlined in Table 2-1.

Table 2-1 *Control* Class Members

Member Name	Description
ClientID	A property that returns the ID of the *HTML* control rendered in the browser (as described in Chapter 1, "The Web Forms Environment"). Use this value to create JavaScript that will reference a Web Form control on the client.
Controls	A property that gets a *ControlCollection* object that references the child controls (if any) for the specified control.
EnableTheming	A property that gets or sets a value indicating whether themes apply to this control. Chapter 3, "Web Form Layout," covers Web Form layout in general, and specifically theming.
EnableViewState	A property that gets or sets a value indicating whether the control persists its view state and the view state of any client controls to the requesting client. View state is maintained on the client for the current page and returned to the server with each posting. Disabling view state can greatly reduce the size of the page sent to the client. Many controls, however, do not function as expected with view state disabled.
ID	A property that gets or sets the ID of the server control. Note that this ID is likely to be different from the *ClientID* property described previously.
Page	A property that gets a reference to the *Page* instance on which the server control is contained.
Parent	A property that gets a reference to the server control's parent control in the page control hierarchy. The parent of most controls will be the same as the *Page* property, but it could instead be a panel or some other control that contains other controls.
Site	A property that gets information about the container that hosts the current control on the design surface.
SkinID	A property that gets or sets the skin to apply to the control. Skins will be covered in Chapter 3.

Table 2-1 *Control* Class Members

Member Name	Description
UniqueID	A property that gets the unique, fully qualified identifier for the server control. This is a property that in some ways is similar to the *ClientID* property, which allows you to safely reference a control in JavaScript, regardless of what container a control resides on. The *UniqueID* property does a similar thing for the server side.
Visible	A property that gets or sets a value that indicates whether a server control is drawn (or rendered) in the browser. One less-than-obvious implication of setting the *Visible* property to false is that the control is not present at all in the HTML sent to the browser. So, if you have client-side code that references a control that is not visible, the client-side code will not be able to find the control because the control will not be rendered in the HTML.
ApplyStyleSheetSkin	A method that applies the style properties defined in the page style sheet to the control.
FindControl	A method that searches the current control for a specified server control.
Focus	A method that sets input focus to a control.
HasControls	A method that determines whether the server control itself contains any child controls.
RenderControl	A method that outputs content and emits trace information, if tracing is enabled.

Note For all controls covered in this chapter, not every property or method is described in the tables. MSDN is the authoritative source for complete listings of class members. The tables presented in this chapter cover the most important of the properties for the purpose of this discussion. Although lists such as this can be tedious, I believe the abbreviated lists presented in this chapter will be of great assistance to developers moving to Web Forms development.

Properties of controls on Web Forms can generally be set programmatically (in the code in *Object.Property=value* format) or declaratively (in the tags of the Web control). If you have any doubt about how to declaratively set properties in the Web control tags, set the properties in the Visual Studio Properties window, and then switch to Source view and look at the changes to the control.

These properties and methods are present in all controls that inherit from *System.Web.UI.Control*, which includes all the controls in *System.Web.UI.WebControls*. The controls that derive directly from *System.Web.UI.Control* are described in the following sections.

Literal

The *Literal* control reserves a location for static text on a Web Form. Table 2-2 lists the one and only significant addition to what the *Control* class offers.

Table 2-2 *Literal* Control Members

Member Name	Description
Text	Gets or sets the text to display in the *Literal* control.

The *Literal* control is rarely used, because the *Label* control (described later in this chapter) is more often used to display static text. Of course, for static text, the *Literal* control is more efficient to use, since it does not maintain view state and results in somewhat more efficient HTML. I think that the preference for the *Label* control over the *Literal* control has to do with a developer's experience using label controls in other development environments and the relative placement of the *Label* control vs. the *Literal* control in the Visual Studio Toolbox. The *Label* control is the top control in the Toolbox, and the *Literal* control is much farther down. Where efficiency really matters, and where the text really is static, the *Literal* control is your best bet.

In Classic ASP, it was common to write out text using the *Write* method of the *Response* object. Why you would use the *Literal* control, rather than using *Response.Write()*, is explained in the following discussion of the *PlaceHolder* control.

PlaceHolder

The *PlaceHolder* control holds dynamically added server controls to the page at a particular location. You might wonder why such a control is required. In Classic ASP, when you added an HTML control to a page, you would often use *Response.Write()* to write out the HTML required for a new control. The problem with doing this in ASP.NET is best explained with an example.

I created a new project named Controls, which will be used by all examples in this chapter. To this project, I added a new Web page by right-clicking the Web site in Solution Explorer, selecting Add New Item from the context menu, selecting WebForm as the file type in the resulting dialog box, and naming the page WhyPlaceholder.aspx. I added nothing to the .aspx page in Design view, and I pressed F7 to access the source code for the page. Inside the *Page_Load* event handler, I added the following line of code.

```
Response.Write("<INPUT type='Submit' ID='btn' />");
```

The expected result is a page with a single button, as shown in Figure 2-1.

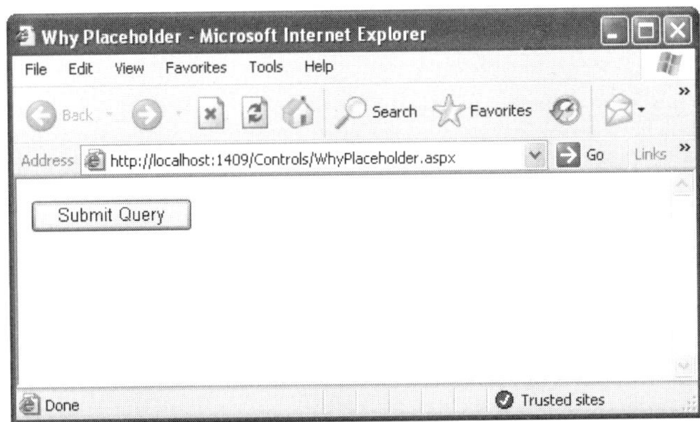

Figure 2-1 A page with a submit button added in the *Page_Load* event handler

So, if using *Response.Write()* results in a button on the page, why would we need a PlaceHolder control? There are two reasons. First, and most important, the control is not properly placed on the page. If you look at the source (click View in the browser, and then click Source), you will see the following.

```
<input type='submit' ID='btn'/>

<!DOCTYPE html PUBLIC "-//W3C//DTD XHTML 1.1//EN"
    "http://www.w3.org/TR/xhtml11/DTD/xhtml11.dtd">

<html xmlns="http://www.w3.org/1999/xhtml" >
<head><title>
    Default Page
</title></head>
<body>
    <form method="post" action="WhyPlaceholder.aspx" id="form1">
<div>
<input type="hidden" name="__VIEWSTATE" id="__VIEWSTATE"
    value="/wEPDwUJNzgzNDMwNTMzZGS8kuieTjLiGMkER51KF6YNnBcsrw==" />
</div>
    <div>
    </div>
    </form>
</body>
</html>
```

The submit control is added at the top of the resulting source, not within the form inside the HTML code. Placing the button outside the form causes a few problems. In general, the form will not be submitted as you would want it to be. In a more complex page in which you place controls declaratively (by dragging the controls onto the form in Design view in Visual Studio), the button is not likely to be placed in the position you want. Even if you use a style attribute to force the control to be positioned visually in a particular location (something I argue against in almost all cases–browsers come in all shapes and sizes), the control will not be correctly placed *logically* in the structure of the page. In Classic ASP, code could be placed anywhere in the page, and it would be evaluated and run where it was placed as the page was evaluated, top to bottom. In contrast, all code in an .aspx page must be contained inside methods in classes, rather than simply where convenient. Because all code in ASP.NET is methods of classes, the code does not have any notion of location within the page.

A second, more important problem with inserting a control as I did in the WhyPlaceholder.aspx example is that the control as inserted is only a client-side control. There is no convenient way to access the contents or events of the control on postback. When you dynamically insert controls on a page, you generally want to insert a control you can access on the server side. The *PlaceHolder* control allows you to add server-side controls at the location of the *PlaceHolder* control. You can then interact with the control on the server side, as well as the client side.

With this background, I will describe in Table 2-3 one of the properties inherited by and used extensively with the *PlaceHolder* control.

Table 2-3 *PlaceHolder* Control Members

Member Name	Description
Controls	A property that gets a *ControlCollection* object that references the child controls (if any) for the specified control. For the *PlaceHolder* control, more importantly, the *.Add* method of the *Controls* collection allows a developer to add controls at a specific location.

To see the *PlaceHolder* control in action, I created a new Web Form named WhyPlaceholder2.aspx. I added a *PlaceHolder* control to the new page by dragging it from the Toolbox onto the form in Design view. Then I pressed F7 to open the code for the page and added the following lines to the *Page_Load* event.

```
System.Web.UI.WebControls.TextBox tb = new TextBox();
tb.ID = "tb";
tb.Text = "Hello World";
this.PlaceHolder1.Controls.Add(tb);
```

The two properties that I set here are not strictly required. However, you should usually set the *ID* property so that you can identify the control when handling a postback. Figure 2-2 shows the page with the preceding code adding the control.

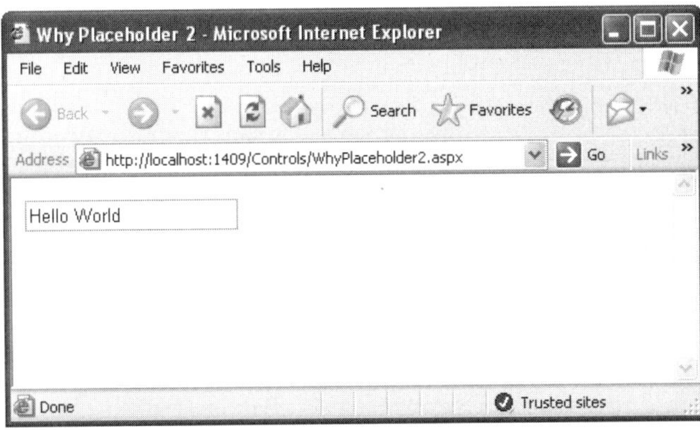

Figure 2-2 A page with a text box added to a *PlaceHolder* control in the *Page_Load* event handler

More important than what the page looks like (Figure 2-1 looked OK in the browser), the HTML source sent to the browser is correct, placing the newly added control inside the form.

```
<!DOCTYPE html PUBLIC "-//W3C//DTD XHTML 1.1//EN"
    "http://www.w3.org/TR/xhtml11/DTD/xhtml11.dtd">

<html xmlns="http://www.w3.org/1999/xhtml" >
<head><title>
    Default Page
</title></head>
<body>
    <form method="post" action="WhyPlaceholder2.aspx" id="form1">
<div>
```

```
<input type="hidden" name="__VIEWSTATE" id="__VIEWSTATE"
    value="/wEPDwUKMTUyNzUzNTM5OGRkv9jclrspkrNAsYfe3C3tJlF6RSU=" />
</div>
    <div>
        <input name="tb" type="text" value="Hello World" id="tb" />
    </div>
    </form>
</body>
</html>
```

Note that the *PlaceHolder* control, added in Design view, does not render any HTML. The text box (named *tb*, with text set to *Hello World*) is placed where the placeholder was in the .aspx page.

> **Note** The *Literal* control does for plain text what the *PlaceHolder* control does for server controls. Rather than using *Response.Write()* to add text to a page, dropping a *Literal* control on the page and adding the text to the *.Text* property allows a developer to control precisely where text will appear on the page. It is still possible to use the <%=*variableName*%> syntax to place text where you want it on the page, but it is not a good idea. Developers creating a framework, like the developers of ASP.NET, have in mind a specific programming model. If you want to add text and controls to a page, the *Literal* and *PlaceHolder* controls (respectively) are the way to go.

Repeater

The *Repeater* control is a data-bound control, often used in conjunction with tables, that allows the developer to specify a set of templates that control how a header, a footer, and items (and optionally, alternating items) appear. Table 2-4 describes the properties added to the *Repeater* control that are not included in the *Control* class that serves as the *Repeater* control's base.

Table 2-4 *Repeater* Control Members

Member Name	Description
AlternatingItemTemplate, *ItemTemplate*	Properties that get or set the *System.Web.UI.ITemplate* that determines how alternating items and items in the control are displayed. *ITemplate* is an interface that defines the behavior for populating a templated ASP.NET control (such as the *Repeater* control) with child controls. The *ItemTemplate* property defines the format and style to be used for each item on the page, unless an *AlternatingItemTemplate* property is defined—in this case, the two templates are used for every other line. By using the *ItemTemplate* and *AlternatingItemTemplate* properties, you can, for instance, create a report in which alternating colors are used on each line for the text or the background. Although it is possible to manipulate these templates programmatically, they are almost always set declaratively on the .aspx page.

Table 2-4 *Repeater* Control Members

Member Name	Description
DataBind	A method that binds the data source to the control.
DataMember	A property that gets or sets the specific table in the data source to bind to the control. The data source provides the data used to feed the *Repeater* control. This property will be discussed in Chapter 5, "Data Binding."
DataSource	A property that gets or sets the data source that provides data for populating the list. This must be set to an object that implements the *IEnumerable* or *IListSource* interface.
DataSourceID	A property that gets or sets the *ID* property of the data source control that should be used to provide data to populate the list. If the *DataSourceID* property is set, the *DataSource* property must not be set, and vice versa.
FooterTemplate, *HeaderTemplate*	Properties that get or set the *System.Web.UI.ITemplate* that determines how the footer (the bottom of the *Repeater* control) or header (the top of the *Repeater* control) in the control are displayed. Although it is possible to manipulate these templates programmatically, they are almost always set declaratively on the .aspx page.
Items	A property that gets the collection of *RepeaterItem* objects in the *Repeater* control. The *RepeaterItem* object represents one of the items to be rendered by the *Repeater* control.
SeparatorTemplate	A property that gets or sets the *System.Web.UI.ITemplate* that defines how the separator between items is displayed.

Imagine that you have a list of people and their pets. You want to create a list of sentences identifying these people and pets, but you don't want to manually read through the list and write out the sentences one by one. The *Repeater* control allows you to easily create a simple page like the one shown in Figure 2-3.

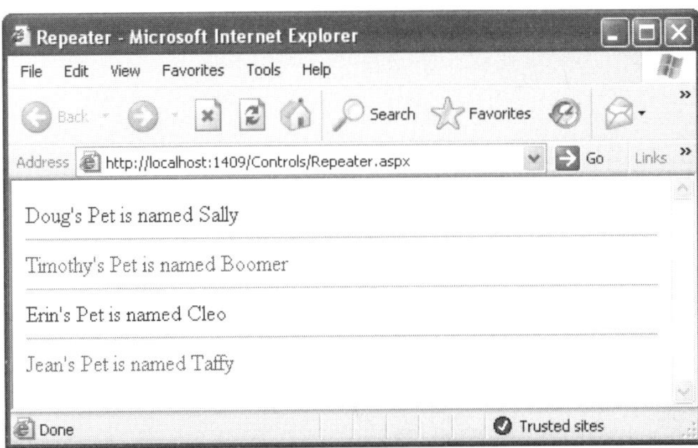

Figure 2-3 The *Repeater* control displaying people and their pets

To create this page, I added a new page to the Controls Web application named Repeater.aspx. I dragged a *Repeater* control onto the page in Design view, switched to Source view, and then added markup into the *Repeater* control, so that the code looked like the following.

```
<asp:Repeater ID="Repeater1" runat="server">
<ItemTemplate>
    <font color=blue>
    <%#Eval("Name") %>'s Pet is named
    <%#Eval("Pet") %></font>
</ItemTemplate>
<AlternatingItemTemplate>
    <font color=red>
    <%#Eval("Name") %>'s Pet is named
    <%#Eval("Pet") %></font>
</AlternatingItemTemplate>
<SeparatorTemplate>
    <hr />
</SeparatorTemplate>
</asp:Repeater>
```

The *<ItemTemplate>* section defines what the items bound to the repeater look like. The *<AlternatingItemTemplate>* section allows you to describe (optionally) what alternating items look like. If you wanted to create a standard "gray bar" report, you could set a background using *<AlternatingItemtemplate>*. The *<%#Eval(FieldName)%>* syntax allows data-bound fields to appear in the item-related templates in the repeater. Generally, the *<%# %>* syntax is used to allow inline items to be data bound. The *Eval()* function allows the developer to access fields in the data source. In this example, the names of the fields are "Name" and "Pet." The *<ItemTemplate>* and *<AlternatingItemTemplate>* sections in this example use a different font color for alternating items. The *<SeparatorTemplate>* section in this example uses a simple horizontal rule tag to draw a line between items.

After the markup is entered, the next step is to enter some code. Pressing F7 brings you to the code file. A couple of steps are required to get the *Repeater* control working. First, an additional *using* clause must be entered.

```
using System.Collections.Generics;
```

Generics are a new feature in C# 2.0. Repeatedly developing the same object is a recurring problem for developers of all sorts of applications. Generics offer a way to create a class once and use that class with all sorts of objects. A common program requirement is to manage lists of items. Before C# 2.0 was available, developers could use an *ArrayList* object to manage collections of objects. The *ArrayList* class can contain any number of any objects. Unfortunately, if they intended to create an *ArrayList* object containing only names, it would be possible to do something like the following.

```
ArrayList al=new ArrayList();
al.Add("Doug");
al.Add("Tim");
al.Add(4);
```

The *Add* method expects an *object* to be passed in as a parameter; because all classes inherit from the *object* class, there is no restriction on what can be added to the *ArrayList* object. This code will compile, and it might even run, depending on what the code does later with the items in the *ArrayList* object. Generics offer a type-safe alternative.

The next step is to create a class to use to supply the *Repeater* control. Often, database results will act as the data source for repeaters, and binding to database results will be covered in Chapter 5. This example uses a list of objects named *People*. The *People* class should be added to the source file outside the page class. The *People* class is shown here.

```
public class People
{
    private string _name;
    private string _pet;

  public People(string newName, string newPet)
  {
    _name = newName;
    _pet = newPet;
  }
  public string Name
  {
    get
    {
      return _name;
    }
  }
  public string Pet
  {
    get
    {
      return _pet;
    }
  }
}
```

The *People* class is a simple class that exposes two properties, *Name* and *Pet*, as well as a public constructor that accepts two arguments used to initialize the properties.

Note A property of a class allows the designer of the class to expose an object by using get and set methods, rather than by making an underlying data member public. More importantly, properties allow the designer of a class to expose a synthesized value, a value that does not actually exist directly in the underlying class. For instance, a class could contain private data members for the unit cost and quantity of a line of an order, and expose a *LineTotal* property that, when called, calculates the line total by multiplying quantity by unit cost. In other cases, properties can be used to allow lazy initialization. For instance, a class might have a property that is derived from a time-consuming database query. If the property is not needed, the database query will never be made. If the property is needed, it is calculated when needed (and perhaps cached for future use). The properties in the *People* class have only getters defined, and so the properties are read-only.

The next step is to add some code to the *Page_Load* event handler to create the list of people and set that list as the *DataSource* property. The *DataSource* property on many controls specifies where the data for the control will come from. Most often, the *DataSource* property is set to a database-related data source, which will be discussed in Chapter 5. Here is the code.

```
List<People> peeps=new List<People>();
peeps.Add(new People("Doug","Sally"));
peeps.Add(new People("Timothy","Boomer"));
peeps.Add(new People("Erin","Cleo"));
peeps.Add(new People("Jean", "Taffy"));

this.Repeater1.DataSource=peeps;
this.Repeater1.DataBind();
```

The *List<T>* class is one of the generic classes. When a generic class is described, *<T>* is used as a placeholder of any type. In the preceding code from the *Page_Load* event handler, the *<T>* is replaced by *<People>*, creating a list of people named *peeps*. Using the *List<T>* class, the *.Add()* method is type-safe and will only allow addition of objects of the correct type. The next four lines each add a new instance of the *People* class to the *peeps* list. The last two lines set the *DataSource* property of the *Repeater* class and call *DataBind()*, which sets the *Items* collection of the *Repeater* class.

Note In the MSDN documentation for the *WebControls* classes, the *Repeater* control is not grouped with either the list controls or the data list controls, although arguably it might be grouped with either of these.

Xml

The *Xml* control can be used to transform an XML document using Extensible Stylesheet Language Transformations (XSLT). The *Xml* control also inherits directly from the *System.Web.UI.Control* class. Some additional properties and methods are added to the *Xml* control, and the important ones are described in Table 2-5.

Table 2-5 *Xml* Control Members

Member Name	Description
DocumentContent	A property that sets a string that contains the XML document to display in the *Xml* control.
DocumentSource	A property that gets or sets the path to an XML document to display in the *Xml* control.
Transform	A property that gets or sets the path to the XSLT transform object that formats the XML document before it is written to the output stream.
TransformArgumentList	A property that gets or sets a list of optional arguments passed to the style sheet used for XSLT.
TransformSource	A property that gets or sets the path to an XSLT style sheet that formats the XML document before it is written to the output stream.

The *Xml* control is commonly used to take an XML document and transform it using an XSLT style sheet. For example, an XML document might contain information on a menu and the URLs the menu items refer to, and the XSLT style sheet will transform that information into appropriate HTML to display a menu.

The *System.Web.UI.WebControl* Class

The bulk of Web controls derive from the *System.Web.UI.WebControl* class. The *WebControl* class derives from the *Control* class, and so do all of the properties and methods mentioned in the preceding section on the *System.Web.UI.Control* class. Most of the properties added in the *WebControl* class fall into two categories: properties that assist with a control gaining focus, and properties that control the appearance of the control. These are described in Table 2-6.

Table 2-6 *WebControl* Class Members

Member Name	Description
AccessKey	A property that gets or sets the access key that allows you to quickly set focus on the control.
Attributes	A property that gets a collection of arbitrary attributes that can be added to the rendered client control. For instance, a bad use of this collection is to add a *Value* attribute to a text box control set to Password mode. Text boxes in Password mode do not allow default text (because of the security risk), but by using the *Attributes* property, you can overcome this limitation. But you should not!
BackColor, BorderColor, BorderStyle, BorderWidth, Font, ForeColor, Height, Style, Width	Properties that control the appearance of the control, as you would expect. The *Font* property is a complex data type that describes all aspects of the font, and the *Style* property is a collection of text attributes to be rendered as the style attribute of the outer HTML control.
CssClass	A property that gets or sets the cascading style sheet class. More information is provided in Chapter 3.
Enabled	A property that gets or sets a value indicating whether the control is enabled. Disabled controls are commonly displayed so that it is apparent that they are disabled.
EnableTheming	A property that gets or sets a value indicating whether themes will apply to this control.
TabIndex	A property that gets or sets the tab index of the control. This defines the order in which controls will be visited as the user presses the Tab key. Generally, using the default order (left to right, top to bottom) is best.
ToolTip	A property that gets or sets text used for the ToolTip, which appears in a popup window when the mouse rests on the control.

A couple dozen controls derive directly or indirectly from the *WebControl* class. I will cover the majority of those controls in this section, omitting the table-related controls and the *AdRotator* control.

Button

Almost every page will have a button, and the *Button* control is used on virtually every example in this book. Traditionally, Web applications required a button to initiate a postback. With creative use of JavaScript, all sorts of controls can now cause a postback, but the button is still the most frequently used. Table 2-7 describes the additional properties, methods, and events of the *Button* control that are not included in the *WebControl* class.

Table 2-7 *Button* Control Members

Member Name	Description
CausesValidation	A property that gets or sets a value that controls whether the button causes validation. Validator controls (discussed later in this chapter) can prevent submission of a form with invalid or incomplete information. This is not always the right thing to do; for instance, a Cancel button should not check for correct and complete entries.
CommandName	A property that gets or sets the name passed to the *Command* event.
OnClientClick	A property that gets or sets the client-side script that will be executed on the client when the button is clicked.
PostBackUrl	A property that gets or sets the URL of the page to post back to when the button is clicked. ASP.NET 1.x did not allow postbacks to a different page, but ASP.NET 2.0 does. This is a feature that I have seldom found useful, because I prefer to have all the logic associated with a particular page on that page. All example pages in this book will post back to themselves.
Text	A property that gets or sets the text for the button caption. *Text* is a property common to many controls that derive from the *WebControl* class.
UseSubmitBehavior	A property that gets or sets a value indicating whether the button uses the client browser's submit mechanism or the ASP.NET framework. If *true*, the standard HTML submit behavior is used; if *false*, JavaScript is used.
ValidationGroup	A property that gets or sets the group of controls for which the button causes validation. In ASP.NET 1.1, all validators were fired for any form submission. ASP.NET 2.0 allows the developer to assign each button to a group of validators so that multiple zones on the form can be validated independently. For instance, a single Web Form with a set of controls that allows a user to log in and register can validate the control sets separately, depending on whether the Login or Register button is clicked.
Click, Command	Events fired when the button is clicked.

Checkbox

The *Checkbox* control is used to select a true or false value. The *Checkbox* control is usually rendered as a box that toggles a check mark in the box when clicked. Multiple check boxes are often used together to allow selection of multiple, non-exclusive items. Often, the *CheckBoxList* control, described later in this chapter, is more appropriate for creating multiple check boxes that should act as a single group. Table 2-8 shows significant *Checkbox* control members.

Table 2-8 *Checkbox* Control Members

Member Name	Description
AutoPostback	A property that gets or sets a value that controls whether the check box automatically posts back when the control is clicked. Many of the controls that derive from the *WebControl* class contain an *AutoPostback* property. Note that the *AutoPostback* behavior is dependent on JavaScript working on the client.
Checked	A property that gets or sets a value indicating whether the check box is selected.
Text	A property that gets or sets the text associated with the check box.
TextAlign	A property that gets or sets a value from the *TextAlign* enumeration, either *Left* or *Right*, indicating whether the text should appear to the left or right of the check box.
CheckedChanged	An event fired when the checked state of the control is changed. This event is fired immediately if *AutoPostback* is *true* and the client browser supports JavaScript.

RadioButton

The *RadioButton* control inherits directly from the *Checkbox* control, so the two controls are similar and share the properties and event shown in Table 2-8. The *RadioButton* control is often rendered as a circle, and when clicked, a dot inside the circle toggles. When two or more radio buttons (also called option buttons) are placed together, any currently selected button is deselected when any one of the buttons is clicked. The action is similar to the mechanical buttons used on car radios in the 1970s and earlier, hence the name. Often the *RadioButtonList* control, described later in this chapter, is more appropriate for creating multiple radio buttons that should act as one.

HyperLink

The *HyperLink* control creates a link on a Web page, commonly used to allow a user to jump to another page. Table 2-9 shows the important members of the *Hyperlink* control class.

Table 2-9 *Hyperlink* Control Members

Member Name	Description
ImageUrl	A property that gets or sets a URL to use for an image when an image link is desired over a text link.
NavigateUrl	A property that gets or sets the URL that the user will navigate to when the *HyperLink* control is clicked.
Text	A property that gets or sets the text for the *HyperLink* control. If both the *Text* property and the *ImageUrl* property are set, the *ImageUrl* property will prevail, and the image will be displayed rather than the text specified in this property.

Image

The *Image* control allows you to display an image on the page. Table 2-10 introduces significant members of the *Image* control class.

Table 2-10 *Image* Control Members

Member Name	Description
AlternateText	A property that gets or sets text to display when the image is unavailable. Alternate text is especially useful for visually impaired users.
ImageUrl	A property that gets or sets a URL to use for the image that you want to display.

ImageButton

The *ImageButton* control's base class is the *Image* control just described. The *ImageButton* control is rendered much like an *Image* control, and it behaves in a way that might seem similar to the *HyperLink* control. The difference is that rather than redirecting the user to another page, the *ImageButton* control causes a post back to the page on which the control resides. The *ImageButton* control does this by using JavaScript; if JavaScript is disabled, or if the underlying JavaScript is in some way broken, the *ImageButton* control will not work.

> **Note** How big of a problem is this? For me, it sometimes can be a major problem. For instance, I have a weblog at *http://weblogs.asp.net/dreilly*. This is a wonderful site, and it provides me with a free place to host my thoughts on all things computer related. Unfortunately, I cannot administer the site from my Pocket PC (something that is often quite convenient) because the site uses some variation on an *ImageButton* control for its login page. And even though the Pocket PC supports JavaScript, it seems not to like the specific JavaScript used on the login page.

Table 2-11 introduces the important members of the *ImageButton* control class.

Table 2-11 *ImageButton* Control Members

Member Name	Description
AlternateText	A property that gets or sets text to display when the image is unavailable. Alternate text is especially useful for visually impaired users.
CausesValidation	A property that gets or sets a value that controls whether the button causes validation. Validator controls (discussed later in this chapter) can prevent submission of a form with invalid or incomplete information. This is not always the right thing to do; for instance, a Cancel button should not check for correct and complete entries.

Table 2-11 *ImageButton* Control Members

Member Name	Description
CommandArgument, *CommandName*	Properties that can be set to allow a single event handler to manage multiple *ImageButton OnClick* events. The *CommandName* and *CommandArgument* properties can be set to allow the single *OnClick* event to determine the source of the click.
Click, *Command*	Events fired when the *ImageButton* control is clicked.

Label

The *Label* control is used to display text in a way very similar to the *Literal* control previously described. The distinction between the *Label* and the *Literal* controls is primarily that the *Label* control contains the properties that it inherits from the *WebControl* class for greater control over the appearance of rendered text.

Panel

The *Panel* control acts as a container for other controls. Using a *Panel* control allows you to control the visibility of a group of controls at once. This can be useful when you select an option on a form that might require entry of additional fields. The panel can be made visible or invisible based on an entry in another field. A few significant properties are added by the *Panel* control, as described in Table 2-12.

Table 2-12 *Panel* Control Members

Member Name	Description
BackgroundUrl	A property that gets or sets the URL of an image to be used as the background of the *Panel* control.
DefaultButton	A property that gets or sets the button to be used as the default button. The default button is the button to be clicked when the Enter key is pressed. This property is also available for the form as a whole.
GroupingText	A property that gets or sets text to be used as the title for a group box to appear around the *Panel* control.
HorizontalAlign	A property that gets or sets a value to align text in the *Panel* control. The value must be from the *HorizontalAlign* enumeration: *Center*, *Justify*, *Left*, *NotSet*, or *Right*. The default is *NotSet*.
ScrollBars	A property that gets or sets a value to control the appearance of scroll bars on the *Panel* control. The value must be from the *ScrollBars* enumeration: *Auto*, *Both*, *Horizontal*, *None*, or *Vertical*. The default is *None*.
Wrap	A property that gets or sets a Boolean value indicating whether content in the panel should wrap.

TextBox

The workhorse of the Web controls is the *TextBox* control. The *TextBox* control allows the user to enter text, and it can be rendered as a simple text box, as a multiline text box (an HTML

TextArea control), or a password text box. Several properties are added by the *TextBox* control, as described in Table 2-13.

Table 2-13 *TextBox* Control Members

Member Name	Description
AutoCompleteType	A property that gets or sets a value indicating the type of automatic completion that should occur. The value must be one of the *AutoCompleteType* enumeration values. There are a large number of values, documented in the MSDN documentation. For example, if you enter "Douglas Reilly" in a *TextBox* control where the *AutoCompleteType* property is set to *DisplayName*, the next time you enter a value into a text box with *AutoCompleteType* set to *DisplayName*, Microsoft Internet Explorer will offer "Douglas Reilly" as an option in the autocomplete drop-down list.
AutoPostBack	A property that gets or sets a Boolean value indicating whether the page should be posted back whenever the text is changed and the user leaves the field. Note that this relies on JavaScript being active, and an event handler for the *TextChanged* event should be defined (more on the *TextChanged* event is provided at the end of this table).
Columns	A property that gets or sets the width, in characters, of the text box. Note that the *MaxLength* property actually sets the maximum number of characters that can be entered into the text box.
ReadOnly	A property that gets or sets a Boolean value that controls whether the *TextBox* control should be rendered as read-only (not allowing modification). Sometimes it is useful to display static text in a text box rather than as part of a label.
Rows	A property that gets or sets an integer value indicating the number of rows in a multiline *TextBox* control. See the *TextMode* property for more information on creating a multiline text box.
Text	A property that gets or sets a string to be displayed in the *TextBox* control.
TextMode	A property that gets or sets a value indicating the type of text box that should be rendered. This must be one of the values in the *TextBoxMode* enumeration: *MultiLine*, *Password*, or *SingleLine*. *SingleLine* is the default, and it renders as a traditional text box. *MultiLine* renders as an HTML *TextArea* control rather than an *Input* control, and *MaxLength* is not honored. When the *TextMode* property is set to *Password*, characters entered are echoed as asterisks. Also, the *Text* property is not rendered to the browser, because the text would appear in plain text in the browser. This can be overcome by explicitly setting an attribute of the *TextBox* control, but this is not recommended.
Wrap	A property that gets or sets a Boolean value indicating whether text should wrap in a multiline text box.
TextChanged	An event fired when the text in a *TextBox* control is changed and the user leaves the control. Note that this method is generally only useful when the *AutoPostBack* property is *true*.

Note The *Panel* and *TextBox* controls both expose a *Wrap* property. These properties are independently implemented in both of these controls, but they do point out an important reason why using the controls in the *WebControls* namespace is preferable to using the controls in the *HtmlControls* namespace. The controls in the *WebControls* namespace provide a more consistent object model; properties that do the same thing have the same name. The *HtmlControls* programming model merely mimics the underlying HTML tags and therefore has very little consistency from a programming model perspective.

Calendar

A common requirement for any data entry screen, whether Web Form or Microsoft Windows Form, is date entry. The *Calendar* control displays a single month at a time, and it allows the user to navigate between months. The *Calendar* control exposes several new properties, as described in Table 2-14.

Table 2-14 *Calendar* Control Members

Member Name	Description
Caption	A property that gets or sets a string to be used as a caption, or title, for the calendar.
CaptionAlign	A property that gets or sets a value indicating the alignment of the caption. The value must be a member of the *TableCaptionAlign* enumeration: *Bottom*, *Left*, *NotSet*, *Right*, or *Top*. *NotSet* is the default.
CellPadding	A property that gets or sets a value indicating the amount of space between the content and the border of the cell.
CellSpacing	A property that gets or sets a value indicating the amount of space between cells.
DayHeaderStyle, *DayStyle*, *NextPrevStyle*, *OtherMonthDayStyle*, *SelectedDayStyle*, *SelectorStyle*, *TodayDayStyle*, *WeekendDayStyle*	Properties that get or set the style indicated, which is of type *TableItemStyle*. The names of the properties are self explanatory, with the possible exception of *OtherMonthDayStyle*, which is used to control the appearance of days in a month other than the currently selected month. Commonly, these styles are set in the Visual Studio editor, and there are even predefined color schemes that will be explained shortly.
DayNameFormat	A property that gets or sets a value indicating how day names should be presented. The value must be a member of the *DayNameFormat* enumeration: *FirstLetter*, *FirstTwoLetters*, *Full*, *Short*, or *Shortest*. For U.S. English, *FirstTwoLetters*, *Short*, and *Shortest* all produce the same day formats.
FirstDayOfWeek	A property that gets or sets a value indicating what should appear as the first day of the week. The value must be a member of the *FirstDayOfWeek* enumeration, which includes each day of the week as well as *Default*, which uses system settings to control the first day of the week.

Table 2-14 *Calendar* Control Members

Member Name	Description
NextMonthText, PrevMonthText	Properties that get or set a string that is displayed for the Next or Prev month navigation control. The default values are *>* and *<*, respectively, which render in a browser as > and <, respectively.
SelectedDate	A property that gets or sets the currently selected date as a *DateTime* object.
SelectedDates	A property that gets a collection of *DateTime* objects that are currently selected. The *SelectionMode* property determines whether more than a single date can be selected and whether any dates at all can be selected.
SelectionMode	A property that gets or sets a value indicating the mode used for selecting dates. The value must be a member of the *CalendarSelectionMode* enumeration: *Day, DayWeek, DayWeekMonth,* or *None. DayWeek* allows selection of a day or a week, and *DayWeekMonth* allows selection of a day, week, or month.
SelectWeekText, SelectMonthText	Properties that get or set a string used for the link to select a week or month.
ShowDayHeader, ShowGridLines, ShowNextPrevMonth, ShowTitle	Properties that get or set a Boolean value indicating whether the indicated items should appear in the rendered *Calendar* control.
TitleFormat	A property that gets or sets a value indicating the format for the title of the calendar control. The value must be a member of the *TitleFormat* enumeration: *Month* or *MonthYear* (for instance, "January" or "January 2006").
TodaysDate	A property that gets or sets the *DateTime* object representing a specific date that appears as today's date.
VisibleDate	A property that gets or sets the *DateTime* object that controls which month is currently visible.
SelectionChanged, VisibleMonthChanged	Event handlers fired when the selection or the visible month are changed.

The *Calendar* control, although not the most complex control (that honor goes to the *GridView* control, covered in Chapter 5), is the most complex single control covered in this chapter. One of the good things about using the *Calendar* control, however, is that when using Visual Studio you do not need to know all the details of how styles are set.

Perhaps the coolest new feature of Visual Studio 2005 is the availability of "smart tags" that allow you to perform common tasks on the complex controls. For instance, if you click the right arrow on the right side of the *Calendar* control, a menu appears with tasks specific to the control, as shown in Figure 2-4.

If you click Auto Format on the menu, a dialog box similar to the one shown in Figure 2-5 appears.

If you select Simple from the list of schemes on the left, the sample calendar appears more like the one shown in Figure 2-6.

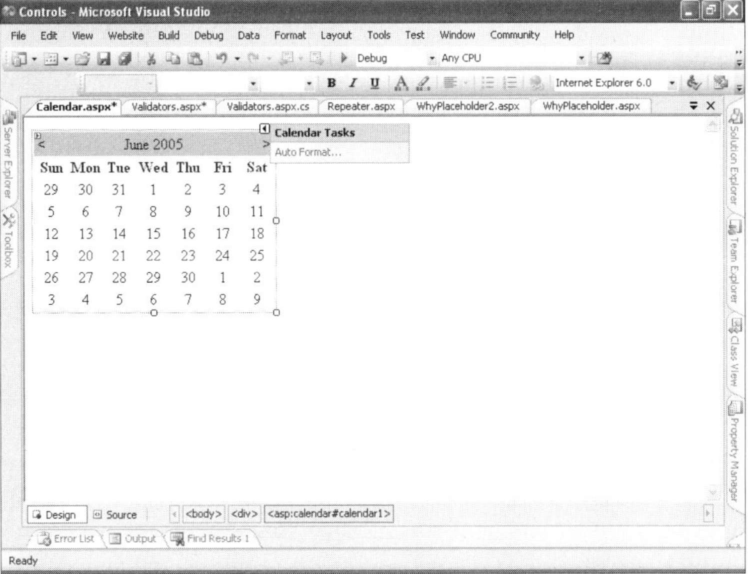

Figure 2-4 The Calendar Tasks menu in Visual Studio 2005

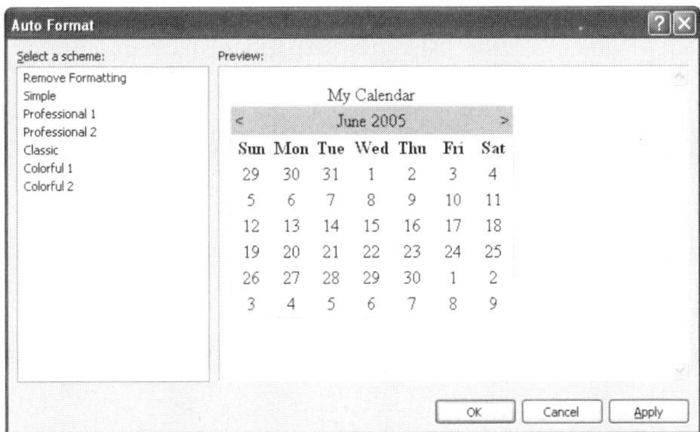

Figure 2-5 The Auto Format dialog box for the Calendar control

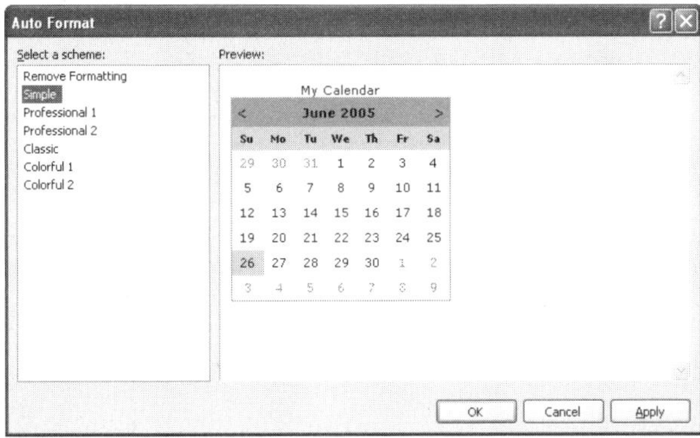

Figure 2-6 The Auto Format dialog box with a scheme applied to the Calendar control

Each of the preset formats presents a different look, allowing a developer to easily change the appearance of a *Calendar* control quickly, without needing to know all the details of the control styles.

ListControl

The *ListControl* class is an *abstract* class that acts as a base for all list controls. An abstract class is a class that is incomplete, with at least one method that has no implementation, and thus cannot be directly instantiated or used. List controls are an important element of most applications. Often list controls are bound to a database table or view. A more detailed discussion of data binding will be deferred until Chapter 5. Still, the descendants of the *ListControl* class can be useful even in the absence of a bound data source.

Note Several interesting and important properties are exposed in the *ListControl* class that are related to data binding. Those properties are common to many data-bound controls and will be covered in Chapter 5.

Table 2-15 explains the significant new properties and events exposed by the *ListControl* class.

Table 2-15 *ListControl* Class Members

Member Name	Description
Items	A property that gets the collection of items in the *ListControl* class. Each element in the collection is of type *ListItem*. Common properties of *ListItem* are *Selected*, *Text*, and *Value*.
SelectedIndex	A property that gets or sets the index of the selected item.
SelectedItem	A property that gets the first selected item in the *Items* collection. Some list controls allow multiple selection.
SelectedValue	A property that gets the value (a string) of the first selected item in the *Items* collection.
SelectedIndexChanged	An event that is fired whenever the selected index is changed. The *SelectedIndexChanged* event is often used in conjunction with the *AutoPostBack* property to allow the page to change as a result of the selected item changing.
ClearSelection	A method that clears the *Selected* property of all the *ListItem* objects in the *Items* collection.

Again, *ListControl* is an abstract base class for other non-abstract list controls that can actually be instantiated. Descriptions of those controls follow.

DropDownList

The *DropDownList* control, which descends directly from the *ListControl* abstract class, appears in the browser to be similar to the *ComboBox* control used in Windows Forms applications. The similarity is superficial, however. Unlike the *ComboBox* control, which can allow entry of arbitrary text into the text box at the top of the control when so configured, the *DropDownList* control only allows selection of an item from the list. *ComboBox* controls often allow incremental searches as well. So, if I enter "R" in one of these *ComboBox* controls, the list advances to the first entry starting with "R." If I type "e," the list advances to the first entry starting with "Re," and so on. Enter the same characters in the *DropDownList* control, and the list moves to the first name starting with "e" as I type "e," ignoring the previously entered "R." The only properties added by the *DropDownList* control are *BorderColor*, *BorderStyle*, and *BorderWidth*, which do exactly what you would expect.

ListBox

The *ListBox* control is similar to the *DropDownList* control. The *ListBox* control looks like the bottom portion of the *DropDownList* control when the list is showing. *ListBox* is a control that can be used when multiple selections are required. Multiple selections can be made using Ctrl+Click and Shift+Click actions, exactly as with standard Windows controls. Ctrl+Click allows selection of random items in a list, and Shift+Click allows selection of a region of the list. The *ListBox* control adds a single significant property, described in Table 2-16, that is not already included in the *DropDownList* control.

Table 2-16 *ListBox* Control Members

Member Name	Description
SelectionMode	A property that gets or sets a value indicating how selections can be made in the *ListBox* control. The value must be a member of the *ListSelectionMode* enumeration: *Multiple* or *Single*.

The *DropDownList* and *ListBox* controls are convenient, and the *DropDownList* control is relatively efficient in terms of use of space on a Web Form. One awkward aspect of the *ListBox* control is how multiple selections are made, relying on mouse clicks and Shift key combinations. The next two controls described offer an alternative to single and multiple selection of items.

RadioButtonList

The *RadioButtonList* control provides a convenient way to display a list of mutually exclusive choices. Using a *RadioButtonList* control is much more convenient than adding several option button controls together on a form. Table 2-17 describes some of the properties of the *RadioButtonList* control that are not included in the *ListControl* base class.

Table 2-17 *RadioButtonList* Control Members

Member Name	Description
CellPadding	A property that gets or sets the distance, in pixels, between the border and the contents of the table cell.
CellSpacing	A property that gets or sets the distance, in pixels, between adjacent cells.
RepeatColumns	A property that gets or sets the number of columns used to display items.

Table 2-17 *RadioButtonList* Control Members

Member Name	Description
RepeatDirection	A property that gets or sets a value indicating the direction of the repeating columns. The value must be a member of the *RepeatDirection* enumeration: *Horizontal* or *Vertical*.
RepeatLayout	A property that gets or sets a value indicating the way items should be laid out. The value must be a member of the *RepeatLayout* enumeration: *Flow* or *Table*.
TextAlign	A property that gets or sets a value indicating the position of text with respect to the option button. The value must be a member of the *TextAlign* enumeration: *Left* or *Right*.

CheckBoxList

The *CheckBoxList* control provides a convenient way to display a list of choices that allow selection of multiple items. Using a *CheckBoxList* control is much more convenient than adding several *Checkbox* controls together on a form. The *CheckBoxList* control adds the same additional properties as the *RadioButtonList* control.

***RadioButtonList* and *CheckBoxList* Example** Although very often the *RadioButtonList* and *CheckBoxList* controls are populated from databases (which will be covered in Chapter 5), you can also add items manually to each of the controls.

In Visual Studio, in the Controls solution, I added a page named RadioAndCheckBoxLists.aspx. Then I added a *RadioButtonList* control, a *CheckBoxList* control, and labels. As in the Calendar example, both controls display a smart tag that allows you to select common tasks from a list, as shown in Figure 2-7.

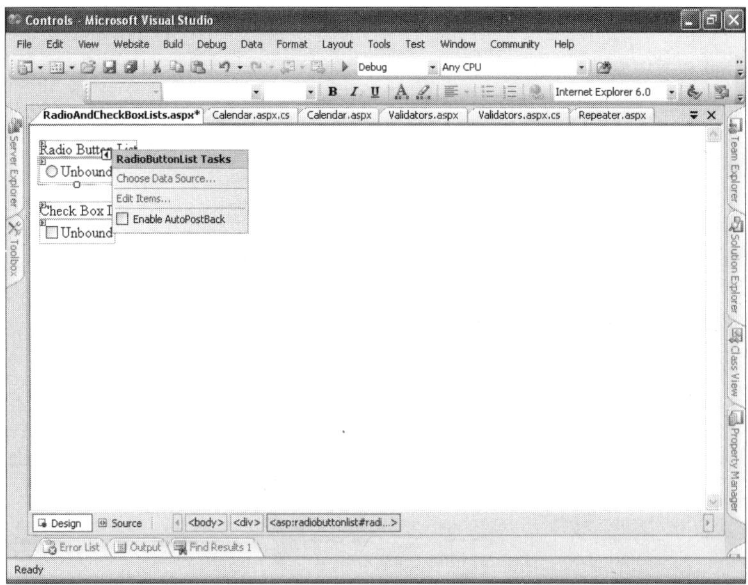

Figure 2-7 The RadioButtonList Tasks menu in Visual Studio 2005

In the Tasks list for both controls is an Edit Items option that opens the dialog box shown in Figure 2-8.

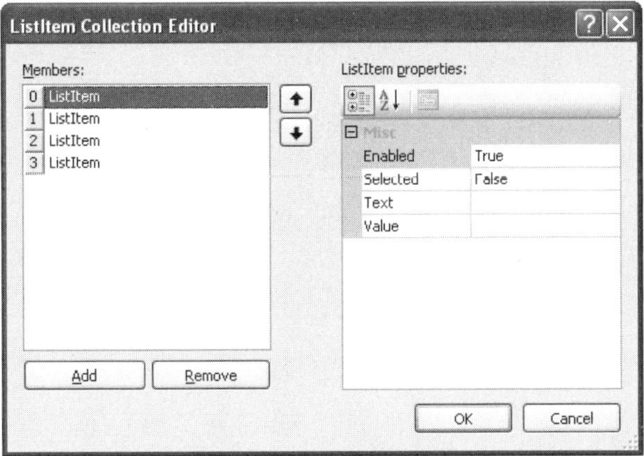

Figure 2-8 The dialog box for editing items in Visual Studio 2005

Figure 2-8 shows the result of clicking Add four times. You should set the *Text* and *Value* properties for each item, because the defaults are not what you want to use. Figure 2-9 shows both the *RadioButtonList* and *CheckBoxList* controls with several items entered. The *CheckBoxList* control has its *RepeatColumns* property set to 2 and its *RepeatDirection* property set to *Horizontal*.

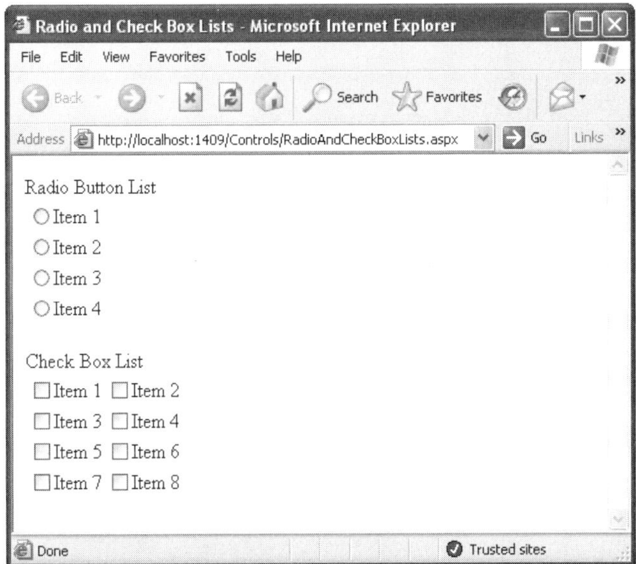

Figure 2-9 The RadioAndCheckBoxLists.aspx page

BaseValidator

Using validators is an important part of developing Web Forms. One of the tedious aspects of traditional Web Forms development is checking values entered by the user. It is easy to validate most data entered, but forgetting to do so is even easier. Validator controls allow the developer to declaratively set up validation checks. The *BaseValidator* class is an abstract class that all validators inherit from; it inherits from the *Label* control and implements the *IValidate* interface. The significant members added by the *BaseValidator* class are described in Table 2-18.

Table 2-18 *BaseValidator* Control Members

Member Name	Description
ControlToValidate	A property that gets or sets the name of the control that the validator validates.
Display	A property that gets or sets a value indicating how the validator should be displayed. The possible values are from the *ValidatorDisplay* enumeration. The values are *None* (meaning no display, ever), *Dynamic* (meaning that the validation text takes up no space on the form unless the text is visible), and *Static* (meaning that the validation text takes up space on the form whether or not the validation has failed, and the text is visible). *None* may seem unusual, but when used in conjunction with the *ValidationSummary* control, it can be a reasonable option.
EnableClientScript	A property that gets or sets a Boolean variable indicating whether the validation should occur on the client, presuming client validation is even possible (this depends on whether JavaScript is available on the client). For this reason, and because a user intending damage could intentionally bypass the client-side validation, client-side validation should not be solely relied on. More information on this is included in the validation example later in this chapter.
ErrorMessage	A property that gets or sets the text for the error message.
IsValid	A property that gets or sets a Boolean value indicating whether the *ControlToValidate* property contains valid content.
SetFocusOnError	A property that gets or sets a Boolean value indicating whether the *ControlToValidate* property should gain focus when there is an error.
Text	An overridden property used to display text when the *ControlToValidate* property is invalid. Note that this is the text that appears at the site of the validator, and the *ErrorMessage* property is the text that will appear in a *ValidationSummary* control (described later).
ValidationGroup	A property that gets or sets the validation group of the validator. Note that this can be any arbitrary string, and if non-blank, should probably match the validation group of some control that causes a postback, such as a *Button* or *ImageButton* control.
Validate	A method that performs the validation on the *ControlToValidate* property and updates the *IsValid* property.

BaseCompareValidator

The *BaseCompareValidator* class is derived directly from the *BaseValidator* class, and like *BaseValidator*, it is an abstract class. The *BaseCompareValidator* class acts as the base class for all typed comparison validators. It adds properties to allow for comparisons of multiple controls, or even just a comparison against a particular type, such as a date. The one significant property added by the *BaseCompareValidator* class is described in Table 2-19.

Table 2-19 ***BaseCompareValidator* Class Members**

Member Name	Description
Type	A property that gets or sets a value indicating the type of data that the entered text should be evaluated as. The value must be a member of the *ValidationDataType* enumeration. The values are *Currency, Date, Double, Integer,* and *String*. The default value is *String*. Note that the comparison is performed on the server, and thus uses the server's locale for dates and currency unless the developer makes special allowances.

Comparisons are evaluated in a type-dependent manner. For example, "5/1/2005" would be greater than "7/24/2004" if the *Type* parameter were set to *Date*, but evaluation would be reversed if the *Type* parameter were set to *String*.

CompareValidator

Of course, *BaseCompareValidator* is an abstract class that cannot be used directly. So that you can create your own control that inherits from the *BaseCompareValidator* class, the *CompareValidator* control is provided in the standard set of Web controls.

The *CompareValidator* control is a flexible validator that can be used in a variety of ways, such as the following:

- To validate that an entered value is of a particular type
- To validate that an entered value has a relationship to some literal value specified
- To validate that an entered value has a relationship to some other control

To do all this, several properties are added to the *CompareValidator* control that are not included in the class it inherits from, *BaseCompareValidator*. The significant added properties are shown in the Table 2-20.

Table 2-20 ***CompareValidator* Class Members**

Member Name	Description
ControlToCompare	A property that gets or sets the name of the control to compare with the control specified by the *ControlToValidate* property. Note that in some cases, you could just swap the values in *ControlToValidate* and *ControlToCompare* and invert the operator specified, and the program would still work as expected. However, it is generally better to have *ControlToValidate* as the later control in the tab order of the form so that the validator will be fired when the last control is exited.

Table 2-20 *CompareValidator* Class Members

Member Name	Description
Operator	A property that gets or sets a value specifying the operation that should take place when the comparison takes place. It must be one of the values in the *ValidationCompareOperator* enumeration. The allowable values are *Equal, NotEqual, GreaterThan, GreaterThanEqual, LessThan, LessThanEqual,* and *DataTypeCheck*. If *DataTypeCheck* is specified, the *ControlToCompare* and *ValueToCompare* properties are ignored.
ValueToCompare	A property that gets or sets a literal value that is used to compare against the value entered in the control specified by the *ControlToCompare* property. If the *ValueToCompare* and *ControlToCompare* properties are both set, *ControlToCompare* is used and *ValueToCompare* is ignored.

CustomValidator

Although the *CompareValidator* control and the other validator controls (described in the following sections) can perform an amazing number of validations, some validations cannot be performed easily, or at all, with the standard validators. The *CustomValidator* control was created for just such a situation.

For instance, imagine that you are allowing only new values (not currently in a database) to be entered into a field. You cannot possibly validate against the database directly by using a *CompareValidator* control, and none of the other standard validators will help in this case. The *CustomValidator* control allows you to specify a client-side and server-side event to be fired to validate a control. This example (validating that an entered value is not in the database) generally requires server-side logic.

New properties and events in the *CustomValidator* control are outlined in Table 2-21.

Table 2-21 *CustomValidator* Class Members

Member Name	Description
ClientValidationFunction	A property that gets or sets the name of the validation function to be called on the client to test input for validity. Note that this function will generally be a JavaScript function, and it must be available on the client.
ValidateEmptyText	A property that gets or sets a Boolean value indicating whether empty text should be validated. This corrects a problem with the ASP.NET 1.x *CustomValidator* control, which is not called to validate empty controls.
ServerValidate	The event fired on the server when validation is called for. The event handler accepts two parameters, one the *Sender* (which is the source of the event and is passed as an *Object,* the base type for all objects in .NET), and one of type *ServerValidateEventArgs*. The server validation event handler must set the *.IsValid* property of the *ServerValidateEventArgs* parameter.

RangeValidator

The *RangeValidator* control validates that an entered value is within a specified range. Validation is dependent on the setting of the *Type* parameter. Table 2-22 shows the two significant members added by the *RangeValidator* control class.

Table 2-22 *RangeValidator* Control Members

Member Name	Description
MaximumValue, *MinimumValue*	Properties that get or set the maximum and minimum values to use for range validation.

RegularExpressionValidator

Many types of input can be validated based on the pattern of characters entered. Examples of such input include telephone numbers, U.S. Social Security numbers, Zip Codes and Postal Codes, and so on. Regular expressions are a pattern against which a specific string is compared, and if the string doesn't match the pattern, the string is rejected. Regular expressions are incredibly versatile, but a detailed tutorial is well beyond the scope of this text. Fortunately, Visual Studio provides a tool with standard regular expressions already loaded, such as the following:

French phone number: (0(\d|\d))?\d\d \d\d(\d \d| \d\d)\d\d

Internet e-mail address: \w+([-+.']\w+)*@\w+([-.]\w+)*\.\w+([-.]\w+)*

U.S. Zip Code: \d{5}(-\d{4})?

In the simplest example, the U.S. Zip Code, looking from left to right, the regular expression expects digits ("\d"), five of them ("{5}"), followed by zero or one occurrences ("?") of a dash and four digits ("(-\d{4})").

The *RegularExpressionValidator* control has the *BaseValidator* control as its base class, and it adds one significant property, shown in Table 2-23.

Table 2-23 *RegularExpressionValidator* Class Members

Member Name	Description
ValidationExpression	A property that gets or sets a string representing the regular expression used to validate the control.

RequiredFieldValidator

A common cause of confusion when using validators is that most validators will not fire unless the *ControlToValidate* property has some text entered. One noteworthy exception in ASP.NET 2.0 is the *CustomValidator* control, which provides a *ValidateEmptyText* property. Because of this, in many cases two validators (a *RequiredFieldValidator* control and some other validator) are required to correctly validate entries. A single property, described in Table 2-24, is new in the *RequiredFieldValidator* control.

Table 2-24 *RequiredFieldValidator* Class Members

Member Name	Description
InitialValue	A property that gets or sets a string representing initial value of the *ControlToValidate* property. By using the *InitialValue* property, you can have a *RequiredFieldValidator* control validate a control with an initial text value (for instance, "Enter a Number") that is considered the same as an empty field.

ValidationSummary

One option for the *Display* property that all validation controls have is *None*, meaning that nothing will ever display in the validation control. This may seem useless, but sometimes it is best to display a validation message someplace other than right next to the control being validated. For instance, a Web Forms are displayed using a markup language, so precise control is not always easy or possible.

The solution is to use a *ValidationSummary* control. This control, unlike the other validation controls, inherits from the *WebControl* class. The *ValidationSummary* control can display text on the form or, where possible, in a message box with the validation errors. The *ValidationSummary* control adds several significant properties, shown in Table 2-25, to those in the base class, *WebControl*.

Table 2-25 *ValidationSummary* Control Members

Member Name	Description
DisplayMode	A property that gets or sets a value indicating the display mode of the *ValidationSummary* control. This value must be a member of the *ValidationSummaryDisplayMode* enumeration. The allowed values are *BulletList*, *List*, and *SingleParagraph*.
EnableClientScript	A property that gets or sets a Boolean value indicating whether client script should be used to display the validation summary.
HeaderText	A property that gets or sets a string to use as the header for the validation summary.
ShowMessageBox	A property that gets or sets a Boolean value indicating whether a message box on the client side should appear.
ShowSummary	A property that gets or sets a Boolean value indicating whether the validation summary should appear inline on the page.

A Validation Example

Perhaps the best way to understand how all of these validators work is to look at an example. In this example, there is only a single line of actual code involved, in this case to set the date on a *CompareValidator* control to allow only dates earlier than today.

In the Visual Studio project called Controls (used for all examples in this chapter, and included with the code for the book), I added a Web Form named Validators.aspx that ultimately appeared as shown in Figure 2-10.

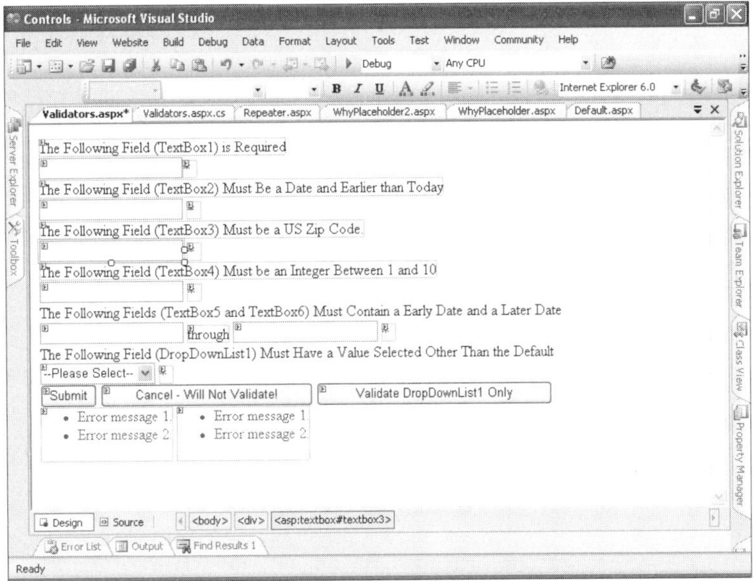

Figure 2-10 The Validators.aspx Web Form in Design view in Visual Studio

Note This form is laid out using line breaks between the labels and the data entry controls. However, there are better ways to lay out a Web Form, and they will be covered in Chapter 3.

To create this form, I dragged a label onto the form, positioned the cursor to the left of the label, pressed Enter, and then add the *TextBox* and *RequiredFieldValidator* controls on the next line. I changed the *Text* property of the label to display the text seen on the screen ("The Following Field (TextBox1) is Required") using the Properties window. Then I clicked the *RequiredFieldValidator* control and modified the following properties:

ControlToValidate: TextBox1

ErrorMessage: "TextBox1 Must Be Filled In"

SetFocusOnError: True

Text: "*"

I repeated the addition of the label and text box, modified the label text as shown in Figure 2-10, and then added a *CompareValidator* control. On the *CompareValidator* control, I modified the following properties:

ControlToValidate: TextBox2

ErrorMessage: "TextBox2 Must Be a Date Earlier Than Today"

Operator: LessThan

SetFocusOnError: True

Text: "*"

Type: Date

The changes to the properties of the *CompareValidator* control are designed to allow TextBox2 to be compared to a date, but note that I did not set the *ValueToCompare* property in the Visual Studio Properties window. Because I want the date entered to be earlier than today (whatever that date might be), I cannot set the date in the tab–I have to set it in code. In the *Page_Load* event of the form, I added the following line of code:

```
this.CompareValidator1.ValueToCompare = DateTime.Today.ToShortDateString();
```

Using this one line of code, the *ValueToCompare* property will always be set to today's date, formatted as a short date string (mm/dd/yyyy in the U.S.). Setting the *Operator* property to *LessThan* causes the validator to look for a date less than (in the case of a date, earlier than) today.

I repeated the addition of the label and text box, modified the label text as shown in Figure 2-10, and then added a *RegularExpressionValidator* control. On the *RegularExpressionValidator* control, I modified the following properties:

ControlToValidate: TextBox3

ErrorMessage: "TextBox3 Must Be a US Zip Code"

SetFocusOnError: True

Text: "*"

ValidationExpression: \d{5}(-\d{4})?

I repeated the addition of the label and text box, modified the label text as shown in Figure 2-10, and then added a *RangeValidator* control. On the *RangeValidator* control, I modified the following properties:

ControlToValidate: TextBox4

ErrorMessage: "TextBox4 Must Be an Integer Between 1 and 10"

MaximumValue: 10

MinimumValue: 1

SetFocusOnError: True

Text: "*"

Next I added a label, a text box label, a second text box, and a *CompareValidator* control on the next line. I modified the labels as shown in Figure 2-10. On the *CompareValidator* control, I modified the following properties:

ControlToCompare: TextBox5

ControlToValidate: TextBox6

ErrorMessage: "TextBox5 Must Be Later than TextBox6"

Operator: GreaterThan

Type: Date

SetFocusOnError: True

Text: "*"

The final data entry and validation control set was entered in much the same way as the first four sets, but rather than adding a text box, I added a drop-down list with a *RequiredField-Validator* control. I modified several properties of the *RequiredFieldValidator* control:

ControlToValidate: DropDownList1

ErrorMessage: "DropDownList1 Must Have a Value Selected"

InitialValue: "--Please Select--"

SetFocusOnError: True

Text: "*"

ValidationGroup: DDL

The *RequiredFieldValidator* control ensures that a value is selected in the drop-down list. For this to work, I needed to enter at least two items into the *Items* collection of the *DropDownList* control, using the Collection Editor dialog box shown in Figure 2-8. It is important that the initial item (or the item set as the default value, if it is not the initial item) has a value that *exactly* matches the *InitialValue* property of the *RequiredFieldValidator* control. In this case, I added the list items "--Please Select--," "Red," "Green," and "Blue."

Note I will often set the *InitialValue* property programmatically, rather than declaratively, by using the *SelectedText* property. This ensures that if the initial value changes, my code will continue to work.

Setting the *ValidationGroup* property to *DDL* allows the *DropDownList* control to be validated separately from the other controls on the page.

On a new line of the form, I added three buttons with the text values "Submit," "Cancel - Will Not Validate" (with the *CausesValidation* property set to *False*), and "Validate DropDownList1 Only" (with the *ValidationGroup* property set to *DDL*, the same as the *ValidationGroup* property of DropDownList1).

On the bottom line on the page, I added two *ValidationSummary* controls, one with no *ValidationGroup* property set, and one with the *ValidationGroup* property set to *DDL*.

Running the Validators.aspx page results in the screen shown in Figure 2-11.

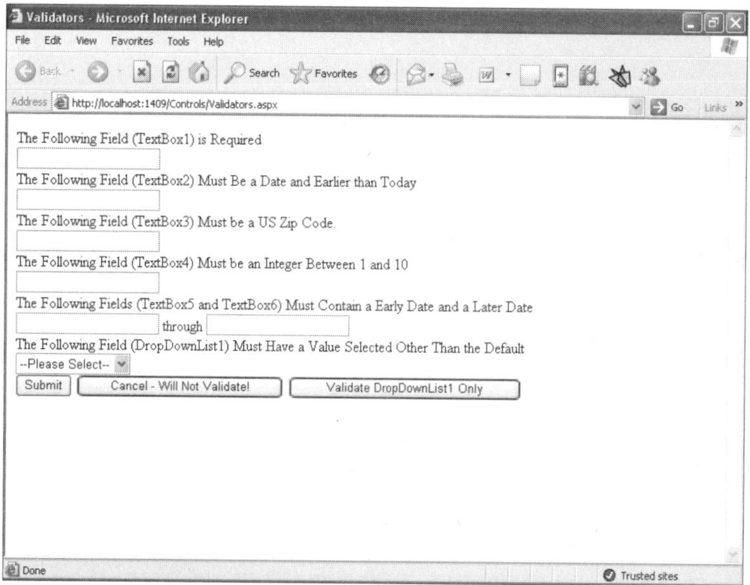

Figure 2-11 The Validators.aspx Web Form running

If you click Submit without entering anything, the screen appears as shown in Figure 2-12.

You should notice a few things about this figure. First, only a single validator has fired, the validator on the first field, TextBox1. Looking at the validators on the page, note that there are only two *RequiredFieldValidator* controls. Why did the second one not fire? Easy: The *Required-FieldValidator* control on the *DropDownList1* control belongs to a different validation group.

Next, when the Submit button is clicked and there is no value in the TextBox1 field, the *Set-FocusOnError* property is set to *True*. This is very convenient, because often you will want the user to immediately correct the problem.

Finally, notice that there is an asterisk (*) next to the TextBox1 field. The longer error message (from the *ErrorMessage* property) is displayed at the bottom of the form by the *ValidationSum-mary* control. The asterisk is from the *Text* property of the *RequiredFieldValidator* control.

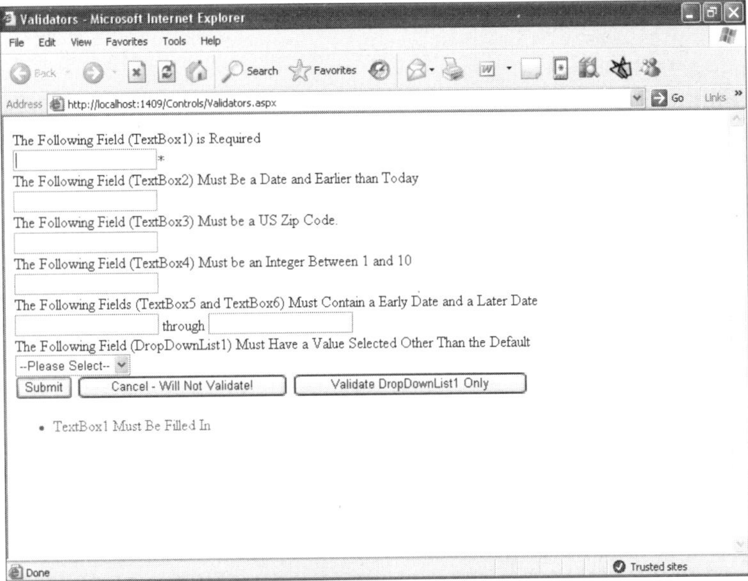

Figure 2-12 The Validators.aspx Web Form after clicking Submit

If you click Validate DropDownList1 Only without adding text to any of the controls and without changing the selection in the drop-down list, the screen appears as shown in Figure 2-13.

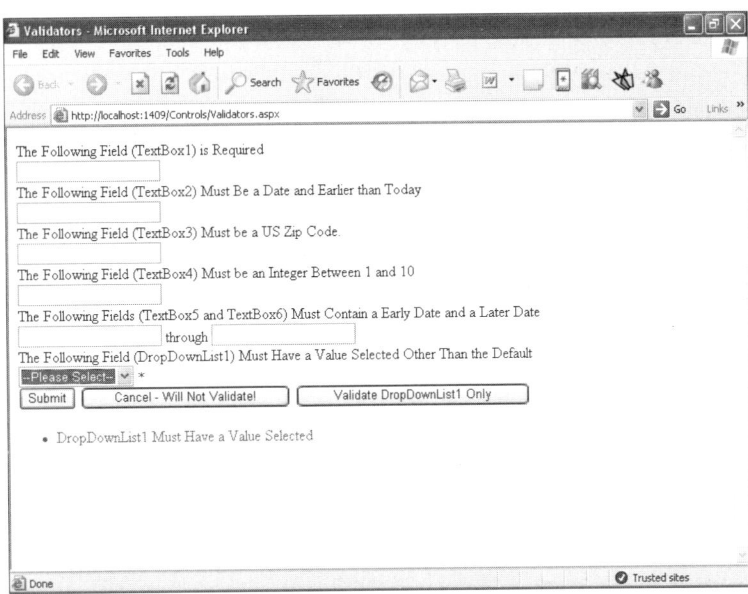

Figure 2-13 The Validators.aspx Web Form after clicking Validate DropDownList1 Only

Note that the second validation summary shows the error message related to the drop-down list, the asterisk near the first text box is gone, and an asterisk appears next to the drop-down list, which now has focus. The ability to separately validate sections of the page is a useful new feature of ASP.NET 2.0.

Next, I entered a value (this could be any value) in the TextBox1 field and clicked Submit to clear all error messages. Then I clicked the TextBox1 field and pressed the Tab key. An asterisk immediately appeared next to the text box. Note that the validation summary did not appear, because it appears only when the form is submitted.

I closed the page and made one modification to the *ValidationSummary* controls, setting the *ShowMessageBox* property of both to *True*.

> **Note** I could have clicked one of the *ValidationSummary* controls, set its *ShowMessageBox* property to *True* in the Properties window, and then repeated the process for the second *ValidationSummary* control. Instead I clicked one *ValidationSummary* control in Design view, pressed Shift while clicking the second *ValidationSummary* control, and set the *ShowMessageBox* property for both controls in the Properties window at the same time. This feature is really useful when you have a large number of controls for which you want to modify a common property.

When I re-ran the page and clicked Submit without entering anything, the screen appeared as shown in Figure 2-14.

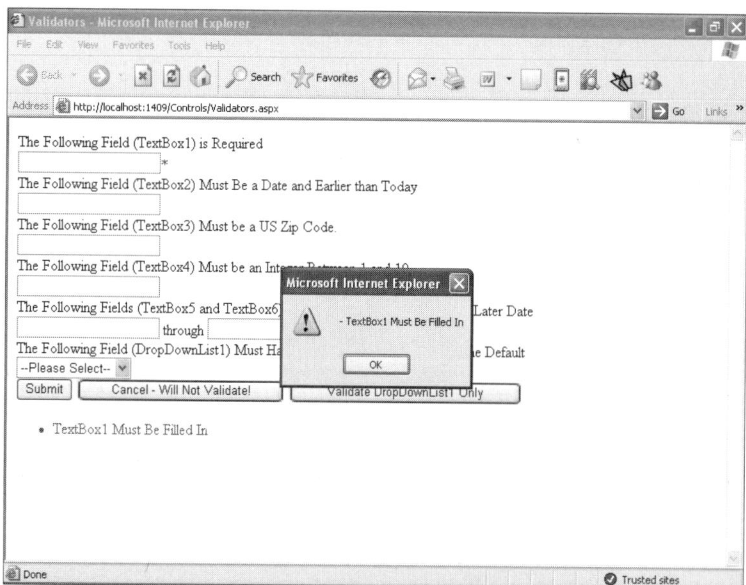

Figure 2-14 The message showing the validation summary text

You can play with the other controls, entering invalid values to see the error messages. As you work with the validators, you will notice that in most cases you will want to add a *RequiredFieldValidator* control. Multiple validators can point to the same *ControlToValidate* property.

One last issue: All of the examples in this section on validators have shown client-side validation. When the Submit button was clicked on my browser, the form was not actually submitted to the server. If I used a browser that did not support JavaScript, or if I had JavaScript disabled, the form would have been submitted. To handle this eventuality, you should use code such as the following in any button click event handler.

```
// Validate the String.Empty ValidationGroup
this.Validate(string.Empty);
if (this.IsValid!=true)
{
    // Do something...
}
```

The *Validate* method has an overload that accepts a string parameter to name the validation group. In this case, the button in question validates controls that do not have any validation group set, so I pass in *string.Empty*, a property of the string class representing an empty string–that is, "". I then check the *IsValid* property of the page, and if it is false, I need to handle it in the area of code with the *Do something...* comment.

Other Controls

In addition to the controls described in this chapter, ASP.NET provides several other controls. First, there is the *GridView* control, which is generally used with databases and will be described in detail in Chapter 5. The older *DataGrid* control will get brief mention, but it is included in ASP.NET 2.0 only for compatibility. Also in Chapter 5, some additional properties of the *ListControl* class and its descendents will be described.

Another broad class of controls is Web Parts. Web Parts are new to ASP.NET 2.0, and they are borrowed from Microsoft SharePoint Products and Technologies. Web Parts allow you to create controls that can be added, removed, and modified (for both content and location) in the browser by the user. Web Parts are covered in Chapter 4, "Working with Web Parts."

A popular strategy for entering large amounts of information on a Web Form that cannot reasonably be fit on a single page is to use a wizard. Wizards contain multiple screens that allow you to navigate back and forth among smaller, more manageable steps. In earlier versions of ASP.NET, you had to manually create your own wizard, often using panel controls that were hidden and revealed in a particular order. Fortunately, ASP.NET 2.0 has a new Wizard control that makes creating wizard applications easier. This new control will be covered in Chapter 3. The *MultiView* control is simpler than the Wizard control, allowing multiple screens, or views, with only one view visible at a time, but without any built-in binding support. The *MultiView* control will be used in an example in Chapter 5.

Although the controls described in this chapter can handle many of the tasks you might have, there might still be times when a custom control allows you to do things easily that might not be easy or even possible using the standard controls. Chapter 6, "Custom Controls," will show you all you need to know about creating custom controls.

Finally, ASP.NET provides some new controls that allow fairly complete handling of user security. The numerous login-related controls will be covered in Chapter 7, "Security and Administration."

Conclusion

In this chapter, you have had an introduction to the standard controls included with ASP.NET 2.0. In the tables, I covered properties, methods, and events that are critical to your understanding of each control. Of course, MSDN is still the definitive source for information on all of these controls, and unlike my tables, the MSDN documentation contains all members of each of the classes.

Next, in Chapter 3, I will cover Web Form layout. Few areas of Web Form development generate as much interest as the details of exactly how Web Forms should be laid out. The forms in this chapter were laid out somewhat awkwardly, using line breaks. By the end of the next chapter, you should be able to do much more elegant Web Form layout.

Chapter 3

Web Form Layout

In this chapter:

Web Form developers tend to be split into two groups. In the first group are developers who came from an HTML and JavaScript background and moved from Web page development to Web Forms development, adding knowledge of server-side programming along the way. The second group of Web Form developers is smart-client or server-side developers who moved to Web Forms development because that was where all the cool development was happening. I fall into the latter group. I know enough HTML to develop fairly complex forms and create a structure, whereas a gifted designer can make my complex Web Forms look pretty. I know my limits, so this chapter will in no way endeavor to make you a complete Web Form designer. Entire books have been written on the topic. Instead, this chapter will give you the knowledge you need to take full advantage of several of the tools that Microsoft ASP.NET 2.0 has to offer, including Master Pages and the Wizard control.

One of the controversies in the Web Forms development world involves the use of HTML tables vs. pure cascading style sheets design. As with most such disagreements, the middle ground is where I believe most developers should stand. Are HTML tables overused and abused? Sure. Have cascading style sheets reached the point where perhaps 98 percent of the visitors to your Web site will use browsers that offer adequate support for cascading style sheets? Sure. The problem with abandoning HTML tables entirely is that there are some tasks that HTML tables support better than cascading style sheets. One of these tasks is the layout of forms. Although I can imagine laying out a form using pure cascading style sheets, it is something I have neither done nor expect to do anytime soon.

Note The next two sections of this chapter, "HTML Tables 101" and "Cascading Style Sheets 101," provide information that is important for anyone creating Web Forms applications in ASP.NET 2.0. However, most of this information is not ASP.NET-specific. If you are very experienced in HTML and cascading style sheets, I encourage you to skip ahead to the section titled "Themes and Skins."

HTML Tables 101

HTML pages can be, and are, created with any text editor. Microsoft Notepad can work perfectly well for creating even the most complex Web Forms, presuming that you have a very good memory for HTML syntax. The reality is, most developers will do a lot better using an editor that actually supports HTML. One of the best options for ASP.NET developers is Microsoft Visual Studio 2005.

In the examples in Chapter 1, "The Web Forms Environment," I used the HTML <br /> tag to create line breaks for form layout. In the real world, most sites use HTML tables to create appealing form layouts, often with cascading style sheets classes assigned to the tables as well. HTML tables are powerful tools for Web Form layout, and a basic understanding is critical. First, a couple of examples will help illustrate some of the features of HTML tables.

In a new Web site created in Visual Studio named WebFormLayout, I created a page named SimpleTable.aspx. In Source view, I added the following HTML markup inside the <form> tag.

```
<table border="1">
    <tr>
        <td>This is the left column.</td>
        <td>This is the right column.</td>
    </tr>
</table>
```

Note In this and most of the introductory examples in this chapter, I set the border attribute of the table to a non-zero value so that my tables will be obvious when the form is viewed in Visual Studio Design view or a browser. This is almost never a good idea in working Web sites, because the border can be a needless distraction from the overall design. In addition to setting the border of a table, you can set attributes such as *cellpadding* and *cellspacing* to pad contents within cells and set spacing between cells.

Inside the opening and closing table tags, several other tags are allowed. The most important of these are the *tr* and *td* tags. The *tr* tag is used for a row in a table, and the *td* tag is used for a column in a table. The *td* tag is for Table Data; a similar tag, *th* (for Table Header), will not be used in any examples here. Unless you specify differently, with a few exceptions, the number of columns in each row of a table should be the same.

Note In my examples, I format the HTML in a way that I find pleasing (indented with opening and closing tags lined up). Previous versions of Visual Studio would have politely allowed my formatting, and then eaten it up and formatted the HTML however it pleased when I changed from Source view to Design view and back. The actual formatting of HTML, for the most part, makes no difference in the way that the HTML is rendered in a browser. However, for a developer, the layout can be important in understanding the structure of the HTML document. Visual Studio 2005 leaves your HTML formatting alone, a feature that is more important than it might sound. Just ask any HTML developer who has used earlier versions of Visual Studio!

When SimpleTable.aspx is displayed in a browser, it appears as shown in Figure 3-1.

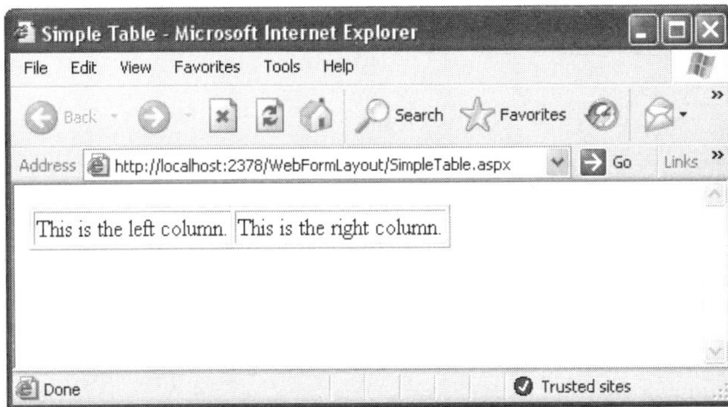

Figure 3-1 SimpleTable.aspx in a browser

As mentioned in the preceding note, Visual Studio 2005 does not modify the layout of entered HTML markup as earlier versions did. More importantly, IntelliSense support in Visual Studio 2005 makes it much easier to select appropriate attributes and values for standard HTML tags, as well as Web control tags. For instance, if you press the Spacebar inside a *table* tag in the Source view in Visual Studio, a list of attributes appears, as shown in Figure 3-2.

HTML Table Width

One of the first things you will probably want to modify in a table is the width. For instance, the following table was created in Visual Studio, with no content inside a two-column table.

```
<table><tr><td></td><td></td></tr></table>
```

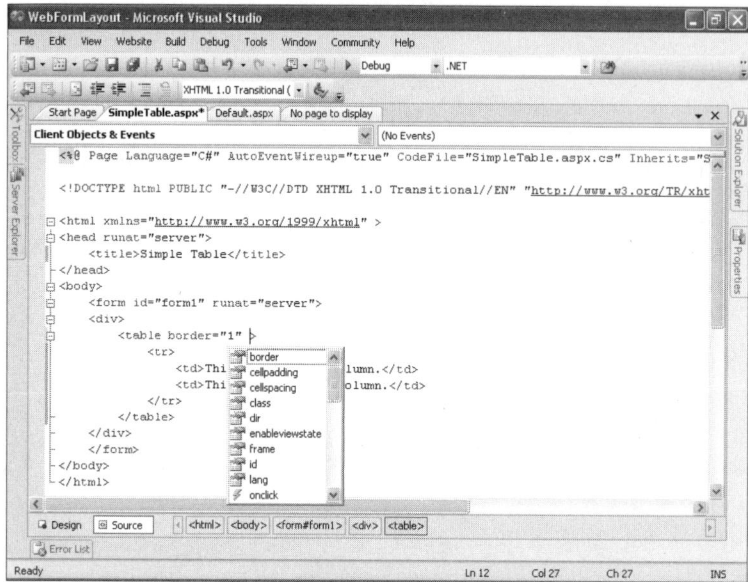

Figure 3-2 IntelliSense technology in Visual Studio showing available attributes for the *table* tag

In Design view, the table appears as shown in Figure 3-3.

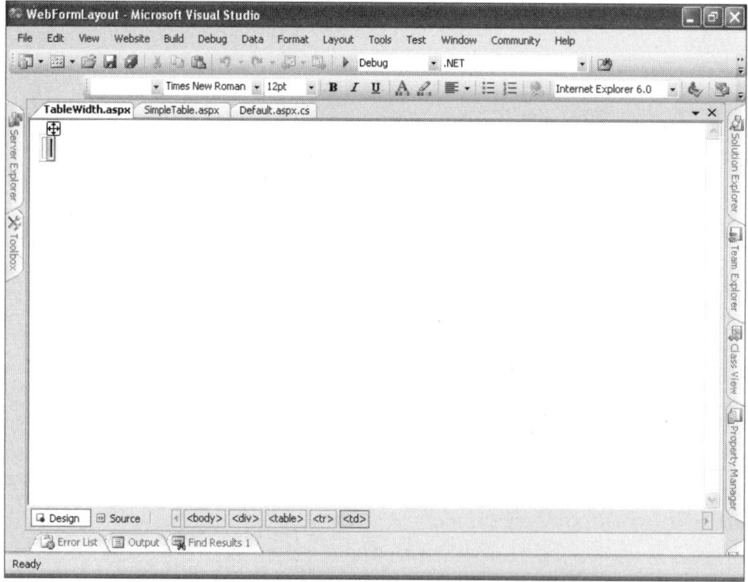

Figure 3-3 An HTML table with no content in Design view

One of the nice features of Visual Studio is the ability to drag and drop controls onto a form. When you are planning to create a table-based form design, the layout shown in Figure 3-3 is not very helpful. You certainly could drag and very carefully drop a control into one of the columns in the table in Figure 3-3, but adding a width attribute to the *table* tag, as shown here,

```
<table border="1" width="500"><tr><td></td><td></td></tr></table>
```

results in the table appearance shown in Figure 3-4.

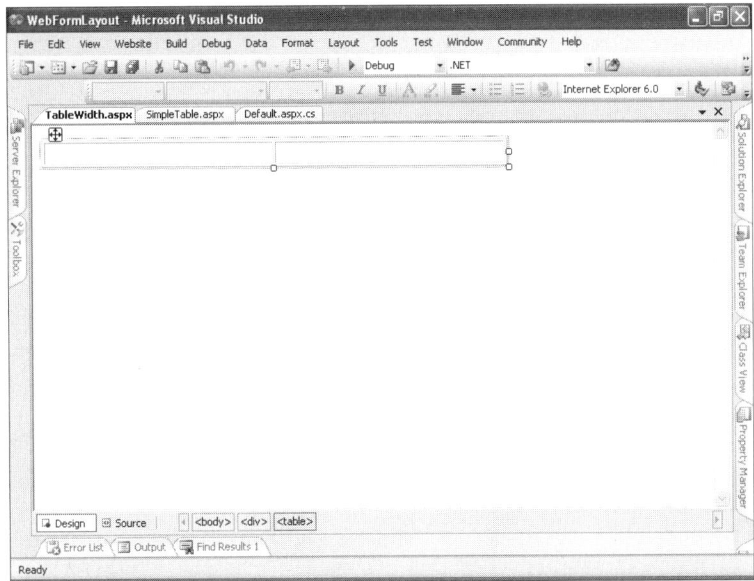

Figure 3-4 An HTML table with a width of 500 and no content in Design view

It is far easier to drag and drop controls into the columns in the table shown in Figure 3-4. In addition to setting a table width to an absolute size (in this case 500 pixels, because pixels are the default scale), you can also set a table width to a percentage. For instance, I added the following markup to a page named TableWidth.aspx.

```
The following table will be 500 pixels wide:
<table border=1 width=500>
   <tr>
         <td>This is the left Column.</td>
         <td>This is the right Column.</td>
   </tr>
</table>
<br />
The following table will be 100% of the width of the browser window:
<table border=1 width=100%>
   <tr>
      <td>This is the left Column.</td>
      <td>This is the right Column.</td>
   </tr>
</table>
<br />
```

When run in a browser, the result was the screen shown in Figure 3-5.

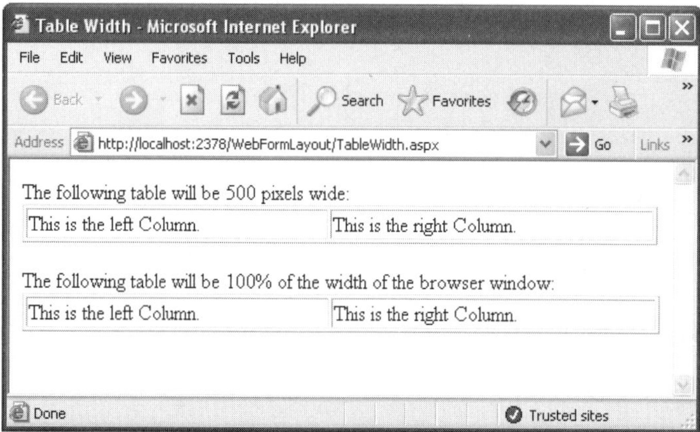

Figure 3-5 TableWidth.aspx in a browser with a normal width

When I changed the width of the browser, the first table remained the same size. The second table (the table with the width set to 100 percent) was reduced in size so that the text in the columns wrapped. The result is shown in Figure 3-6.

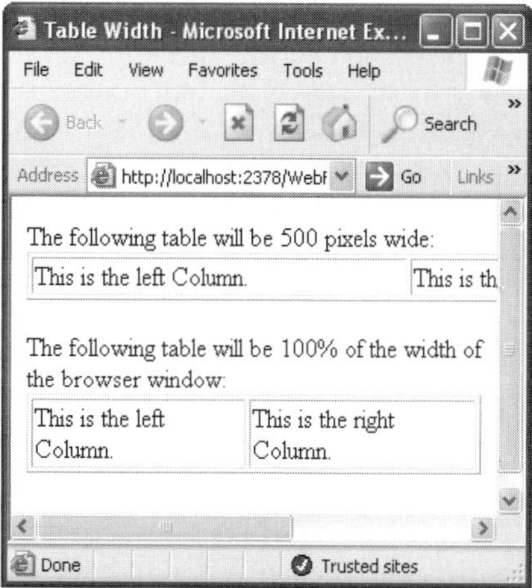

Figure 3-6 TableWidth.aspx in a browser with a reduced width

In addition to setting the width of a table, it is possible to set the width of columns as well. The width of a *td* tag can also be set in pixels or as a percentage of the total table width. In theory, you could even mix and match—make one column 200 pixels wide and another column 30 percent. But the result can vary from browser to browser, and this sort of mixing is generally a bad idea. However, tables can be nested, with one table inside another, and setting the width of one table in pixels and the other as a percentage is not only acceptable, it is common.

One thing to remember is that HTML is a markup language, and in many cases, the attributes you set are more like suggestions than precise placement directions. Look at Figure 3-7.

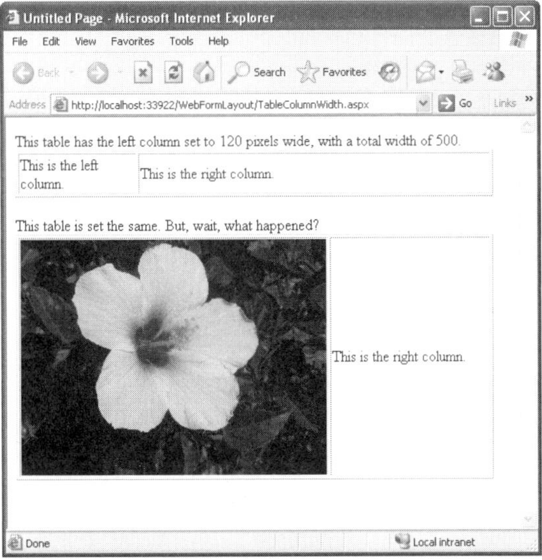

Figure 3-7 TableColumnWidth.aspx in a browser

In the WebFormLayout project, I added a new page named TableColumnWidth.aspx. To the markup in this form, I added the following HTML.

```
This table has the left column set to 120 pixels wide, with a total width of 500.
<table border="1" width="500">
    <tr>
        <td width="120">This is the left column.</td>
        <td>This is the right column.</td>
    </tr>
</table>
<br />
This table is set the same.  But, wait, what happened?
<table border="1" width="500">
    <tr>
        <td width="120"><img src="flower.jpg"
        id="flower" alt="Flower from Hawaii" /></td>
        <td>This is the right column.</td>
    </tr>
</table>
```

> **Note** In all cases, when I display an image, I include an *alt* attribute, which provides alternate text that is especially useful for visually impaired users.

Two HTML tables are defined in this markup, and both have the left column set to a width of 120 pixels (the pixels unit is the default because no other unit type is specified). In the first table, I added the text declaring which column the text should appear in. In the second table, I placed an HTML image control in the left column. The image control, identified by the *img* tag, has its *src* (for source) attribute set to "flower.jpg." An image file is basically unbreakable, meaning that unlike text with embedded spaces, it cannot be conveniently broken into multiple lines. When the flower image, which is 320 x 240 pixels, is placed in the 120-pixel-wide column, the column expands to accommodate the image. If I made the image width 120 pixels and the height 90 pixels, the image would maintain the correct aspect ratio and the column width would not expand. Adding the following code to the page accomplishes this (resizing the image using *height* and *width* attributes).

```
This table is also set the same. But this time, I have resized the image.
<table border=1 width=500>
    <tr>
        <td width=120><img src="flower.jpg" id="Img1"
           alt="Flower from Hawaii" height=90 width=120 /></td>
        <td>This is the right column.</td>
    </tr>
</table>
```

This additional table appears as shown in Figure 3-8.

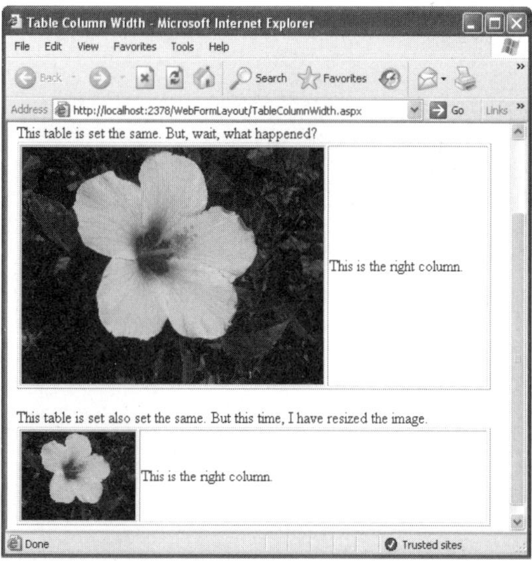

Figure 3-8 TableColumnWidth.aspx in a browser showing the third table with a resized image

One thing to remember about setting the height and width of an image as I did here is that this is not a good way to display a thumbnail image. Generally, thumbnail images are displayed to save download time and network space when an image is displayed. Reducing the height and width in the browser, as shown in the previous example, results in no savings of download time or network space—the same large image is downloaded and then displayed in a smaller size, which is wasteful.

> **Note** The *height* and *width* attributes can also be added even when you don't need to resize the image. Setting these attributes allows the page layout to remain correct even if the image is not found, and it provides a hint to the browser that can make page loading more efficient.

HTML Table Alignment

In addition to sizing an HTML table, you might also want to align the table overall or align content within a column. When considering the alignment of a table overall, you should think about how HTML tables are often used. One use, for example, is to set the overall structure of the page. Often, all content on a page is placed within a single table, by using a complex set of attributes that I will explain later.

If all content is placed inside a single table, what happens when the table is narrower than the overall size of the browser window? For instance, I am writing this book on a PC with a 21.3-inch LCD display, and the resolution is set to 1280 x 1024. However, when I create a Web Form application, I commonly target it to look good at 600 x 800. (The vast majority of PCs come with the screen resolution set to at least 600 x 800, meaning that your Web Form layout should work for most users.) So, when the table containing the content is narrower than the screen, what happens to the rest of the screen? That all depends on how you align the table.

In the WebFormLayout project, I created a new Web Form named TableAlign.aspx and added the following markup.

```
This table is 500 pixels wide.
<table border=1 width=500>
    <tr>
        <td>This is the left column.</td>
        <td>This is the right column.</td>
    </tr>
</table>
<br />
This table is 500 pixels wide, with align set to center.
<table border=1 width=500 align=center>
    <tr>
       <td>This is the left column.</td>
       <td>This is the right column.</td>
    </tr>
</table>
```

This markup creates two tables, each 500 pixels wide. The second table also has an *align* attribute set to *center*, meaning that the table should be centered in the browser. The result is shown in Figure 3-9.

Figure 3-9 TableAlign.aspx showing a table without alignment and a centered table

Another option when creating an overall table to contain content on a Web Form is to set the width to 100 percent (leaving align unset, because it will not matter). This creates a page that will always take up the entire width of the browser. In some cases, allowing the Web Form to be the width of the browser is appropriate. Before doing so, it is useful to view the page on a high-resolution display to ensure that the Web Form layout remains reasonable when the table is quite wide.

Columns can also be aligned, both horizontally and vertically. Vertical alignment is useful only when the height of the cell is set or is higher than the content of the current cell because the content in another cell in the same row is taller. I created a new Web Form, TableColumnAlign.aspx, and added the following markup to show all the possible combinations of alignment.

```
<table border=1 width=500>
    <tr>
        <td align=left>This is left aligned.</td>
        <td align=center>This is center aligned.</td>
        <td align=right>This is right aligned.</td>
    </tr>
    <tr>
        <td align=center valign=middle>This is content that is centered
            vertically and horizontally.</td>
        <td>This is a great deal of text, repeated a number of
            times, in order to ensure that the cell wraps.
            This is a great deal of text, repeated a number of
            times, in order to ensure that the cell wraps.
            This is a great deal of text, repeated a number of
            times, in order to ensure that the cell wraps.
            This is a great deal of text, repeated a number of
            times, in order to ensure that the cell wraps.
       </td>
       <td align=right valign=bottom>This is right aligned and valigned to
            bottom.
       </td>
    </tr>
</table>
```

When run, TableColumnAlign.aspx looks as shown in Figure 3-10.

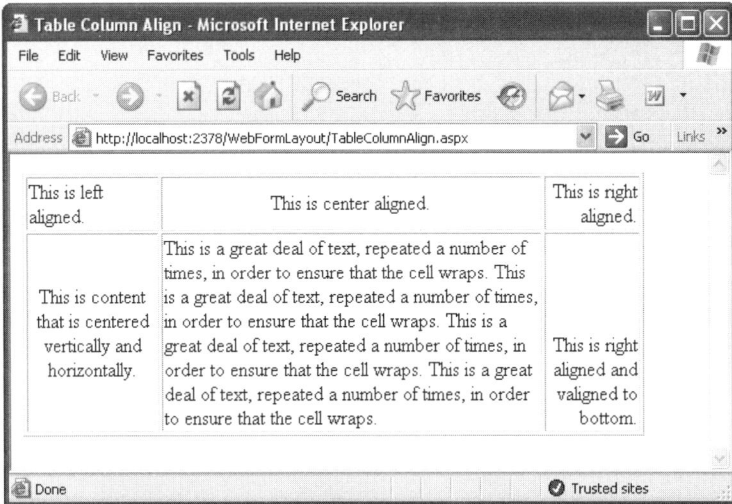

Figure 3-10 TableColumnAlign.aspx showing tables with various alignments set

When setting the *align* attribute, allowed values are *left*, *right*, and *center*. When setting the *valign* attribute, allowed values are *baseline*, *bottom*, *middle*, and *top*. The *baseline* setting is useful only with Netscape, and it aligns the text to the first line of text in other cells in the row.

Spanning Columns and Rows in HTML Tables

In addition to sizing and aligning content within tables, sometimes you need a different number of rows in one column, or a different number of columns in one row. For example, a common overall page layout is shown in Figure 3-11.

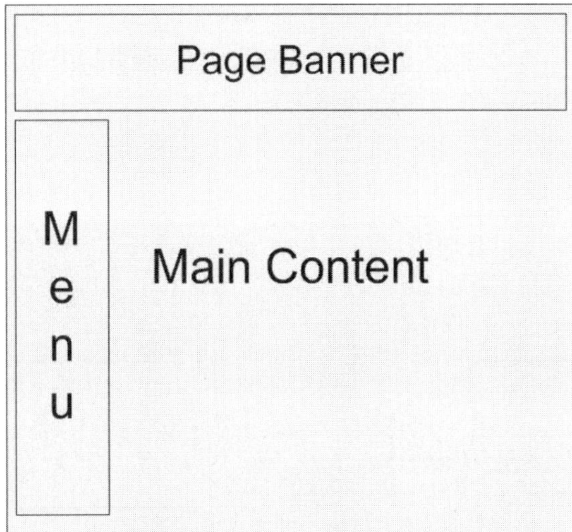

Figure 3-11 A common page layout structure

This sort of page can be constructed in several ways. One way would be to create the Page Banner as a single-row, single-column table, and the Menu and Main Content as a two-column, single-row table. There is one problem with this structure: If the content in any of the cells exceeds the required size, one of the tables will be wider than the other.

To demonstrate a page layout such as that shown in Figure 3-11, I added a page named TablePageLayout.aspx with the following table markup.

```
<table border=1 width=500>
    <tr>
        <td colspan=2 bgcolor="#3399cc" align=center><h1>Banner</h1></td>
    </tr>
    <tr height=300>
        <td width=100 bgcolor="#3399cc" align=center><b>Menu</b></td>
        <td align=center valign=middle><b>Main Content</b></td>
    </tr>
</table>
```

A couple of new attributes are used in this example. First, the background color is set by using the *bgcolor* attribute. In HTML markup, colors are described by using the names of common colors or by using a number sign (#) followed by six hexadecimal digits. Each two of the digits represents the intensity of one of three colors: red, green, and blue.

Another new attribute used in this example is *colspan*. In this example, I created a two-column, two-row table. In the first row, I wanted one wide column. To achieve this, I created a single *td* element and used the *colspan* attribute to indicate that the *td* element should span two columns. I also explicitly set the width of the left cell in the second row (which is where I would expect the menu to be).

Finally, for the banner, I used an *h1* tag. The *h1* tag is used on a single line to indicate that the line should be displayed as a header. Several header tags (*h1*, *h2*, and so on) can specify how text inside the tag should be rendered. Unlike some other ways of controlling the formatting of text, these tags do not specify the exact font, font size, or other precise formatting. Rather, the *h1* tag specifies a general look (that is, a heading) and allows the browser to determine the exact font and formatting to use.

When run, the page appears as shown in Figure 3-12.

Your table layout can be quite complex. For example, I have a classic ASP application that uses both the *colspan* attribute and the *rowspan* attribute (an equivalent attribute that allows a *td* attribute to span multiple rows) to create a very complex display that nicely groups all hospital patients assigned to each resident.

Putting It All Together: A Simple Web Form

Using the table attributes just discussed, as well as the Web controls introduced in Chapter 2, "A Multitude of Controls," you can create a simple Web Form. SimpleWebForm.aspx, added to the WebFormLayout project, will be our example for laying out a form by using tables and Web controls. Figure 3-13 shows SimpleWebForm.aspx in a browser.

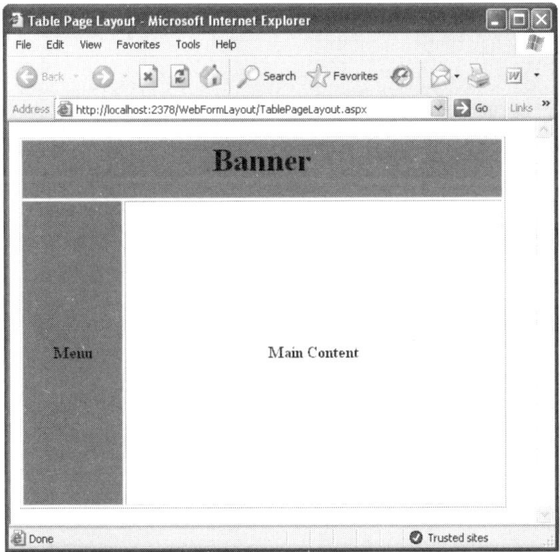

Figure 3-12 TablePageLayout.aspx in a browser

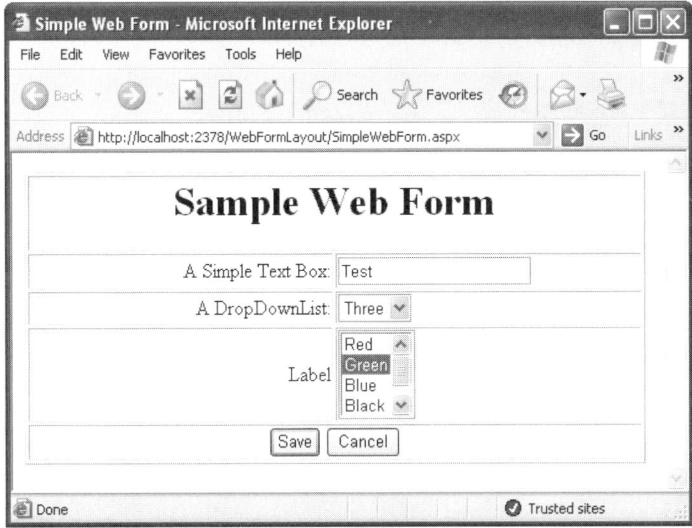

Figure 3-13 SimpleWebForm.aspx in a browser

Recall that in all examples so far, I set the *border* attribute to 1 to show all tables clearly. Here, setting the *border* attribute to 0 will perhaps give a better view of what a completed form might look like. Figure 3-14 shows the same form with no border showing.

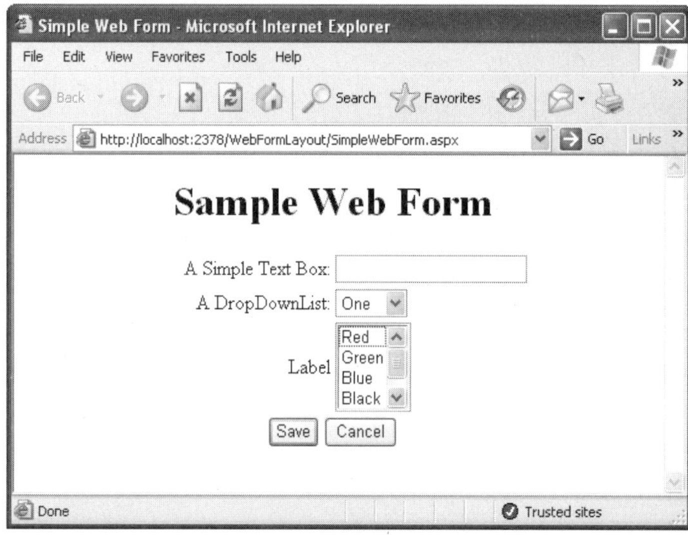

Figure 3-14 SimpleWebForm.aspx in a browser with table borders not visible

The markup to create the table to hold the form is shown here.

```
<table border=0 width=500>
    <tr>
        <td colspan=2 align=center><h1>Sample Web Form</h1></td>
    </tr>
    <tr>
        <td align=right width=50%>
            <asp:Label ID="Label1" runat="server" Text="A Simple Text Box:">
            </asp:Label></td>
        <td>
            <asp:TextBox ID="TextBox1" runat="server"></asp:TextBox></td>
    </tr>
    <tr>
        <td align=right width=50%>
            <asp:Label ID="Label2" runat="server" Text="A DropDownList:">
            </asp:Label></td>
        <td>
            <asp:DropDownList ID="DropDownList1" runat="server">
                <asp:ListItem>One</asp:ListItem>
                <asp:ListItem>Two</asp:ListItem>
                <asp:ListItem>Three</asp:ListItem>
                <asp:ListItem>Four</asp:ListItem>
                <asp:ListItem>Five</asp:ListItem>
            </asp:DropDownList></td>
    </tr>
    <tr>
        <td align=right width=50%>
            <asp:Label ID="Label3" runat="server" Text="Label">
            </asp:Label></td>
        <td>
            <asp:ListBox ID="ListBox1" runat="server">
                <asp:ListItem>Red</asp:ListItem>
```

```
                <asp:ListItem>Green</asp:ListItem>
                <asp:ListItem>Blue</asp:ListItem>
                <asp:ListItem>Black</asp:ListItem>
                <asp:ListItem>White</asp:ListItem>
            </asp:ListBox></td>
    </tr>
    <tr>
        <td align=center colspan=2>
            <asp:Button ID="Button1" runat="server" Text="Save" />
            <asp:Button ID="Button2" runat="server" Text="Cancel" /></td>
    </tr>
</table>
```

Both the row with the title and the row with the buttons have a single cell that spans both columns of the table. In the other rows, the left column widths are set to 50 percent of the table width, and each column is right justified. The drop-down list and list box have their items declared in the markup. Starting in Chapter 5, "Data Binding," we'll look at list controls fed by data sources.

It is important to remember that the example shown in Figure 3-14 is a very simple form. In most cases, form layout will be much more complex. For example, as I am writing this book, I am converting a Microsoft Office Access application to a Web application. One of the major forms in the application is 17 inches long! More importantly, the individual sections of the form are quite complex, with many individual rows containing varying numbers of controls. When converting the form to a Web Form, the first step was to break up the form into several steps by using a Wizard control (which will be covered later in this chapter). One of the more complex pages in the Wizard control is shown in Figure 3-15. Note that the form is a little too wide to display at the resolution of the screen on which the application is displayed.

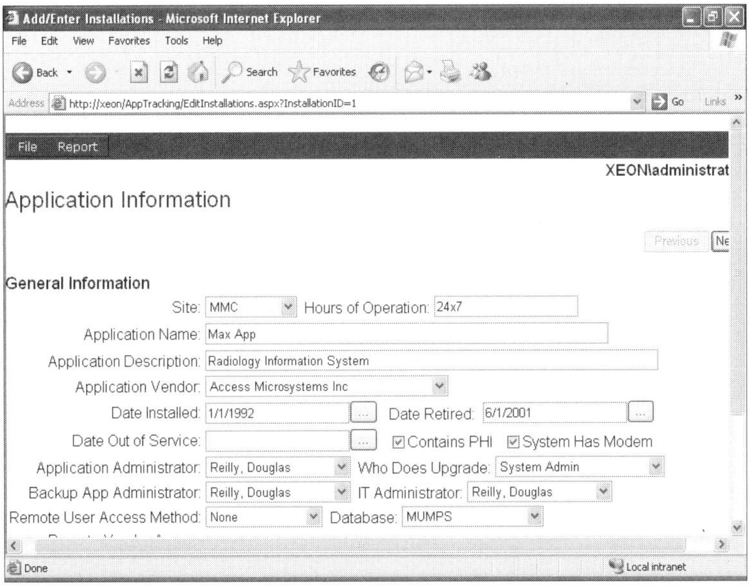

Figure 3-15 A real-world application showing a complex form

In the Access form, many of the controls were aligned in ways that were not convenient for a Web Form. For instance, in the original form, the labels "Who Does Upgrade" and "IT Administrator" were directly aligned on the colons, and the associated combo boxes were aligned on the left. In the Web Form, such an alignment would require complex nesting of tables that would make the page unmanageable. In Figure 3-15, controls after the first label/control pair are placed by using space characters (generally an HTML nonbreakable space, * *).

A great number of other items can be manipulated to modify the appearance of the rendered tables and controls. In addition to colors, as we have seen in previous examples, fonts can be changed as well, by setting a style, or, in the case of Web controls, by setting the font on the individual Web controls.

In addition to using markup to control the properties of HTML controls, you can also set the properties of HTML controls programmatically. Recall that in Chapter 2, I mentioned that in addition to the *System.Web.UI.WebControls* namespace, where most of the Web controls that I use in this book are located, there is an alternate namespace for controls, *System.Web.UI.HtmlControls*. The controls in the *HtmlControls* namespace are merely a thin layer on top of the existing HTML controls; they provide a less consistent object model than the controls in the *WebControls* namespace.

By adding the *runat=server* attribute to any HTML element and giving it a unique ID, you can reference the control in code. For example, imagine that you created a table and, depending on some condition determined at run-time in code, you needed to hide one row of the table. Let's use the following table markup for this example.

```
<table>
    <tr>
        <td>Left column</td>
        <td>Right column</td>
    </tr>
    <tr runat="server" ID="trHide">
        <td>Left column that might be hidden</td>
        <td>Right column that might be hidden</td>
    </tr>
</table>
```

In code, you would be able to make the row identified as *trHide* invisible by setting the *Visible* property of the *trHide* object, as shown here.

```
trHide.Visible=false;
```

All properties of the various HTML controls can be set programmatically if the *runat=server* attribute is added to the tag. The MSDN documentation on HTML controls describes all of the properties of all of the HTML controls.

There are some problems with laying out a Web Form by using traditional HTML markup. For instance, imagine that you have dozens of elements on the page, and you need to change the font. If the font is defined for each element (each label, each text box, and so on), changing the font requires each style to be manually manipulated. I have manually manipulated styles in several large-scale systems, including one that allowed a single application to generate what ended up being a very different appearance so that the same application could be used by customers of many different clients, with each client's customers getting their own look and feel. Manipulating styles involved changing a large number of inline *<FONT>* tags. Even as I worked on that project, I knew that there had to be a better way. Fortunately, there is.

Cascading Style Sheets 101

Cascading style sheets is a specification that allows developers to control all aspects of the appearance of a page. Cascading style sheets styles can be applied at different levels. You can apply a style to all instances of an HTML tag–for instance, all *<P>* tags, or all *<TEXTAREA>* tags. You can also apply a style to a class of controls. For example, you could declare an *error* class, apply that class to several different tags by including a *class* attribute, and then control the appearance of many objects with a single class. Finally, cascading style sheets styles may be applied to specific IDs.

Note It is useful to think about the different ways in which cascading style sheets styles can be applied, and when to use each. For example, when you want to style all instances of a given HTML element, applying the style to that HTML tag makes sense. If, on the other hand, you have a style that you want to apply to some, but not all, of a particular HTML tag, or even some of a number of different HTML tags, applying the style to a class and identifying the tags you want styled as belonging to that class makes the most sense. Finally, if you have a style that you want to apply to a particular element, and only that element, applying the style to a particular ID makes sense. In the examples in this book, cascading style sheets styles will be applied at each of these three levels.

Thinking about the layout in Figure 3-12, it might be useful to first look at a similar page created by using cascading style sheets. Figure 3-16 shows such a page.

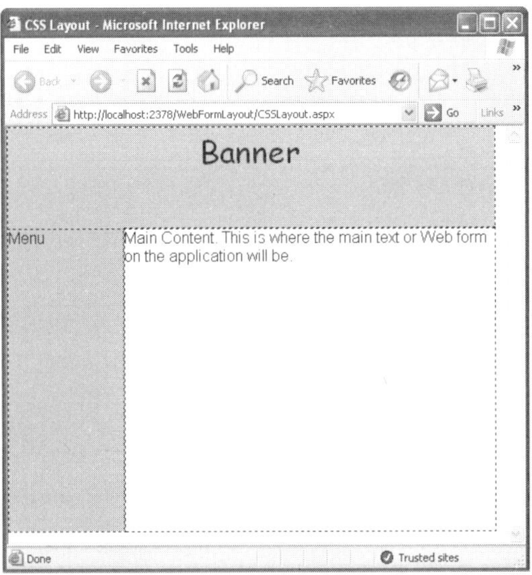

Figure 3-16 A page layout similar to that shown in Figure 3-12, using cascading style sheets

The markup for the page shown in Figure 3-16 is in the WebPageLayout project in a file called CSSLayout.aspx, shown in Listing 3-1.

Listing 3-1 CSSLayout.aspx

```
<%@ Page Language="C#" AutoEventWireup="true" CodeFile="CSSLayout.aspx.cs" Inherits="CSS
Layout" %>

<!DOCTYPE html PUBLIC "-//W3C//DTD XHTML 1.1//EN"
   "http://www.w3.org/TR/xhtml11/DTD/xhtml11.dtd">

<html xmlns="http://www.w3.org/1999/xhtml" >
<head runat="server">
    <title>Cascading Style Sheets Layout</title>
    <link href="StyleSheet.css" rel="stylesheet" type="text/css" />
</head>
<body>
    <form id="form1" runat="server">
        <div id="menu">Menu</div>
        <div id="banner">Banner</div>
        <div id="mainContent">Main Content.  This is where the main text or
           Web form on the application will be.</div>
    </form>
</body>
</html>
```

A great deal of this markup is the standard Visual Studio–generated template markup. At the very top of a Web page markup is the *@ Page* directive. The *Language* attribute specifies the programming language used in the page, in this example, C#. The *AutoEventWireup* attribute specifies whether events are automatically wired up, based on the name of event handlers in the class. The default value is *true*, and Visual Studio 2005, unlike earlier versions, sets the attribute to *true*. With *AutoEventWireup* set to *true*, event wireup is automatic, and a method named *Page_Load* will automatically be called when the page is loaded. *CodeFile* points to the file where the code of the page will be located, and *Inherits* points to the name of the class (which must be directly or indirectly based on the *Page* class). *CodeFile* replaces the previous *Codebehind* attribute, although the older attribute is still supported.

Here is the line that specifies the cascading style sheets (.css) file to use when rendering the page.

```
<link href="StyleSheet.css" rel="stylesheet" type="text/css" />
```

One important feature of Visual Studio is the ability to easily create these .css file link tags. When you add a .css file to the solution, you can simply drag the file from Solution Explorer and drop it on the form, and a link similar to the one shown in the sample will be added to the markup on the page.

Inside the form on the page (again, the form is part of the standard template that Visual Studio creates), I added a few *div* tags. A *div* tag can be used to divide a Web page into separate sections, either to logically group sections or, more commonly, to apply different formatting to different sections of the page. In this example, I created separate *div* tags with self-explanatory IDs of *menu*, *banner*, and *mainContent*. Note that the order of the *div* tags is in fact not the order in which I most likely would want the content to appear. Generally, the banner would be at the very top of the page, with the menu and main content below the banner. In this example, the physical order of the *div* tags does not matter, because of the .css file linked above. Before looking at the .css file in detail, it is interesting to see what CSSLayout.aspx would look like if the link to the .css file were removed. Figure 3-17 shows this scenario.

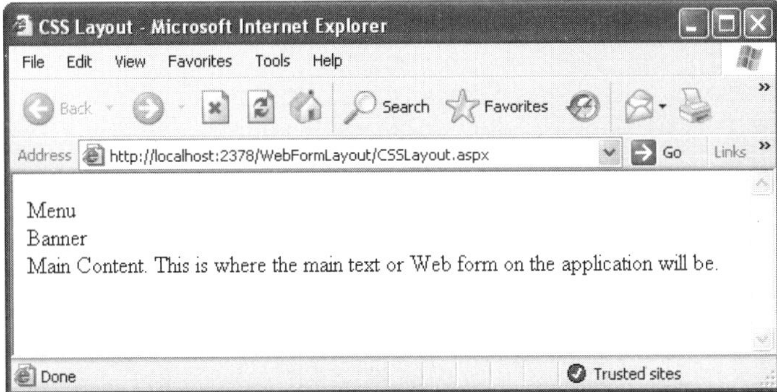

Figure 3-17 CSSLayout.aspx without the .css file link

The output is quite different without the .css file. So, what exactly is in StyleSheet.css that creates such a different appearance? Listing 3-2 shows the entire file.

Listing 3-2 StyleSheet.css

```
body
{
   font-family:Arial;
}
DIV#banner
{
   position:absolute;
   left:0;
   top:0;
   height:100px;
   width:500px;
   background-color:Silver;
   font-family:Comic Sans MS;
   font-size:xx-large;
   text-align:center;
   border:dotted 1px;
}
DIV#menu
{
   position:absolute;
   left:0;
   top:100px;
   height:300px;
   width:120px;
```

```
    background-color:Silver;
    border:dotted 1px;
}
DIV#mainContent
{
    position:absolute;
    left:120px;
    top:100px;
    height:300px;
    width:380px;
    border:dotted 1px;
}
```

First, the style sheet defines a font family to be applied to the *body* tag, essentially applying the style to all elements of the page. Although the style for the *body* tag refers to a single font, this attribute could specify more than a single font in the same family, to ensure that one of the specified fonts will be found. For instance, to ensure that any client would see the page using one of the popular sans serif fonts, the body style could have been defined as follows.

```
body
{
    font-family:Arial Verdana Sans Serif;
}
```

The next three styles defined in StyleSheet.css are to be applied, specifically, to a *div* element identified by a particular ID. For instance, the first style is identified by *DIV#banner*, meaning that it applies only to a *div* tag with an ID of *banner*. Again, the implication of using this sort of style is that the style will apply to a single element only. In this example, that is exactly the desired effect.

Several cascading style sheets attributes are applied to all of the *DIV#<id name>* styles. First, each defines a *border* property with a value of *dotted 1 px*. This is solely for illustrative values, but the *border* property can be used to create some interesting effects. In this example, I used the *border* property as a shortcut to access some individual properties, such as *border-width* and *border style*. A complete explanation of the *border* settings possible with cascading style sheets is beyond the scope of this book, but many books and online resources completely document this property.

The *position* property is set to *absolute*. The alternative values for *position* are *static*, *relative*, *fixed*, and *inherit*. Using any of the other values for *position* would result in wildly different layouts on this standard page, generally displaying the page elements in the order in which the *div* tags appear on the page.

The next set of common properties specified are also related to the position of the elements on the page, but in this case specifying *left*, *top*, *height*, and *width*. These properties can be set to absolute values, commonly in pixels (as in this example) or percentages of the height or width of the containing block. The specific values set in this example are not arbitrary. For instance, the banner has a top and left of 0, a height of 100, and a width of 500. The top property of the menu and mainContent are both set to 100, so that they nest directly under the banner. The left of the menu style is set to 0, and the left of mainContent is set to 120, which is the same as the width property of the menu.

The banner and the menu have the *background-color* property set to *silver*, one of the allowed named colors. The banner also has several properties set. In addition to the previously visited *font-family* property (set to Comic Sans MS for the banner), the *font-size* property is set to *xx-large* and the *text-align* property is set to *center*.

If you compare this example to the example using HTML tables to lay out a page, you might wonder what advantage cascading style sheets offers. Rather than a single page with markup, you have a page with markup and a separate page with the styles to apply to the markup. One advantage is that the same styles can be applied to a great number of pages, simply by linking StyleSheet.css. More important, perhaps, is the ability to dramatically change the appearance of a page by modifying styles. The modifications include styles that would be difficult, if not impossible, to duplicate by using HTML tables. For instance, look at Figure 3-18, showing CSSLayout2.aspx. This file has the exact same markup as CSSLayout.aspx, shown in Figure 3-16, but it uses a different style sheet.

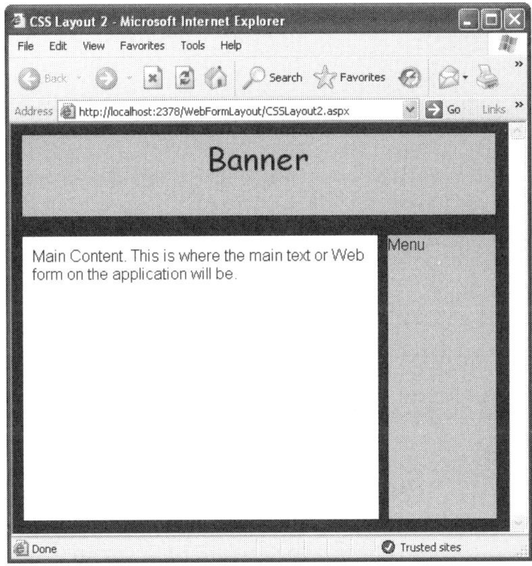

Figure 3-18 The same page as shown in Figure 3-16 (CSSLayout.aspx), with a different .css file

The style sheet, StyleSheet2.css, is shown in Listing 3-3.

Listing 3-3 StyleSheet2.css

```
body
{
    font-family:Arial;
    background-color:Blue;
}
DIV#banner
{
    position:absolute;
```

```
    left:10px;
    top:10px;
    height:80px;
    width:480px;
    background-color:Silver;
    font-family:Comic Sans MS;
    font-size:xx-large;
    text-align:center;
    border:dotted 1px;
}
DIV#menu
{
    position:absolute;
    left:380px;
    top:110px;
    height:280px;
    width:110px;
    background-color:Silver;
    border:dotted 1px;
}
DIV#mainContent
{
    padding: 10px 10px 10px 10px;
    position:absolute;
    left:10px;
    top:110px;
    height:260px;
    width:340px;
    background-color:White;
    border:dotted 1px;
}
```

You will notice several differences in this style sheet. First, the body style has an added *background-color* attribute. In practice, this could be a background image, or anything to add interest to the design.

Next, the position of each style ensures that the background appears around all of the other elements on the page. Also, the *mainContent* style adds a background color (white), to ensure that it stands out from the page background. Finally, when I changed the background color, the text in the main content section looked a little strange, so I added a *padding* property and set the padding for the top, bottom, left, and right.

With relatively simple changes to the style sheet, the look of the page changed dramatically. Using style sheets allows developers to separate the content from the presentation. Looking at the markup in Listing 3-1, you will see that nothing specifies the appearance of the rendered page. Other than a bit of boilerplate markup, the only markup on the page is the link to the .css file and the *div* tags that contain the content.

One question you might have is, How will I remember all of the possible properties possible in a cascading style sheets style? Fortunately for Visual Studio users, the answer is by editing their .css files in Visual Studio. Figure 3-19 shows IntelliSense options that are available when you edit a .css file.

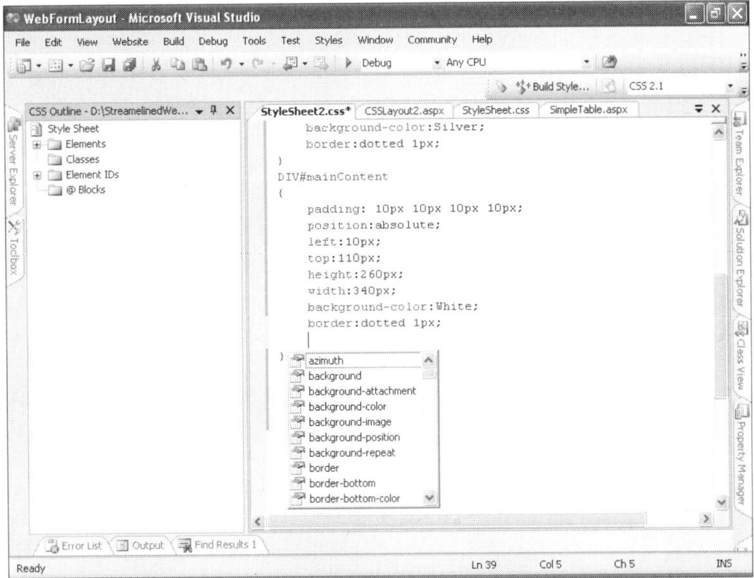

Figure 3-19 IntelliSense options available when editing a .css file in Visual Studio

As an alternative, you can view the Properties window while editing a style, as shown in Figure 3-20.

Figure 3-20 The Properties window, available while editing a .css file in Visual Studio

If you click the button with ellipses (...), a dialog box such as that shown in Figure 3-21 appears, allowing you to edit all aspects of the style by using convenient editors.

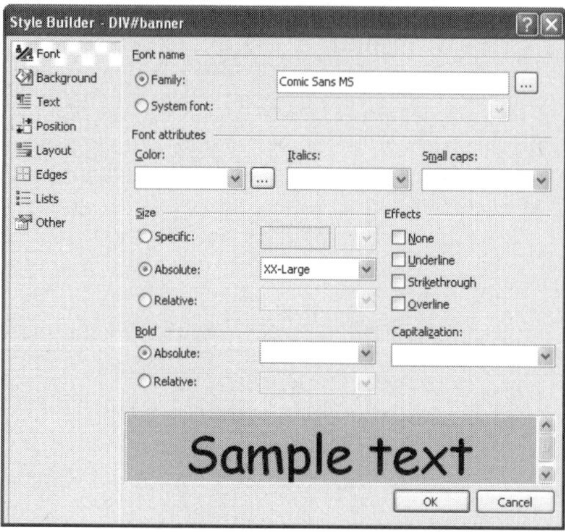

Figure 3-21 The Style Builder dialog box in Visual Studio

Themes and Skins

ASP.NET 2.0 introduces a new way to style Web Forms. In many respects, themes are an alternative to cascading style sheets, but just as often they are used in conjunction with cascading style sheets to conveniently alter the appearance of a Web page without changing the content. Themes are not useful for changing the overall layout of the page; however, ASP.NET 2.0 offers a new tool to help with that, called Master Pages, covered in the next section.

A theme is used as a sort of server-side style sheet to allow controls to appear differently based on the theme applied. To see what a theme can do, let's look at a page we have seen previously. The page shown in Figure 3-22 is the same page as in Figure 3-13, with a theme applied.

Clearly, compared with Figure 3-13, this form is different. The backgrounds of the controls are gray, and the borders around the controls are different, as is the appearance of the buttons. How exactly do themes work?

First, the structure of an ASP.NET application folder is important. There are several special folders, generally beginning with *App_*. When you create a new skin file, it is placed in a folder named App_Themes. Inside App_Themes is another folder named for the specific theme. Figure 3-23 shows the App_Themes folder and the SkinFile folder. The appearance of these folders in Solution Explorer exactly mirrors the folder structure where the application exists.

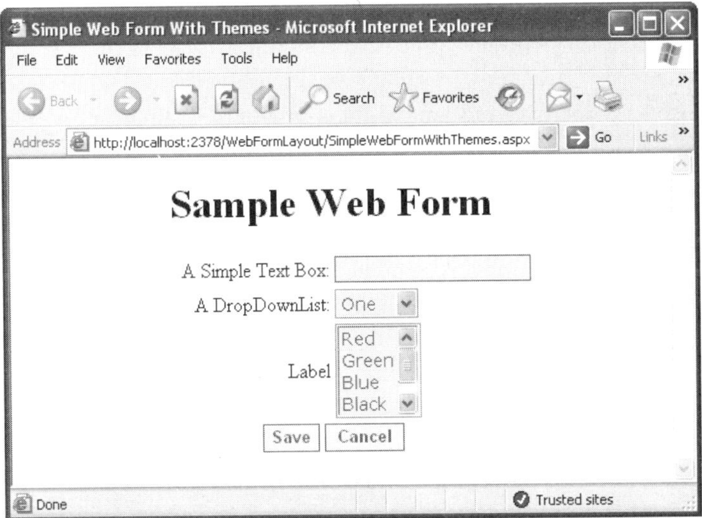

Figure 3-22 SimpleWebFormWithThemes.aspx, the same form as Figure 3-13, with a theme applied

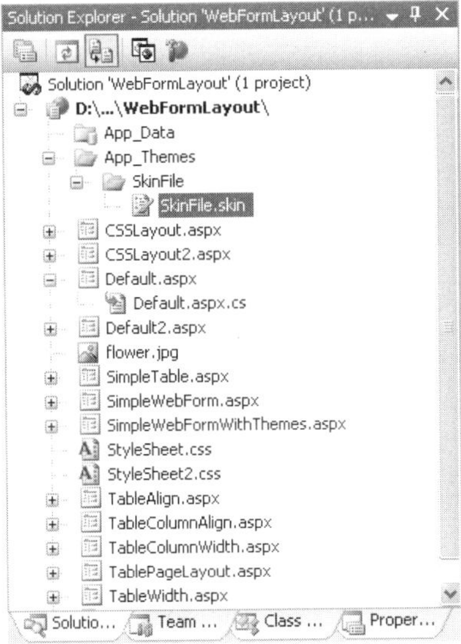

Figure 3-23 Solution Explorer, showing the contents of the App_Themes folder

> **Note** When you create your first theme, Visual Studio 2005 asks whether you want to create the App_Themes folder. This is a kinder and gentler Visual Studio, verifying significant actions before performing them.

A skin file consists of ASP.NET control markup tags, with the ID removed. As a matter of fact, because there is no IntelliSense technology in a skin file, it often makes sense to create sample controls in an .aspx file, copy them into the skin file, and remove the ID attribute and value. The skin file used to modify the page in Figure 3-22 is shown in Listing 3-4.

Listing 3-4 SkinFile.skin

```
<asp:TextBox runat="server"
    BackColor="#efefef" BorderStyle="Solid"
    Font-Size="0.9em" Font-Names="Verdana"
    ForeColor="#585880" BorderColor="#585880"
    BorderWidth="1pt" />

<asp:DropDownList runat="server"
    BackColor="#efefef" BorderStyle="Solid"
    Font-Size="0.9em" Font-Names="Verdana"
    ForeColor="#585880" BorderColor="#585880"
    BorderWidth="1pt" />

<asp:ListBox runat="server"
    BackColor="#efefef" BorderStyle="Solid"
    Font-Size="0.9em" Font-Names="Verdana"
    ForeColor="#585880" BorderColor="#585880"
    BorderWidth="1pt" />

<asp:Button  runat="server"
    BorderColor="#585880" Font-Bold="true"
    BorderWidth="1pt" ForeColor="#585880"
    BackColor="#f8f7f4" />
```

Any control for which you want to create a changeable appearance, or "skin," should be defined in the skin file. A theme can be set declaratively in the @ *Page* directive, as in the SimpleWebFormWithThemes.aspx.

```
<%@ Page Language="C#" AutoEventWireup="true"
   CodeFile="SimpleWebFormWithThemes.aspx.cs"
   Inherits="SimpleWebFormWithThemes" Theme="SkinFile" %>
```

The name specified in the *Theme* attribute is the name of the folder, in the App_Themes folder for the application, or a global theme, found in the %WINDIR%\Microsoft.NET\Framework\ <*version*>\Themes folder (where %WINDIR% is the Microsoft Windows folder and <*version*> is the exact version number of the Microsoft .NET Framework you are using. Note that themes are not available for .NET 1.*x* applications.)

Note In early beta versions, Microsoft shipped ASP.NET 2.0 with several global themes. There were cut, and they are not in the final product. Themes for download will be available at *www.asp.net*.

Themes can also be applied programmatically, by setting the *Theme* property of the *Page* class. You might expect that setting a theme is something naturally done in the *Page_Load* event. However, this is not possible. You must use a newly created event, *Page_PreInit*, as follows.

```
protected void Page_PreInit()
{
    Page.Theme = Server.HtmlEncode(Request.QueryString["Theme"]);
}
```

In this example, the theme is set based on a value passed in on the query string. Of course, in a production application, the theme would be set via a configuration file or in some other way that would ensure that a selected theme is actually available.

Master Pages

After you have created a few Web Forms for a site, it will become apparent that a great deal of common markup is used on every page. You can see such common markup in several of the examples in this chapter that use HTML tables and cascading style sheets for page layout. But if we wanted to create a site with several Web Forms that share a common look and feel, doing so the way in which we have done it so far would be tedious.

In Classic ASP, the solution to this problem was server-side includes. By using include files containing markup (and possibly code), developers could create, with some difficulty, pages that could take on an overall look and feel. ASP.NET 1.*x* changed the model for handling common page elements. Rather than server-side includes, user controls were the preferred way to create reusable blocks of markup and code. The user control has its own event model that mirrors the event model of the page. This was a workable model, but there were limitations. For example, you had to manually add the user control or controls providing the boilerplate markup and code to each page. Often, several user controls were needed (one for the header, one for the menu, one for the footer, and so on).

ASP.NET 2.0 offers a much better solution. Master Pages can be created in a way similar to creating a normal Web Form. A Master Page contains the markup for a page, in addition to one or more *contentplaceholder* tags that can contain default content, which can be modified by the pages that use the Master Page. Table 3-1 lists important properties of the *MasterPage* class.

Table 3-1 Important Master Page Properties

Member Name	Description
ContentPlaceholders	A property that gets a list of *contentplaceholder* controls that the Master Page uses to define different content regions.
Master	A property that gets the parent Master Page of the current Master Page, when Master Pages are nested.

> **Note** Although it is completely legal in ASP.NET 2.0 for a Master Page to itself have a Master Page (and there might be particular scenarios that are best served by nesting Master Pages), this is not supported in Design view in Visual Studio. After trying to use nested Master Pages in Visual Studio, I found this limitation to be significant enough that I do not use nested Master Pages.

To create a Master Page in Visual Studio, right-click the Web site and select Add New Item. In the Add New Item dialog box, select Master Page, enter a name, and then click Add. The Add New Item dialog box is shown in Figure 3-24.

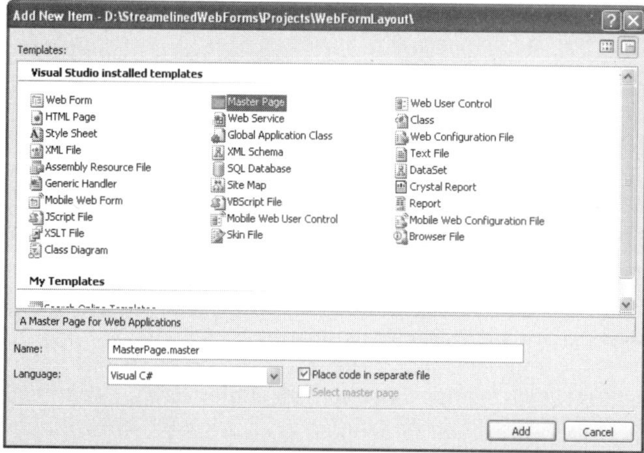

Figure 3-24 Adding a Master Page in Visual Studio

Listing 3-5 shows the markup for the Master Page created by Visual Studio.

Listing 3-5 MasterPage.master Template Content

```
<%@ Master Language="C#" AutoEventWireup="true"
   CodeFile="MasterPage.master.cs" Inherits="MasterPage" %>

<!DOCTYPE html PUBLIC "-//W3C//DTD XHTML 1.1//EN"
   "http://www.w3.org/TR/xhtml11/DTD/xhtml11.dtd">

<html xmlns="http://www.w3.org/1999/xhtml" >
<head runat="server">
    <title>Untitled Page</title>
</head>
<body>
    <form id="form1" runat="server">
    <div>
        <asp:contentplaceholder id="ContentPlaceHolder1" runat="server">
        </asp:contentplaceholder>
    </div>
    </form>
</body>
</html>
```

The @ *Master* directive looks very similar to the @ *Page* directive seen previously, and the attributes have similar meaning. Inside the form tags is a *comtentplaceholder* control, with a name of *ContentPlaceHolder1*. In most cases, I kept the default value provided by Visual Studio for the control IDs. This particular ID is used not only in this Master Page, but also as a link from any page that uses this Master Page. Thus, a meaningful name is important.

Using the cascading style sheets layout from CSSLayout2.aspx as a base, I modified MasterPage.master (from Listing 3-5) so that it contained the same layout as CSSLayout2.aspx. Listing 3-6 shows the resulting markup.

Listing 3-6 MasterPage.master with Layout like CSSLayout2.aspx

```
<%@ Master Language="C#" AutoEventWireup="true"
   CodeFile="MasterPage.master.cs" Inherits="MasterPage" %>

<!DOCTYPE html PUBLIC "-//W3C//DTD XHTML 1.1//EN"
   "http://www.w3.org/TR/xhtml11/DTD/xhtml11.dtd">

<html xmlns="http://www.w3.org/1999/xhtml" >
<head runat="server">
    <title>Master Page</title>
    <link href="StyleSheet2.css" rel="stylesheet" type="text/css" />
</head>
<body>
    <form id="form1" runat="server">
        <div id="menu">Menu</div>
        <div id="banner">Banner</div>
        <div id="mainContent">
            <asp:contentplaceholder id="cphMainContent" runat="server">
            Main Content.  This is the default text from the master page.
            </asp:contentplaceholder>
        </div>
    </form>
</body>
</html>
```

The markup in Listing 3-6 should look familiar. Between the form tags, the markup is almost identical to CSSLayout2.aspx, with the addition of the *contentplaceholder* tag. Text and markup placed inside the *contentplaceholder* tag are used as default content when the page using the Master Page does not provide content for that *contentplaceholder* tag. When viewed in Visual Studio in Design view, the screen appears as shown in Figure 3-25.

You can drag components onto the form and edit existing text, just as you can when editing a Web page. After you create a Master Page, you have the option of selecting a Master Page whenever you create a new Web page. When you create a new Web page (by right-clicking the Web site in Solution Explorer and selecting Add New Item), note the Select Master Page check box toward the bottom of the Add New Item dialog box, as shown in Figure 3-26.

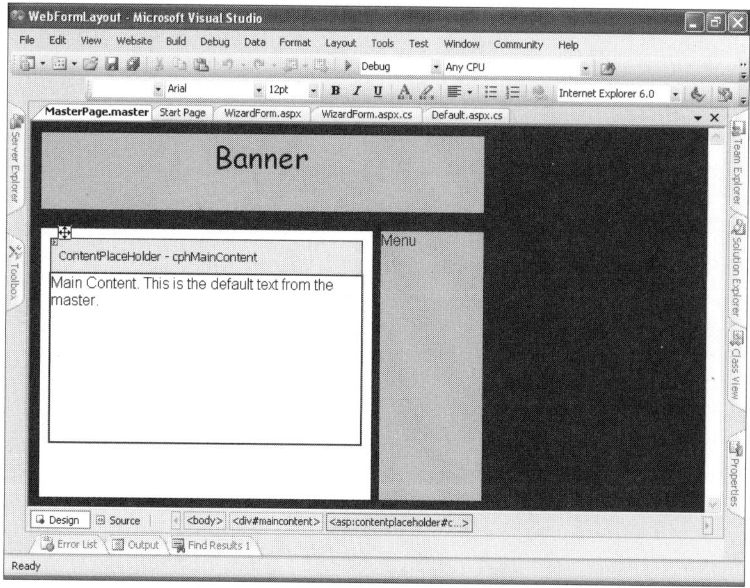

Figure 3-25 A Master Page in Design view in Visual Studio

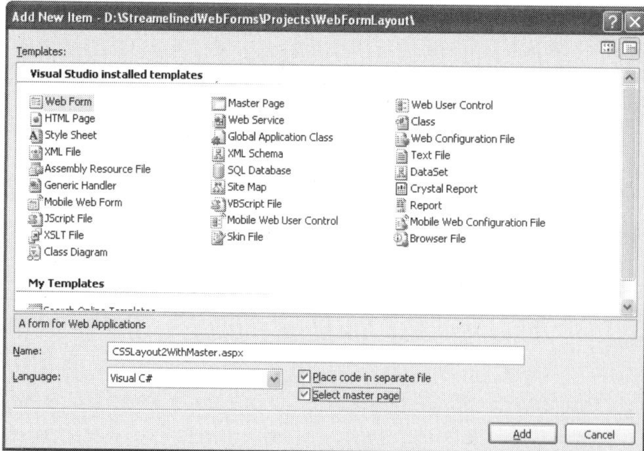

Figure 3-26 The Add New Item Dialog box in Visual Studio, with the Select Master Page check box selected

When you enter the file name you want to use (in this case, CSSLayout2WithMaster.aspx) and click Add, a dialog box appears that allows you to select a Master Page, as shown in Figure 3-27.

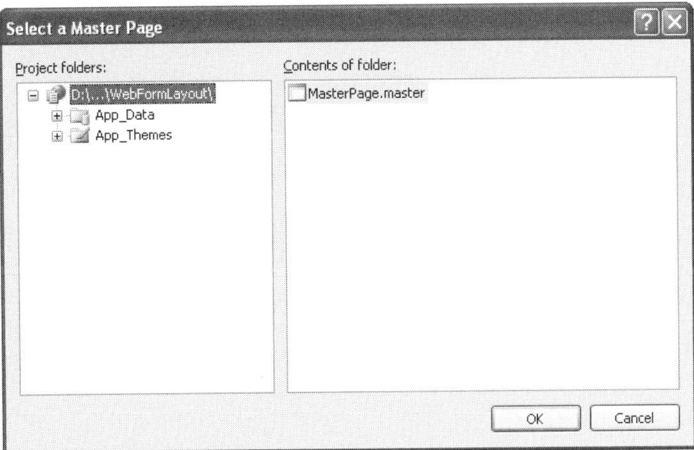

Figure 3-27 The Select A Master Page dialog box in Visual Studio

The Master Pages in the project are available in this dialog box, and you should select one from the list. What is most revealing about the markup in the newly created page is its brevity.

```
<%@ Page Language="C#" MasterPageFile="~/MasterPage.master"
   AutoEventWireup="true" CodeFile="CSSLayout2WithMaster.aspx.cs"
   Inherits="CSSLayout2WithMaster" Title="Untitled Page" %>
<asp:Content ID="Content1" ContentPlaceHolderID="cphMainContent"
   Runat="Server">
</asp:Content>
```

The markup is wrapped here for clarity, but it is on three separate lines in the file. Most of the attributes of the *@ Page* directive should be familiar by now; however, there is one noteworthy addition. The *MasterPageFile* attribute allows you to specify the Master Page to use for the page. The only other markup is a single *Content* tag, already linked to the *contentplaceholder* tag in the Master Page from Listing 3-6.

In Design view, a Web Form with a Master Page allows editing and dragging components only onto the area defined in the *Content* tag. The rest of the screen is locked, which makes complete sense, because when editing a page based on a Master Page, you should be able to modify only the content that is on that page. CSSLayout2WithMaster.aspx is shown in Design view in Figure 3-28.

Because there is no text inside the *Content* tag in CSSLayout2WithMaster.aspx, the main content area of the form will be blank when the page is run. If, rather than leaving the *Content* tag without text, you deleted the tag entirely (leaving just the *@ Page* directive in the markup), the default content from the Master Page would appear as shown in Figure 3-29.

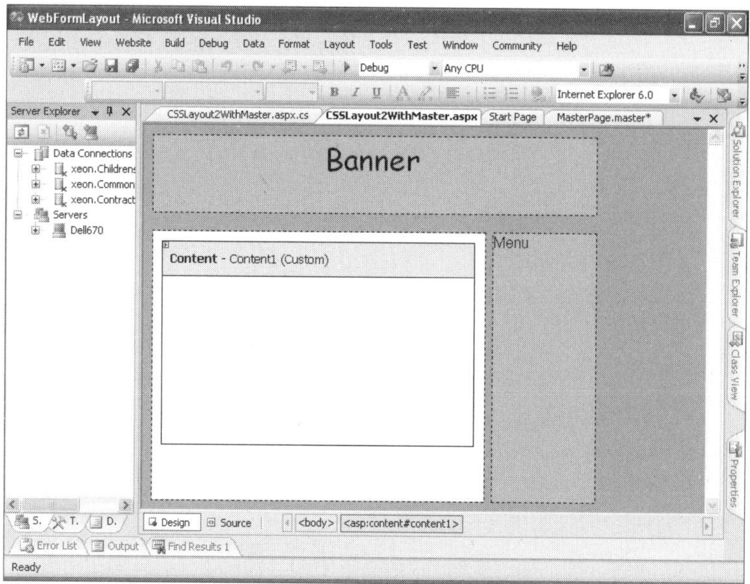

Figure 3-28 CSSLayout2WithMaster.aspx in Design view in Visual Studio

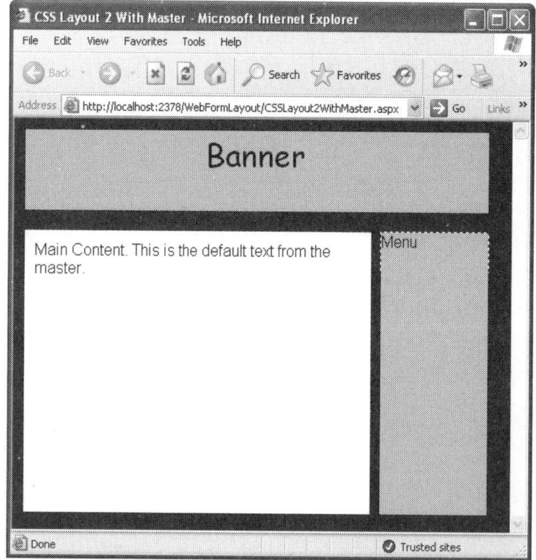

Figure 3-29 CSSLayout2WithMaster.aspx after the *Content* tag is deleted, showing default content from the Master Page

Of course, a more useful example of using a Master Page is the creation of custom content to add to the *Content* tags that overrides the default content from the Master Page. By dropping in some markup similar to that in SimpleWebForm.aspx, the resulting markup in CSSLayout2WithMaster.aspx is as shown in Listing 3-7.

Listing 3-7 CSSLayout2WithMaster.aspx

```
<%@ Page Language="C#" MasterPageFile="~/MasterPage.master"
   AutoEventWireup="true" CodeFile="CSSLayout2WithMaster.aspx.cs"
   Inherits="CSSLayout2WithMaster" Title="Untitled Page" %>
<asp:Content ID="Content1" ContentPlaceHolderID="cphMainContent"
   Runat="Server">
<table width=100% border=1>
    <tr>
        <td align=right width=50%>
            <asp:Label ID="Label1" runat="server" Text="Text Box:">
            </asp:Label></td>
        <td>
            <asp:TextBox ID="TextBox1" runat="server"></asp:TextBox></td>
    </tr>
    <tr>
        <td align=right width=50%>
            <asp:Label ID="Label2" runat="server" Text="Drop Down List:">
            </asp:Label></td>
        <td>
            <asp:DropDownList ID="DropDownList1" runat="server">
                <asp:ListItem>Red</asp:ListItem>
                <asp:ListItem>Green</asp:ListItem>
                <asp:ListItem>Blue</asp:ListItem>
            </asp:DropDownList></td>
    </tr>
    <tr>
        <td align=right width=50%>
            <asp:Label ID="Label3" runat="server" Text="List Box:">
            </asp:Label></td>
        <td>
            <asp:ListBox ID="ListBox1" runat="server">
                <asp:ListItem>Red</asp:ListItem>
                <asp:ListItem>Green</asp:ListItem>
                <asp:ListItem>Blue</asp:ListItem>
            </asp:ListBox></td>
    </tr>
    <tr>
        <td align=center colspan=2></td>
    </tr>
</table>
</asp:Content>
```

The great thing about using Master Pages is that each page has only the markup required for that page. By factoring out all common markup and functionality, the developer is better able to focus on what is important—the unique content on the page.

When run, CSSLayout2WithMaster.aspx looks like Figure 3-30.

The Master Page examples here use only markup. The real power in Master Pages can be seen when, in addition to visual features, common code is also included in the Master Page. For instance, I created a Master Page that includes buttons and button handlers that allow all standard CRUD code (Create, Read, Update, and Delete) to reside in the Master Page, with the page that uses the Master Page required only to set a few properties.

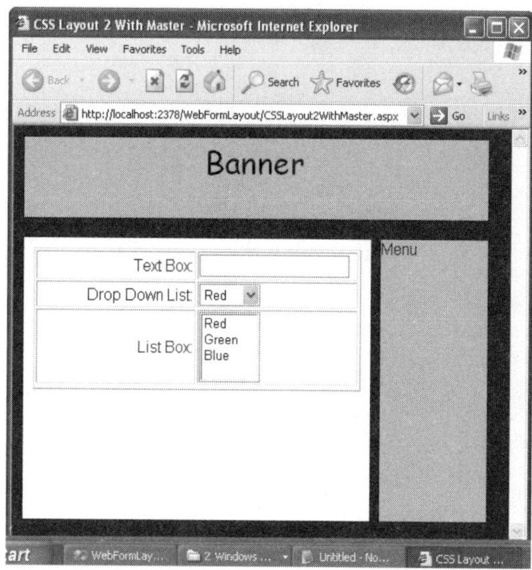

Figure 3-30 CSSLayout2WithMaster.aspx running in a browser

Sometimes, it might be useful to refer to properties or methods of the Master Page from the page using it. The *Page* class has a *Master* property so that from a page, you can refer to the Master Page in code by referencing the *Master* property of the current page.

If you are trying to get to a custom property or method of the Master Page rather than some standard property, you must cast the *Master* property to the correct type. For instance, if you have a Master Page in which the class is named *MyMasterPage*, you can access an instance of the class like so.

```
MyMasterPage myMaster=(MyMasterPage)this.Master;
```

The Wizard Control

A common pattern in form design is the wizard pattern. You probably are familiar with the way that wizards work. When you start the wizard, you progress from page to page by using Next and Previous buttons. On the final page, you can complete the wizard by clicking Finish. You'll almost always have the option of canceling the wizard. Sometimes you are allowed to jump from screen to screen by using a menu on the side, but often the developer needs to ensure that the user steps through screen 1 before going to screen 2, and so on in a linear fashion.

Developers using earlier versions of ASP.NET resorted to using panel controls to create individual areas of a page that could be made visible and invisible as needed. Fortunately, ASP.NET 2.0 provides a new Wizard control to streamline development of wizard Web Forms.

To show the power of the Wizard control, I created a new Web page in the WebPageLayout project, named WizardForm.aspx. After dragging and dropping a Wizard control onto the form, the Wizard Tasks smart tag appeared, as shown in Figure 3-31.

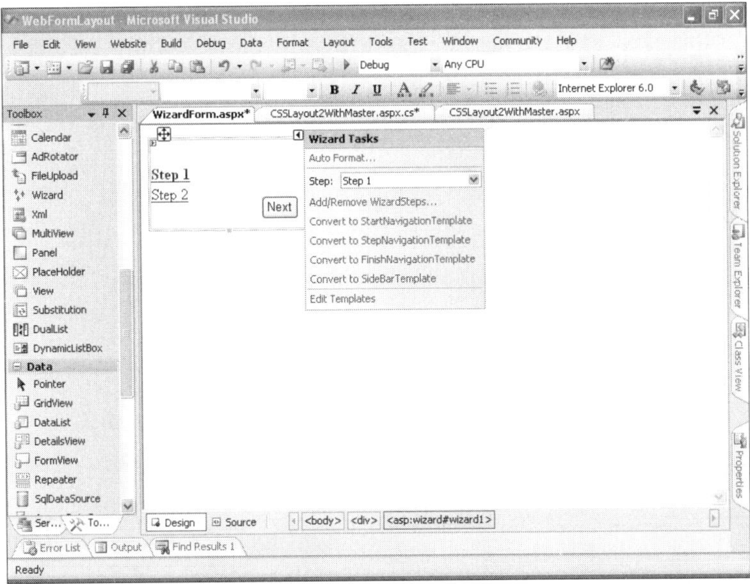

Figure 3-31 The Wizard control and the Wizard Tasks smart tag

The first task when creating a wizard Web Form is usually to add and remove wizard steps. The WizardStep Collection Editor dialog box is shown in Figure 3-32.

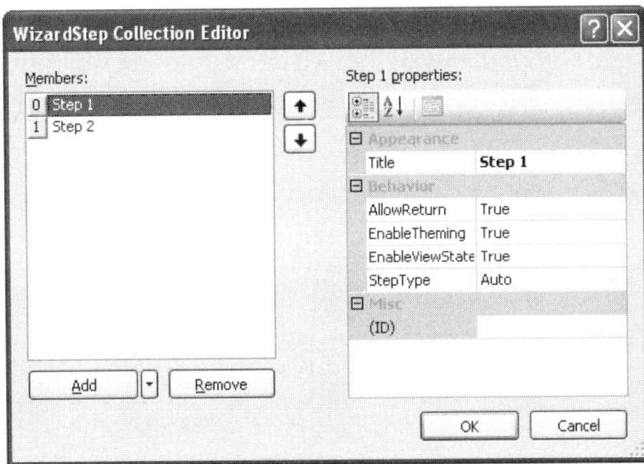

Figure 3-32 The WizardStep Collection Editor dialog box

For this example, I wanted four steps:

1. Enter text in a text box
2. Select from drop-down list

3. Select or clear a check box
4. Finish

I clicked Add until I had four steps, and then I changed the names. The resulting WizardStep Collection Editor dialog box appears in Figure 3-33.

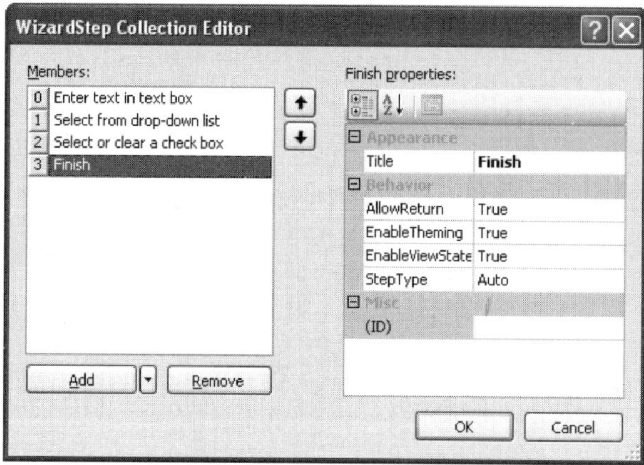

Figure 3-33 The WizardStep Collection Editor dialog box with four steps defined

In the WizardStep Collection Editor dialog box, you can change the order of the steps and force the wizard step to be a particular *StepType*. The possible types are:

- **Auto** Allows the Wizard control to determine what type of step this is. There is almost never a need to change from this default.
- **Complete** A complete step, with no buttons.
- **Finish** A step with the Next button rendered as a Finish button. No Previous button is rendered.
- **Start** The first step to appear, with a Next button but no Previous button.
- **Step** A step between the Start and Finish steps.

After the four steps are entered, the markup in the WizardForm.aspx file appears as shown in Listing 3-8.

Listing 3-8 WizardForm.aspx with Steps Added

```
<%@ Page Language="C#" AutoEventWireup="true" CodeFile="WizardForm.aspx.cs" Inherits=
    "WizardForm" %>

<!DOCTYPE html PUBLIC "-//W3C//DTD XHTML 1.1//EN"
    "http://www.w3.org/TR/xhtml11/DTD/xhtml11.dtd">

<html xmlns="http://www.w3.org/1999/xhtml" >
```

```
<head runat="server">
    <title>Untitled Page</title>
</head>
<body>
    <form id="form1" runat="server">
    <div>
        <asp:Wizard ID="Wizard1" runat="server">
            <WizardSteps>
                <asp:WizardStep runat="server" Title="Enter Text in Text Box">
                </asp:WizardStep>
                <asp:WizardStep runat="server" Title="Select From
                   DropDownList">
                </asp:WizardStep>
                <asp:WizardStep runat="server" Title="Checking or
                    Unchecking CheckBox">
                </asp:WizardStep>
                <asp:WizardStep runat="server" Title="Finish">
                </asp:WizardStep>
            </WizardSteps>
        </asp:Wizard>
    </div>
    </form>
</body>
</html>
```

If you look back at Figure 3-31, you will see that the smart tag menu includes an Auto Format option. The Auto Format dialog box allows you to look at the various format settings by clicking the format name in the list of schemes on the left. Figure 3-34 shows one format that I like.

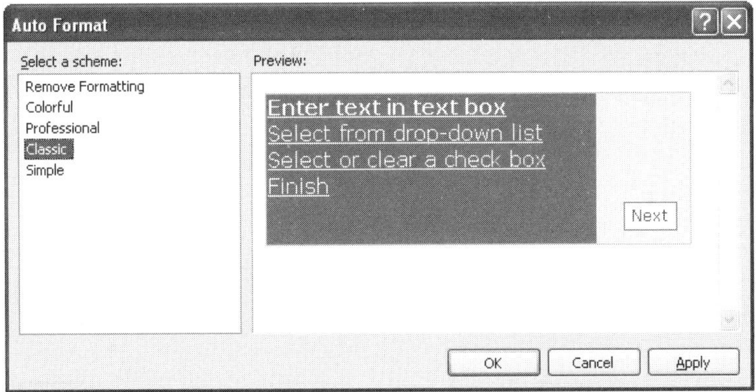

Figure 3-34 The Auto Format dialog box showing one of the Auto Format settings

If you click OK, the format is applied to your Wizard control. Because of the screen constraints and the verbosity of the step names, you should hide the side bar. With focus on the Wizard control in Design view, you can disable the side bar in the Properties window by setting the

DisplaySideBar property to *False*. To make the Wizard control easier to work with, you can click and drag the lower right corner. The control changes color and the size appears as you drag the corner, as shown in Figure 3-35.

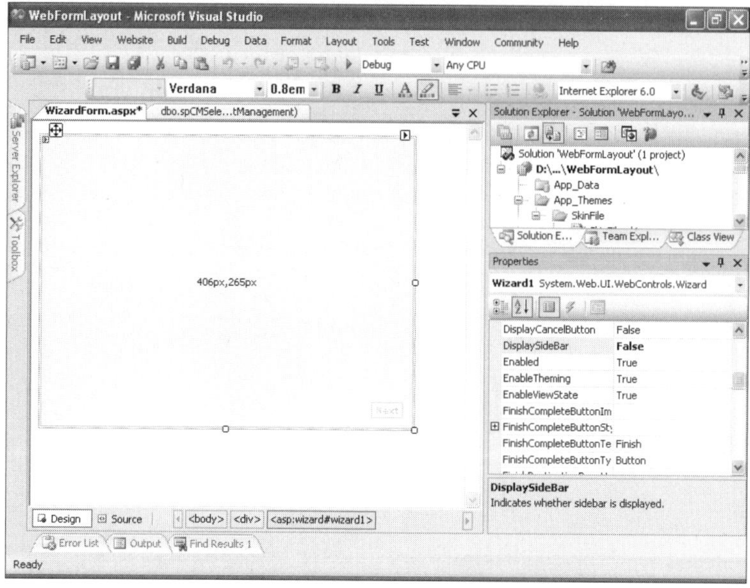

Figure 3-35 Resizing the Wizard control in Visual Studio

Now you can drag and drop controls onto the form. For Step 1, drag two *Label* controls (each on a separate line) and a *TextBox* control, and set the label text and *TextBox* name as shown in the Properties window. In the first *Label* control, enter "Step 1" as the text, and in the second *Label* control, enter "Your Dog's name is:". When running, WizardForm.aspx appears for Step 1 as shown in Figure 3-36.

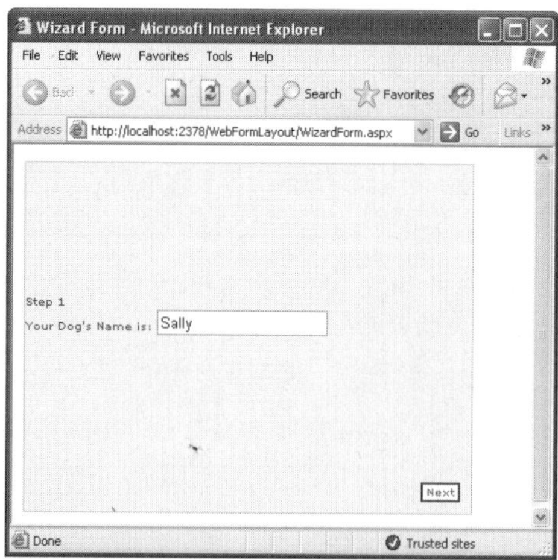

Figure 3-36 WizardForm.aspx on Step 1

Look back at Figure 3-31, and notice the drop-down list with the names of the steps. Selecting a different step in this list allows you to design that step. For Step 2, perform the same tasks described previously, but in the "Select from drop-down list" step, add two labels and a *drop-down list* control with Red, Green, and Blue list items. The first *Label* control should have the text "Step 2", and the second should have "Your Favorite Color:" for the text. When running, Step 2 appears in WizardForm.aspx as shown in Figure 3-37.

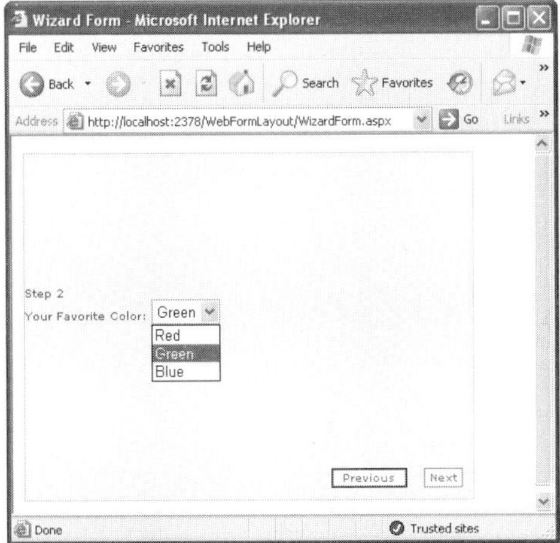

Figure 3-37 WizardForm.aspx on Step 2

For Step 3, add a *Label* control to the "Select or clear a check box" screen with "Step 3" as the text, and on the next line drag and drop a check box with "I am allergic to cats" as the text. WizardForm.aspx appears when it is run for Step 3 as shown in Figure 3-38.

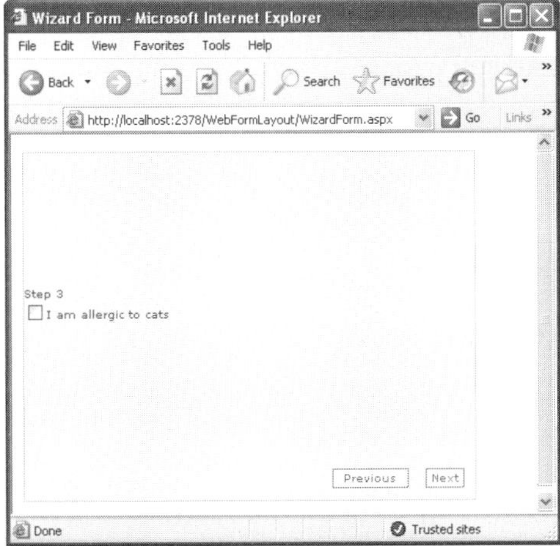

Figure 3-38 WizardForm.aspx on Step 3

For the final page, Step 4, add two labels. The first *Label* control should have "Step 4" as its text, and the second *Label* control should have no text and should be named "FinishLabel" because this Label control will be accessed from code. Step 4 appears in WizardForm.aspx as shown in Figure 3-39.

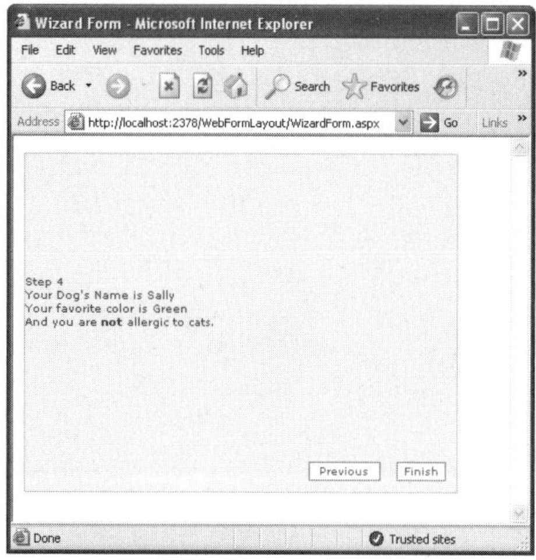

Figure 3-39 WizardForm.aspx on Step 4

In the end, the markup for the page should be similar to Listing 3-9.

Listing 3-9 WizardForm.aspx with Controls Added to Steps

```
<%@ Page Language="C#" AutoEventWireup="true" CodeFile="WizardForm.aspx.cs"
   Inherits="WizardForm" %>

<!DOCTYPE html PUBLIC "-//W3C//DTD XHTML 1.1//EN"
   "http://www.w3.org/TR/xhtml11/DTD/xhtml11.dtd">

<html xmlns="http://www.w3.org/1999/xhtml" >
<head runat="server">
    <title>Untitled Page</title>
</head>
<body>
    <form id="form1" runat="server">
    <div>
        <asp:Wizard ID="Wizard1" runat="server" ActiveStepIndex="0"
           BackColor="#EFF3FB" BorderColor="#B5C7DE" BorderWidth="1px"
           DisplaySideBar="False" Font-Names="Verdana" Font-Size="0.8em"
           Height="265px" Width="406px">
            <WizardSteps>
                <asp:WizardStep runat="server" Title="Enter Text in Text Box">
                    <asp:Label ID="Label1" runat="server" Text="Step 1">
                    </asp:Label>
                    <br />
```

```
            <asp:Label ID="Label2" runat="server" Text="Your Dog's Name is:">
            </asp:Label>
            <asp:TextBox ID="DogName" runat="server"></asp:TextBox>
        </asp:WizardStep>
        <asp:WizardStep runat="server" Title="Select From DropDownList">
            <asp:Label ID="Label3" runat="server" Text="Step 2">
            </asp:Label>
            <br />
            <asp:Label ID="Label4" runat="server" Text="Your Favorite Color:">
            </asp:Label>
            <asp:DropDownList ID="DropDownList1" runat="server">
                <asp:ListItem>Red</asp:ListItem>
                <asp:ListItem>Green</asp:ListItem>
                <asp:ListItem>Blue</asp:ListItem>
            </asp:DropDownList>
        </asp:WizardStep>
        <asp:WizardStep runat="server" Title="Checking or
           Unchecking CheckBox">
            <asp:Label ID="Label5" runat="server" Text="Step 3">
        </asp:Label>
            <br />
            <asp:CheckBox ID="CheckBox1" runat="server" Text=
               "I am allergic to cats" />
        </asp:WizardStep>
        <asp:WizardStep runat="server" Title="Finish">
            <asp:Label ID="Label6" runat="server" Text="Step 4">
            </asp:Label>
            <br />
            <asp:Label ID="FinishLabel" runat="server"></asp:Label>
        </asp:WizardStep>
    </WizardSteps>
    <StepStyle Font-Size="0.8em" ForeColor="#333333" />
    <SideBarStyle BackColor="#507CD1" Font-Size="0.9em"
        VerticalAlign="Top" />
    <SideBarButtonStyle BackColor="#507CD1" Font-Names="Verdana"
        ForeColor="White" />
    <HeaderStyle BackColor="#284E98" BorderColor="#EFF3FB"
        BorderStyle="Solid" BorderWidth="2px"
        Font-Bold="True" Font-Size="0.9em" ForeColor="White"
        HorizontalAlign="Center" />
    <NavigationButtonStyle BackColor="White" BorderColor="#507CD1"
        BorderStyle="Solid"
        BorderWidth="1px" Font-Names="Verdana" Font-Size="0.8em"
        ForeColor="#284E98" />
</asp:Wizard>

    </div>
    </form>
</body>
</html>
```

In addition to the controls that were manually added to the form, several tags related to the Auto Format settings appear toward the bottom of the markup. On the last page, I renamed the second label from the default to "FinishLabel" to make it easier to identify.

After setting the look of the wizard, the next step is to add code that does something with the entered information. In many cases, this involves adding data to a database. In this example, however, I simply summarize the entered information.

Before I perform this summarization, you should be aware of several helpful Wizard control properties and events. Table 3-2 summarizes the most important of them.

Table 3-2 Important Wizard Control Properties and Events

Member Name	Description
ActiveStep	A property that gets the step in the *WizardSteps* collection that is currently displayed to the user.
ActiveStepIndex	A property that gets or sets the index of the current step.
FinishDestinationPageUrl	A property that gets or sets the URL that the user is redirected to when the Finish button is clicked.
WizardSteps	A property that sets a collection of *WizardStepBase* objects defined in the control.
ActiveStepChanged	An event that occurs when the user switches to a new step in the control.
CancelButtonClick	An event that occurs when the Cancel button is clicked.
FinishButtonClick	An event that occurs when the Finish button is clicked.
NextButtonClick	An event that occurs when the Next button is clicked.
PreviousButtonClick	An event that occurs when the Previous button is clicked.
SideBarButtonClick	An event that occurs when a button on the side bar is clicked.

The *ActiveStepChanged* event is the most important of the events. You will often need to perform some action when active steps are changed. Although it might be tempting to use one of the button click events to perform some action, it is almost always not the best way to handle the change of the screen. The most significant problem is that handling a button click does not address all the possible ways in which a step can be reached. A step can be reached by clicking Next or Previous, or possibly even by clicking one of the side bar menus, if they are present.

When the *ActiveStepChanged* event handler is called, you can determine which step is active in a couple of ways. You can look at the *ActiveStepIndex* property, or you can check some property (such as the *Name* property) of the *ActiveStep* property.

In this example, I want to summarize the selections made in the wizard. To create an event handler, click the Wizard control in the Visual Studio Design view, and then in the Properties window, click the Event button (which looks like a lightning bolt) to see a list of events. The Event button is shown in Figure 3-40.

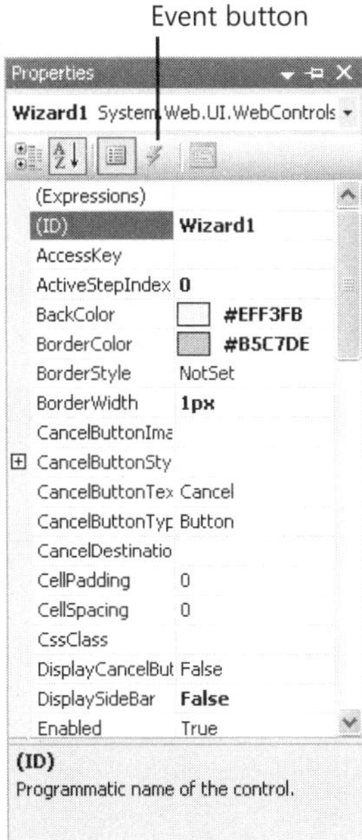

Figure 3-40 Event button in the Properties window

Double-clicking the area to the right of the *ActiveStepChanged* event name in the Properties window opens the code file inside an event handler. To set the text of the *FinishLabel* control, I added the following code.

```
protected void Wizard1_ActiveStepChanged(object sender, EventArgs e)
{
      if (this.Wizard1.ActiveStepIndex == 3)
      {
            this.FinishLabel.Text =
                  "Your Dog's Name is " +
                  this.DogName.Text + "<br />";
            this.FinishLabel.Text +=
                  "Your favorite color is " +
                  this.DropDownList1.SelectedItem.Text +
                  "<br />";
            if ( this.CheckBox1.Checked==true )
            {
                  this.FinishLabel.Text +=
                        "And you are allergic to cats.";
            }
            else
            {
                  this.FinishLabel.Text +=
                        "And you are <b>not</b> allergic to cats.";
            }
      }
}
```

This code checks the *ActiveStepIndex* property of the *Wizard1* control, looking for an *ActiveStepIndex* of 3.

> **Note** In some cases, you'll want to use the *OnFinish* event that is fired when the Finish button is clicked to handle the end of a Wizard operation. In this case, I wanted to display something special as the Finish step starts, so I used the *ActiveStepChanged* event and checked the index of the step.

When you run the page and step through the wizard, the last step will look something like the screen shown earlier in Figure 3-39.

Of course, the details will vary depending on the user's pet history and color preferences. The neat thing about the Wizard control is that the properties of all controls anywhere in the wizard are available in every step, even when the controls in question are not visible to the user.

Note that my earlier advice about using the button click events does not apply to the Finish button event handler. You will often want to perform specific actions when the user has indicated that he or she is finished with the wizard.

Conclusion

In this chapter, you have been introduced to the various ways that you can lay out a Web Form. The topic of HTML tables vs. cascading style sheets is an area fraught with strong feelings on both sides. I have taken a middle ground. Both HTML tables and cascading style sheets have their place. Looking at the source of any number of very popular Web pages, you will often see a mixture of HTML tables and cascading style sheets, and I think that is likely to remain for some time, especially with respect to form layout. Themes and Master Pages provide a way to leverage the power of HTML and cascading style sheets along with the power of server-side programming that ASP.NET offers. Finally, you learned about the Wizard control, one of several powerful new controls offered by ASP.NET 2.0 designed to markedly reduce the amount of code required for a powerful Web Forms application.

Next, in Chapter 4, "Working with Web Parts," I will cover a new and exciting feature of ASP.NET 2.0. One of the things that users often wish for on Web pages is a way to rearrange the page to suit their needs. For instance, a portal page might have an area with the weather, another area with stock quotes, and yet another with company news. If the user is a bicyclist, having the weather most prominent on the page might be most useful; however, a user with a great deal invested in the stock market might prefer to see stock quotes most prominently. Web Parts allow users to rearrange, and even hide, sections of the page to suit their specific needs. This is a powerful new tool that will add that something extra to your Web Forms applications.

Chapter 4

Working with Web Parts

In this chapter:

Web applications have a lot going for them. For example, they can be run on a large number of diverse clients. A particular Web application might run on a PC, a Macintosh computer, a Pocket PC, or, in many cases, all of these environments. The user experience might not always be perfect on all devices, but often it is good enough.

Web applications can also be run remotely by users who are not at the location of the actual application. The exact location of the server that houses the application is of virtually no consequence to users of the application. Whether the server is in the next room or around the world, in most cases a well-designed Web application performs equally well. Those of us who have been around long enough to create large-scale client/server applications may recall the process of carefully crafting a network structure to ensure that the clients and servers were joined via a fast connection. With Web applications, this task is eliminated.

However, some serious limitations exist when it comes to allowing users to customize Web applications. By cleverly applying themes and cascading style sheets (covered in Chapter 3), a Web developer can allow users to change the overall look of the application. Even the layout of the application can be changed—for example, by using cascading style sheets, you can allow users to move a menu from the left side of the page to the right side. However, for other kinds of changes, such as adding a stock ticker or removing a pane that displays the current weather, some other technology is required.

Fortunately, Microsoft ASP.NET 2.0 offers a new feature, borrowed from Microsoft SharePoint Products and Technologies, called Web Parts. Web Parts are little bits of functionality that can be added or removed by users as they run the application. What Web Parts can do is limited only by the imagination of the developer.

Web Parts in Action

To understand what Web Parts can do, you have to see them in action. In a new Web site that I named WebParts, I added a few Web Parts and a drop-down list. The Web site runs in Browse mode by default, as shown in Figure 4-1.

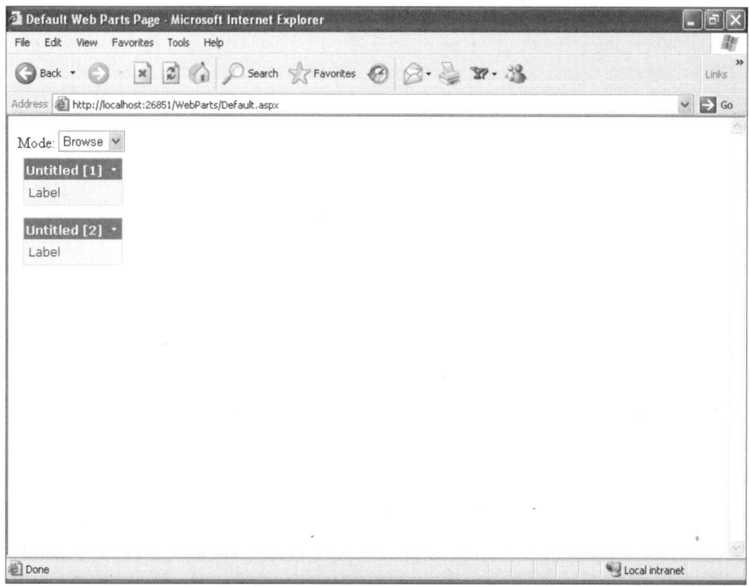

Figure 4-1 Default.aspx in the WebParts Web site, shown in Browse mode

In addition to the label and the drop-down list, this page has two other controls, identified as Untitled [1] and Untitled [2]. These are Web Parts. If you click the down arrows in one of the title bars, a menu appears that allows you to minimize or close the Web Part. Note that if you close the Web Part, the page remembers this action, and the Web Part will still be closed when you return to the page.

When you change the mode from Browse to Design, the page reloads and looks as shown in Figure 4-2.

In addition to the controls that were visible in Browse mode, a couple of other elements appear in Design mode. Two parts of the page are enclosed in boxes. These are Web Part zones. Web Part zones are parts of the page into which you can drag and drop Web Parts. For instance, as you drag one of the Web Parts from WebPartZone1 into WebPartZone2, you see a visual indicator that the Web Part zone is ready to accept the Web Part–in this case, a blue line that appears in WebPartZone2, as shown in Figure 4-3.

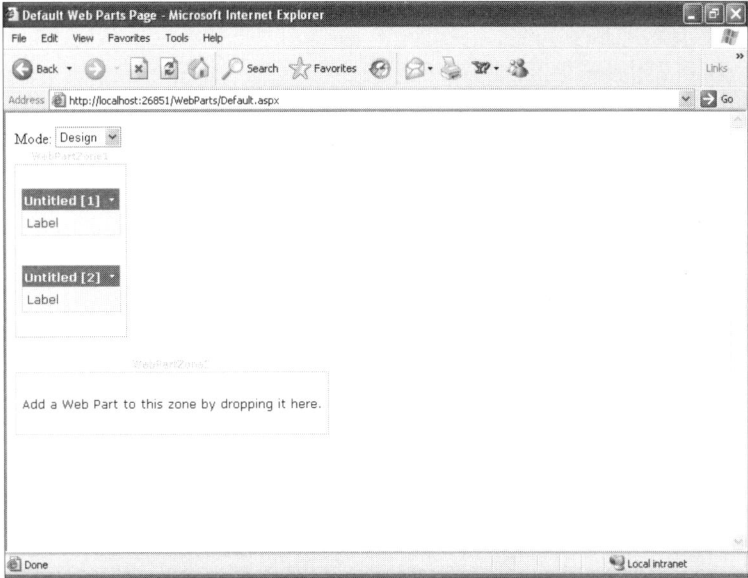

Figure 4-2 Default.aspx in the WebParts Web site, shown in Design mode

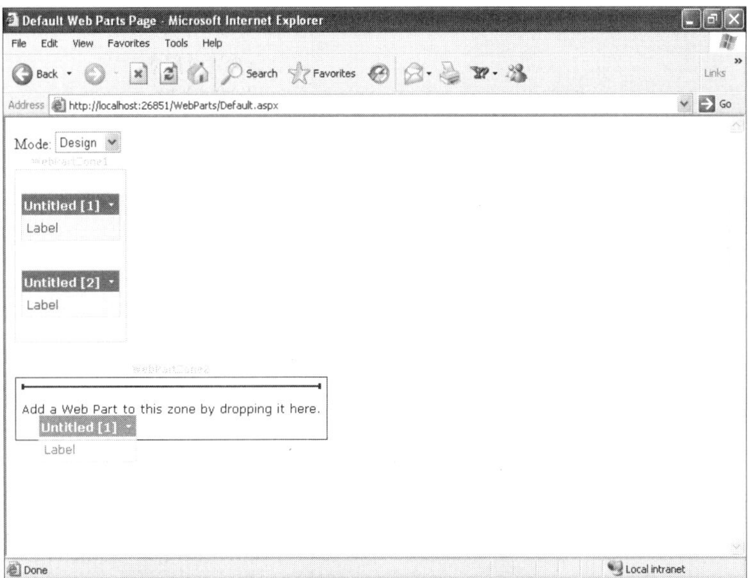

Figure 4-3 Default.aspx while dragging a Web Part in Design mode

This is very cool! You, as the developer, can create little bits of functionality, which your users can customize and combine in ways that are convenient for them.

Note The full drag-and-drop experience works only with Microsoft Internet Explorer.

The Parts of Web Parts

When you first start to work with Web Parts, the number of controls available is somewhat daunting. Figure 4-4 shows the Web Parts available in the Microsoft Visual Studio Toolbox.

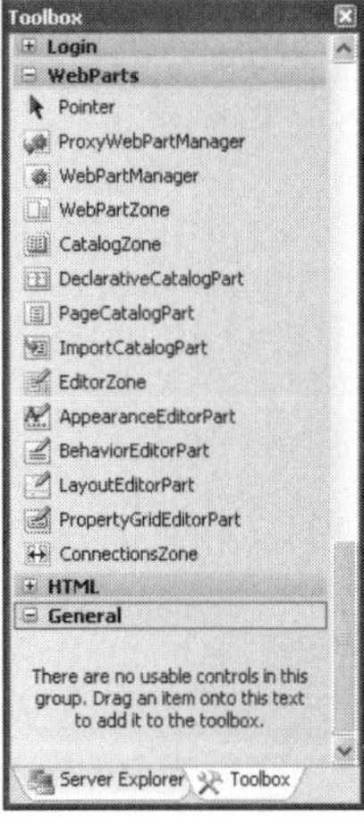

Figure 4-4 Web Parts in the Visual Studio Toolbox

To fully understand how Web Parts work, you must first understand the individual elements of Web Parts. Table 4-1 describes most of the Web Parts components, as well as how they might be used.

Table 4-1 Web Parts Components

Component	Description	Use
WebPartManager	The central class in the Web Part control set. This is a non-visual control that will never appear to the user.	Always required for Web Parts to work.
ProxyWebPartManager	The class used when the *WebPartManager* component is on the Master page in use by the page in question.	Used when you have the *WebPartManager* component on a Master page.
WebPartZone	The central class in the Web Parts control set for hosting Web Parts.	Always used. A place for the user to drag and drop controls onto the form.
CatalogZone	The central class in the Web Parts control set for hosting *CatalogPart* controls in the control set for hosting Web Parts. The next three types are *CatalogPart*-type controls.	Used to give users the ability to view a catalog of available Web Parts in Visual Studio Design view.

Table 4-1 **Web Parts Components**

Component	Description	Use
DeclarativeCatalogPart	A *CatalogZone* component that allows developers to add a set of server controls declaratively on a page.	Commonly used to make controls available by simply adding markup for controls inside the DeclarativeCatalogPart zone.
PageCatalogPart	A *CatalogZone* component that allows users to re-activate controls previously closed.	Used only if the page allows controls to be closed.
ImportCatalogPart	A component that allows users to import a description file that describes the settings on a Web Part control or server control that they want to add to a Web page.	Used when the user has exported the description from a control that supports the *Export* verb from the Web Part Verb menu.
EditorZone	A component that allows users to modify Web pages according to their preferences. The following three controls in this table must be contained in the *EditorZone* component.	Used to contain components to allow users to edit the appearance, behavior, and layout of Web Part properties.
AppearanceEditorPart	A component that allows users to edit several user interface properties of an associated Web Part.	Used to allow a user to edit the appearance of a Web Part.
BehaviorEditorPart	A component that allows users to edit several properties to affect the behavior of the associated Web Part.	Used to change the visibility of verbs such as *close*, *minimize*, and *restore*.
LayoutEditorPart	A component that allows users to edit several properties to affect the layout of the associated Web Part.	Used to change the location of a Web Part.

Note If you are going to allow users to close Web Parts, it is critical to have a *PageCatalogPart* component on the page to allow users to retrieve the Web Parts they have closed.

When designing with Web Parts, you will first drag and drop a variety of Web Part–related controls onto the form. A *WebPartManager* control must be the first control dragged onto the form. You will also want to drag at least one *WebPartZone* control onto the form; adding at least two *WebPartZone* controls makes the most sense, because you will want to give users the ability to alter the look of the page. You will also want to provide some way for users to change modes. The default mode is Browse. You will almost always want to allow Edit mode, so that users can move Web Parts from zone to zone, and Catalog mode, to allow users to make closed Web Parts visible again.

Now that you have a basic introduction to these controls, it makes sense to look at the markup and code of a simple example, as shown in Listing 4-1, later in this section. Of course, in the world of Web Parts, even a simple example can be a little involved.

Setting Up ASP.NET for Web Parts

ASP.NET uses a database to store information about the personalization of the page so that the changes made to the location and visibility of Web Parts on the page can be persisted or stored. If you are using Visual Studio with Microsoft SQL Server 2005 Express Edition (which is the new version of Microsoft SQL Server 2000 Desktop Engine, or MSDE), the database should be created for you automatically. If you do not have SQL Server Express installed, you might have to manually create the database in either SQL Server 2005 or SQL Server 2000 and add the connection information to the Web.config file in the Web site. The first time you try to run a page using Web Parts, you will get an error message related to a SQL Server timeout if the database has not been created. For example, my Web.config file had the following entries added to the *ConnectionStrings* section (I have added line breaks for readability).

```
<remove name="LocalSqlServer"/>
<add name="LocalSqlServer"
        connectionString="data source=.;
        Integrated Security=SSPI;Initial Catalog=aspnetdb"
        providerName="System.Data.SqlClient"/>
```

The Microsoft .NET Framework contains a program named *aspnet_regsql.exe* that can be run to create the database that ASP.NET requires, if it cannot be created automatically. *aspnet_regsql.exe* presents a wizard that allows you to decide where the database should be installed. The second page of the wizard allows you to configure the database that ASP.NET uses, as shown here.

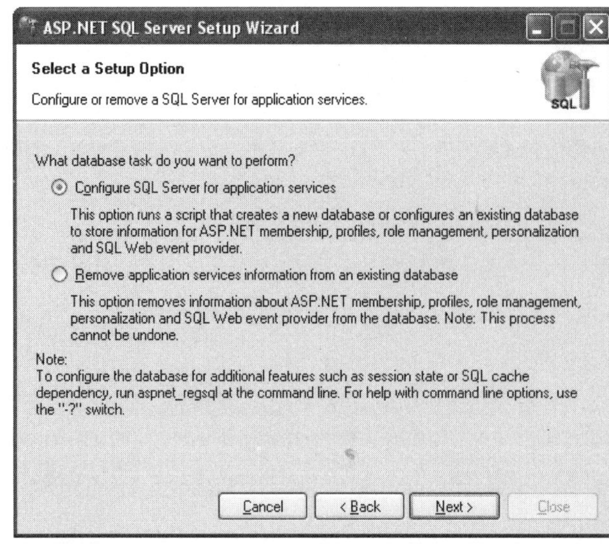

The next page allows you to select the server and database to use, as well as user credentials, as shown here.

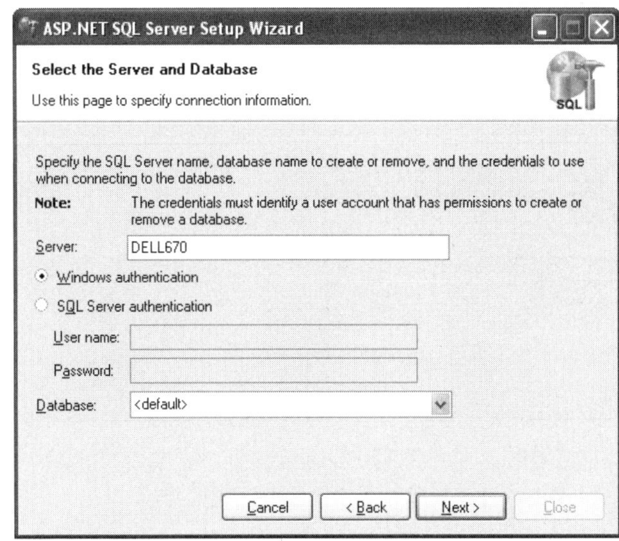

When you finish the wizard, the database creates the following tables, and you will be able to use Web Part personalization.

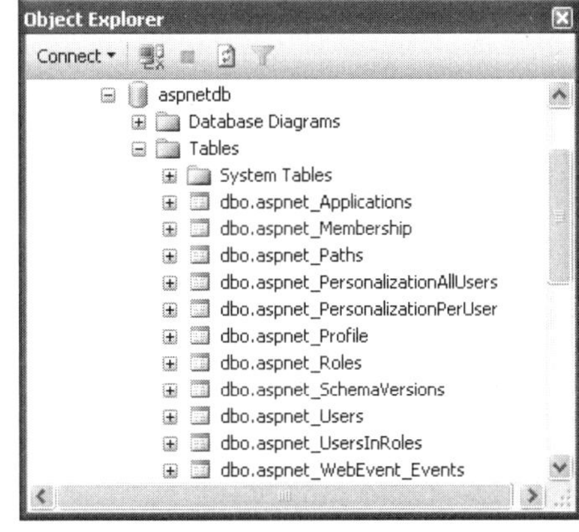

I created a Web site in Visual Studio named WebParts. On the Web Form created by Visual Studio, named Default.aspx, I dragged several controls onto the form. First I dragged a *WebPartManager* control onto the form, which must be the first Web Part–related control on the form. Then I dragged a *DropDownList* control onto the page; by using the control's smart tag, I opened the DropDownList Tasks menu that allowed me to edit the items in the drop-down list. I added three items, and I changed the *Text* property of the three items to Browse, Design, and Catalog.

Next, I dragged two *WebPartZone* controls onto the form. More than one *WebPartZone* control makes a Web Form much more useful. Then I added a *CatalogZone* component to the Web Form. To give me something to work with, I dragged two label controls onto the first *WebPartZone* control. Note that any control can be dragged onto a *WebPartZone* control, and the control will become a Web Part. Finally, I added a *PageCatalogPart* control to the *CatalogZone* component. The *PageCatalogPart* control must be added to a *CatalogZone* component.

The default look for *WebPartZone* controls is rather bleak, as shown in Figure 4-5.

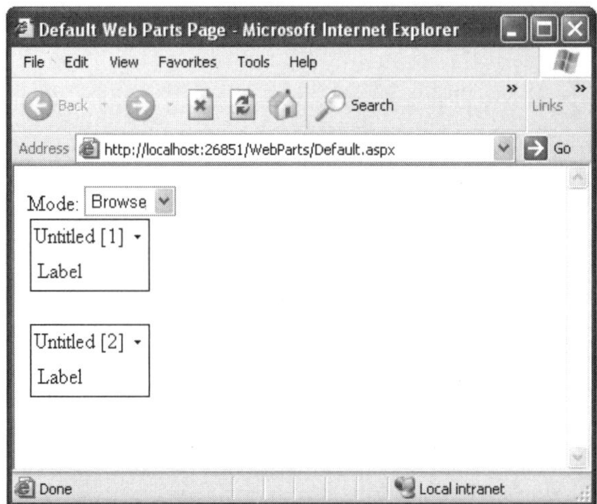

Figure 4-5 The default appearance of a Web Form with Web Parts

To make the *WebPartZone* components a little more attractive, I used the smart tags for the controls to open the WebPartZone Tasks menu. From that menu, I selected Auto Format, and in the resulting dialog box, I selected the Professional scheme. The resulting markup is shown in Listing 4-1.

Listing 4-1 Markup for Simple Web Part Example

```
<%@ Page Language="C#" AutoEventWireup="true"
        CodeFile="Default.aspx.cs" Inherits="_Default" %>

<!DOCTYPE html PUBLIC "-//W3C//DTD XHTML 1.1//EN"
"http://www.w3.org/TR/xhtml11/DTD/xhtml11.dtd">

<html xmlns="http://www.w3.org/1999/xhtml" >
<head runat="server">
    <title>Default Web Parts Page</title>
</head>
<body>
    <form id="form1" runat="server">
        <div>
            <asp:WebPartManager ID="WebPartManager1" runat="server">
            </asp:WebPartManager>
            Mode: <asp:DropDownList ID="DropDownList1" runat="server"
```

```
            AutoPostBack="True"
            OnSelectedIndexChanged=
            "DropDownList1_SelectedIndexChanged">
          <asp:ListItem Selected="True">Browse</asp:ListItem>
          <asp:ListItem>Design</asp:ListItem>
          <asp:ListItem>Catalog</asp:ListItem>
      </asp:DropDownList>
  </div>
  <asp:WebPartZone ID="WebPartZone1" runat="server"
      BorderColor="#CCCCCC" Font-Names="Verdana"
      Padding="6">
      <PartChromeStyle BackColor="#F7F6F3" BorderColor="#E2DED6"
          Font-Names="Verdana" ForeColor="White" />
      <MenuLabelHoverStyle ForeColor="#E2DED6" />
      <EmptyZoneTextStyle Font-Size="0.8em" />
      <MenuLabelStyle ForeColor="White" />
      <MenuVerbHoverStyle BackColor="#F7F6F3"
          BorderColor="#CCCCCC" BorderStyle="Solid"
          BorderWidth="1px" ForeColor="#333333" />
      <HeaderStyle Font-Size="0.7em" ForeColor="#CCCCCC"
          HorizontalAlign="Center" />
      <ZoneTemplate>
          <asp:Label ID="Label1" runat="server"
             Text="Label"></asp:Label>
          <asp:Label ID="Label2" runat="server"
             Text="Label"></asp:Label>
      </ZoneTemplate>
      <MenuVerbStyle BorderColor="#5D7B9D" BorderStyle="Solid"
          BorderWidth="1px" ForeColor="White" />
      <PartStyle Font-Size="0.8em" ForeColor="#333333" />
      <TitleBarVerbStyle Font-Size="0.6em" Font-Underline="False"
          ForeColor="White" />
      <MenuPopupStyle BackColor="#5D7B9D" BorderColor="#CCCCCC"
          BorderWidth="1px" Font-Names="Verdana"
          Font-Size="0.6em" />
      <PartTitleStyle BackColor="#5D7B9D" Font-Bold="True"
          Font-Size="0.8em" ForeColor="White" />
  </asp:WebPartZone>
    
  <asp:WebPartZone ID="WebPartZone2" runat="server"
      BorderColor="#CCCCCC" Font-Names="Verdana"
      Padding="6">
      <PartChromeStyle BackColor="#E3EAEB" BorderColor="#C5BBAF"
          Font-Names="Verdana" ForeColor="#333333" />
      <MenuLabelHoverStyle ForeColor="Yellow" />
      <EmptyZoneTextStyle Font-Size="0.8em" />
      <MenuLabelStyle ForeColor="#333333" />
      <MenuVerbHoverStyle BackColor="#E3EAEB" BorderColor="#CCCCCC"
          BorderStyle="Solid"
          BorderWidth="1px" ForeColor="#333333" />
      <HeaderStyle Font-Size="0.7em" ForeColor="#CCCCCC"
          HorizontalAlign="Center" />
      <MenuVerbStyle BorderColor="#1C5E55" BorderStyle="Solid"
          BorderWidth="1px" ForeColor="White" />
      <PartStyle Font-Size="0.8em" ForeColor="#333333" />
```

```
            <TitleBarVerbStyle Font-Size="0.6em" Font-Underline="False"
                ForeColor="White" />
            <MenuPopupStyle BackColor="#1C5E55" BorderColor="#CCCCCC"
                BorderWidth="1px" Font-Names="Verdana"
                Font-Size="0.6em" />
            <PartTitleStyle BackColor="#1C5E55" Font-Bold="True"
                Font-Size="0.8em" ForeColor="White" />
        </asp:WebPartZone>
        <asp:CatalogZone ID="CatalogZone1" runat="server">
            <ZoneTemplate>
                <asp:PageCatalogPart ID="PageCatalogPart1"
                    runat="server" />
            </ZoneTemplate>
        </asp:CatalogZone>
         
    </form>
</body>
</html>
```

This looks like quite a bit of markup; however, all of the markup related to styles inside the *WebPartZone* tags was added automatically when I applied the scheme in the Auto Format dialog box.

At the top of the page is the *WebPartManager* control. This is a non-visual control, meaning that it is present at design time but will not appear to the end user. Several events and methods are exposed by the *WebPartManager* control; the most important of these are described in Table 4-2.

Table 4-2 *WebPartManager* Events and Methods

Event or Method	Description
DisplayModeChanged	Event fired when the display mode has changed.
DisplayModeChanging	Event fired before the display mode is changed, offering the ability to cancel the change.
WebPartAdded	Event fired when a Web Part has been added.
WebPartAdding	Event fired before a Web Part is added, offering the ability to cancel the addition.
WebPartClosed	Event fired when a Web Part has been closed.
WebPartClosing	Event fired before a Web Part is closed, offering the ability to cancel the closing.
WebPartMoved	Event fired when a Web Part has been moved.
WebPartMoving	Event fired before a Web Part is moved, offering the ability to cancel the move.
AddWebPart	Method to add a Web Part to a page programmatically.
CanConnectWebParts	Method to test whether Web Parts can connect.
CreateWebPart	Method to create a Web Part from a standard control.
ImportWebPart	Method to import a Web Part from an XML stream.

Next in the markup is a drop-down list that includes the Browse, Design, and Catalog options. Most importantly, the *AutoPostback* attribute is set to *true*, meaning that the control will post back when the selection is changed. The event handler for the selected index change is shown in the following code.

```
protected void DropDownList1_SelectedIndexChanged(object sender,
        EventArgs e)
{
    if (DropDownList1.SelectedValue.ToLower() == "browse")
    {
        WebPartManager1.DisplayMode = WebPartManager.BrowseDisplayMode;
    }
    else if (DropDownList1.SelectedValue.ToLower()=="design" )
    {
        WebPartManager1.DisplayMode = WebPartManager.DesignDisplayMode;
    }
    else // DropDownList1.SelectedValue.ToLower() == "catalog"
    {
        WebPartManager1.DisplayMode = WebPartManager.CatalogDisplayMode;
    }
}
```

This code sets the *DisplayMode* property of the *WebPartManager1* object based on the selection made in the drop-down list. For many developers of simple applications, this might be the only interaction with the *WebPartManager* non-visual control. I will cover the *DisplayMode* property settings in the next section.

After the drop-down list are two *WebPartZone* tags. The markup for the *WebPartZone* controls includes several styles (added using the Auto Format dialog box in Visual Studio, described previously). For instance, the following markup describes the style that should be used for the *WebPartZone1* control, specifying the font size, foreground color, and horizontal alignment.

```
<HeaderStyle Font-Size="0.7em" ForeColor="#CCCCCC"
    HorizontalAlign="Center" />
```

See the MSDN documentation for a complete listing of all the possible style elements and all the areas of the *WebPartZone* control that allow the application of styles.

Inside the first *WebPartZone* tag is a *ZoneTemplate* tag that contains the default content for the zone—in this example, two labels that I dragged onto the Web Part zone. Note that in addition to using objects specifically created as Web Parts, any user control or server control can be dragged onto a *WebPartZone* control or manually added inside a *ZoneTemplate* tag.

Finally, a *CatalogZone* tag contains a *ZoneTemplate* tag, which contains a *PageCatalogPart* tag that I dragged onto the *CatalogZone* control in Visual Studio. The *PageCatalogPart* tag allows the user to reopen previously closed Web Parts. Other than providing the *CatalogZone* control and the *PageCatalogPart* control, you don't have to do anything else to allow your users to access previously closed controls in the *CatalogZone* control.

Display Modes and Web Parts

Recall that the event handler for the drop-down list for Default.aspx in the WebParts project changed the *DisplayMode* property of the *WebPartManager1* object. The *DisplayMode* property must be one of the *WebPartDisplayMode* enumerations, as outlined in Table 4-3.

Table 4-3 *WebPartDisplayMode* Enumerations

DisplayMode Property	Description
BrowseDisplayMode	Displays Web Parts for normal, end user use. This is the default mode.
DesignDisplayMode	Displays the Web Part zone user interface (UI), enabling users to drag and drop Web Part components to change the layout of the page.
EditDisplayMode	Displays special editing UI elements and allows end users to edit the controls on the page.
CatalogDisplayMode	Displays a special catalog UI to allow end users to add and remove page controls.
ConnectDisplayMode	Displays a special connections UI to allow end users to connect Web Part controls.

Browse, Design, and Catalog are the three display modes you will use most. The *BrowseDisplayMode* enumeration can be seen in Figure 4-1, and the *DesignDisplayMode* enumeration can be seen in Figure 4-2 and Figure 4-3. To use the *CatalogDisplayMode* enumeration, you must first close one of the Web Parts on the page. In Figure 4-6, the menu for one of the Web Parts appears on the Default.aspx page.

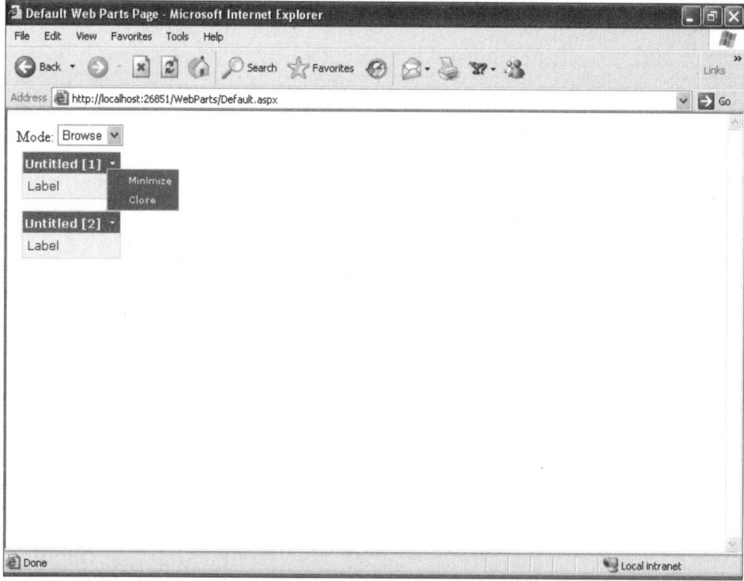

Figure 4-6 The menu that allows you to close or minimize a Web Part

When you click Close, the page appears as shown in Figure 4-7.

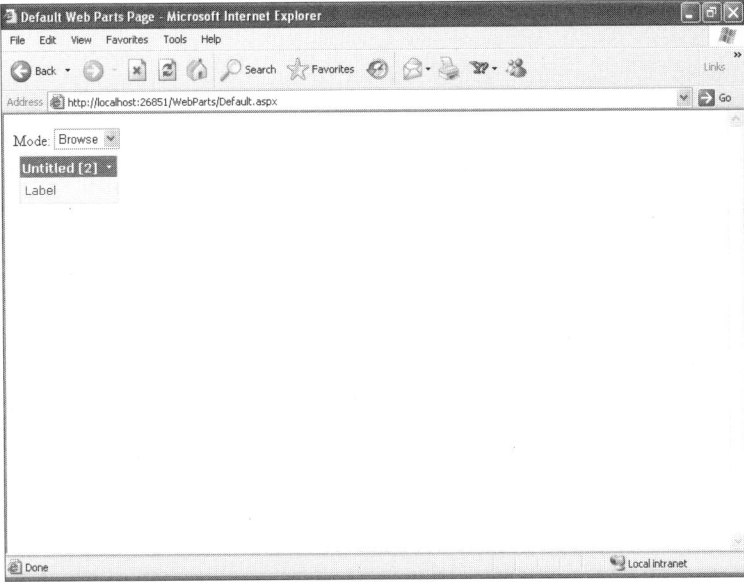

Figure 4-7 Default.aspx after one Web Part is closed

The first thing I noticed when I first played with Web Parts is that when you close a Web Part, it stays closed! The state of the page is saved, even if you have not logged in to the site. This is known, rather oddly, as anonymous personalization.

To get the closed Web Part back, you must enter Catalog mode. In Default.aspx, select Catalog from the drop-down list, and the page appears as shown in Figure 4-8.

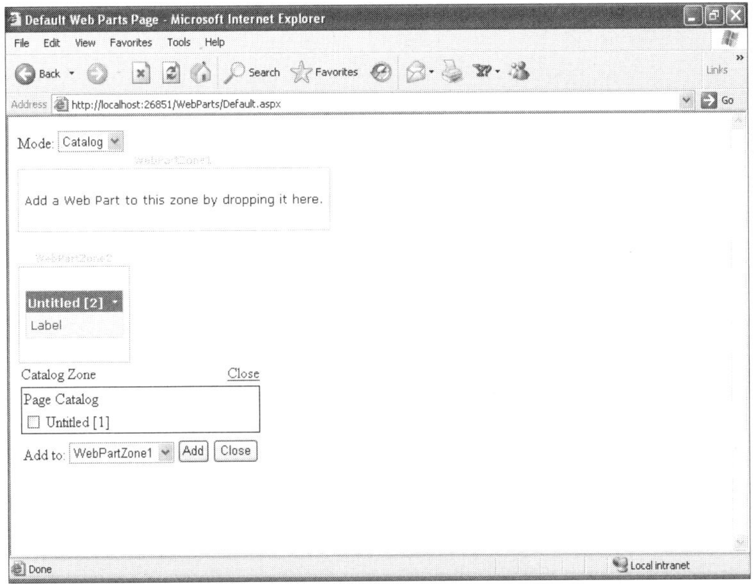

Figure 4-8 Default.aspx in Catalog mode after one Web Part is closed

The interesting portion of the page is the Page Catalog inside of the Catalog Zone. Untitled [1] is in the list of Web Parts in the catalog. When you select the check box next to Untitled [1] and click Add, the Web Part is added to the selected zone, WebPartZone1, as shown in Figure 4-9.

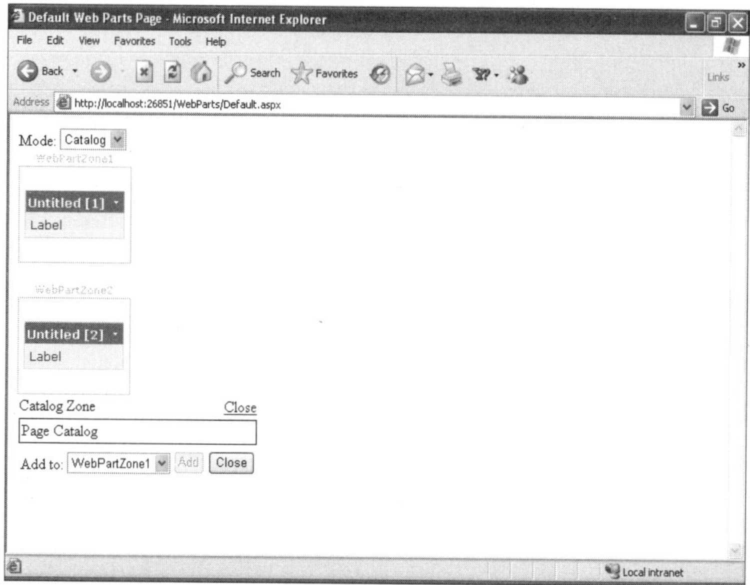

Figure 4-9 Default.aspx in Catalog mode after adding the previously closed Web Part

Adding Components

Now that we have seen Web Parts in use, it makes sense to build a page from the ground up. I added a new page to the WebParts site in Visual Studio, named WebPartsSample.aspx. First, I added a *WebPartManager* component. Nothing else must be done with this component, although it will be used in code. Next, I added a table, using the Layout/Insert table menu option in Visual Studio Design view. I created a table with two rows and two columns, with a width of 500 pixels.

To use Web Parts, I added a Web Part zone to each of the four cells of the table, which appeared in Visual Studio Design view as shown in Figure 4-10.

To allow previously closed Web Parts to be reopened, I added a *PageCatalogPart* control to the page. You cannot simply drag a *PageCatalogPart* control onto the page. You must first add a *CatalogZone* control, and then you can drag a *PageCatalogPart* control into the *CatalogZone* control. The result should be similar to the page shown in Figure 4-11.

To allow editing, you must add an Editor zone to the page. This control can be dragged and dropped onto the page anywhere you like; I dropped it at the bottom of the page.

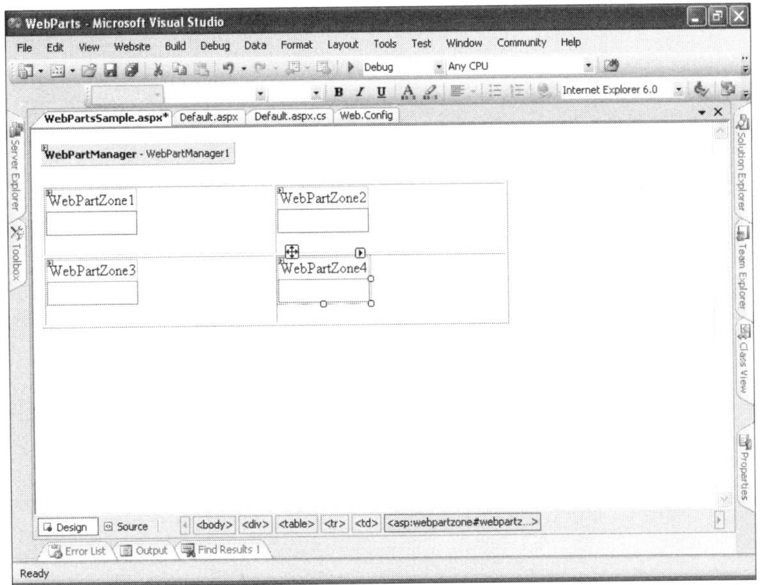

Figure 4-10 WebPartsSample.aspx after adding the *WebPartManager* control and four Web Part zones

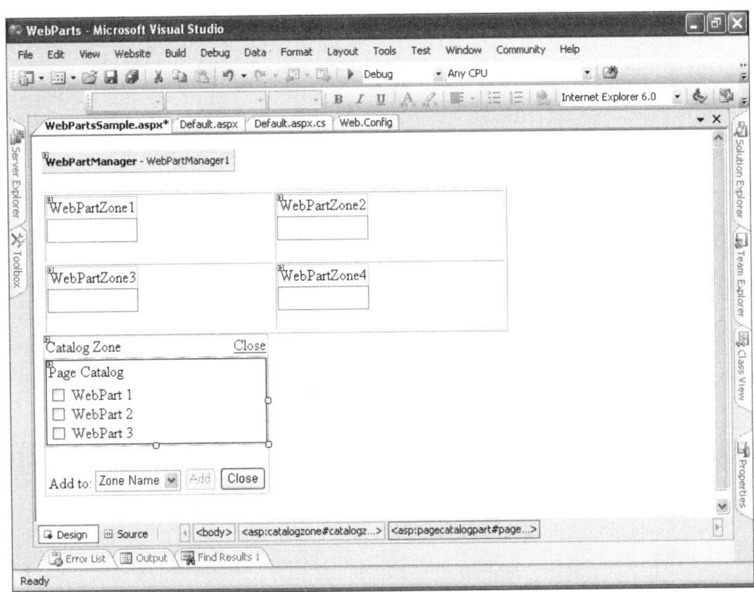

Figure 4-11 WebPartsSample.aspx after adding the *CatalogZone* and *PageCatalogPart* controls

To each of the Web Part zones, I added a component. It does not matter specifically what you add, but I added a calendar, a check box list, a bulleted list, and a label. When run, the page looks almost like it would have had I not used any Web Parts. The difference is that each Web Part has a title bar by default, with the name Untitled [*n*], where *n* is a number from 1 to 4. The title bars also have menus that allow you to close or minimize the Web Parts. Figure 4-12 shows the page running with all Web Parts in the default mode.

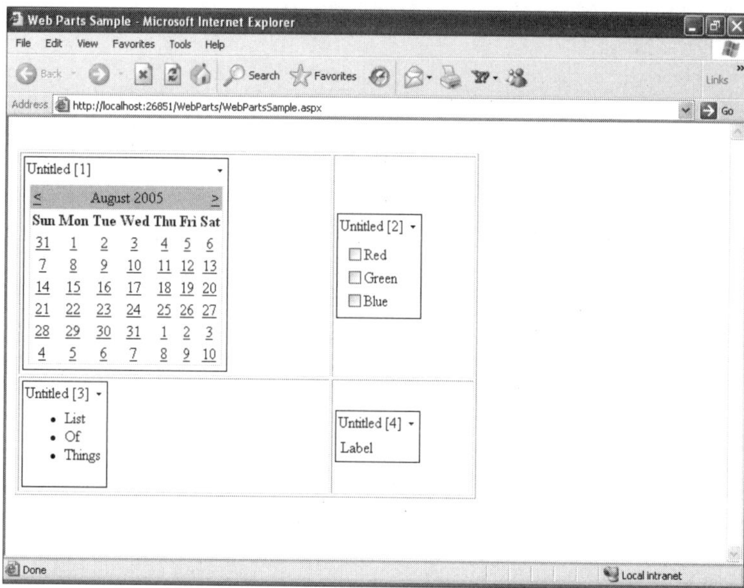

Figure 4-12 WebPartsSample.aspx running in Browse mode

Figure 4-13 shows the page running after I minimized the Web Part containing the calendar.

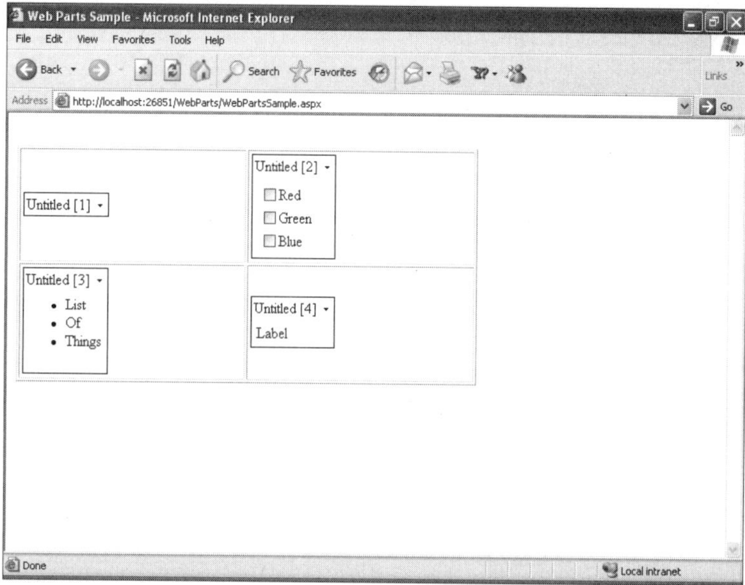

Figure 4-13 WebPartsSample.aspx running in Browse mode, after minimizing the Web Part containing the calendar

To do anything else with the Web Parts (such as rearrange or restore Web Parts), you must set the *DisplayMode* property of the *WebPartManager* component. You can allow users to set the display mode in several ways. You have seen an example using a drop-down list in the Default.aspx page, but the display mode can also be set with check boxes, option buttons, or whatever works for you. In this example, I added an option button list (*RadioButtonList* in the code) at the top of the form with three items, with both text and values set to "Browse," "Edit," and "Catalog." I set the *RepeatColumns* property to 3, meaning that the items will be displayed three across, and I left the default *RepeatDirection* property set to Horizontal. Although it's not required, I set the Browse item as the default selection, so that it will appear with a check mark when the page is first run. I set the *AutoPostback* property to *true*, and then I double-clicked the *RadioButtonList* control so that Visual Studio would create the event handler. I then added code very similar to the code in the *SelectionChanged* event handler in Default.aspx.

```
protected void RadioButtonList1_SelectedIndexChanged(object sender, EventArgs e)
{
    if (this.RadioButtonList1.SelectedValue.ToLower() == "browse")
    {
        this.WebPartManager1.DisplayMode =
            WebPartManager.BrowseDisplayMode;
    }
    else if (this.RadioButtonList1.SelectedValue.ToLower() == "edit")
    {
        this.WebPartManager1.DisplayMode = WebPartManager.EditDisplayMode;
    }
    else // this.RadioButtonList1.SelectedValue.ToLower() == "catalog"
    {
        this.WebPartManager1.DisplayMode =
            WebPartManager.CatalogDisplayMode;
    }
}
```

When you run WebPartsSample.aspx, you should be able to switch from Browse mode to Edit mode, move Web Parts from one zone to another, return to Browse mode, close one of the Web Parts, and then use Catalog mode to add the closed Web Part back into one of the zones. When you look at the page, it is functional, but not very attractive. You can remedy this by clicking the smart tag arrow and selecting Auto Format on the menu. Figure 4-14 shows the page running in Browse mode with all Web Part zones set to the Simple Auto Format scheme.

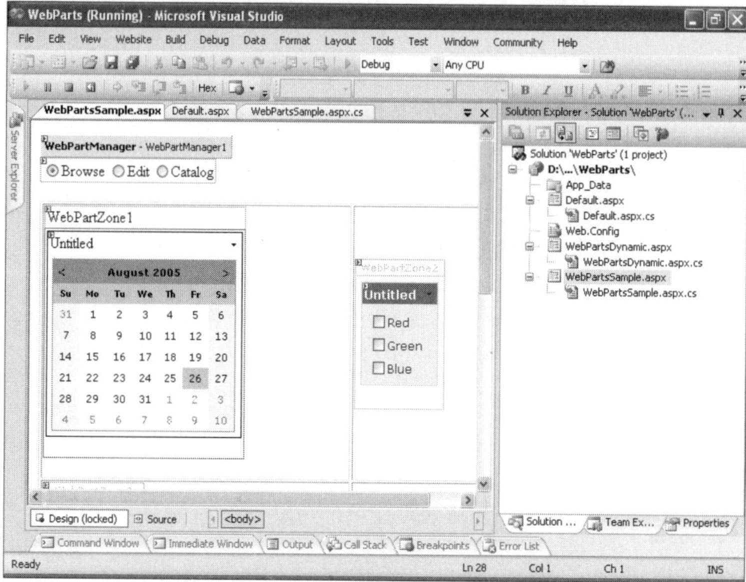

Figure 4-14 WebPartsSample.aspx running in Browse mode with the Simple Auto Format scheme applied

Programmatically Controlling Web Parts

Allowing users to modify the layout of the page is a major benefit of using Web Parts, but programmatically controlling the addition and deletion of Web Parts also provides benefits. Although a major goal of ASP.NET 2.0 is reduction in the amount of code, there is certainly a place for code. For example, you might want to dynamically create and display a Web Part only if certain criteria were met, such membership in the Admin role or one or more items existing in a shopping cart.

Using WebPartsSample.aspx as a base, I created a similar page, named WebPartsDynamic.aspx. All the controls and layout in WebPartsDynamic.aspx are the same as in WebPartsSample.aspx, with the addition of two buttons, one to add a Web Part dynamically, and another to remove a Web Part dynamically. The final page is as shown in Figure 4-15.

Clicking the Add Web Part button adds a Web Part to WebPartZone1, as shown in Figure 4-16.

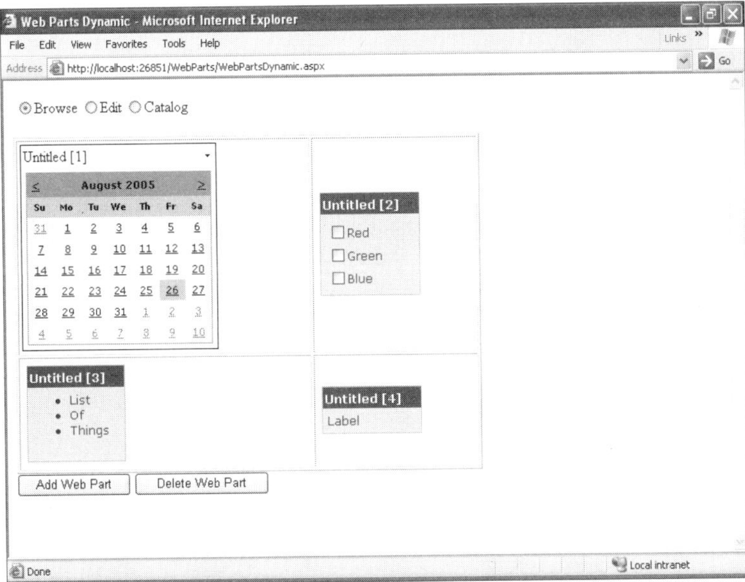

Figure 4-15 WebPartsDynamic.aspx running in Browse mode

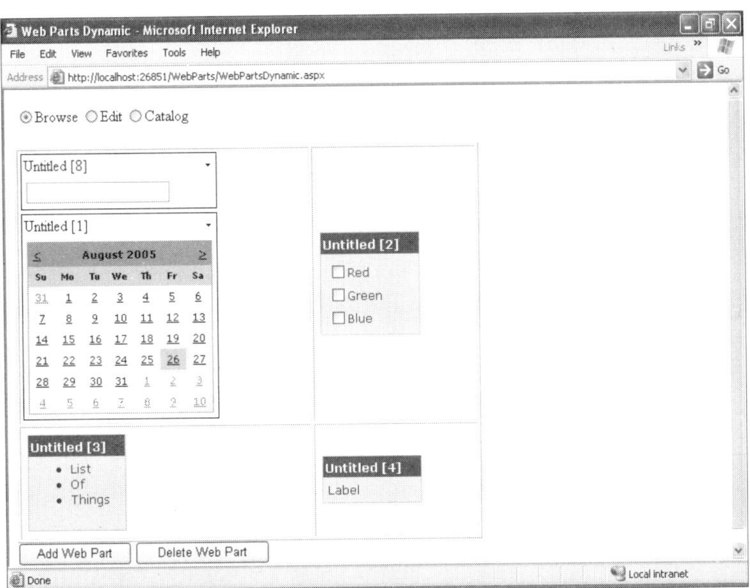

Figure 4-16 WebPartsDynamic.aspx running in Browse mode after clicking Add Web Part

Clicking the Delete Web Part button removes the Web Part, resulting in a screen that looks exactly like Figure 4-15. The server-side code for WebPartsDynamic.aspx is shown in Listing 4-2.

Listing 4-2 WebPartsDynamic.aspx.cs

```
using System;
using System.Data;
using System.Configuration;
using System.Collections;
using System.Web;
using System.Web.Security;
using System.Web.UI;
using System.Web.UI.WebControls;
using System.Web.UI.WebControls.WebParts;
using System.Web.UI.HtmlControls;

public partial class WebPartsDynamic : System.Web.UI.Page
{
    protected void Page_Load(object sender, EventArgs e)
    {

    }
    protected void RadioButtonList1_SelectedIndexChanged(object sender,
        EventArgs e)
    {
        if (this.RadioButtonList1.SelectedValue.ToLower() == "browse")
        {
            this.WebPartManager1.DisplayMode =
                WebPartManager.BrowseDisplayMode;
        }
        else if (this.RadioButtonList1.SelectedValue.ToLower() == "edit")
        {
            this.WebPartManager1.DisplayMode =
                WebPartManager.EditDisplayMode;
        }
        else // this.RadioButtonList1.SelectedValue.ToLower() ==
                "catalog"
        {
            this.WebPartManager1.DisplayMode =
                WebPartManager.CatalogDisplayMode;
        }
    }
    protected void Button1_Click(object sender, EventArgs e)
    {
        TextBox tb = new TextBox();
        tb.Text = "Hello!";
        tb.ID = "DynamicWebPart";
        GenericWebPart gwp = this.WebPartManager1.CreateWebPart(tb);
        this.WebPartManager1.AddWebPart(gwp, this.WebPartZone1, 0);
    }
    protected void Button2_Click(object sender, EventArgs e)
    {
        if (this.WebPartZone1.WebParts.Count > 0)
        {
            this.WebPartManager1.DeleteWebPart(
                this.WebPartZone1.WebParts[0]);
        }
    }
}
```

The interesting part of this code are the two button click event handlers. *Button1_Click* is the event handler for the Add Web Part button. The *CreateWebPart* method of the *WebPartManager* class expects as a parameter an object that derives from the *Control* class. A text box certainly qualifies, and so I first created a new *TextBox* object, and then I set the *Text* property and the *ID* property. Controls cannot be directly added to a Web Part zone, although Visual Studio Design view makes it appear that they can. Behind the scenes, when you drag and drop a normal control onto a Web Part zone, a wrapper is created. That is what I did when I called the *CreateWebPart* method of the *WebPartManager1* control. The return value from the *CreateWebPart* method is a *GenericWebPart* object. I stored the returned object in the variable *gwp*. Finally, I added the Web Part to WebPartZone1. The last parameter to the *AddWebPart* method is the index, and 0 means that the control will be added at the top of the Web Part zone.

Button2_Click is the event handler for the Delete Web Part button. First I checked the *Count* property of the *WebParts* collection on WebPartZone1. If it is greater than 0 (meaning that there is at least one Web Part in WebPartZone1), the first Web Part (at index 0) is deleted. Note that this code can delete any Web Part, not just the Web Parts added by using the Add Web Part button. There is no distinction between Web Parts created declaratively in markup and Web Parts created dynamically in code at runtime.

The *WebPartManager* control can also be used to prevent mode changes, as well as to prevent moving and closing of particular Web Parts. To prevent a change to Edit mode, you can use code similar to the following.

```
protected void WebPartManager1_DisplayModeChanging(object sender,
      WebPartDisplayModeCancelEventArgs e)
 {
     if (e.NewDisplayMode == WebPartManager.EditDisplayMode)
     {
         e.Cancel = true;
         e.NewDisplayMode = WebPartManager.BrowseDisplayMode;
         this.RadioButtonList1.SelectedIndex = 0;
     }
 }
```

This event handler is called just before the display mode changes. Initially, when I worked on this example, I simply set the *Cancel* property of the *WebPartDisplayModeCancelEventArgs* argument to *true*. However, I learned that this is not sufficient; you must set the *NewDisplayMode* property as well. In practice, this is not a terrible problem, and it might be useful if you wanted to cause one display mode change to trigger a different display mode. Normally, you might want to just disable whatever widget you use to change the display mode, rather than use an event handler to cancel a change. In the end, having events that can be handled is always best, because the developers of the framework can never anticipate all scenarios for all developers. The downside of preventing a mode change via handling the *DisplayModeChanging* event is that a round trip to the server is required.

Also, to keep the user interface in sync with the actual mode, I reset the RadioButton1 *SelectedIndex* property to 0 (meaning that Browse will be selected by default in the option button list).

Conclusion

In this chapter, I presented an overview of Web Parts and how they are used and controlled on a Web page. Web Parts are not appropriate for every application, perhaps not even most, but they are perfect for some types of applications. If you are creating portal Web applications, with lots of utility-type functions on a single page, Web Parts are ideal. You can make all sorts of Web Parts available, allowing users to personalize the page so that they always see exactly what they want to see, in the order they prefer. There are, of course, some limitations to what users can do. In general, they can make Web Parts visible or invisible and move them around, but only within the constraints of the developer's design. Web Parts can be dragged and dropped only into Web Part zones; a Web Part zone must exist on the page before a user can drop a Web Part into it.

One significant aspect of using Web Parts has not been addressed in this chapter. Rather than using individual controls as Web Parts, you will often want to create custom controls that act as Web Parts; this lets you do a variety of special things, such as allow users to edit information in the Web Part. In addition, unlike the default title bar text "Untitled" that results from dropping standard controls into a Web Part zone, custom Web Parts can have defined titles. User controls can also be used as Web Parts, and by overriding a single interface, many of the Web Part properties can be set. Building custom Web Parts and using user controls as Web Parts will be covered in Chapter 6, "Custom Controls."

Next, in Chapter 5, you will learn all about data binding. Virtually all Web sites rely on data from a database to customize content for the user. Data binding makes it all happen. ASP.NET 2.0 provides some powerful new controls that allow the developer to do more with less code. Still, when working with data, you might find yourself occasionally working with code to make the magic happen.

Chapter 5

Data Binding

In this chapter:

Most Web Forms these days are fed by, and feed, databases. By using a database, in fact, Web applications can do virtually everything that traditional Microsoft Windows or smart client applications can do, with the advantage that there is generally no client installation required. Using a traditional Windows application that accesses a database usually requires that some sort of database driver be loaded on the machine accessing the application, in addition to the actual application. For a Web application, any database drivers need only be loaded on the Web server. The client machine accessing a Web application does not need to know anything about the database connection. Web application user interfaces are not as rich as Windows applications, and they require a constant connection, but these are the only significant downsides.

Creating the Sample Database

The examples in the book will generally use the BikeBlog database. Included with the source for the book is a file named CreateBikeBlog.sql. To create the database from the SQL file, open Microsoft SQL Server Management Studio. Next, right-click the name of any database in Object Explorer, and then click New Query on the context menu, as shown in the following screen shot.

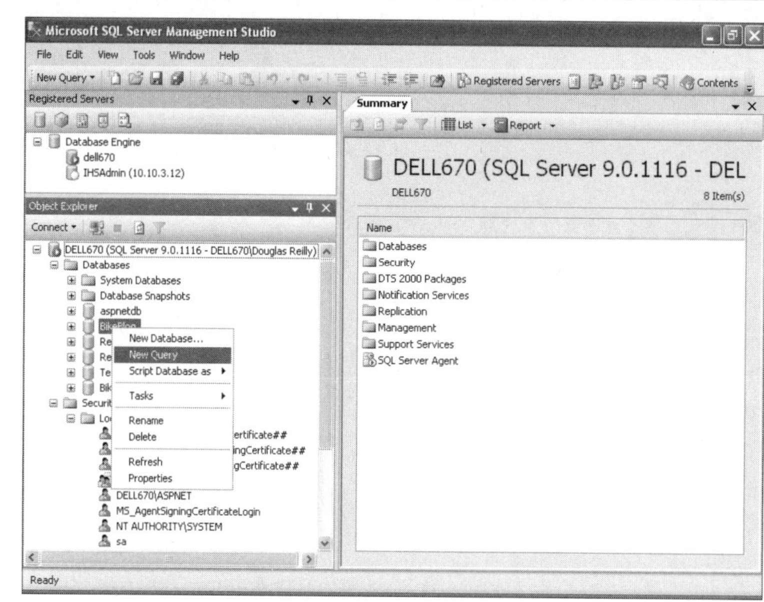

A new window appears. Point to Open on the File menu, click CreateBikeBlog.sql, and then click OK. The resulting screen looks like this.

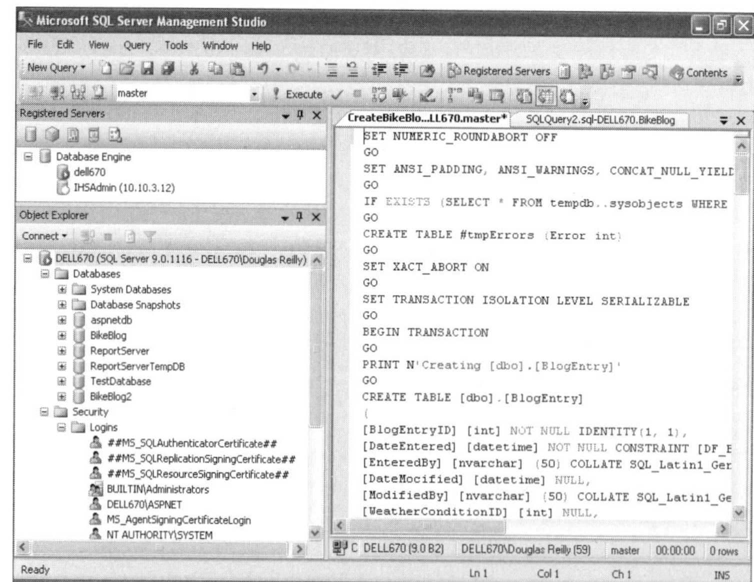

Click Execute, and the database, tables, views, and stored procedures are created, and the tables are populated with some default data.

When Classic ASP was first introduced, databases were accessed via classic ADO. Microsoft Visual Basic Scripting Edition (VBScript) supported the use of ADO; however, the ASP framework itself offered no special support for data-bound applications. Classic ADO had what amounted to a one-size-fits-all database object, the *Recordset*. The *Recordset* object could be connected and disconnected, it could use a server-side or client-side cursor, and dozens of different properties could be set to modify its behavior. However, an individual data source might or might not support any number of these properties, and would generally give no hint that a property setting was being ignored.

Microsoft ASP.NET 1.x was a complete rewrite, with special emphasis on server controls, including several controls that made data binding easier. Microsoft ADO.NET 1.x introduced a totally new model for database access. In contrast to classic ADO, in which all database access was through the *Recordset* object, ASP.NET introduced several classes that together allowed a developer to do most, but not quite all, of what was possible with classic ADO. ADO.NET added features that gave the developer much greater control over certain aspects of database access.

The *DataSource* Control

One thing missing from ASP.NET 1.x was a good way to use Rapid Application Development (RAD) tools to develop database-oriented Web Forms. I personally found myself using code whenever I needed to access data, either in a bound control or for other sorts of manipulations. Microsoft Visual Studio .NET (the previous version of Visual Studio, used to support 1.x applications) allowed you to bind data in code, but some of the implementation details were not great, and you generally needed to use code to initiate loading the data and the data binding.

ASP.NET 2.0 offers a major improvement, the various *DataSource* controls. A *DataSource* control is a non-visual control that encapsulates all the information needed to retrieve (and optionally insert, update, and delete) data without using code. Using a *DataSource* control relieves the developer from having to create a great deal of boilerplate code to bind the results of a query to a data control, allowing virtually all work to be done declaratively. Rather than a single *DataSource* control, there are several. The standard *DataSource* controls are:

- ***SqlDataSource*** For SQL Server databases
- ***AccessDataSource*** For Microsoft Office Access databases
- ***ObjectDataSource*** For business objects
- ***XmlDataSource*** For XML data
- ***SiteMapDataSource*** For connecting to a valid site map

All *DataSource* controls inherit from the *DataSourceControl* class, which implements the *IDataSource* and *IListSource* interfaces. The examples in this book will use the *SqlDataSource* control.

Using *SqlDataSource* allows me to connect to SQL Server databases. SQL Server 2005 Express Edition offers a no-cost way to develop applications targeted to SQL Server 2005; for performance reasons, using a server-based database, as opposed to a file-based database (such as Access), makes a great deal of sense for a Web application.

The *SqlDataSource* Control

All the examples in this chapter are placed in a Web site named DataBinding. I created the Web site by using the File/New/Web Site menu option. In the newly created DataBinding Web site, open the Web Form generated by Visual Studio (named Default.aspx). Open the Toolbox, and drag an *SqlDataSource* control from the Data section onto the Web Form. It doesn't matter exactly where you place the control, because *SqlDataSource* is a non-visual control. After you place the control on the form, the SqlDataSource Tasks menu appears, as shown in Figure 5-1.

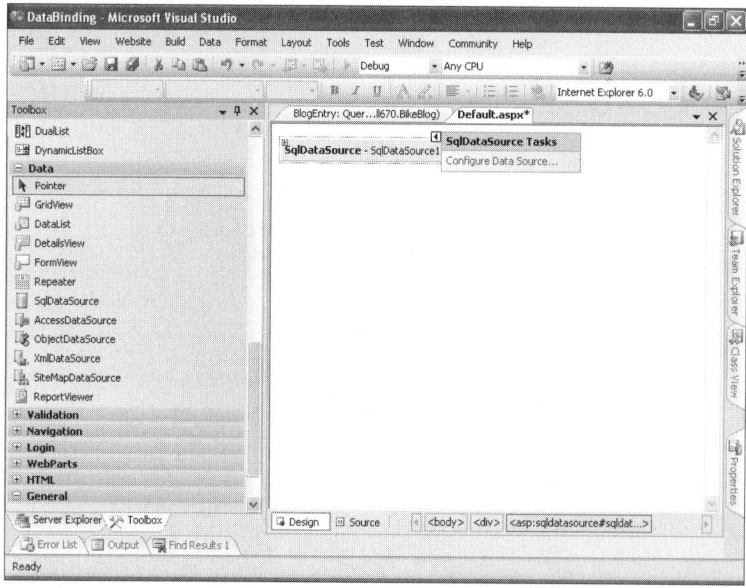

Figure 5-1 The *SqlDataSource* control, with the SqlDataSource Tasks menu displayed

Click Configure Date Source, the only option on the SqlDataSource Tasks menu, and the Configure Data Source wizard appears, as shown in Figure 5-2.

Because this is a new Web site, no database connections are configured. To generate connection configurations, click New Connection. The Add Connection dialog box appears, as shown in Figure 5-3.

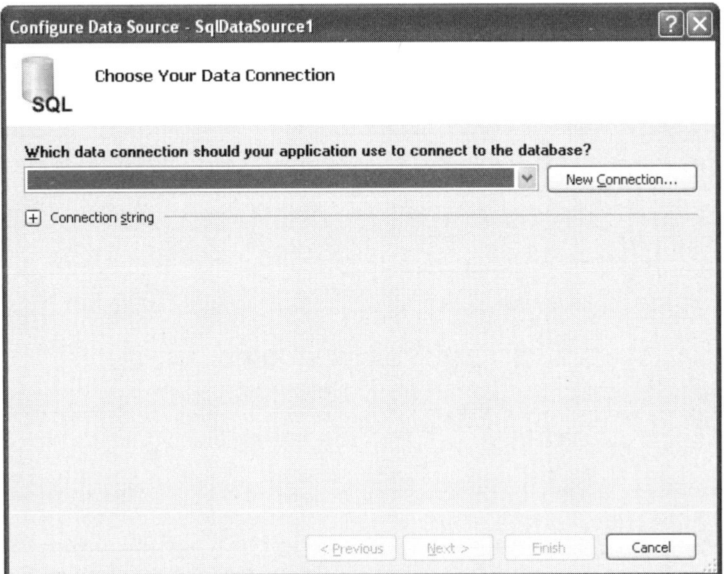

Figure 5-2 The first page of the Configure Data Source wizard

Figure 5-3 The Add Connection dialog box

In the Server Name box, you can enter the name of the server that you want to use. If you are unsure of the name of the server (or if you don't want to type), you can click the down arrow to see a list of available servers, like the list shown in Figure 5-4.

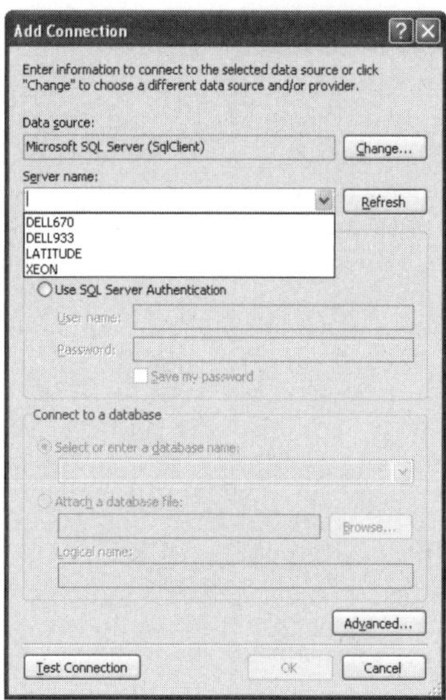

Figure 5-4 The Add Connection dialog box showing a list of available servers

For this example, I selected the machine I was working on, named DELL670. In the Log On To The Server section, click Use Windows Authentication, rather than Use SQL Server Authentication.

Note Using Windows Authentication for the connection will work properly as long as you are testing the Web site using the Web server built into Visual Studio 2005. Recall from Chapter 1, "The Web Forms Environment," that the built-in Web server runs as a normal application, whereas a "real" Web server runs as a service. When I move the application into production, presumably using Internet Information Services (IIS), I must do one of two things. I could change the connection to use SQL Server authentication, and then supply an explicit user name and password. Or I could add the user whose security context an ASP.NET application will run under in IIS (in this case, the user is <*machinename*>\ASPNET) as a user in SQL Server and continue using Windows Authentication.

In the Connect To A Database section, select the BikeBlog database from the list of databases, and then click OK. In the Configure Data Source wizard, you can see the resulting connection string by clicking the plus sign (+). The result should be something like Figure 5-5.

Click Next, and the second page of the wizard appears, as shown in Figure 5-6.

Saving the connection string is generally useful, and the default name is usually reasonable. On the third page of the Configure Data Source wizard, you can determine exactly how data should be obtained for the data source you are creating. You can specify a custom SQL statement or a stored procedure (which we will do later in this chapter), or you can specify the columns to include, and in other ways customize the SQL SELECT statement by using a convenient user interface.

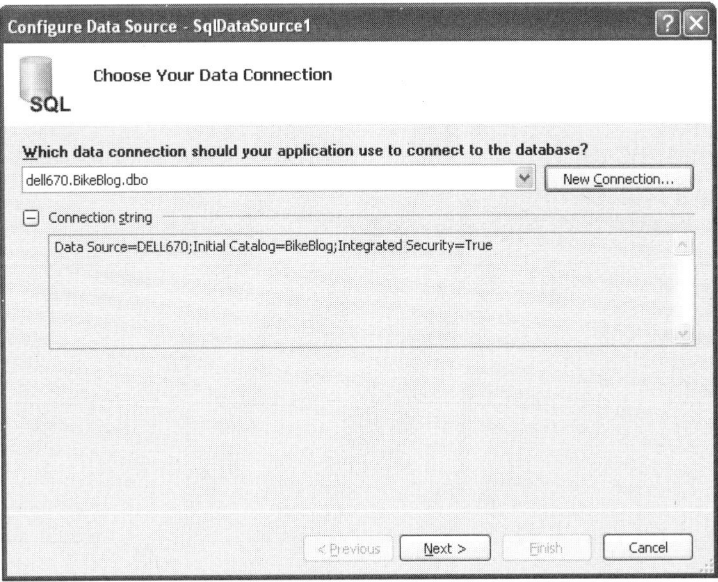

Figure 5-5 The Configure Data Source wizard with the connection string displayed

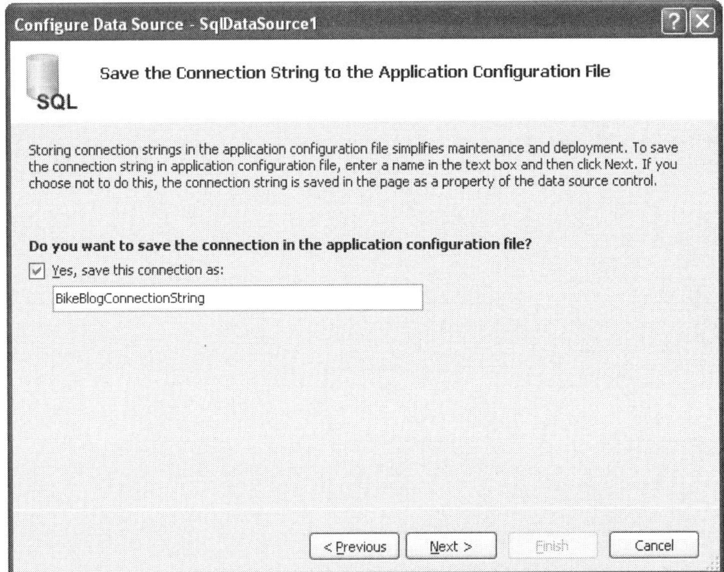

Figure 5-6 The second page of the Configure Data Source wizard

> **Note** Whether you should use dynamically generated SQL statements or stored procedures is an issue that can cause heated debates in the developer community. For a discussion of the issues involved, with pointers to opinions that differ from mine, see my article "To SP or not to SP in SQL Server" at *http://www.simpletalk.com/2005/04/11/to-sp-or-not-to-sp-in-sql-server/*.

In this example, the BlogEntry table should be the default table. Figure 5-7 shows the columns that should be selected. Note that as you select columns, the SELECT statement appears at the bottom of the page. Selecting the columns and specifying the WHERE clause and the ORDER BY clause, and then looking at the resulting SELECT statement, can serve as a way to learn SQL syntax.

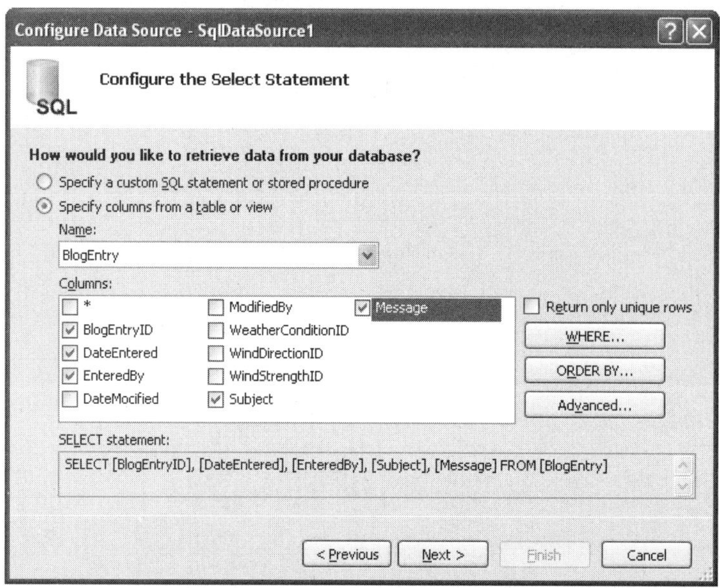

Figure 5-7 The Configure Data Source wizard with several columns selected

In SQL, a WHERE clause is used to restrict the number of rows returned by the query. Click WHERE, and the Add WHERE Clause dialog box shown in Figure 5-8 appears. In Figure 5-8, I added some data for an example WHERE clause.

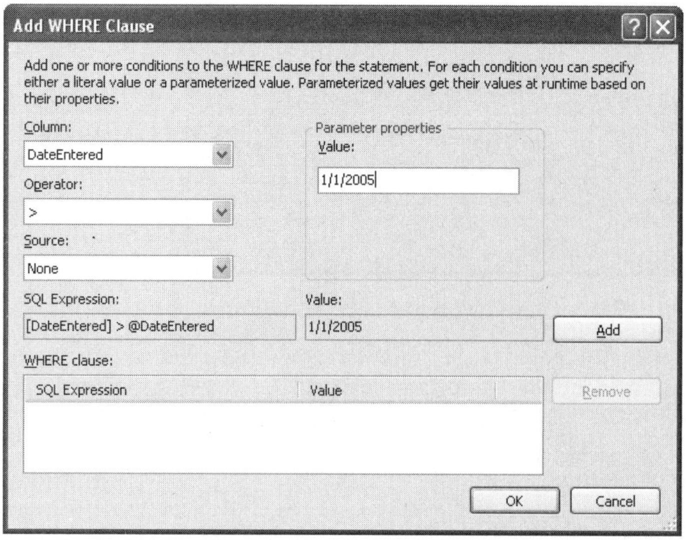

Figure 5-8 The Add WHERE Clause dialog box with a WHERE clause entered

The Column list shows the columns in the table involved in the SELECT statement. I selected DateEntered for illustrative purposes. The Operator list allows you to select an operator to use in the WHERE clause. Several operators are available only for columns that are string-type columns. These string-only operators include LIKE, NOT LIKE, and CONTAINS. Finally, you can select the source of the right side of the SQL expression in the Source list. This is where some of the magic happens that allows for substantial reduction in the number of lines of code. In this example, I selected None as the source, which allowed me to enter a literal value in the Value box (in this example, 1/1/2005). The other options for source are:

- **Control** The value to compare comes from a control on the current form.
- **Cookie** The value to compare comes from a cookie.
- **Form** The value to compare comes from a value on the form. Generally, Control is a better choice, unless you are trying to access a form element that is not in an ASP.NET *runat=server* form. Using Control allows you to use the server-side ID of the control. If you use Form, you must ensure that the ID you are using is the final ID that ASP.NET renders, which might or might not be the same as the server-side ID.
- **Profile** The value to compare comes from a Profile value, part of the personalization and membership system that will be covered in Chapter 7, "Security and Administration."
- **QueryString** The value to compare comes from a value passed in on the query string of the URL. If you select this option, you are prompted to specify the session variable key, and you can offer a default value. A URL can be in the following format: *MyPage.aspx?var1=val1&var2=val2*. Given this string, using QueryString as the source, if we specify var1 as the QueryStringField, val1 will be used as the value.
- **Session** The value to compare comes from session state. If you select this option, you are prompted to specify the session variable key, and you can offer a default value.

When you click Add in the dialog box shown in Figure 5-8, the dialog box shown in Figure 5-9 appears.

When you click OK, you return to the Configure Data Source wizard, where you can see that the WHERE clause has been added to the SELECT statement at the bottom of the page, as shown in Figure 5-10.

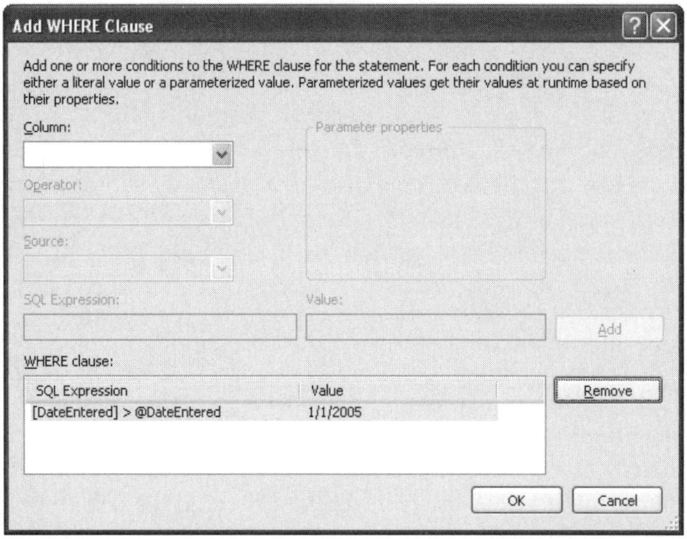

Figure 5-9 The Add WHERE Clause dialog box with a WHERE clause added

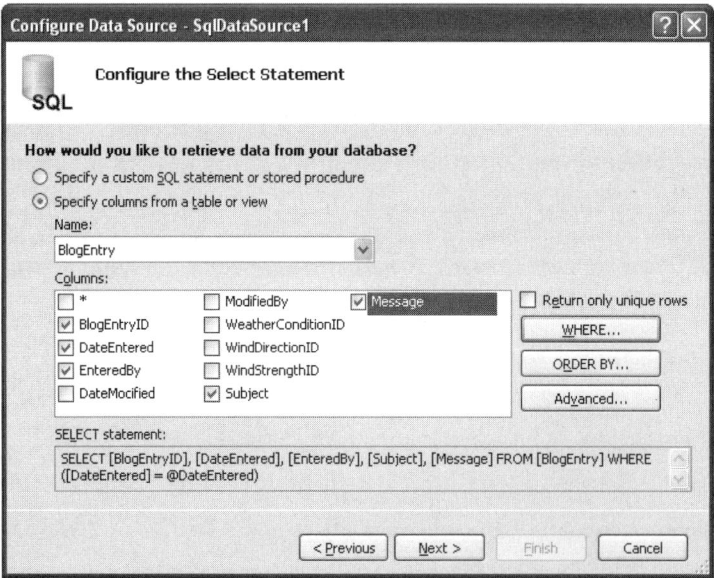

Figure 5-10 The Configure Data Source wizard with a WHERE clause added to the SELECT statement

Next, click ORDER BY to open the Add ORDER BY Clause dialog box. ORDER BY is the part of the SQL SELECT statement that determines the order in which rows are returned. In an SQL SELECT statement, without an ORDER BY clause, the order of rows returned is undefined (even if it seems as if the rows returned are in some specific order). You can select three columns, choosing whether each is ascending or descending. In this example, it is reasonable to sort entries by DateEntered in descending order. This results in the dialog box shown in Figure 5-11. Note the SELECT statement at the bottom of the dialog box.

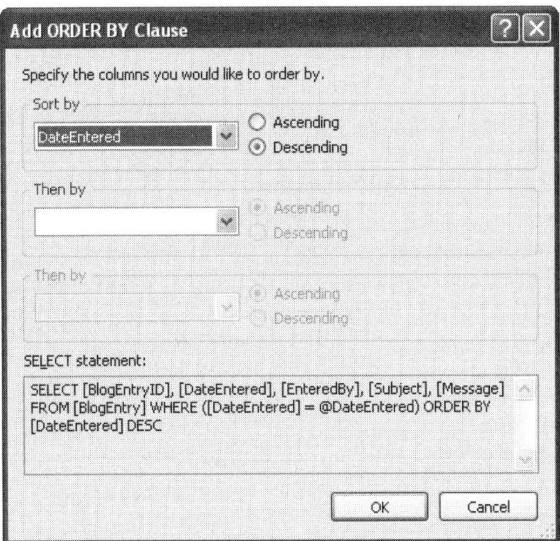

Figure 5-11 The Add ORDER BY Clause dialog box with the DateEntered column selected

After you add the ORDER BY clause, click Advanced in the Configure Data Source wizard to open the dialog box shown in Figure 5-12.

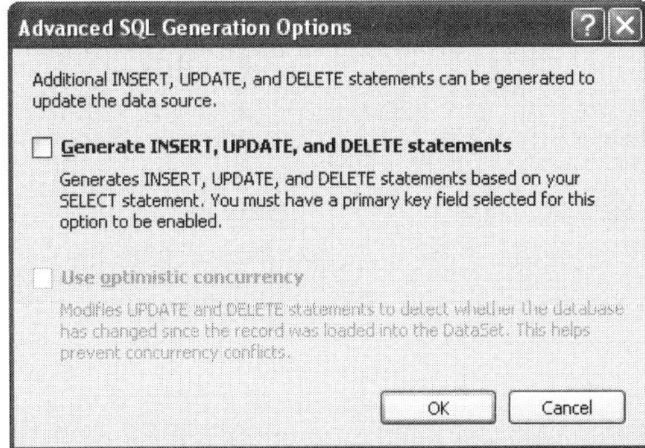

Figure 5-12 The Advanced SQL Generation Options dialog box

In this dialog box, you can allow data to be added or deleted from the configured data source and enable optimistic concurrency. One of the problems with any multi-user database system is what happens when two users simultaneously modify the same data. In many applications, the user who saves last saves best. For example, imagine that user Doug reads a row, and then user Jean also reads that row, and then user Jean saves changes to the row. When user Doug tries to save the data, his changes will overwrite Jean's changes. Often this is completely acceptable. If it is not, after selecting the first check box shown in Figure 5-12 to create INSERT, UPDATE, and DELETE statements, select the second check box. Selecting the Use Optimistic Concurrency check box modifies the UPDATE and DELETE statements to determine whether another user modified the data since it was loaded. For our example, select the first check box only.

Note In this particular example, enabling optimistic concurrency will result in invalid SQL, because one column in the table is a *text* column. I could have avoided this by using a new feature of SQL Server 2005 to create a very long *nvarchar* column (up to 4000 Unicode characters in length) instead of the *text* type column, but doing so would mean that the database would load only in SQL Server 2005. Using a new feature in a new version of a database server is sometimes worth the cost. This time, on balance, I didn't feel that using the new feature of SQL Server 2005 was worth it for the minor possible gain.

After clicking OK in the Advanced SQL Generation Options dialog box and clicking Next in the wizard, the final page of the Configure Data Source wizard appears, which allows you to test the query. If you click Test Query, the Parameter Values Editor dialog box allows you to modify the value used in the WHERE clause. Click OK, and the dialog box that appears should be a similar to Figure 5-13.

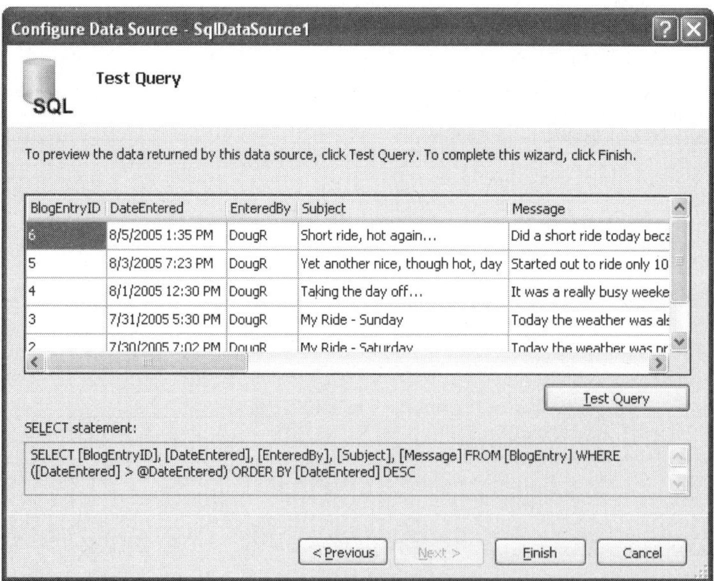

Figure 5-13 The final screen of the Configure Data Source wizard, showing test data returned

Click Finish to return to the Design view of Default.aspx. The SqlDataSource Tasks menu now has an additional option, Refresh Schema. This option is useful if you change the name or type of any of the columns returned in the query.

The *GridView* Control

Developers of ASP.NET 1.x were initially thrilled because ASP.NET rescued them from the tedium of manually reading through result sets and building tables to display tabular data. As time passed, however, the limitations of the *DataGrid* control became obvious. Although it was possible to do many things with the *DataGrid* control, it was not easy to do many things *well*. To maintain backward compatibility, the *DataGrid* control is still available. However, there is no reason I can think of for using it for new Web Forms development. Why? Because ASP.NET 2.0 introduces the new *GridView* control.

The *GridView* control replaces the *DataGrid* control. The *GridView* control offers all of the features of the *DataGrid* control, and it adds several features that improve the ability to display and edit data without adding any code.

Let's drop a *GridView* control onto the Default.aspx form, created when the DataBinding project was created. The GridView Tasks menu appears next to the *GridView* control. This menu allows you to complete most of the tasks required to configure the *GridView* control. From top to bottom, we will step through those menu items.

Clicking the Auto Format menu option opens the Auto Format dialog box. You can scroll through and preview the possible schemes (a fairly large number). I like the Slate scheme, shown in Figure 5-14.

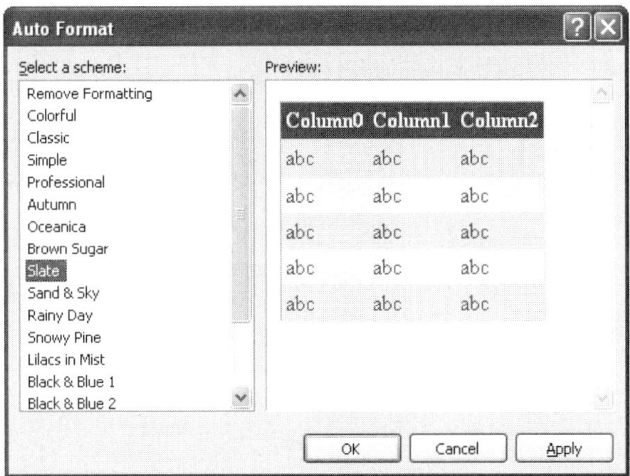

Figure 5-14 The Auto Format dialog box for the *GridView* control, showing the Slate scheme

The next option on the GridView Tasks menu is Choose Data Source. Select the data source just added (named SqlDataSource1 by default), and the GridView Tasks menu expands a bit, as shown in Figure 5-15.

The next two menu options allow you to configure the data source, stepping through the same wizard that you used to create the data source, and refresh the schema, useful when data types or the number of columns returned change. The next menu option that I selected is Edit Columns. I selected columns to appear in SqlDataSource, but at least one of those fields (BlogEntryID) is not something that you generally want to show, although having the columns available in the returned data is useful. BlogEntryID is not a meaningful column for the end user, but the developer might use it when, for instance, creating a hyperlink column. Often hyperlinks need to identify a row in the database, and BlogEntryID is a good candidate for that.

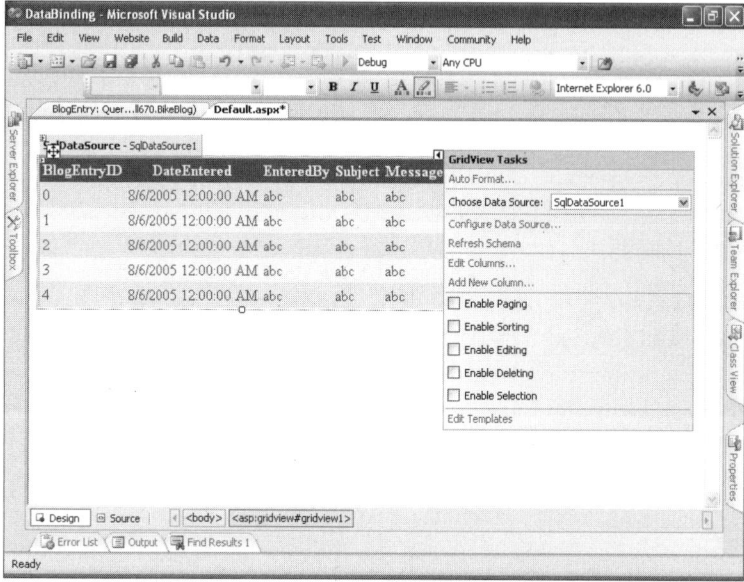

Figure 5-15 The GridView Tasks menu after selecting a data source

When you click Edit Columns, the resulting dialog box displays a list of the currently selected fields, with a variety of ways to add and remove them from the display. Click one of the fields (for instance, BlogEntryID), and the dialog box looks like Figure 5-16.

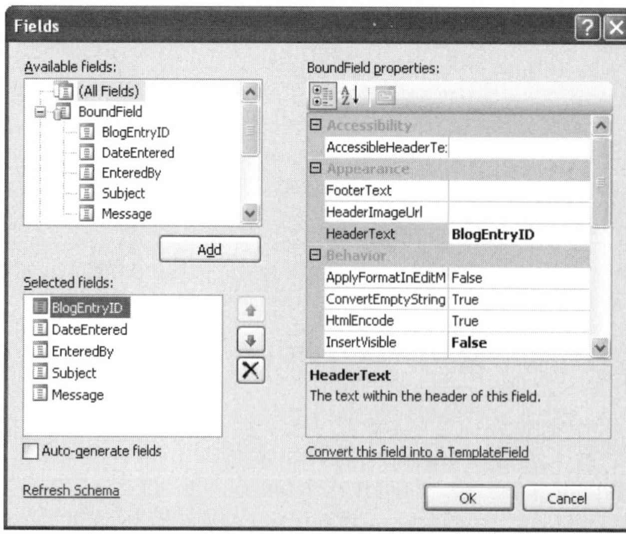

Figure 5-16 The Fields dialog box, allowing selection of fields to display in the *GridView* control

Look at the properties of the field currently selected (in this case, BlogEntryID). Presuming you follow best practices for naming database columns (no spaces, no special characters), one property you will often modify is the *HeaderText* property. In this example, "Blog #" might be a better column name than "BlogEntryID" if we want to keep this column in the display. Another property that might be useful is the *NullDisplayText* property. For instance, if I had included the DateModified column for display in the *GridView* control, setting *NullDisplayText* to "Not Modified" could be useful.

Here's something interesting to consider when using the *GridView* control. Note that the *ReadOnly* property is generally set based on the column constraints. Because BlogEntryID is an IDENTITY column, and also the primary key for the BlogEntry table, it is reasonable that the field be set to *ReadOnly*, and it is. The *DataField* property will be set to the correct column when the *GridView* control is associated with the data source. A useful related property is the *DataFormatString* property. For an integer value such as *BlogEntryID*, the default formatting is generally reasonable; however, a common field type that requires special formatting is the date field type. The default formatting for a DateTime column is (in the U.S.) MM/dd/yyyy hh:mm:ss. This might be appropriate, or it might not be. For this example, mostly to show the available formatting flexibility, I set the *DataFormatString* property for the DateEntered column to "{0:ddd, MM/dd/yyyy}," which means that the first value passed in (in this case, the single field *DateEntered*) should be formatted showing the three-character day of the week ("ddd"), followed by a comma (the literal "," after "ddd"), followed by "MM/dd/yyyy" (for two-digit month, a slash, two-digit day, a slash, and four-digit year). A large number of character strings are possible for the *DataFormatString* property. A search on MSDN for "Formatting Overview" should get you to a page that contains links to all sorts of details on the *DataFormatString* property.

On the GridView Tasks menu shown in Figure 5-15, the next item is Add New Column. This option is a little redundant, because the previous menu option, Edit Columns, also allows for the addition of a column. The next five menu items are check boxes that specify how the *GridView* control will allow users to control the page. The check boxes are:

- **Enable Paging** Shows only a page of data at a time, allowing the user to get to the next and previous page (if next and previous pages are available).
- **Enable Sorting** Makes the heading text a hyperlink that allows the user to sort the column. Click the column once, and it is sorted in ascending order; click it again, and it is sorted in descending order.
- **Enable Editing** Adds a column with a hyperlink that, when clicked, allows the user to edit the information in the *GridView* control in place. This sounds more useful than it often really is, because to control the look of the row while editing, you have to do so much work that you might just want to do the editing in one of the numerous other ways that ASP.NET offers. I will explain more about this later.
- **Enable Deleting** Adds a column with a hyperlink that, when clicked, allows the user to delete a row.

- **Enable Selection** Adds a column with a hyperlink that, when clicked, allows the user to select the row. What happens when the row is selected is up to the developer.

For now, leave all of these check boxes cleared. We will discuss each of these options shortly.

Edit Template Mode

The final menu option on the GridView Tasks menu is Edit Templates. When you click this option, the display changes quite a bit, as shown in Figure 5-17.

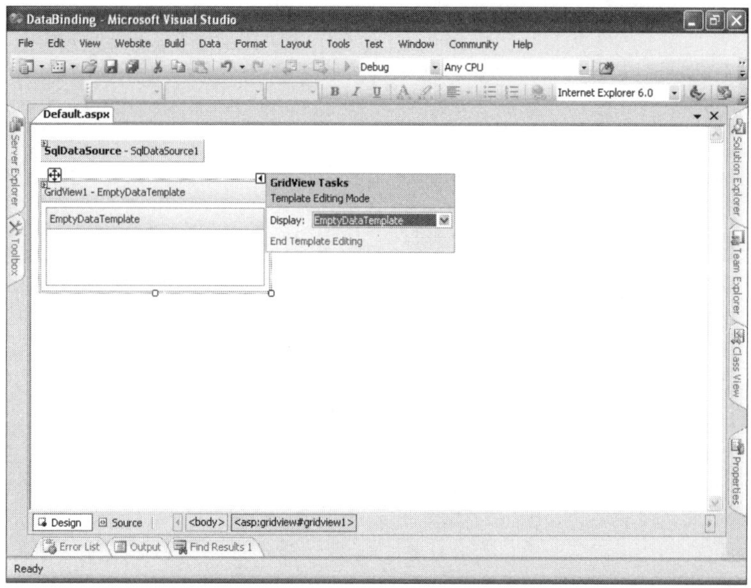

Figure 5-17 The *GridView* control in Template Editing Mode showing the EmptyDataTemplate template

One of the maddening aspects of using the *DataGrid* control in ASP.NET 1.x was the need to do special processing to display an appropriate message when no data was present. Figure 5-17 shows one of the two templates that can be edited, EmptyDataTemplate, which is displayed when no data is present. In this case, I simply typed "No Blog Entries to Display" into the template, but you can drag and drop any control into the template, and you can enter any HTML directly into the template by using Source view if you prefer.

The other template that can be edited is PagerTemplate, as shown in Figure 5-18.

The PagerTemplate template allows you to control the look and feel of the pager in grid views that allow paging. I left this template blank. (Paging will also be discussed in the next section.) To exit Template Editing Mode, click End Template Editing on the smart tag menu.

Before experimenting with any additional properties, it might be useful to see the *GridView* control in action. On the Debug menu, choose Start Debugging. If this is the first time you have run this Web site, a message asks whether you want to create a Web.config file to be modified to allow debugging. You should leave the default selected (which will modify the Web.config file) and click OK. The resulting page should look like the screen shown in Figure 5-19.

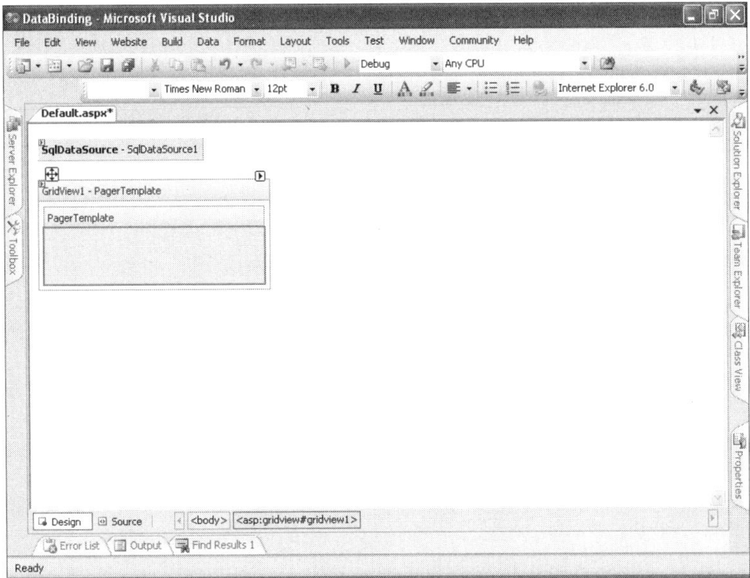

Figure 5-18 The *GridView* control in Template Editing Mode showing the PagerTemplate template

Default Page - Microsoft Internet Explorer

Address http://localhost:3673/DataBinding/Default.aspx

BlogEntryID	DateEntered	EnteredBy	Subject	Message
7	8/9/2005 8:43:13 AM	DougR	No riding yesterday	No riding yesterday, due to the rain.
6	8/5/2005 1:35:00 PM	DougR	Short ride, hot again...	Did a short ride today because of other plans (going to the Allentown PA Drum Corps. International show). Had lunch at the root beer stand in Point Pleasant. Really warm, the wind tired me out a bit heading back West from the beach.
5	8/3/2005 7:23:00 PM	DougR	Yet another nice, though hot, day	Started out to ride only 10 miles or so, but felt so good that I continued to Brick Beach 3, about a 17 mile round trip. Very nice ride, felt amazingly good most of the ride.
4	8/1/2005 12:30:00 PM	DougR	Taking the day off...	It was a really busy weekend of riding, and so I took the day off. I did walk out to the store (perhaps a 2.5 mile round trip).
3	7/31/2005 5:30:00 PM	DougR	My Ride - Sunday	Today the weather was also very nice, though a little warm. I road with another Doug, and we rode all the way into Island Beach State Park. Very cool ride, a little wind out of the NNE (seemed like East until we were heading north...)
2	7/30/2005 7:02:00 PM	DougR	My Ride - Saturday	Today the weather was pretty good for riding (limited wind, not too hot) and I was able to get about 20 miles in. I rode out past Brick Beach 3 and then headed back. Wind not too bad.

Done Trusted sites

Figure 5-19 Default.aspx in the DataBinding Web site, running with no paging, sorting, editing, or selecting

One thing to notice about the page shown in Figure 5-19 is that the individual entries are rather long. With the screen resolution used in Figure 5-19, less than seven complete entries are visible. In a real application, there might be several hundred entries. When the number of rows gets that high, it is unreasonable to send all rows from the server to the browser each time the page is requested. In addition to the fact that the user might be using a slow connection, finding particular data among so many entries is difficult.

Paging

The solution is to use the *GridView* control's automatic paging. The *GridView* control can be configured to show a certain number of rows on each of multiple pages. The automatic paging support offered by the *GridView* control might be all you will ever need when it comes to paging a large result set.

Close the browser and go back to the GridView Tasks menu (by clicking the smart tag arrow on the right side of the control), where you can select the check box marked Enable Paging. If you run the application again, you will see no difference. The reason for this is the *PageSize* property of the *GridView* control. Figure 5-20 shows the Properties dialog box for the *GridView* control.

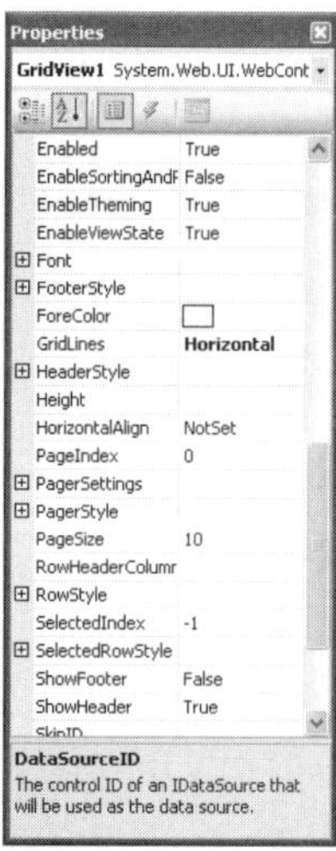

Figure 5-20 The *GridView* control's Properties dialog box

The *PageSize* property defaults to 10. If all rows in a *GridView* control are a single line in length, using 10 as a *PageSize* value is entirely reasonable. However, in this example, some of the entries are four rows long (and a real blog site might have even longer entries), so paging based on 10 rows is not quite enough. Changing the *PageSize* property to 4 is a reasonable choice here. Figure 5-21 shows Default.aspx with paging enabled. Note the links at the bottom right, indicating that the entries are split among two pages.

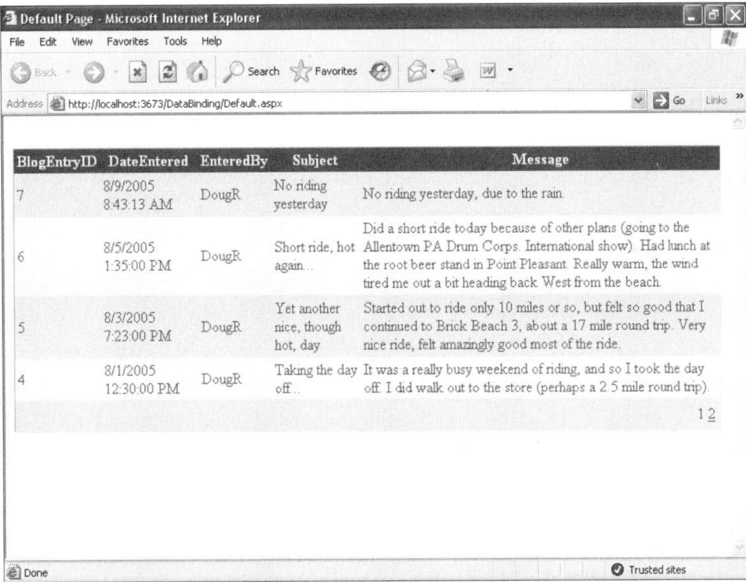

Figure 5-21 Default.aspx with paging enabled, showing page 1

When you click 2 at the bottom of the page, the page looks like Figure 5-22.

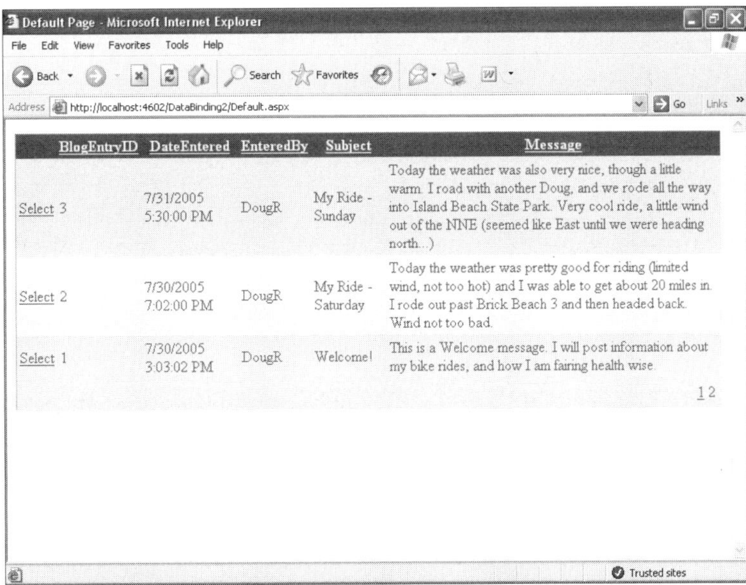

Figure 5-22 Default.aspx with paging enabled, showing page 2

Sorting

Another useful feature of the *GridView* control is the ability to sort the grid view. Very often, the row you are looking for can be found by sorting the rows in one order or another. To enable sorting, all you have to do is select the Enable Sorting check box on the GridView Tasks menu. Enabling sorting on the grid view in Default.aspx in the DateBinding Web site results in the screen shown in Figure 5-23. In this figure, I clicked Subject once to sort the entries in ascending order.

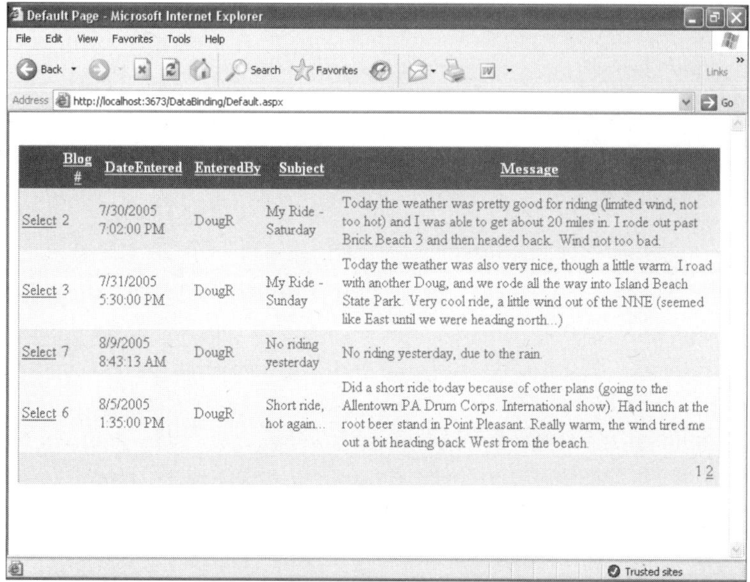

Figure 5-23 Default.aspx with sorting enabled and entries sorted by Subject

Editing

The next thing to try in the grid view is editing. Select the Enable Editing check box, as shown in Figure 5-24.

An additional column appears with an Edit hyperlink. When the page is run and the Edit link is clicked on one of the rows in the *GridView* control, the screen looks like Figure 5-25.

The first thing you should notice is that the Edit link in the row you are editing has been replaced with Update and Cancel links. When the user has made changes, the Update link saves the changes, and the Cancel link ignores the changes. Also notice that the Blog # column is not editable; that column was marked as read-only. In a real Web application, fields such as DateEntered and EnteredBy might also be read-only.

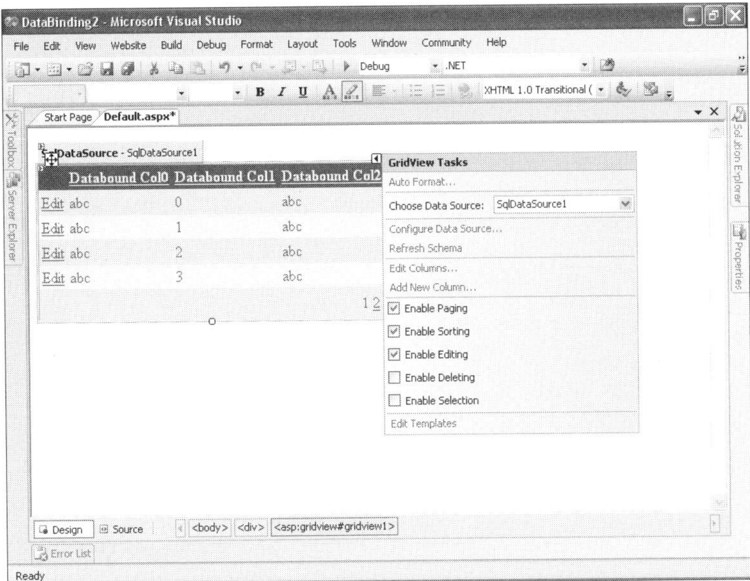

Figure 5-24 Default.aspx in Design view with editing enabled

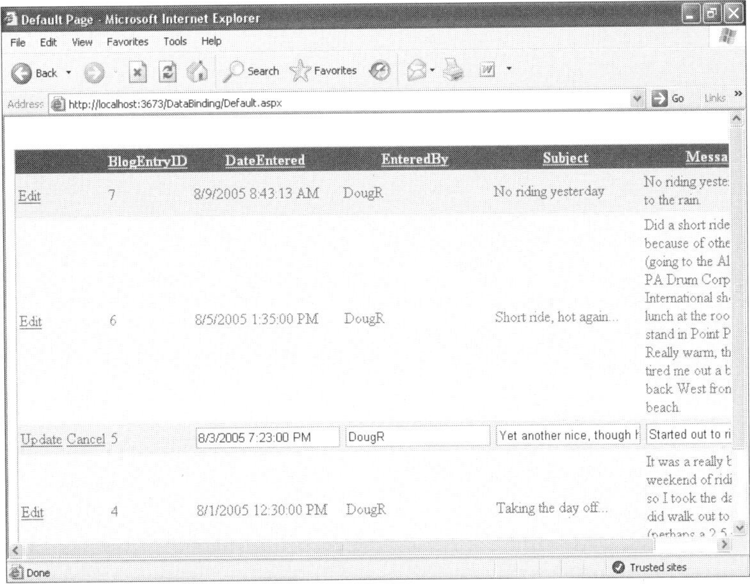

Figure 5-25 Editing a row in Default.aspx

You will also notice that the editing view is not very good. The text boxes for the Subject and Message fields are not appropriately sized. They should both be multiline text boxes. Finally, when the *GridView* control is placed in edit mode, the line is formatted so that the *GridView* control is wider than the screen, making a horizontal scroll bar necessary. Although it is not a firm rule, restricting a page so that it does not scroll horizontally at your target resolution is a good idea.

One solution to the problems caused when a *GridView* control is placed in edit mode is to create a custom editing template. This can work for certain kinds of data. Later in this chapter, I will explain several options for editing data selected from a *GridView* control, as well as the custom editing templates.

Deleting

Looking back at the GridView Tasks menu shown in Figure 5-24, the next option is Enable Deleting. To make the grid fit a little better, select the Enable Deleting check box, and clear the Enable Editing check box. The page in Design view should look like Figure 5-26.

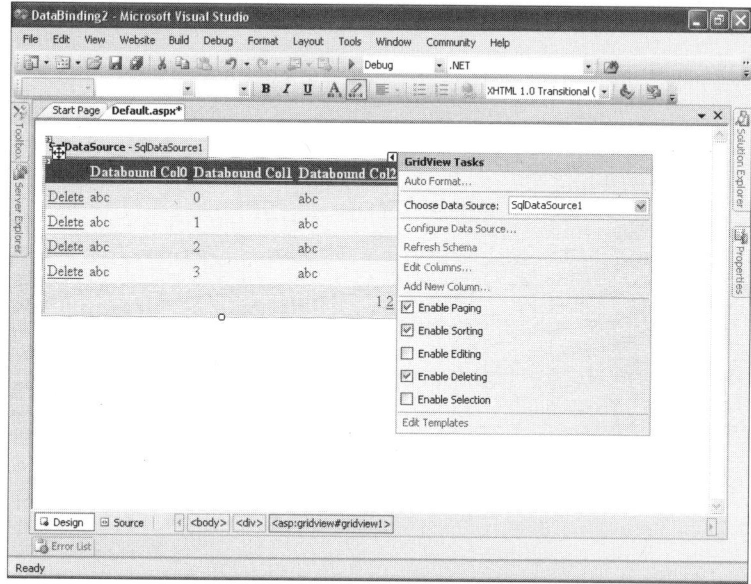

Figure 5-26 Default.aspx in Design view with deleting enabled

When the page is run, the Delete link appears, just like the Edit link in Figure 5-25.

Selecting

The last check box in the GridView Tasks menu is Enable Selection. Selecting this check box (and clearing Enable Deleting to allow the grid to fit better) replaces the Delete links with Select links, as shown in Figure 5-27.

When you run the page, the most interesting thing to note is that clicking the Select link posts back the page and changes the color of the row selected. This is not a very interesting feature; you can do several more interesting things with the Select feature. The section of this chapter on the *DetailsView* control will use the Select feature to edit the data in different ways.

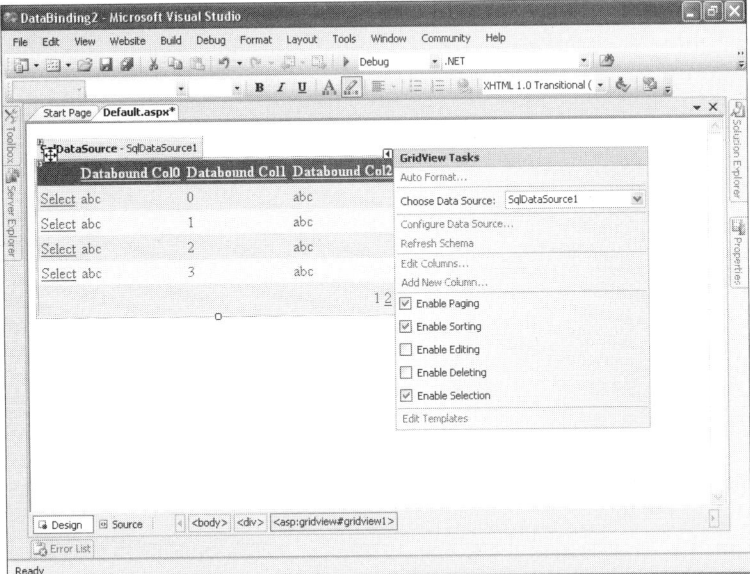

Figure 5-27 Default.aspx in Design view with selection enabled

Using a Custom EditItemTemplate

The *GridView* control provides a default appearance when a row in the *GridView* control is being edited. Often this default appearance is not sufficient. For those occasions, the developer can customize the appearance when editing by creating custom *EditItemTemplate* markup. The markup inside an *EditItemTemplate* is used whenever an item is being edited, and it can contain any number of controls. The easiest way to create an *EditItemTemplate* in a *GridView* control is to use the Edit Columns option on the GridView Tasks menu. To demonstrate how editing templates work, I created a new page named EditTemplate.aspx. I dragged new *SqlDataSource* and *GridView* controls onto the page, connected the *SqlDataSource* control to the BikeBlog database, and connected the *GridView* control to the *SqlDataSource* control.

When you come to the Fields dialog box, the Auto-generate Fields check box is selected by default. Clear this option, and then add the fields that you want to appear in the *GridView* control. I added the fields shown in Figure 5-28.

Note in Figure 5-29 that, in the Selected Fields list, the Subject and Message fields have a slightly different icon next to them. The different icon means that these fields are template fields. The Subject field should always be filled in, so adding a *RequiredFieldValidator* control is a good idea. The Message field can contain a great deal of text, so the default behavior when editing (creating a short, single-line text box) is not always appropriate. In Figure 5-29, I clicked Convert This Field Into A TemplateField for both the Subject field and the Message field. I also made the EnteredBy field read-only by using the properties window in the Fields dialog box.

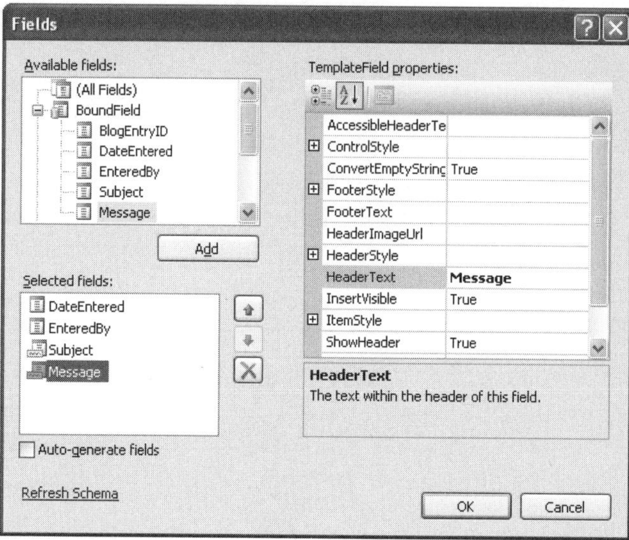

Figure 5-28 Fields dialog box showing Subject and Message fields

If you want to allow editing, one more column must be added in the Fields dialog box. In the Available Fields list, expand the CommandField element and add an Edit, Update, Cancel field, and move it so that it is the first field in the Selected Fields list in the bottom left of the Fields dialog box, as shown in Figure 5-29. Click OK to accept the changes.

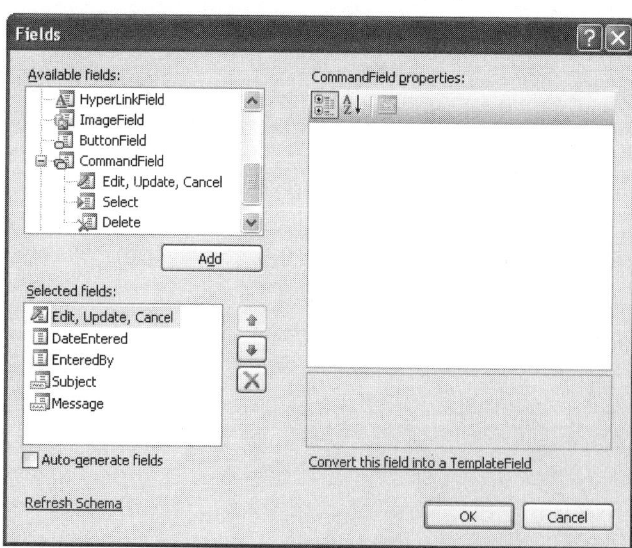

Figure 5-29 Fields dialog box with an Edit, Update, Cancel field

After you have converted the two fields into templates, the *GridView* control markup will be similar to the following.

```
<asp:GridView ID="GridView1" runat="server" AutoGenerateColumns="False"
    BackColor="White"
    BorderColor="#E7E7FF" BorderStyle="None" BorderWidth="1px"
    CellPadding="3" DataSourceID="SqlDataSource1"
    GridLines="Horizontal">
    <FooterStyle BackColor="#B5C7DE" ForeColor="#4A3C8C" />
    <Columns>
        <asp:CommandField ShowEditButton="True" />
        <asp:BoundField DataField="DateEntered" HeaderText="DateEntered"
            SortExpression="DateEntered" />
        <asp:BoundField DataField="EnteredBy" HeaderText="EnteredBy"
            ReadOnly="True" SortExpression="EnteredBy" />
        <asp:TemplateField HeaderText="Subject" SortExpression="Subject">
             <EditItemTemplate>
                 <asp:TextBox ID="TextBox2" runat="server"
                    Text='<%# Bind("Subject") %>'></asp:TextBox>
             </EditItemTemplate>
             <ItemTemplate>
             <asp:Label ID="Label2" runat="server"
                Text='<%# Bind("Subject") %>'>
             </asp:Label>
             </ItemTemplate>
        </asp:TemplateField>
        <asp:TemplateField HeaderText="Message" SortExpression="Message">
            <EditItemTemplate>
                <asp:TextBox ID="TextBox1" runat="server"
                    Text='<%# Bind("Message") %>'></asp:TextBox>
            </EditItemTemplate>
            <ItemTemplate>
                <asp:Label ID="Label1" runat="server"
                    Text='<%# Bind("Message") %>'></asp:Label>
            </ItemTemplate>
        </asp:TemplateField>
    </Columns>
    <RowStyle BackColor="#E7E7FF" ForeColor="#4A3C8C" />
    <SelectedRowStyle BackColor="#738A9C" Font-Bold="True"
        ForeColor="#F7F7F7" />
    <PagerStyle BackColor="#E7E7FF" ForeColor="#4A3C8C"
        HorizontalAlign="Right" />
    <HeaderStyle BackColor="#4A3C8C" Font-Bold="True"
        ForeColor="#F7F7F7" />
    <AlternatingRowStyle BackColor="#F7F7F7" />
</asp:GridView>
```

Note In addition to the *EditItemTemplate* markup block, an *ItemTemplate* markup block is also present for each field. It is rare that the *ItemTemplate* provided by default is not sufficient.

Inside the *<EditItemTemplate>* tags for the controls converted to templated fields is a single *TextBox* control. In each case, the *Text* property is set to the return of the *Bind* method, with the field name passed as a parameter. By modifying the tags that describe the controls used for editing, we can modify the look and feel of the *GridView* control while editing. I added a *RequiredFieldValidator* control to the *EditItemTemplate* for the Subject field, resulting in the following.

```
<asp:TemplateField HeaderText="Subject" SortExpression="Subject">
    <EditItemTemplate>
        <asp:TextBox ID="TextBox2" runat="server"
            Text='<%# Bind("Subject") %>'>
        </asp:TextBox>
        <asp:RequiredFieldValidator runat="server"
            ControlToValidate="TextBox2" ErrorMessage="*" Text="*" />
    </EditItemTemplate>
    <ItemTemplate>
        <asp:Label ID="Label2" runat="server"
            Text='<%# Bind("Subject") %>'></asp:Label>
    </ItemTemplate>
</asp:TemplateField>
```

Next, I modified the *EditItemTemplate* for the Message field, making the *TextBox* control a multiline text box, and set a height and width that would not cause the *GridView* control to grow wider than the screen in edit mode. The resulting markup for the Message *EditItemTemplate* is shown here.

```
<asp:TemplateField HeaderText="Message" SortExpression="Message">
    <EditItemTemplate>
        <asp:TextBox ID="TextBox1" runat="server"
            TextMode="MultiLine" Height="120" Width="220"
            Text='<%# Bind("Message") %>'></asp:TextBox>
    </EditItemTemplate>
    <ItemTemplate>
        <asp:Label ID="Label1" runat="server"
            Text='<%# Bind("Message") %>'></asp:Label>
    </ItemTemplate>
</asp:TemplateField>
```

When run and placed in edit mode by clicking the Edit link, EditTemplate.aspx looks like Figure 5-30.

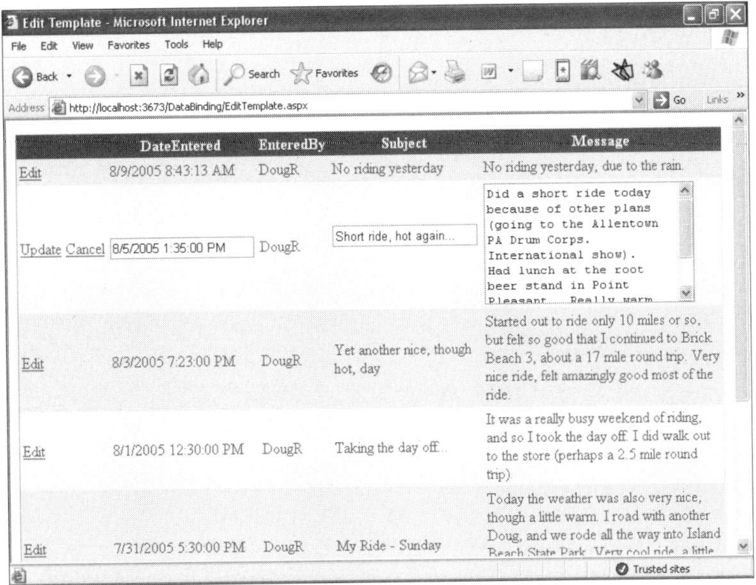

Figure 5-30 EditTemplate.aspx running in Edit mode, showing the templated interface

The *DetailsView* Control

In addition to the *GridView* control, the *DetailsView* control also allows you to create Web Forms with a minimum of code. The *DetailsView* control allows you to view and edit the details of a particular row. The *DetailsView* control is in the Data section of the Toolbox, just as the *GridView* control is. When you drag a *DetailsView* control onto the form, the DetailsView Tasks menu appears, as shown in Figure 5-31.

The first item on the DetailsView Tasks menu is Auto Format, which works exactly the same way that Auto Format works for the *GridView* control. Here I selected Slate, the same scheme that I used for the *GridView* control. I also selected the same data source (SqlDataSource1) that I used for the *GridView* control. The Configure Data Source and Refresh Schema menu options are the same as for the *GridView* control, as are Edit Fields and Add New Fields.

As with the GridView Tasks menu, there are several check boxes on the menu. For the *DetailsView* control, these are:

- **Enable Paging** Allows the user to page through multiple pages when there is a large number of columns (because the *DetailsView* control shows one column per line).
- **Enable Inserting** Allows the user to insert new data. The data source must be set to allow insertions.

- **Enable Editing** Allows the user to edit existing data. The data source must be set to allow editing.
- **Enable Deleting** Allows the user to delete existing data. The data source must be set to allow deletion.

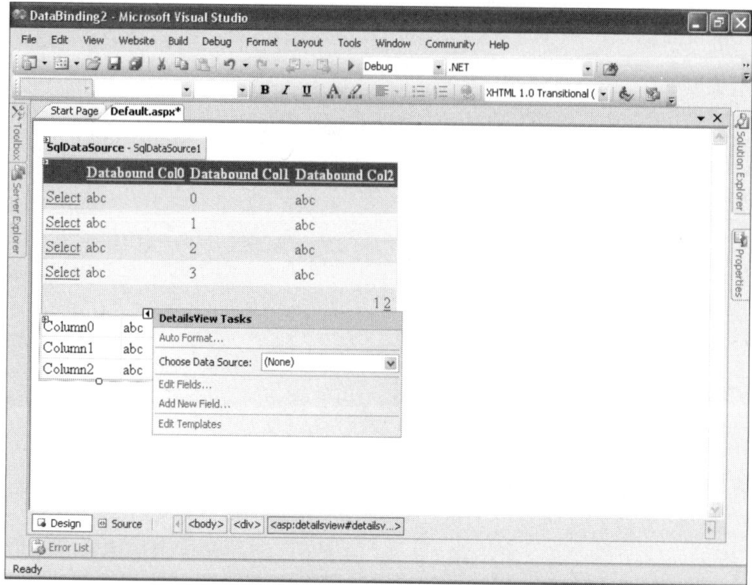

Figure 5-31 Default.aspx in Design view, with the *DetailsView* control added and the DetailsView Tasks menu visible

The final option on the DetailsView Tasks menu is Edit Templates. Several templates can be edited in the *DetailsView* control:

- **FooterTemplate** Template for the footer of the *DetailsView* control
- **HeaderTemplate** Template for the header of the *DetailsView* control
- **EmptyDataTemplate** Template for the page appearance when there is no data for the *DetailsView* control
- **PagerTemplate** Template for the pager, when paging is enabled

To view the *DetailsView* control in a reasonable format, I set the *Width* property of the *DetailsView* control to 100%. When I ran the page, it appeared as shown in Figure 5-32. (I also set the *PageSize* property of *GridView1* to 2 so that more of the *DetailsView* control appeared.)

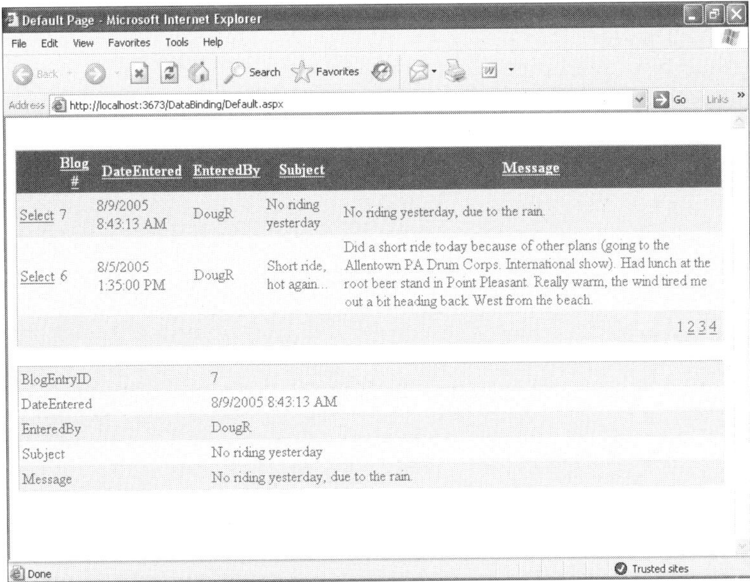

Figure 5-32 Default.aspx running, showing the *DetailsView* control

Selecting a Row in the *GridView* Control to View in the *DetailsView* Control

The *DetailsView* control is commonly used in conjunction with a *GridView* control. They are a natural fit: the *GridView* control provides the big picture, and the *DetailsView* control allows you to drill down into a particular record.

The *DetailsView* control could be used in *ReadOnly* mode to allow viewing of details that are not in the *GridView* control. For example, with selection enabled, we might want to have the *DetailsView* control show the details of a selected row. So far, there has been no coding at all; one line of code will be required to have the *DetailsView* control navigate to the correct row.

The *DetailsView* control has a large number of events that can be handled to manage the way that the control works. Two events are associated with the *SelectedIndex* property changing. (The *SelectedIndex* property tracks which row of the data source is currently selected.) The first is the *SelectedIndexChanging* event, which is fired before the index is actually changed. It accepts two parameters. The first is *Sender*, of type *Object*. The second, *e*, is of type *GridView-SelectEventArgs*. *GridViewSelectEventArgs* has one property that is particularly useful in this case, *NewSelectedIndex*. This property is the index of the newly selected row. One other property of *GridViewSelectEventArgs* that can be useful is *Cancel*, which allows you to cancel the selection.

The second *SelectedIndex*-related event occurs after the selected index has actually changed, named *SelectedIndexChanged*. This event handler has a signature similar to the *SelectedIndex-Changing* event handler, with a second parameter of type *EventArgs*.

For the purpose of moving the *DetailsView* control to the selected row, the *SelectedIndexChanging* event is most useful. To add the *SelectedIndexChanging* event, click the *GridView* control in Design view. In the Properties window, click the Events button (which looks like a lightning bolt), and then double-click in the field next to *SelectedIndexChanging* in the list of events. This opens the code page, where you will add one line to the event handler so that it looks like this.

```
protected void GridView1_SelectedIndexChanging(object sender, GridViewSelectEventArgs e)
{
    this.DetailsView1.PageIndex = e.NewSelectedIndex;
}
```

> **Note** The naming of properties is unfortunately a little unclear here. You might guess that the *DataItemIndex* property would set the location of the row to be displayed in the *Details-View* control. Not so. The *DataItemIndex* property is read-only. The *PageIndex* property sets the location in the data source.

When you run the page and click the second row in the grid view (blog number 6), that entry appears in the details view, as shown in Figure 5-33.

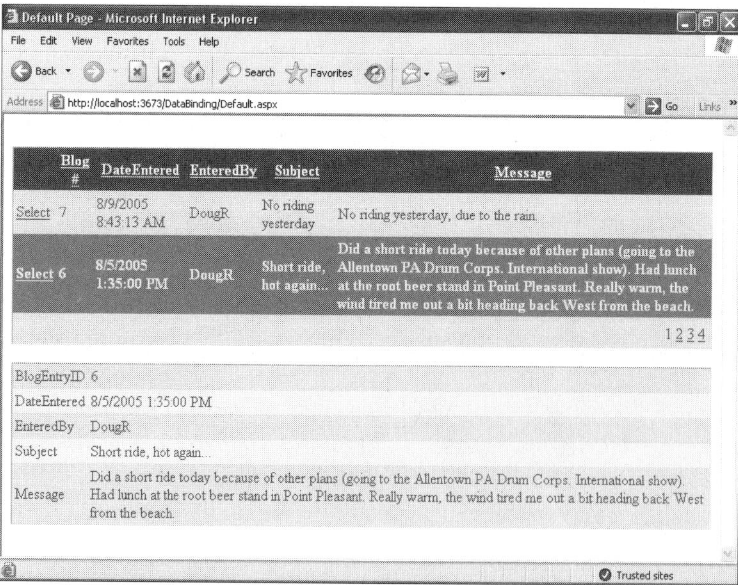

Figure 5-33 Default.aspx running, with blog 6 selected in the grid view and shown in the details view

Selecting a Row in the *GridView* Control to Edit in the *DetailsView* Control

A more common use of the *DetailsView* control is to allow editing of a single row. In Design view, with the application not running, selecting the Enable Editing check box on the DetailsView Tasks menu enables editing. One other property that must be set to allow editing to occur is the *DefaultMode* property. In the Properties window, the *DefaultMode* property is set to *ReadOnly* by default. Setting the *DefaultMode* property to *Edit* causes the *DetailsView* control to default to Edit mode. When the application is run and blog number 6 is selected, the screen looks like Figure 5-34.

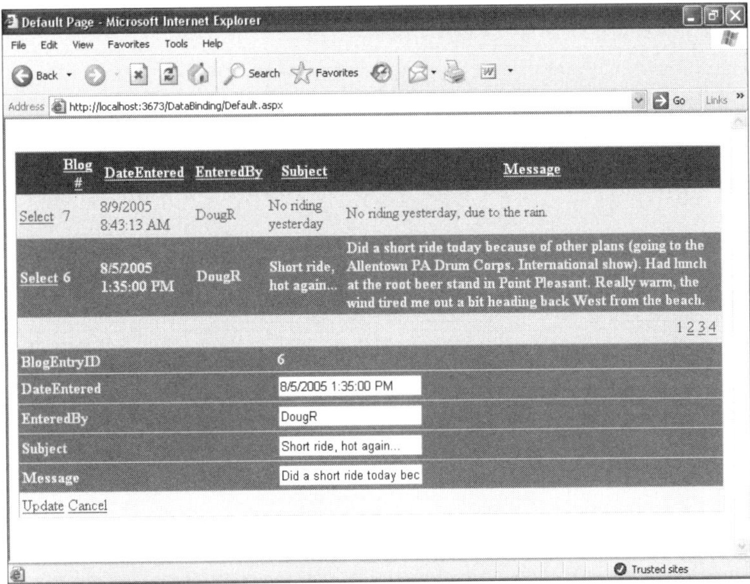

Figure 5-34 Default.aspx running, with blog 6 selected in the grid view and shown in Edit mode in the details view

Once again, the data entry fields are not set up ideally. This problem can be overcome by creating a custom template for one or more of the fields in the *DetailsView* control. The easiest way to do this is to click the Edit Fields option on the DetailsView Tasks menu, select the field that needs a non-default appearance, and click the Convert This Field Into A TemplateField link in the bottom right of the Fields dialog box, as shown in Figure 5-35.

A template field is different from the other field types in a *DetailsView* control (for instance, a bound field) in that the developer can provide a markup template that will be used to render the field. In the example shown in Figure 5-33, the Subject and Message fields are the obvious choices for converting to a template field, just as they were in the previous EditTemplate.aspx example. The markup shown in Listing 5-1 shows the default template created for the Subject and Message fields (in bold).

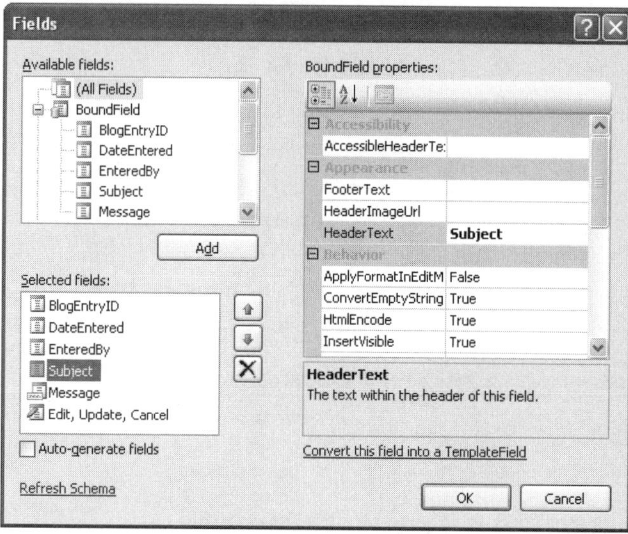

Figure 5-35 The Fields dialog box, set to convert the Subject field to a template field

Listing 5-1 Markup for the *DetailsView* Control after Converting Subject and Message Fields to TemplateFields

```
<asp:DetailsView ID="DetailsView1" runat="server" AutoGenerateRows="False"
    BackColor="White"
    BorderColor="#E7E7FF" BorderStyle="None" BorderWidth="1px"
    CellPadding="3" DataKeyNames="BlogEntryID"
    DataSourceID="SqlDataSource1" GridLines="Horizontal" Height="50px"
    Width="100%" DefaultMode="Edit">
    <FooterStyle BackColor="#B5C7DE" ForeColor="#4A3C8C" />
    <RowStyle BackColor="#E7E7FF" ForeColor="#4A3C8C" />
    <PagerStyle BackColor="#E7E7FF" ForeColor="#4A3C8C"
        HorizontalAlign="Right" />
    <Fields>
        <asp:BoundField DataField="BlogEntryID" HeaderText="BlogEntryID"
            InsertVisible="False"
            ReadOnly="True" SortExpression="BlogEntryID" />
        <asp:BoundField DataField="DateEntered" HeaderText="DateEntered"
            SortExpression="DateEntered" />
        <asp:BoundField DataField="EnteredBy" HeaderText="EnteredBy"
            SortExpression="EnteredBy" />
        <asp:TemplateField HeaderText="Subject" SortExpression="Subject">
            <ItemTemplate>
                <asp:Label ID="Label2" runat="server"
                   Text='<%# Bind("Subject") %>'></asp:Label>
            </ItemTemplate>
            <EditItemTemplate>
                <asp:TextBox ID="TextBox2" runat="server"
                    Text='<%# Bind("Subject") %>'></asp:TextBox>
            </EditItemTemplate>
            <InsertItemTemplate>
                <asp:TextBox ID="TextBox2" runat="server"
```

```
                    Text='<%# Bind("Subject") %>'></asp:TextBox>
            </InsertItemTemplate>
        </asp:TemplateField>
        <asp:TemplateField HeaderText="Message" SortExpression="Message">
            <ItemTemplate>
                <asp:Label ID="Label1" runat="server"
                    Text='<%# Bind("Message") %>'></asp:Label>
            </ItemTemplate>
            <EditItemTemplate>
                <asp:TextBox ID="TextBox1" runat="server"
                    Text='<%# Bind("Message") %>'></asp:TextBox>
            </EditItemTemplate>
            <InsertItemTemplate>
                <asp:TextBox ID="TextBox1" runat="server"
                    Text='<%# Bind("Message") %>'></asp:TextBox>
            </InsertItemTemplate>
        </asp:TemplateField>
        <asp:CommandField ShowEditButton="True" />
    </Fields>
    <HeaderStyle BackColor="#4A3C8C" Font-Bold="True"
        ForeColor="#F7F7F7" />
    <EditRowStyle BackColor="#738A9C" Font-Bold="True"
        ForeColor="#F7F7F7" />
    <AlternatingRowStyle BackColor="#F7F7F7" />
</asp:DetailsView>
```

By default, the *DetailsView* control renders the edit controls as single-line text boxes with the default width. To modify the appearance of the Subject and Message fields in the *DetailsView* control and make data entry of large blocks of text easier, I made the following changes in the *EditItemTemplate* markup block:

- Added *Width=80%* to the *EditItemTemplate* and *InsertItemTemplate* markup blocks for the Subject field.
- Added *Width=80%*, *Height=200px*, and *TextMode=MultiLine* to the *EditItemTemplate* and *InsertItemTemplate* markup blocks for the Message field.

Running the modified code results in a page like that shown in Figure 5-36.

One problem with the page shown in Figure 5-36 is the appearance of the text in the Message field. The font in the Message field is different from the font in the other text boxes because, when a *TextMode* property in a text box is set to *MultiLine*, the HTML is rendered not as a normal INPUT tag, but as a TEXTAREA tag. To make the text in the *TextArea* control appear similar to the text in the other edit controls, I added a new style to the style sheet (StyleSheet.css).

```
textarea
{
    font-family:Arial;
    font-size:12px;
}
```

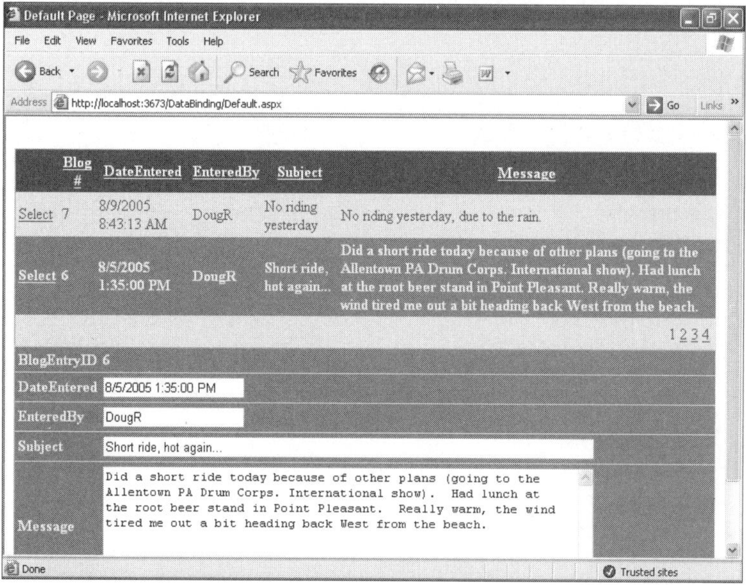

Figure 5-36 Default.aspx after converting Subject and Message fields to template fields and modifying templates

This style sets the font of a *TextArea* control to be Arial 12 px (which is 12 points, not pixels), and the result is shown in Figure 5-37. Another consequence of a multiline text box being rendered as a TEXTAREA tag is that the *MaxLength* property is ignored. If you need to limit the length of a multiline text box, you must do so by using JavaScript.

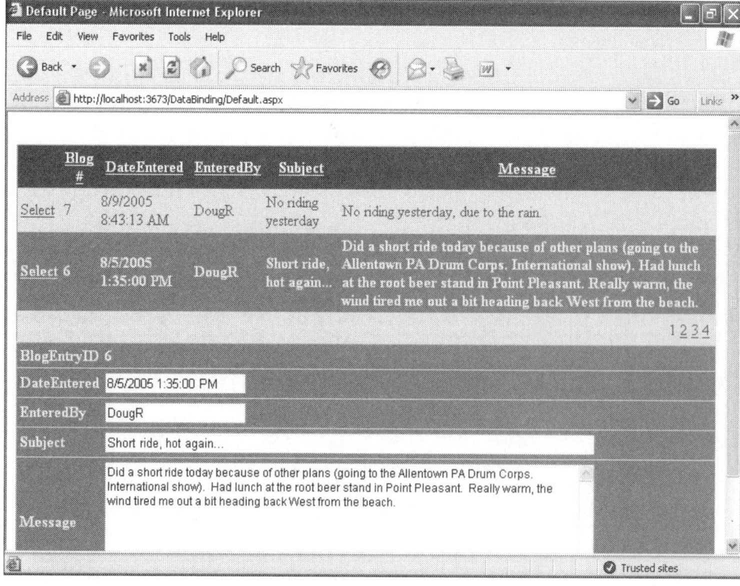

Figure 5-37 Default.aspx after adding the *textarea* style to StyleSheet.css

That looks better!

The *MultiView* Control

You can allow data to be edited on a Web Form in many ways. In addition to using the *DetailsView* control or editing templates, as shown in the previous examples, you can also create a single page to handle display and editing of data by using a *MultiView* control. A *MultiView* control can contain any number of sections of markup, called views, with only a single view visible at a time. Using the *MultiView* control falls somewhere between using multiple *Panel* controls, covered in Chapter 2, "A Multitude of Controls," and using the Wizard control, covered in Chapter 3, "Web Form Layout."

The previous iteration of the Default.aspx page allowed for relatively convenient and attractive editing of blog entry details. One problem remains. Let's look back at the structure of the underlying BlogEntry table. In addition to the columns that have been used in the *GridView* control, several other columns were not included because their appearance in the *GridView* control would be problematic. Here is the SQL CREATE script that allows you to create the BlogEntry table in SQL Server, which also shows all the columns in the BlogEntry table.

```
CREATE TABLE [dbo].[BlogEntry] (
    [BlogEntryID] [int] NOT NULL ,
    [DateEntered] [datetime] NOT NULL ,
    [EnteredBy] [nvarchar] (50) NULL ,
    [DateModified] [datetime] NULL ,
    [ModifiedBy] [nvarchar] (50) NULL ,
    [WeatherConditionID] [int] NULL ,
    [WindDirectionID] [int] NULL ,
    [WindStrengthID] [int] NULL ,
    [MilesBiked] [smallint] NULL ,
    [Subject] [nvarchar] (255) NULL ,
    [Message] [text] NULL
) ON [PRIMARY] TEXTIMAGE_ON [PRIMARY]
```

For example, the WeatherConditionID, WindDirectionID, and WindStrengthID columns are just ID columns that point to the real data in supporting tables. Displaying a number would be meaningless. Rather than editing a number for the various weather-related ID columns, the user would certainly prefer to see the string values pointed to by these ID columns.

Data editing can be allowed in several ways. A common way is to create a second page that is called when the user edits one of the rows. However, this creates a clutter of pages required for a single task. An alternative is to create a single page with a control new to ASP.NET 2.0 called a *MultiView* control.

On a new page, named BetterEdit.aspx, I dropped an *SqlDataSource* control onto the form, configured it, and then dropped a *MultiView* control onto the form. Then, in Source view, I added two *View* tags to the *MultiView* control, which resulted in the markup shown in Listing 5-2.

Listing 5-2 BetterEdit.aspx after Adding an *SqlDataSource* Control, a *MultiView* Control, and Two *View* Elements

```
<%@ Page Language="C#" AutoEventWireup="true" CodeFile="BetterEdit.aspx.cs"
    Inherits="BetterEdit" %>

<!DOCTYPE html PUBLIC "-//W3C//DTD XHTML 1.1//EN"
    "http://www.w3.org/TR/xhtml11/DTD/xhtml11.dtd">

<html xmlns="http://www.w3.org/1999/xhtml" >
<head runat="server">
    <title>Untitled Page</title>
</head>
<body>
    <form id="form1" runat="server">
    <div>
        <asp:SqlDataSource ID="SqlDataSource1" runat="server"
           ConnectionString=
              "<%$ ConnectionStrings:BikeBlogConnectionString %>"
              DeleteCommand="DELETE FROM [BlogEntry] WHERE [BlogEntryID] =
              @original_BlogEntryID"
            InsertCommand="INSERT INTO [BlogEntry] ([DateEntered],
                [EnteredBy], [DateMocified], [ModifiedBy], [Subject],
                [Message])
            VALUES (@DateEntered, @EnteredBy, @DateMocified, @ModifiedBy,
                @Subject, @Message)"
            SelectCommand="SELECT [BlogEntryID], [DateEntered],
                [EnteredBy], [DateMocified], [ModifiedBy], [Subject],
                [Message]
                FROM [BlogEntry] ORDER BY [DateEntered] DESC"
            UpdateCommand="UPDATE [BlogEntry] SET [DateEntered] =
                @DateEntered, [EnteredBy] = @EnteredBy, [DateMocified] =
                @DateModified, [ModifiedBy] = @ModifiedBy,
                [Subject] = @Subject, [Message] = @Message
            WHERE [BlogEntryID] = @original_BlogEntryID">
            <DeleteParameters>
                <asp:Parameter Name="original_BlogEntryID" Type="Int32" />
            </DeleteParameters>
            <UpdateParameters>
                <asp:Parameter Name="DateEntered" Type="DateTime" />
                <asp:Parameter Name="EnteredBy" Type="String" />
                <asp:Parameter Name="DateMocified" Type="DateTime" />
                <asp:Parameter Name="ModifiedBy" Type="String" />
                <asp:Parameter Name="Subject" Type="String" />
                <asp:Parameter Name="Message" Type="String" />
                <asp:Parameter Name="original_BlogEntryID" Type="Int32" />
            </UpdateParameters>
            <InsertParameters>
                <asp:Parameter Name="DateEntered" Type="DateTime" />
                <asp:Parameter Name="EnteredBy" Type="String" />
                <asp:Parameter Name="DateMocified" Type="DateTime" />
                <asp:Parameter Name="ModifiedBy" Type="String" />
                <asp:Parameter Name="Subject" Type="String" />
```

```
                <asp:Parameter Name="Message" Type="String" />
            </InsertParameters>
        </asp:SqlDataSource>

    </div>
        <asp:MultiView ID="MultiView1" runat="server">
            <asp:View ID="Grid" runat=Server>
            </asp:View>
            <asp:View ID="DetailsEdit" runat=server>
            </asp:View>
        </asp:MultiView>
    </form>
</body>
</html>
```

The markup for the *SqlDataSource1* control is generated by the wizard; however, looking at this markup and understanding it will help if you need to modify your code after the initial creation of the data source. Directly inside the *SqlDataSource* tag, the markup sets the *ConnectionString* attribute, using special syntax that retrieves the value from the Web.config file, as shown here.

```
ConnectionString=
    "<%$ ConnectionStrings:BikeBlogConnectionString %>"
```

Next, the markup defines a series of commands: *DeleteCommand*, *InsertCommand*, and *SelectCommand*. The values for these attributes are SQL strings that include, where appropriate, parameter placeholders, in this case specified by a variable name that begins with an at sign (@). These commands can be manually modified; however, if the number or names of parameters change, the parameters in the next section must be modified to match. Parameters are declared in the markup as shown here.

```
<DeleteParameters>
    <asp:Parameter Name="original_BlogEntryID" Type="Int32" />
</DeleteParameters>
```

Each of the commands have a corresponding parameters section that must match the parameters in the corresponding command.

Inside the markup for the *MultiView* control, I added the two *View* controls. The *View* controls work in a way that is very similar to the earlier *EditItemTemplate* markup blocks shown in previous examples. The *View* controls act as containers for other controls. I named the views appropriately: Grid and DetailsEdit. In Design view in Visual Studio, the page looks like Figure 5-38.

There is not much support in Design view for the *MultiView* control, so adding the *View* tags manually is the easiest way to create the views. After the views are added, you can drag and drop controls onto the views as you would on any standard page. I dropped a *GridView* control onto the first view (named Grid), and then I created a table formatted as a data entry form (two columns, one right justified for labels, one left justified for the edit controls, both set to 50 percent of the width of the table).

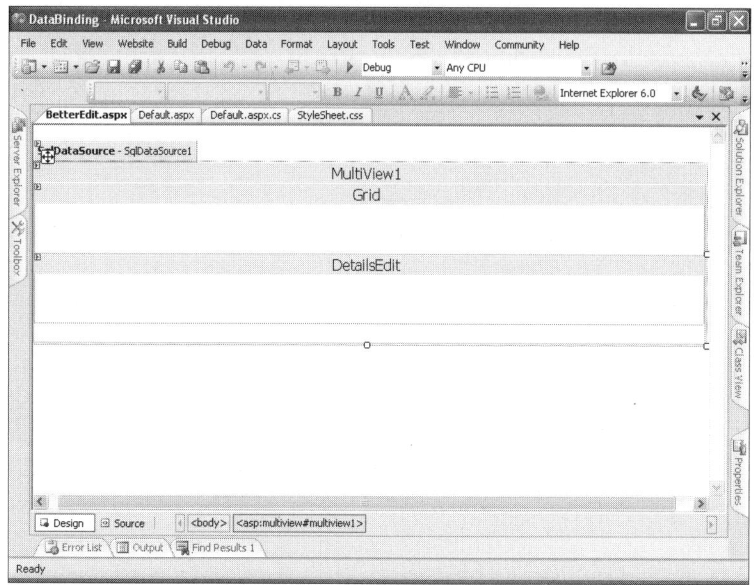

Figure 5-38 BetterEdit.aspx after adding the *MultiView* control

Next, I added three *SqlDataSource* controls to the form. These are used to select data from the WeatherCondition, WindDirection, and WindStrength tables. In Chapter 2, I introduced the *DropDownList* control and indicated that, normally, it is populated from a database. This data entry form will be an example of that, with each of the columns, WeatherConditionID, WindDirectionID, and WindStrengthID, displayed and edited by using a *DropDownList* control. After configuring the *SqlDataSource* controls to select data from the respective tables and changing the names from the default names to meaningful names, I added labels, text boxes, and combo boxes as needed to the DetailsEdit view, and I modified the names of the controls as appropriate. Note that none of these *SqlDataSources* controls required anything other than a SELECT statement, because the data will not be edited with this form.

After the *SqlDataSource* controls are configured and the *DropDownList* controls are renamed appropriately, the next step is to select a *DropDownList* control in Visual Studio and open the Properties window. After the *DataSourceID* property is correctly set (in the *ddlWeatherCondition* control, for example, this would be the data source named dsWeatherCondtion), two other important properties must be set. First is the *DataTextField* property, which selects the field that will appear as the text in the drop-down list. The other is the *DataValueField* property, which selects the field to use as the underlying value for the control. Figure 5-39 shows the Properties dialog box for the Weather Condition drop-down list.

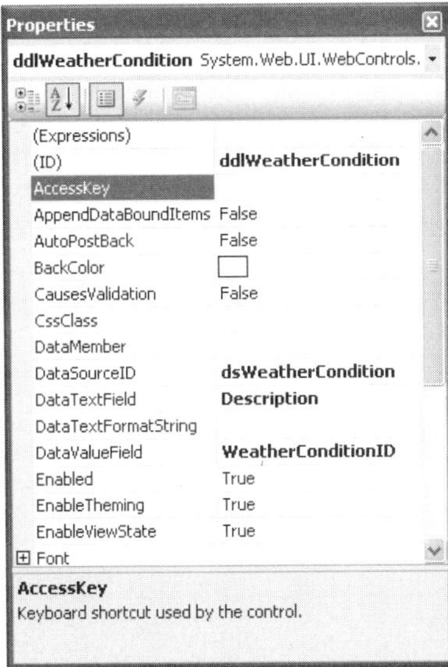

Figure 5-39 Properties dialog box with data-related properties configured

Populating the Details Editing Form

To populate the detail controls in the DetailsEdit view in the *MultiView* control, I had a few possible options. For example, I could have used the *Select* method of the *SqlDataSource* control. In this way, only a line or two of code would be required to get the *SqlDataSource* control to return the specific row from the BlogEntry table. In this example, that would be a viable alternative, but to show programmatic database access, I opted not to use the *Select* method.

The programmatic ways to access data using ADO.NET fall into two general categories:

- ***DataReader*** A one-way, forward-only object for returning data from an ADO.NET data source. There is one *DataReader* for each of the data providers, such as SqlClient and OleDb.
- ***DataSet*** A provider-independent object that provides an in-memory representation of the requested data. To fill a *DataSet*, you generally have to use one of the data provider–specific *DataAdapter* classes.

Whether to use a *DataReader* or *DataSet* object is the subject of some intense discussion. In fact, I have written on the topic myself (*http://www.simple-talk.com/2005/06/10/adonet-data-access/*). My general preference is to use *DataReader* objects for Web Forms. My reasons are:

- The *DataAdapter* uses the *DataReader* to read the data into the *DataSet* anyway, so using the *DataReader* directly is faster.

- The *DataSet* can consume large quantities of memory if the result set is similarly large.
- Advantages of the *DataSet* include the ability to contain multiple tables, the ability to have random access to all rows of the results, and the ability to update and save data.

The Many Faces of ADO.NET

One aspect of ADO.NET that causes significant confusion is the fact that there are some database-agnostic classes and some classes that are specialized for a particular database or type of database access. I will provide much more detail about these classes later in this chapter, but simply understanding which are generic and which are tied to a particular database will be helpful.

The *DataSet* class, for example, is totally isolated from the actual location of the data. In general, your code should ignore where the data might have come from and just use the data from the *DataSet*. The *Command*, *DataReader*, and *DataAdapter* classes are available for several different databases. Each family of classes of database-specific access components is generally thought of, when all tied together, as a *provider*. In Visual Studio, you can choose from providers for SQL Server, OLE DB, and ODBC data. Other providers (including a provider for MySQL) can be obtained from third parties.

Although this might sound confusing (and sometimes it really is), keep in mind that each class provided by each of the providers implements a known interface. So, every one of the *Command* objects (such as *SqlCommand* and *OleDbCommand*) implements a known interface (such as *IDbCommand*). This mapping, however, is imperfect. For example, in ADO.NET 1.1, Microsoft added a property named *HasRows* to the *SqlDataReader* object to allow the developer to determine whether a data reader will return any data. (The significance of this will be covered a bit later). Unfortunately, this property was added only to the *SqlDataReader* class; it is not available in any of the other standard implementations, and it is not part of the *IDataReader* interface, nor any new interface that data readers could implement. This is still true in ADO.NET 2.0.

For now, just remember that a *DataSet* is independent of any provider, and virtually all other database-related objects are tied to a specific provider and implement a known interface.

ADO.NET 1.x provided two basic objects to get data, and both still exist in ADO.NET 2.0. The first is *DataReader*. A *DataReader* object is a one-way, read-only view of the returned result set. To access any data from a *DataReader*, you must call the *Read* method of the *DataReader*. The *Read* method of the *DataReader* returns a Boolean value; it returns *true* when there is a row to navigate to. After the *DataReader* has been read, the developer can access the data in the current row by either indexing the *DataReader* (by using a column name or column ordinal) or using one of the many access routines to get specific types of data. When the *Read* method returns *false*, there are no more rows in the result set.

Interestingly, in the implementation of all *DataReader* objects (except the SqlClient version), there is no non-destructive way to determine whether a *DataReader* is returning any rows. After you call the *Read* method, the pointer is moved to the first row of the *DataReader*, and you cannot move back so that the *DataReader* is in its initial state. As I just mentioned, the SqlClient implementation (named *SqlDataReader*) is an exception: It exposes a *HasRows* property that is a Boolean value of *true* or *false*, indicating whether there are any rows waiting in the *DataReader*. The *DataReader* has the advantage of being very fast and relatively efficient in terms of resources; however, using a *DataReader* can be a problem if lengthy processing must be done on each row returned, because the connection must be held open the entire time the *DataReader* is being accessed. *DataReaders* can return multiple result sets, and you can navigate (one way, from the first result set, to the second, and so on) by using the *NextResult* method.

The second major way to access a database is with the *DataSet* object. A *DataSet* is an in-memory, database-independent representation of one or more tables. To fill a *DataSet*, you must use one of the database-specific *DataAdapter* objects. For instance, the SqlClient provider has the *SqlDataAdapter* object that can be used to fill a *DataSet*. After the *DataSet* has been filled, the data in the resulting tables can be accessed by using the *Tables* collection. Rows are accessed by using the *Rows* collection of the individual *DataTable* objects from the *Tables* collection. The *Rows* collection can be indexed by using both a row ordinal and a column name or column ordinal.

Using the *DataSet* has several advantages. First, the *DataSet* provides random access to the data returned from the database. The developer can look at the first row of the first table, then the third row of the second table, then the twelfth row of the first table, and so on, without causing any problems. Another advantage is that the *DataSet* can be serialized into XML and passed between tiers of a system, even if the tiers are in different process spaces or on different machines. *DataSet* objects can also be cached by ASP.NET, and caching is a very important feature for creating scalable, high-performance Web Forms applications. *DataSet* objects can even be passed back from a Web service. (Many developers consider using a *DataSet* in this way to be a terrible idea, at least in part because the *DataSet* is a relatively heavyweight object to serialize; the *DataSet* is also proprietary and cannot be used by most Web services not created with .NET.)

> **Note** In ADO.NET 2.0, the members of the *DataSet* object's *Tables* collection (*DataTable* objects) are also serializable, meaning that *DataTable* objects can be passed independent of a *DataSet* from tier to tier of an application or returned from a Web service. The difference between serializing a single-table *DataSet* and just the single table is minimal, and it does not address concerns related to broad compatibility.

Although *DataSet* objects can be very useful, they might not always be ideal. For example, because *DataSet* objects are in-memory representations of the data, they take up a great deal of memory, especially if there are many rows or many tables.

For demonstration purposes, I created methods that retrieved the data using both objects. After the data was obtained and ready (in a *DataSet* or *DataReader*), I populated the forms appropriately.

> **Note** The first thing I did to use any of the *SqlClient* objects, such as *SqlDataAdapter* and *SqlDataReader*, was add the following line to the top of the source file.
>
> ```
> using System.Data.SqlClient;
> ```
>
> This line allows you to refer to the classes in the *SqlClient* namespace without including *System.Data.SqlClient*.

You can select and save data in SQL Server in a variety of ways. One way is to use raw SQL SELECT, INSERT, and UPDATE statements. Although it is common practice to create these statements by simply concatenating strings, that is a dangerous thing to do. The safest way to use raw SQL statements is to create the SQL string with parameters, as shown in the markup in Listing 5-2.

An alternative, which is unsafe and subject to an SQL injection attack, is to build up an SQL statement in a string by concatenating literal strings with SQL syntax and variables. Variables that come from user input should not be trusted. Rather than a reasonable value, a user-supplied variable could have additional SQL commands appended. When you use a user-supplied variable, rather than use parameters, to build up an SQL string, you could be bit by an SQL injection attack.

> **Note** SQL strings passed into the *SqlClient* command object should contain named parameters. Named parameters are a wonderful thing. They allow you to add parameters in any order convenient, and, when used with stored procedures, they allow you to provide default values—a useful tactic when you are adding parameters to an existing stored procedure and you don't want to break old code. For OleDb, parameters are positional rather than named. So, when parameters appear in an SQL string, they should appear as ? characters rather than by name. Another consequence of how OleDb parameters work is that they must be added to the *Parameters* collection in the order in which they appear in the SQL string, left to right.

> **Tip** The vast majority of the database code in this chapter can be made to work for the OleDb provider by replacing "Sql" with "OleDb" in the name of the objects used to access data. For instance, change *SqlCommand* to *OleDbCommand* (and ensure that parameters are placed in the SQL string as specified in the previous note,) and most code will work for the OleDb provider. Note that the connection string must be changed as well.

Although it is not required to prevent an SQL injection attack, using stored procedures provides some additional advantages. Stored procedures are blocks of SQL code that can be called by name and can accept virtually any number of parameters. In this respect, stored procedures are similar to functions in programming languages such as C#. Stored procedures can contain any number of SELECT, UPDATE, INSERT, and DELETE statements.

The first advantage is that all the database-related work is done near the database. This can be more efficient, especially when you are combining several operations in a single stored procedure. Listing 5-3 shows the two stored procedures, *spSelectBlogEntry* and *spSaveBlogEntry*, used to select and save BlogEntry rows, respectively.

Listing 5-3 Stored Procedures to Select and Save BlogEntry Rows

```
CREATE PROCEDURE dbo.spSelectBlogEntry

    (
    @BlogEntryID int
    )

AS
    SET NOCOUNT ON

    SELECT BlogEntryID, DateEntered, EnteredBy, DateMocified, ModifiedBy,
        WeatherConditionID, WindDirectionID, WindStrengthID, Subject,
        Message
    FROM BlogEntry
    WHERE BlogEntryID=@BlogEntryID

    RETURN


CREATE PROCEDURE dbo.spSaveBlogEntry

    (
    @BlogEntryID int,
    @Subject nvarchar(128),
    @Message text,
    @WeatherConditionID int,
    @WindDirectionID int,
    @WindStrengthID int,
    @EnteredBy nvarchar(128) = 'DougR'
    )
AS

    IF Exists(SELECT * FROM BlogEntry WHERE BlogEntryID=@BlogEntryID)
    BEGIN
        UPDATE BlogEntry SET
            Subject=@Subject,
            Message=@Message,
            WeatherConditionID=@WeatherConditionID,
```

```
            WindDirectionID=@WindDirectionID,
            WindStrengthID=@WindStrengthID,
            ModifiedBy=@EnteredBy,
            DateModified=GetDate()
        WHERE BlogEntryID=@BlogEntryID
    END
    ELSE
    BEGIN
        INSERT INTO BlogEntry(
            Subject,
            Message,
            WeatherConditionID,
            WindDirectionID,
            WindStrengthID,
            EnteredBy)
        VALUES(
            @Subject,
            @Message,
            @WeatherConditionID,
            @WindDirectionID,
            @WindStrengthID,
            @EnteredBy)
        SET @BlogEntryID=SCOPE_IDENTITY()
    END

    RETURN @BlogEntryID
```

The first stored procedure, *spSelectBlogEntry*, is very straightforward and requires little explanation. It takes a single parameter, *@BlogEntryID*, which is an integer. The first line of the stored procedure, after the parameter declaration, is SET NOCOUNT ON, which instructs SQL Server not to send a message after each statement indicating the number of rows affected. In some cases, not setting NOCOUNT ON can cause problems with reading records, and in any event the row counts being returned will increase network traffic. The guts of the stored procedure is the same sort of SELECT statement used in some previous examples.

The second stored procedure, *spSaveBlogEntry*, is a bit more complicated. The pattern used is worth learning. The parameters passed in are all the parameters required to insert (or update) a row in the BlogEntry table. One of the parameters, *EnteredBy*, has a default value passed in, 'DougR'. Because of the way that *SqlClient* parameters are processed, if a parameter is not passed in and a default value is present, the stored procedure runs as if the default value were actually passed in to the procedure.

Inside the stored procedure, the first step is to determine whether the row specified by the *@BlogEntryID* parameter exists. If the row exists, it is updated; otherwise, the row is inserted. All other parameters except the *@EnteredBy* parameter are used to insert or update the column of the table with the same name. Note that the *@EnteredBy* parameter is used to fill in the EnteredBy column for a row inserted, and the ModifiedBy column for a modified row. If the BlogEntry is inserted, the stored procedure sets the *@BlogEntryID* variable to *SCOPE_IDENTITY()*, a special SQL Server function to retrieve the IDENTITY value just inserted. *SCOPE_IDENTITY()* returns the value of the column in the most recently inserted table that has been identified as the IDENTITY column in the table; in this case the *BlogEntryID* column is the IDENTITY value. Finally, the *@BlogEntryID* parameter is returned from the stored procedure.

You might ask, "Why write a single stored procedure to save the data, rather than a separate Update and Insert stored procedure?" I have found that a single stored procedure used to insert or update, as appropriate, has worked better for me. One benefit of a single stored procedure that will handle both inserts and updates is that it allows the editing of new and existing rows to be handled in the same way in your code.

Before looking at the code, let's look at the screens to see how everything should work. When the page is first loaded, it looks like Figure 5-40.

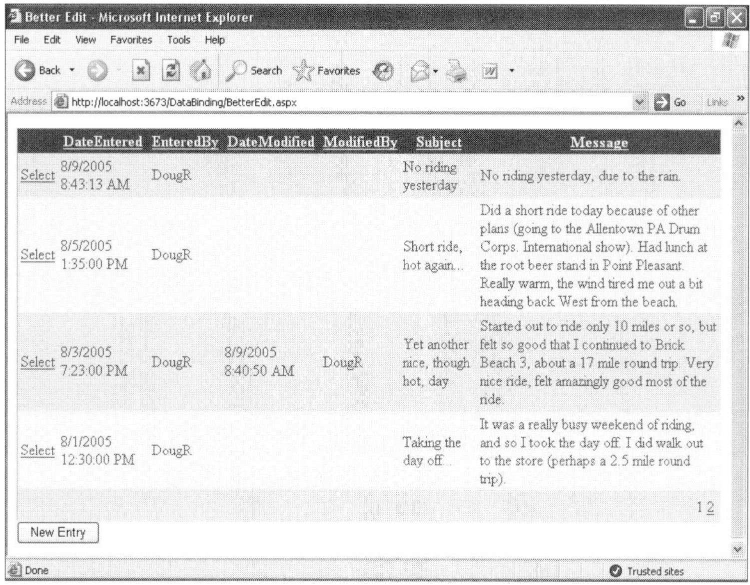

Figure 5-40 BetterEdit.aspx when first loaded, showing the *GridView* control

The four most recent rows are displayed, as well as a button that allows the user to add a new entry. To edit one of the rows, click a Select link, and a page like the one shown in Figure 5-41 appears.

The Cancel button causes the *GridView* control to reappear without any change to the data. The Save button saves the data, rebinds the *GridView* control, and makes the *GridView* control visible again. Listing 5-4 shows the complete code for BetterEdit.aspx.cs.

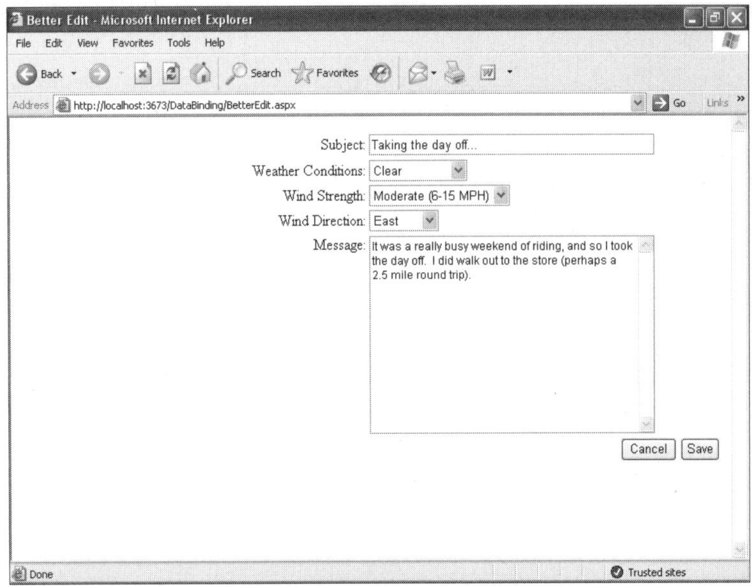

Figure 5-41 Editing the details of a row

Listing 5-4 BetterEdit.aspx.cs

```
using System;
using System.Data;
using System.Data.SqlClient;
using System.Configuration;
using System.Collections;
using System.Web;
using System.Web.Security;
using System.Web.UI;
using System.Web.UI.WebControls;
using System.Web.UI.WebControls.WebParts;
using System.Web.UI.HtmlControls;

public partial class BetterEdit : System.Web.UI.Page
{
    public int EditBlogEntryID
    {
        get
        {
            return ViewState["EditBlogEntryID"] == null ? 0 :
                (int)ViewState["EditBlogEntryID"];
        }
        set
        {
            ViewState["EditBlogEntryID"] = value;
        }
    }
    protected void Page_Load(object sender, EventArgs e)
    {
        if (this.IsPostBack==false)
```

```
        {
            this.MultiView1.SetActiveView(this.Grid);
        }
    }
    protected void GridView1_SelectedIndexChanging(object sender,
        GridViewSelectEventArgs e)
    {
        this.MultiView1.SetActiveView(this.DetailsEdit);
        this.EditBlogEntryID =
            int.Parse(
            GridView1.DataKeys[e.NewSelectedIndex].Value.ToString());
        this.BindDetailsEdit();
    }
    private void BindDetailsEdit()
    {
        // This code is not normal practice. I have set up code that
        //     can be fed using a DataReader or a DataSet
        IDataReader dr;
        DataSet ds;
        ds = this.SelectBlogEntryDS(this.EditBlogEntryID);
        dr = (IDataReader)ds.CreateDataReader();
        // Comment the two lines above and uncomment the line below
        //      to use a DataReader directly.
        //         dr = this.SelectBlogEntryDR(this.EditBlogEntryID);
        try
        {
            if (dr.Read())
            {
                this.edSubject.Text = dr["Subject"].ToString();
                this.edMessage.Text = dr["Message"].ToString();
                this.ddlWeatherCondition.SelectedIndex =
                    this.ddlWeatherCondition.Items.IndexOf(
                        this.ddlWeatherCondition.Items.FindByValue(
                            dr["WeatherConditionID"].ToString()));
                this.ddlWindDirection.SelectedIndex =
                    this.ddlWindDirection.Items.IndexOf(
                        this.ddlWindDirection.Items.FindByValue(
                            dr["WindDirectionID"].ToString()));
                this.ddlWindStrength.SelectedIndex =
                    this.ddlWindStrength.Items.IndexOf(
                        this.ddlWindStrength.Items.FindByValue(
                            dr["WindStrengthID"].ToString()));
            }
            else
            {
                this.edSubject.Text = string.Empty;
                this.edMessage.Text = string.Empty;
                this.ddlWeatherCondition.SelectedIndex = 0;
                this.ddlWindDirection.SelectedIndex = 0;
                this.ddlWindStrength.SelectedIndex = 0;
            }
        }
        finally
        {
            dr.Close();
```

```
    }

}
private DataSet SelectBlogEntryDS(int BlogEntryID)
{
    string spName = "spSelectBlogEntry";
    SqlConnection cn = new SqlConnection(
        ConfigurationManager.ConnectionStrings[
        "BikeBlogConnectionString"].ConnectionString);
    SqlCommand cmd = new SqlCommand(spName,cn);
    cmd.CommandType = CommandType.StoredProcedure;

    cmd.Parameters.AddWithValue("@BlogEntryID", BlogEntryID);

    SqlDataAdapter da = new SqlDataAdapter(cmd);
    DataSet ds = new DataSet();
    try
    {
        da.Fill(ds);
    }
    catch ( Exception Ex )
    {
        // Handle the error...
    }
    return ds;
}

private SqlDataReader SelectBlogEntryDR(int BlogEntryID)
{
    string spName = "spSelectBlogEntry";
    SqlDataReader dr = null;
    SqlConnection cn = new SqlConnection(
        ConfigurationManager.ConnectionStrings[
        "BikeBlogConnectionString"].ConnectionString);
    cn.Open();
    try
    {
        SqlCommand cmd = new SqlCommand(spName, cn);
        cmd.CommandType = CommandType.StoredProcedure;

        cmd.Parameters.AddWithValue("@BlogEntryID", BlogEntryID);
        dr = cmd.ExecuteReader(CommandBehavior.CloseConnection);
    }
    catch
    {
        // Close the connection in case of error...
        cn.Close();
    }
    // If no error, return the DataReader, and the connection
    //     will be closed when the DataReader is closed.
    return dr;
}

private bool SaveBlogEntry(string Subject, string Message,
    int WeatherConditionID, int WindDirectionID, int WindStrengthID,
    int BlogEntryID)
```

```
    {
        bool ret = false;

        string spName = "spSaveBlogEntry";
        SqlConnection cn = new SqlConnection(
            ConfigurationManager.ConnectionStrings[
            "BikeBlogConnectionString"].ConnectionString);
        cn.Open();
        try
        {
            SqlCommand cmd = new SqlCommand(spName, cn);
            cmd.CommandType = CommandType.StoredProcedure;

            cmd.Parameters.AddWithValue("@BlogEntryID", BlogEntryID);
            cmd.Parameters.AddWithValue("@Subject", Subject);
            cmd.Parameters.AddWithValue("@Message", Message);
            cmd.Parameters.AddWithValue("@WeatherConditionID",
                WeatherConditionID);
            cmd.Parameters.AddWithValue("@WindDirectionID",
                WindDirectionID);
            cmd.Parameters.AddWithValue("@WindStrengthID", WindStrengthID);

            cmd.ExecuteNonQuery();
            ret=true;
        }
        finally
        {
            // Close the connection in case of error...
            cn.Close();
        }

        return ret;
    }
    protected void cmdCancel_Click(object sender, EventArgs e)
    {
        this.MultiView1.SetActiveView(this.Grid);
        this.EditBlogEntryID = 0;
    }
    protected void cmdSave_Click(object sender, EventArgs e)
    {
        this.SaveBlogEntry(this.edSubject.Text, this.edMessage.Text,
            int.Parse(this.ddlWeatherCondition.SelectedValue),
            int.Parse(this.ddlWindDirection.SelectedValue),
            int.Parse(this.ddlWindStrength.SelectedValue),
            this.EditBlogEntryID);
        this.EditBlogEntryID = 0;
        this.GridView1.DataBind();
        this.MultiView1.SetActiveView(this.Grid);
    }
    protected void btnNewEntry_Click(object sender, EventArgs e)
    {
        this.MultiView1.SetActiveView(this.DetailsEdit);
        this.EditBlogEntryID = 0;
        this.BindDetailsEdit();
    }
}
```

Error Handling and Connections

When working with databases, it is important to remember that connections should be closed and disposed of as soon as possible. The following code ensures that the connection, if opened, will be closed as soon as the code in the *try* block is executed.

```
cn.Open();
try
{
    // Use the connection...
}
finally
{
    // Close the connection in case of error...
    cn.Close();
}
```

If the connection is not closed, it will eventually be closed when the connection object is collected by garbage collection. However, because of the way that .NET garbage collection works, the connection could remain open for a long time.

What this code does not address is what will happen if the call to the *Open* method of the *cn* variable (an *SqlConnection* object) fails. There are several schools of thought on how to handle an exception that takes place before the connection is actually opened. When code is split between the user interface and the database access code (as it often will be in production code), determining how to handle such an exception can be problematic. A failure of a database connection is often a catastrophic error that cannot be overcome easily. In much of my production code, I allow such an exception to bubble up to the user interface code to either have the user interface code handle it, or just as likely have a global exception handler handle the problem. Alternately, the call to the *Open* method could be moved inside the *try* block, and a *catch* block could be added.

The first thing you should notice in this code is the integer property named *EditBlogEntryID*. This property allows the page to remember the currently edited BlogEntryID. A property is a special type of member of a class. The underlying value of the property can be a private variable of the class, or it can be calculated or retrieved from some sort of persistent storage. In this example, the *EditBlogEntryID* property is persisted in view state. The *get* section of the property contains an interesting bit of code that is not entirely obvious.

```
get
{
    return ViewState["EditBlogEntryID"] == null ?
        0 : (int)ViewState["EditBlogEntryID"];
}
```

C# (like C++ before it) has what is called a tertiary operator. This operator has three parts:

- An expression, in this case ViewState["EditBlogEntryID"] == null
- An expression to use when the first expression is true, in this case 0
- An expression to use when the first expression is false, in this case (int)ViewState["Edit-BlogEntryID"]

The *set* section of the property declaration simply stores the *value*, which is a keyword that represents the value being set, to the *ViewState* collection.

Clicking the Select link opens the details page. When the Select link is clicked, the *Selected-IndexChanging* event is fired. The code for this method controls the action of the page.

```
protected void GridView1_SelectedIndexChanging(object sender,
      GridViewSelectEventArgs e)
{
    this.MultiView1.SetActiveView(this.DetailsEdit);
    this.EditBlogEntryID =
      int.Parse(
         GridView1.DataKeys[e.NewSelectedIndex].Value.ToString());
    this.BindDetailsEdit();
}
```

The first line of the event handler sets the active view of the *MultiView* control. The *MultiView* control allows only one view to be active at a time, so setting a view as the active view hides all other views (in this case, the grid view is hidden). Next, the *EditBlogEntryID* property is set. *EditBlogEntryID* is a property that is used to hold the BlogEntryID that is currently being edited. The *GridViewSelectEventArgs* argument (*e*, in this example) has a property named *NewSelectedIndex*. The code next uses the *NewSelectedIndex* property as an index into the collection of DataKeys, which is a collection of the values of each row specified by the *DataKeyNames* property of the *GridView* control. The *DataKeyNames* property in the *GridView1* object is set to *BlogEntryID*, so the following code returns the BlogEntryID column of the selected row.

```
GridView1.DataKeys[e.NewSelectedIndex].Value.ToString()
```

This value is a string, so it is parsed to get an integer.

The next line, calling the *BindDetailsEdit* method, is what causes the edit controls in the details section of the page to be populated. The *BindDetailsEdit* method first declares several variables. The following bit of code requires some explanation.

```
ds = this.SelectBlogEntryDS(this.EditBlogEntryID);
dr = (IDataReader)ds.CreateDataReader();
//       dr = this.SelectBlogEntryDR(this.EditBlogEntryID);
```

Two methods retrieve a specific blog entry. The one used here is the *SelectBlogEntryDS* method. After the *DataSet* object is returned in the *ds* variable, I use a new method of the *DataSet* object, *CreateDataReader*, to return a *DataReader* object based on the data in the *DataSet*. I use the *CreateDataReader* method here just as a convenience for this example. By using the *CreateReader* method, I can show creation of both a *DataSet* and a *DataReader*, while the code that fills in the text boxes can always use a *DataReader*. Alternately, if the top two lines are commented out and the third line is uncommented, the *DataReader* is returned directly from the other method for selecting a blog entry, named *SelectBlogEntryDR*. In both cases, the routines to select a blog entry are passed the *EditBlogEntryID* property.

The two selection methods are similar, but both deserve discussion because they could both be repeated often in your own code.

Note The two selection methods are members of the page class here. In a real application, you might place these and other data access functions is another class, so that they could be accessed from multiple pages. This degree of isolation allows more code reuse, but it is often awkward for examples in a book.

The *SelectBlogEntryDS* method returns a *DataSet*.

```
private DataSet SelectBlogEntryDS(int BlogEntryID)
{
    string spName = "spSelectBlogEntry";
    SqlConnection cn = new SqlConnection(
        ConfigurationManager.ConnectionStrings[
        "BikeBlogConnectionString"].ConnectionString);
    SqlCommand cmd = new SqlCommand(spName,cn);
    cmd.CommandType = CommandType.StoredProcedure;

    cmd.Parameters.AddWithValue("@BlogEntryID", BlogEntryID);

    SqlDataAdapter da = new SqlDataAdapter(cmd);
    DataSet ds = new DataSet();
    try
    {
        da.Fill(ds);
    }
    catch ( Exception Ex )
    {
        // Handle the error...
    }
    return ds;
}
```

After declaring and setting the stored procedure name, the code creates a connection. To create a connection, you must have a connection string. While creating the first of the *SqlDataSource* controls in Visual Studio, I created a connection string that was saved in the

Web.config file. In the Web.config file, the following section is devoted to connection strings.

```
<connectionStrings>
    <add name="BikeBlogConnectionString"
    connectionString=
    "Data Source=DELL670;Initial Catalog=BikeBlog;Integrated Security=True"
    providerName="System.Data.SqlClient"/>
</connectionStrings>
```

The code uses the *connectionStrings* collection of the *ConfigurationManager* class, indexes it with the name of the connection ("BikeBlogConnectionString" in this case), and uses the *ConnectionString* member of that object, which is a string.

After the connection is created, the code creates a command object, of type *SqlCommand*. The *CommandType* property is set to *CommandType.StoredProcedure*. The three possible values for *CommandType* are:

- *CommandType.Text*
- *CommandType.TableDirect*
- *CommandType.StoredProcedure*

CommandType.Text is the default value, which is used when you are specifying a raw SQL statement, such as SELECT, INSERT, UPDATE, or DELETE. *TableDirect* is used when the command text is the name of a table. *CommandType.TableDirect* is used only by the OleDb provider. *StoredProcedure* is used when the name of a stored procedure is specified by the command text. (Note that rather than setting the *CommandType* property to *CommandType.StoredProcedure*, I could have left it set to *CommandType.Text* and passed in "*EXEC* spSelectBlogEntry @BlogEntryID" as the command text. I always use *StoredProcedure*.) The *BlogEntryID* parameter is then added to the command's *Parameters* collection, using the *AddWithValue* method.

Next, I created a new *SqlDataAdapter* object and a new, empty *DataSet*. Then I called the *Fill* method of the *SqlDataAdapter* object, which fills in the *DataSet* passed as a parameter. Finally, the *DataSet* is returned. One interesting aspect of this code is that the *SqlConnection* object is never opened. When the connection associated with the *DataAdapter* object is closed, it is opened only when required and safely closed when the *DataAdapter* object is done using it. This is a convenient feature, because it eliminates the need for the developer to manually manage the state of the connection.

The *SelectBlogEntryDR* method is similar in many respects to the *SelectBlogEntryDS* method, but it's a little more complex because the state of the connection does need to be managed. The connection is created in this method in the same way that it is created in the *DataSet* returning method. After the connection is created, however, it is opened by calling the *Open* method of the connection. Immediately after the *Open* call, the code has a *try/catch* block, as shown here.

```
cn.Open();
try
{
    SqlCommand cmd = new SqlCommand(spName, cn);
    cmd.CommandType = CommandType.StoredProcedure;

    cmd.Parameters.AddWithValue("@BlogEntryID", BlogEntryID);
    dr = cmd.ExecuteReader(CommandBehavior.CloseConnection);
}
catch
{
    // Close the connection in case of error...
    cn.Close();
}
return dr;
```

In a *try/catch* block, the code in the *try* section is executed, and if an exception occurs, the *catch* section is executed. In this example, I called the *ExecuteReader* method of the command object inside the *try* block. The *ExecuteReader* method can accept a single parameter, and I passed in *CommandBehavior.CloseConnection*. This parameter passed to the *ExecuteReader* method is required when you have a method that will pass a *DataReader* object back to the caller. Without this parameter, when you passed the *DataReader* back to the caller, the underlying connection would remain open until garbage collection. When this parameter is used, the underlying connection is closed when the *DataReader* is closed. In the preceding code, the *catch* block is used so that the connection is closed if there is a problem with executing the command. Finally, the *DataReader* is returned.

Now that I have described the two possible methods to retrieve the data from the database, I will continue with the balance of the explanation of the *BindDetailsEdit* method seen in Listing 5-4. After creating the *DataReader* (either directly or by creating a *DataSet* and converting it to a *DataReader*), the code enters a *try* block. Note that rather than using a *catch* block at the end, I used a *finally* block, so that the code inside the *finally* block will always be executed. Inside the *finally* block, the *DataReader* is closed, which is critical, because when calling *SelectBlogEntryDR* method, the underlying connection will be closed only when the *DataReader* is closed.

In the *try/finally* block in the *BindDetailsEdit* method, the first step is to call the *Read* method on the *DataReader*. This is required, because initially, the *DataReader* is logically pointing to just before the first row returned. If *Read* is not called, the code will cause an exception indicating an attempt to read data when none is present. The *Read* method returns a Boolean value; *if (dr.Read())* means that the code under the *if* clause will be executed only if there is at least one row returned. In this example, we know that only a single row will be returned (because the stored procedure retrieves a row based on a primary key, *BlogEntryID*). In other cases, in which multiple rows will be returned, using *while* rather than *if* will allow the code to execute for each row returned.

If the *Read* method returns true, the individual edit controls will be populated. The *DataReader* is indexed by using the field name. The ordinal of the column can also be used, but in practice this can be awkward to do, because you also need to know the order of rows returned by the command. Just as important, if the order of the returned columns change, you will need to ensure that the ordinal you pass as a parameter is updated as well. In this example, I used a *DataReader*, even though a *DataSet* is the source of the *DataReader*, simply to show creation of both a *DataReader* and a *DataSet*. Accessing data in a *DataSet* is similar to accessing data in a *DataReader*. The code to read the data from a *DataReader* is shown here.

```
if (dr.Read())
{
    this.edSubject.Text = dr["Subject"].ToString();
    // ... and so on ...
```

If the *DataSet* were used directly, the code would appear as follows.

```
if ((ds.Tables.Count > 0) && (ds.Tables[0].Rows.Count>0) )
{
    this.edSubject.Text = ds.Tables[0].Rows[0]["Subject"].ToString();
    // ... and so on ...
```

Warning In both of the preceding cases in which the *Subject* is retrieved, if *Subject* could be null, the value from the column should be tested to determine whether it is null, using *DbNull.Value* as shown here.

```
if ( dr["Subject"]!=DbNull.Value )
{
    this.edSubject.Text=dr["Subject"].ToString();
}
```

The drop-down lists are set to values reflecting the data returned as well. The *SelectedIndex* property is set to the index of the item found by using the *FindByValue* method, passing in the data from the *DataReader*. The code to set each *DropDownList* control looks a little complicated, but it does the job of properly setting the values in the *DropDownList* control.

If the *DataReader* does not contain any rows, the edit controls are all set to default values in the *else* statement associated with the *if (dr.Read())* statement.

The user indicates that he or she wants to save the modified entry by clicking the Save button. The event handler is shown here.

```
protected void cmdSave_Click(object sender, EventArgs e)
{
    this.SaveBlogEntry(this.edSubject.Text, this.edMessage.Text,
        int.Parse(this.ddlWeatherCondition.SelectedValue),
        int.Parse(this.ddlWindDirection.SelectedValue),
        int.Parse(this.ddlWindStrength.SelectedValue),
        this.EditBlogEntryID);
```

```
        this.EditBlogEntryID = 0;
        this.GridView1.DataBind();
        this.MultiView1.SetActiveView(this.Grid);
    }
```

First, the data is saved. The *SaveBlogEntry* method is called, passing in the entered values from the edit controls. Next, the *EditBlogEntryID* property is set to 0, meaning that there is no currently edited row. I called the *DataBind* method on the *GridView1* object to ensure that the changes just made are reflected in the grid view when it is made visible in the final line of the event handler.

The *SaveBlogEntry* method is reasonably straightforward.

```
private bool SaveBlogEntry(string Subject, string Message,
    int WeatherConditionID, int WindDirectionID, int WindStrengthID,
    int BlogEntryID)
{
    bool ret = false;

    string spName = "spSaveBlogEntry";
    SqlConnection cn = new SqlConnection(
        ConfigurationManager.ConnectionStrings[
        "BikeBlogConnectionString"].ConnectionString);
    cn.Open();
    try
    {
        SqlCommand cmd = new SqlCommand(spName, cn);
        cmd.CommandType = CommandType.StoredProcedure;
        cmd.Parameters.AddWithValue("@BlogEntryID", BlogEntryID);
        cmd.Parameters.AddWithValue("@Subject", Subject);
        cmd.Parameters.AddWithValue("@Message", Message);
        cmd.Parameters.AddWithValue("@WeatherConditionID",
            WeatherConditionID);
        cmd.Parameters.AddWithValue("@WindDirectionID", WindDirectionID);
        cmd.Parameters.AddWithValue("@WindStrengthID", WindStrengthID);

        cmd.ExecuteNonQuery();
        ret = true;
    }
    finally
    {
        // Close the connection in case of error...
        cn.Close();
    }
    return ret;
}
```

The connection is created as it was in the selection methods. The connection is opened, and then the code enters a *try* block to ensure that the connection is closed, because the call to close is inside the *finally* block. After creating the command and adding parameters, I called the *ExecuteNonQuery* method of the command object. The *ExecuteNonQuery* method is used to execute SQL statements that do not return any result sets.

> **Note** There is one other method on the command object to execute an SQL command. The *ExecuteScalar* method returns the first column of the first row of the SQL command. Generally, the *ExecuteScalar* method is used when you know that the command will return only a single value.

Two additional event handlers allow the user to add a totally new entry, as well as cancel changes while editing details.

```
protected void btnNewEntry_Click(object sender, EventArgs e)
{
    this.MultiView1.SetActiveView(this.DetailsEdit);
    this.EditBlogEntryID = 0;
    this.BindDetailsEdit();
}
protected void cmdCancel_Click(object sender, EventArgs e)
{
    this.MultiView1.SetActiveView(this.Grid);
    this.EditBlogEntryID = 0;
}
```

The event handler for the new entry button sets DetailsEdit as the active view, sets the *EditBlogEntryID* property to 0, and then calls the *BindDetailsEdit* method. Because the *EditBlogEntryID* property is 0 and *BlogEntryID* cannot be 0, this ensures that no row will be returned and the edit controls will be initialized.

The event handler for the cancel button on the DetailsEdit view sets the grid view as the active view, and then sets the *EditBlogEntryID* to 0.

Future Enhancements

The code shown in Listing 5-4 is marginally functional, and of course there is much room for improvement. First, the appearance of the page leaves a bit to be desired. A more flashy version of this Web site will appear in future chapters. Figure 5-42 shows the main page of the Web site with some additional flair.

This version uses some of the cascading style sheets features covered in Chapter 3. In addition, a simple header image was added to the page. These changes will be used in some examples shown in upcoming chapters.

Anyone who knows anything about weblogs will note a large number of deficiencies with the bike blog shown in this chapter. First, anyone can add an entry. There is no security associated with the site, and when blog entries are saved, they just use my name. Another problem is that the site does not allow comments; I might want anyone entering a comment to register on the site. The security issues will be addressed in Chapter 7.

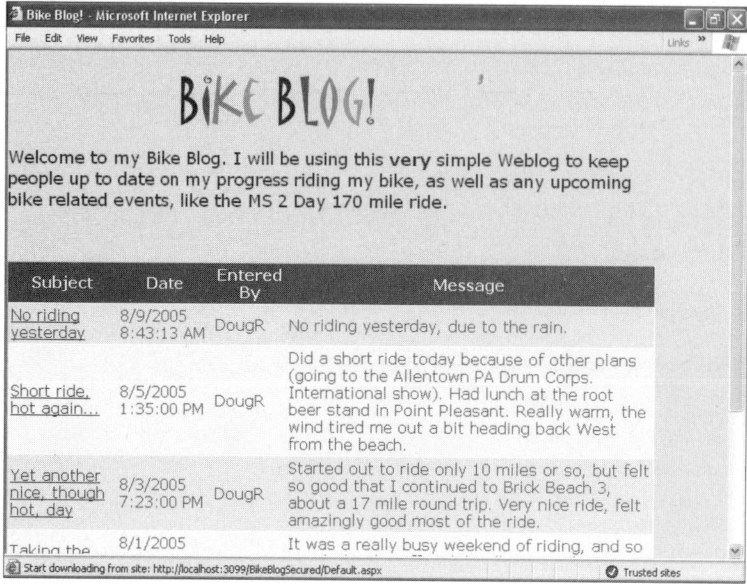

Figure 5-42 A prettier version of the bike blog

Another problem is that, although using the *GridView* control is one possible way to display the entries on the main screen, there are others. For example, a *user control*, which is in many ways a mini-page, allows for a more logical structure, and a page can contain multiple instances of a particular user control. Authoring user controls and server controls will be covered in Chapter 6, "Custom Controls."

One other improvement, beyond the scope of this book, would be to add a Really Simple Syndication (RSS) feed from the blog. This would allow users to read the bike blog from one of the dozens of RSS aggregators without having to visit the page.

Conclusion

We have already learned quite a bit about the Web Forms environment, the standard ASP.NET server controls, laying out Web Forms, and using Web Parts. This chapter introduced data binding. In addition to the many ways in which Web Forms applications can be built to access data from a database declaratively, without any code, we learned how to use the *DataSet* and *DataReader* objects to programmatically access data, as well as how to save data. In addition to the raw SQL SELECT statements used in the *SqlDataSource* controls, we also learned how to use stored procedures to select and save data.

Next, in Chapter 6, we will learn about creating custom controls of all sorts. By using custom controls, one developer can work out all the details of a problem, and then other developers can take that predefined bit of tested functionality and build solutions. Custom controls sound good, and they are. However, they can be tricky to get right. After reading the next chapter, you will be well on your way to creating controls that you and others can use.

Chapter 6

Custom Controls

In this chapter:

As I mentioned earlier in this book, a goal for Microsoft ASP.NET 2.0 was a 70 percent reduction in the amount of code. To the extent that this goal was met, it was because of new controls that eliminate a great deal of coding. For instance, the *DataSource* control, covered in Chapter 5, "Data Binding," eliminates much of the procedural coding required by previous versions of ASP.NET to provide data to controls. The *GridView* control, also covered in Chapter 5, allows fairly complete display of information from the database without any procedural code. In Chapter 7, "Web Forms User Security and Administration," you will learn about a new set of controls that allow you to perform almost all tasks associated with identifying, registering, and logging in users without any significant code. This is the power of controls: the ability to encapsulate a chunk of functionality and then have it reused, by yourself or other developers.

Custom controls, created specifically for an application, or perhaps better yet, for a suite of applications, allow you as the developer to encapsulate chunks of functionality required by your applications, just like the controls included with ASP.NET 2.0. The job of creating an application can be reasonably split among several developers, with each developer concentrating on creating specific controls or on tying controls together to create an application.

For instance, I once worked on a large system (not using ASP.NET or Microsoft SQL Server) with several unusual requirements. First, the application needed to communicate with a database that used unusual data types in certain areas. One was a date/time type that used a string in a particular format, rather than the *DateTime* type provided by the database. The development environment provided a variety of rich controls for interacting with dates, but those dates had to come from the database as *DateTime* types. So that all eight developers on the team didn't have to become experts in the details of this particular part of the system, I was tasked with creating a control that completely encapsulated handling of the date and time; the other developers could simply drag the control onto their forms. When bugs in the control became apparent (as, unfortunately, sometimes happens), I was able to address the problems, and when the application was next built, the fix was applied to all forms that used the control.

Compare this to a scenario in which each developer works out an individual solution on each and every form that he or she creates. Different developers might address a problem in subtly different ways, each with their own set of bugs. A perfect, bug-free solution would be ideal, but in the real world, a single consistent solution, even with a bug or two, is the next best thing. Custom controls allow you to create such consistent, if not perfect, solutions to the problems specific to your application.

Types of Controls You Can Create

All of the standard ASP.NET controls, such as *TextBox*, *DropDownList*, and *Button*, are standard server controls. For the end user of a control, standard server controls offer perhaps the best of all worlds. They can be easily dragged and dropped onto a form, and they offer a very rich design interface that allows the developer to visualize what the Web Form will look like when the page is run.

The design-time experience for your users is the good news about standard server controls. The bad news is that creating them is much more difficult than creating a standard ASP.NET Web Form. Rather than creating the control declaratively, and possibly adding some code where required, you must create standard server controls entirely in code. Testing standard server controls can be troublesome as well. Often, debugging standard server controls involves placing them on a page and examining the HTML source when the page is run.

An alternative type of custom control that you as a developer can create is called a user control. User controls are often seen as the ASP.NET answer to server-side includes that are used in Classic ASP. In Classic ASP, it was common to create reusable chunks of markup and code by creating include files, and then using the *include* directive on every page of the application that needed the chunk of markup and code that the include file contained. Server-side includes are supported by ASP.NET 2.0 for backward compatibility, but their use is discouraged, primarily because user controls offer a better alternative.

You program against properties of user controls. You can also easily use the same chunk of functionality more than once on a single page, and you can dynamically include any number of instances of the user control. In addition, ASP.NET 2.0 offers an improved design interface for user controls. In earlier versions, when you dragged a copy of a user control onto a page from Solution Explorer, only a gray box appeared to represent the user control. ASP.NET 2.0 displays the user control as it will appear when the page is run.

One specialized type of custom control remains: Web Parts. Recall from Chapter 4, "Working with Web Parts," that you can use any server control as a Web Part. But by either creating a custom Web Part or implementing an interface in a user control, you can also customize the look of the Web Part.

Which type of control is right for your application? The answer is, of course, "It depends." It depends on who will be using the control. It depends on the complexity of the user interface you are developing. And it depends on your ability as a developer. This chapter will introduce you to each type of control and help you decide which one is best for your specific application.

User Controls

The *UserControl* class is the base class for all user controls that you create. User controls have their own file extension: .ascx is associated with user controls, just as .aspx is associated with Web pages. User controls can be created with any text editor, and of course Microsoft Visual Studio offers good support for creating user controls. Another important authoring option is to create and test as a Web page, and then convert the page into a user control. I will leave text editor authoring as an exercise for the brave user, and the following sections will explain how to create a user control in Visual Studio directly, cache a user control, and create a new page that can be converted into a user control. Along the way, I will show you how to use user control caching, another significant advantage to using user controls.

Creating a User Control in Visual Studio

Creating a user control in Visual Studio is much like creating any other new item. In a new Web site named CustomControls, right-click the Web site in Solution Explorer, and then select Add New Item from the context menu. In the Add New Item dialog box, select Web User Control from the installed templates, as shown in Figure 6-1. The default name is WebUserControl.ascx. Click Add, and the new user control is added to your solution.

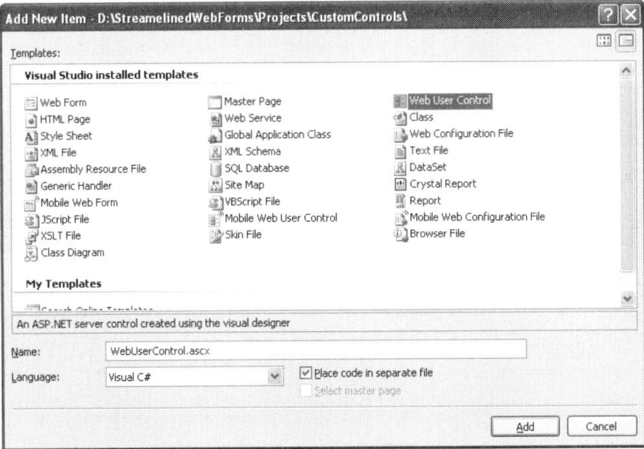

Figure 6-1 Adding a user control in Visual Studio

The Source view of the user control in Visual Studio is shown in Figure 6-2. Note that I added a line break so that all attributes are visible in the screen shot.

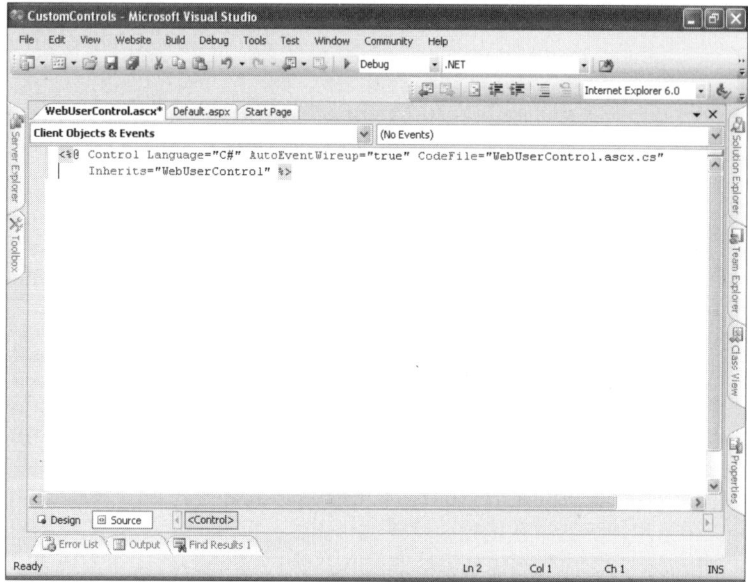

Figure 6-2 A new user control in Source view

The user control has an *@ Control* directive that is very similar to the *@ Page* directive of a Web Form. And that is it. There is nothing else in the markup for the user control (unlike a Web Form, which includes lots of default markup). The markup included in the default page of a Web Form is unnecessary for user controls because user controls are added to an existing page; the HTML and body tags (which can only exist once per page) are part of that existing page rather than the user control.

Switch to Design view, and you see a totally blank screen. Just as with a Web Form, you can drag and drop other controls onto the page, and you can use Source view to add markup to the user control. In this example, I dropped a *Label* control onto the page. I also wanted to modify the label whenever the page was loaded. As with Web Forms, you can double-click the user control in Design view outside of any control to see the source code of the user control. When you do so, the source code for the user control looks like the following code.

```
using System;
using System.Data;
using System.Configuration;
using System.Collections;
using System.Web;
using System.Web.Security;
using System.Web.UI;
using System.Web.UI.WebControls;
using System.Web.UI.WebControls.WebParts;
using System.Web.UI.HtmlControls;
```

```
public partial class WebUserControl : System.Web.UI.UserControl
{
    protected void Page_Load(object sender, EventArgs e)
    {
        // Control initialization code here...
    }
}
```

The most important thing about this default code is that the *WebUserControl* class inherits from *System.Web.UI.UserControl*. The *UserControl* class provides essentially the same properties as the *Page* class. If required, the user control–based class can also access the current page by referencing the *Page* property of the *UserControl* class.

To allow the user control to do something useful, I added a single line of code to the *Page_Load* event handler.

```
this.Label1.Text = DateTime.Now.ToLongTimeString();
```

This code sets the text of the label to the current time. In Visual Studio, go to the Default.aspx page that Visual Studio created by default. From Solution Explorer, drag a copy of the user control onto the page, and the page appears as shown in Figure 6-3.

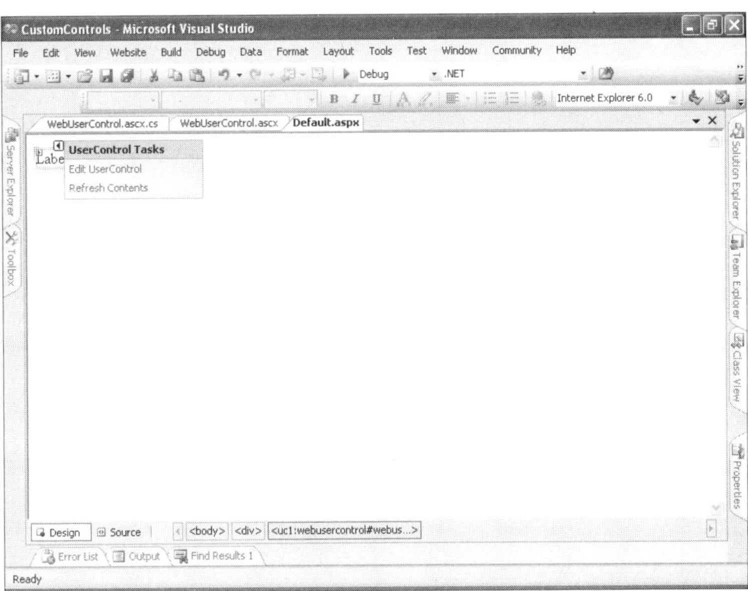

Figure 6-3 The UserControl Tasks menu after dropping a user control onto a form

The UserControl Tasks menu allows you to edit the user control or refresh the contents. By editing the user control, you can modify properties of controls contained in the user control. For instance, you can click the label to modify the properties of the label. Refreshing the contents causes the page display to be refreshed with the latest version of the control.

After you drag a copy of the user control onto the Default.aspx page, the markup is as shown in Listing 6-1.

Listing 6-1 Default.aspx after a User Control Is Added

```
<%@ Page Language="C#" AutoEventWireup="true"  CodeFile="Default.aspx.cs"
   Inherits="_Default" %>
<%@ Register Src="WebUserControl.ascx" TagName="WebUserControl"
   TagPrefix="uc1" %>
<!DOCTYPE html PUBLIC "-//W3C//DTD XHTML 1.1//EN"
   "http://www.w3.org/TR/xhtml11/DTD/xhtml11.dtd">

<html xmlns="http://www.w3.org/1999/xhtml" >
<head runat="server">
    <title>Default Page</title>
</head>
<body>
    <form id="form1" runat="server">
    <div>
        <uc1:WebUserControl ID="WebUserControl1" runat="server" />
    </div>
    </form>
</body>
</html>
```

The bulk of the page is the default markup created by Visual Studio. The two highlighted lines are added as a result of dragging and dropping the user control onto the form. The first highlighted line registers the user control on the page. The attributes of the @ *Register* directive are described in Table 6-1.

Table 6-1 @ *Register* Directive Attributes

Attribute	Description
Src	The location (relative or absolute) of the user control
TagName	The alias to associate with the user control
TagPrefix	The alias to associate with the namespace for the user control

Several other attributes can be used with the @ *Register* directive. However, these are generally associated with custom server controls, which will be covered later in this chapter.

Recall that when you add a *TextBox* control to a Web Form, *asp:TextBox* is the tag that marks the text box control in the markup. Your own controls are referenced by tags in the format *TagPrefix:TagName*. The *TagPrefix* specified in the @ *Register* directive is used as a namespace to ensure that controls are named uniquely. Thus, an instance of the new user control is declared in the source of a page with the following markup.

```
<uc1:WebUserControl ID="WebUserControl1" runat="server" />
```

When you run the Default.aspx page, it looks something like the page shown in Figure 6-4; of course, the time will be different.

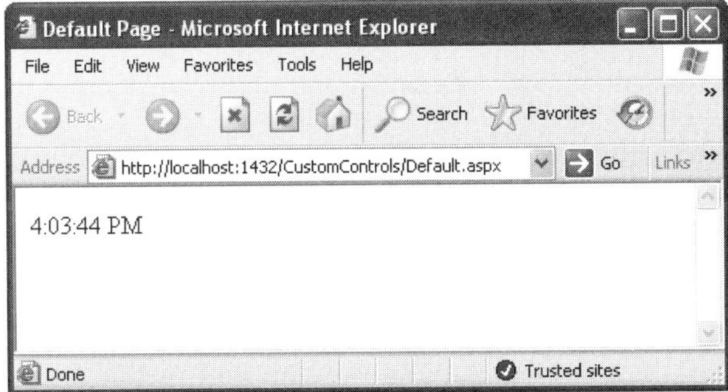

Figure 6-4 Default.aspx running in the browser, showing output from the *WebUserControl* user control

Caching a User Control

What is the fastest way to get data from a database? This is a bit of a trick question. The fastest way to get data out of a database is to remember it from the last time you got it from the database, and just display it again without a new database request. This is the idea behind caching. The user control created in the last section is a very simple control that is easy to render. Imagine, however, that you had a much more complex control that took some time to render, either because of some lengthy general processing or because it had to access a database. In many cases, caching the user control and rendering it only every minute or so can provide a significant performance and scalability advantage in a very busy application.

User controls (and entire pages in ASP.NET 2.0, for that matter) can be cached by using the *@ OutputCache* directive. Any arbitrary object can also be cached. The cache is application-scoped storage, meaning that all users of an application share the same cache. The *@ OutputCache* directive is placed at the top of the .ascx file. For example, adding the following directive to a user control will cause the output of the user control to be cached for 60 seconds.

```
<%@ OutputCache Duration="60" VaryByParam="none" %>
```

In this example, the *Duration* attribute is the amount of time for which the item should be cached, in seconds. The *VaryByParam* attribute is set to *none* to indicate that the caching should not depend on any parameters. Table 6-2 shows all possible values for the *@ OutputCache* directive.

Table 6-2 @ *OutputCache* Directive Attributes

Attribute	Description
Duration	The amount of time, in seconds, that the page or user control will be cached. This is a required attribute.
Location	The location where the item will be cached. This attribute is not supported for user controls. Allowed values are *Any*, meaning that the output cache can be located on the browser client, a proxy server, or any server participating in the request or on the server where the request was processed; *Client*, meaning that the output cache can be located on the browser client where the request originated; *Downstream*, meaning that the output cache can be located on any HTTP 1.1 cache—capable device other than the origin server; *None*, meaning that no caching is enabled; *Server*, meaning that the output cache can be located on the Web server where the request was processed; or *ServerAndClient*, meaning that items can be cached only on the Web server or the requesting browser client. The default value is *Any*.
Shared	A Boolean value that indicates whether user control output can be shared for multiple pages. If the user control does special processing on a page-by-page basis, this should be set to *false*. The default value is *false*.
VaryByCustom	Any text that represents custom output caching requirements. If the string "browser" is specified, the cache is varied by browser name and major browser version. If some other string is specified, you must override the *HttpApplication.GetVaryByCustomString* method in the Global.asax file for your application.
VaryByHeader	A semicolon-delimited list of HTTP headers used to vary the output cache. This attribute is not supported for user controls. A copy of the output is cached for each unique combination of the headers specified. This setting enables caching not only in the ASP.NET cache, but also in all HTTP 1.1 caches.
VaryByParam	A semicolon-delimited list of strings used to vary the cache. The strings represent query string values sent with a *GET* method attribute or a parameter sent using the *POST* method. Possible values are *none*, meaning that no parameters are used to create unique copies in cache; *, meaning that all parameters are used to create unique copies in cache; or a list of specific parameters. *VaryByParam* must be specified in @ *OutputCache* directives in ASP.NET pages, and in user controls as well, unless *VaryByControl* is specified.
VaryByControl	A semicolon-delimited list of strings used to vary the cache. The strings represent the IDs of ASP.NET server controls. This attribute is not supported on ASP.NET pages, and it is required on user controls, unless *VaryByParam* is specified.

Note Although you set the duration for the cached page or user control, it is not absolutely certain that the object will be held in cache for the amount of time specified. The advantage of the cache is that if the server requires more memory for additional load processing, the system can release some cached objects. ASP.NET keeps track of when cached objects are used; when the server requires more memory, it searches for the object in cache for which the last use is furthest in the past. These infrequently used objects are called "least recently used." This applies specifically to the ASP.NET cache and not to other caches in proxy servers or browser clients.

Why are all these attributes needed? Often, you will cache a user control that retrieves specific data. Using the BikeBlog database example from the last chapter, you might create a user control to display a specific row in the BlogEntry table. The BlogEntry row that is displayed might depend on a parameter passed into the page on the URL (for instance, ShowBlogEntry .aspx?BlogEntryID=2), or you might have a *DropDownList* control that specifies the BlogEntry row. Using the *VaryByParameter* or *VaryByControl* parameters, respectively, would allow these scenarios to work correctly.

To test the effect of caching, I created a new user control named CachedWebUserControl.ascx and a page named CacheTest.aspx. CachedWebUserControl.ascx and CachedWebUser-Control.ascx.cs are shown in Listings 6-2a and 6-2b, and CacheTest.aspx and CacheTest .aspx.cs are shown in Listings 6-3a and 6-3b.

Listing 6-2a CachedWebUserControl.ascx

```
<%@ Control Language="C#" AutoEventWireup="true"
   CodeFile="CachedWebUserControl.ascx.cs" Inherits="CachedWebUserControl"  %>
<%@ OutputCache Duration="60" VaryByParam="none" %>
<asp:Label ID="Label1" runat="server" Text="Label"></asp:Label>
```

Listing 6-2b CachedWebUserControl.ascx.cs

```
using System;
using System.Data;
using System.Configuration;
using System.Collections;
using System.Web;
using System.Web.Security;
using System.Web.UI;
using System.Web.UI.WebControls;
using System.Web.UI.WebControls.WebParts;
using System.Web.UI.HtmlControls;

public partial class CachedWebUserControl : System.Web.UI.UserControl
{
    protected void Page_Load(object sender, EventArgs e)
    {
        this.Label1.Text = string.Format(
            "The Time in the User Control is: {0}",
               DateTime.Now.ToLongTimeString());
    }
}
```

Listing 6-3a CacheTest.aspx

```
<%@ Page Language="C#" AutoEventWireup="true" CodeFile="CacheTest.aspx.cs"
   Inherits="CacheTest" %>

<%@ Register Src="CachedWebUserControl.ascx" TagName="CachedWebUserControl"
   TagPrefix="uc1" %>
```

```
<!DOCTYPE html PUBLIC "-//W3C//DTD XHTML 1.1//EN"
   "http://www.w3.org/TR/xhtml11/DTD/xhtml11.dtd">

<html xmlns="http://www.w3.org/1999/xhtml" >
<head runat="server">
    <title>Cache Test/title>
</head>
<body>
    <form id="form1" runat="server">
    <div>
        <asp:Label ID="Label1" runat="server" Text="Label"></asp:Label><br />
        <uc1:CachedWebUserControl id="CachedWebUserControl1"
            runat="server">
        </uc1:CachedWebUserControl> </div>
    </form>
</body>
</html>
```

Listing 6-3b CacheTest.aspx.cs

```
using System;
using System.Data;
using System.Configuration;
using System.Collections;
using System.Web;
using System.Web.Security;
using System.Web.UI;
using System.Web.UI.WebControls;
using System.Web.UI.WebControls.WebParts;
using System.Web.UI.HtmlControls;

public partial class CacheTest : System.Web.UI.Page
{
    protected void Page_Load(object sender, EventArgs e)
    {
        this.Label1.Text = string.Format(
            "The Time in the Web Page is: {0}",
            DateTime.Now.ToLongTimeString());
    }
}
```

CachedWebUserControl.ascx is extremely simple, containing just the *@ Control* directive, an *@ OutputCache* directive, and the label tag. CachedWebUserControl.ascx.cs contains a *Page_Load* event handler that simply sets the text of the label on the user control, clearly identifying itself as coming from the user control and placing the time in the text.

CacheTest.aspx is also a simple page. In addition to the boilerplate markup generated by Visual Studio, it contains a *Label* control and an instance of the *CachedWebUserControl* user control. The code in CacheTest.ascx.cs is very similar to the code in CachedWebUserControl.ascx.cs.

It sets the text of the *Label* control on the page, clearly identifying it as coming from the page, and it places the time in the label text.

When initially run, the page looks something like Figure 6-5, with the same time value displayed in the Web page and the user control.

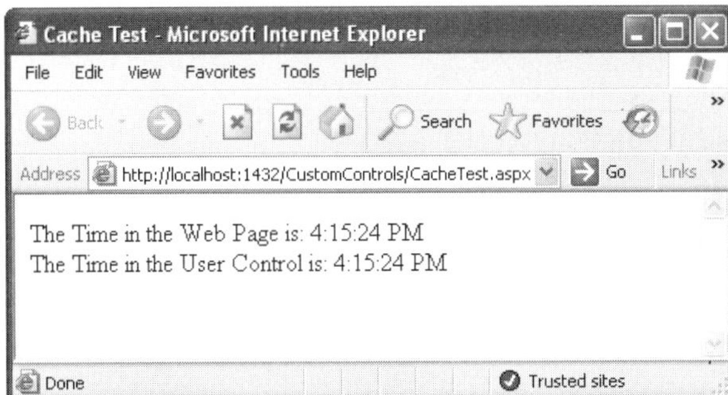

Figure 6-5 CacheTest.aspx running in the browser, showing output from both the page and the *WebUserControl* user control

When you refresh the page, you see something similar to Figure 6-6, with the time in the Web page updated, but the time in the user control the same as the initial post, assuming that you clicked Refresh in less than 60 seconds (the cache duration). This shows that the user control is, indeed, being cached.

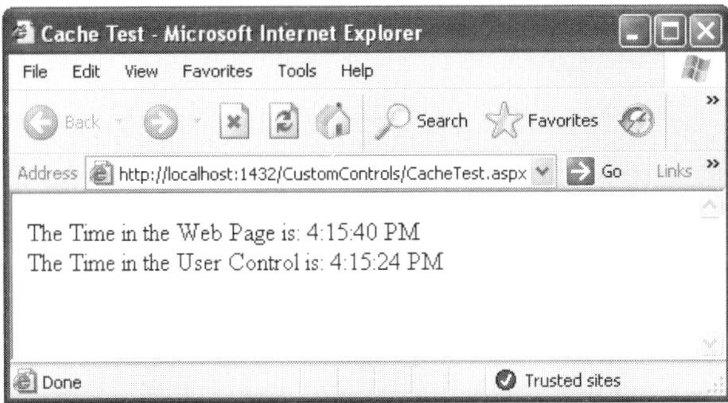

Figure 6-6 CacheTest.aspx running in the browser after refreshing the page, showing the effect of caching the user control

Caching involves some important implications. First, when a user control (or a page) is cached, the events associated with the page (such as the *Page_Load* event) will not be called when the item is requested and retrieved from the cache. Also, users might receive slightly outdated information in some circumstances in which caching is used. For instance, if you cache a user control that displays data from a database, it is possible that, for at least the duration of the cache, users might see old information. In some cases, this can be a reasonable tradeoff if the data isn't very dynamic. In cases in which this is not acceptable, you should not enable caching, or you should consider using the new ASP.NET cache dependency *SqlCacheDependency* class, and programmatically control caching of your user control. The *SqlCacheDependency* class is available, in slightly different forms, for SQL Server 7.0 and later. See the MSDN documentation for details about the *SqlCacheDependency* class. Other cache dependency controls are similarly documented. You can also read *Programming Microsoft ASP.NET 2.0 Core Reference* by Dino Esposito (Microsoft Press, 2005) for a more complete description of ASP.NET caching and cache controls.

Creating a User Control by Converting a Page

If you are creating a complex user control, testing it in a live page might be more difficult than debugging a Web Form. Fortunately, there is a reasonably well-documented way to create a new Web Form, debug it, and then convert it to a user control.

Recall from the Bike Blog example in Chapter 5 that the listing of BlogEntry rows was done in a *GridView* control. *GridView* controls are reasonable options in many cases, but in this particular case, a richer user interface might be desirable.

> **Note** There is nothing in the following example that, strictly speaking, could not be done in a *GridView* control by using some complex templating. However, the technique is broadly applicable and an excellent methodology for creating complex user interfaces that are more easily debugged.

Figure 6-7 shows a page designed to display an individual BlogEntry row. Note that for the page, the BlogEntryID is passed in on the URL.

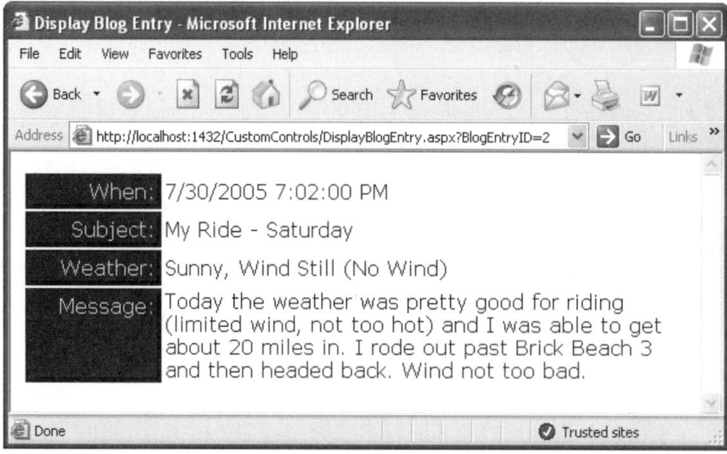

Figure 6-7 DisplayBlogEntry.aspx displaying a single blog entry

The markup in DisplayBlogEntry.aspx is fairly straightforward, although it contains several previously covered features. The source for the page is shown in Listing 6-4.

Listing 6-4 DisplayBlogEntry.aspx, Which Displays a Single Blog Entry Row and Acts as a Base for a User Control

```
<%@ Page Language="C#" AutoEventWireup="true"
   CodeFile="DisplayBlogEntry.aspx.cs" Inherits="DisplayBlogEntry" %>

<!DOCTYPE html PUBLIC "-//W3C//DTD XHTML 1.1//EN"
   "http://www.w3.org/TR/xhtml11/DTD/xhtml11.dtd">

<html xmlns="http://www.w3.org/1999/xhtml" >
<head runat="server">
    <title>Display Blog Entry</title>
    <link href="StyleSheet.css" rel="stylesheet" type="text/css" />
</head>
<body>
    <form id="form1" runat="server">
    <div>
        <table width=100%>
            <tr>
                <td align=right class="leftcol">
                    <asp:Label ID="Label1" runat="server"
                        Text="When:"></asp:Label></td>
                <td>
                    <asp:Label ID="lblWhen"
                        runat="server"></asp:Label></td>
            </tr>
            <tr>
                <td align=right class="leftcol">
                    <asp:Label ID="Label2" runat="server"
                        Text="Subject:"></asp:Label></td>
                <td>
                    <asp:Label ID="lblSubject"
                        runat="server"></asp:Label></td>
            </tr>
            <tr>
                <td align=right class="leftcol">
                    <asp:Label ID="Label3" runat="server"
                        Text="Weather:"></asp:Label></td>
                <td>
                    <asp:Label ID="lblWeather"
                        runat="server"></asp:Label></td>
            </tr>
            <tr>
                <td align=right class="leftcol"
                        valign="top">
                    <asp:Label ID="Label4" runat="server"
                        Text="Message:"></asp:Label></td>
                <td>
                    <asp:Label ID="lblMessage"
                        runat="server"></asp:Label></td>
            </tr>
        </table>
    </div>
    </form>
</body>
</html>
```

The changes I made to the default page that Visual Studio created begin with the inclusion of a style sheet. In the body of the page, there is also a table set to 100 percent of the width of whatever contains it (in this case the enclosing form, which will fill the browser window). Each row has two columns. The left column is aligned right, with the style class set to "leftcol". The right column has a label, with the ID set to a reasonable value and no text value set. StyleSheet.css is shown in Listing 6-5.

Listing 6-5 StyleSheet.css, Used to Style DisplayBlogEntry.aspx

```
body
{
    font-family:Verdana;
}
textarea
{
    font-family:Verdana;
    font-size:12px;
}
.leftcol
{
    width:100px;
    background-color:Blue;
    color:Yellow;
    border-style:outset;
    border-color:Blue;
}
```

The first style sets the font family of the page to Verdana. The next style sets the font family and the font size for any text area control to also be Verdana with a font size of 12. The final style is applied to the left column of the table; the class of everything in the left column is set to "leftcol". The width of the left column is set to 100 pixels. Initially, I allowed the width to be set by the browser. However, when the page is converted to a user control, and multiple instances of the user control are displayed one on top of another, the column width of all instances should be identical (100 pixels was an arbitrary value that was both visually appealing and contained the column text that I wanted to display). The *background-color* and *color* attributes are set to contrasting values, again to present an interesting user interface. Finally, the border style and border color are set to values that ensure that the labels will stand out, as you can see in Figure 6-7.

The code file, DisplayBlogEntry.aspx.cs, is shown in Listing 6-6.

Listing 6-6 DisplayBlogEntry.aspx.cs

```
using System;
using System.Data;
using System.Data.SqlClient;
using System.Configuration;
using System.Collections;
using System.Web;
```

```
using System.Web.Security;
using System.Web.UI;
using System.Web.UI.WebControls;
using System.Web.UI.WebControls.WebParts;
using System.Web.UI.HtmlControls;

public partial class DisplayBlogEntry : System.Web.UI.Page
{
    public int BlogEntryID
    {
        get
        {
            return ViewState["BlogEntryID"] == null ? 0 :
                (int)ViewState["BlogEntryID"];
        }
        set
        {
            ViewState["BlogEntryID"] = value;
        }
    }
    protected void Page_Load(object sender, EventArgs e)
    {
        // This is code that will go away when we convert
        //       to a user control...
        if (this.IsPostBack == false)
        {
            int _BlogEntryID;
            int.TryParse(Request["BlogEntryID"],
                out _BlogEntryID);
            BlogEntryID = _BlogEntryID;
        }
        // This code will be used in the final user control...
        if (this.IsPostBack == false)
        {
            SqlDataReader dr = this.SelectBlogEntryDR(BlogEntryID);
            try
            {
                if (dr.Read())
                {
                    string Weather = string.Empty;
                    Weather = dr["WeatherCondition"].ToString() + ",
                                 Wind " +
                        dr["WindStrength"].ToString();
                    if ( dr["WindStrength"].ToString().
                                        IndexOf("Still") < 0)
                    {
                        Weather += " Out of the " +
                            dr["WindDirection"].ToString();
                    }
                    this.lblWhen.Text =
                        ((DateTime)dr["DateEntered"]).ToString();
                    this.lblSubject.Text =
                        dr["Subject"].ToString();
```

```
                    this.lblMessage.Text =
                        dr["Message"].ToString();
                    this.lblWeather.Text = Weather;
                }
            }
            finally
            {
                dr.Close();
            }
        }
    }
    private SqlDataReader SelectBlogEntryDR(int BlogEntryID)
    {
        string spName = "spSelectBlogEntryAndWeather";
        SqlDataReader dr = null;
        SqlConnection cn = new SqlConnection(
            ConfigurationManager.ConnectionStrings[
            "BikeBlogConnectionString"].ConnectionString);
        cn.Open();
        try
        {
            SqlCommand cmd = new SqlCommand(spName, cn);
            cmd.CommandType = CommandType.StoredProcedure;

            cmd.Parameters.AddWithValue("@BlogEntryID", BlogEntryID);
            dr = cmd.ExecuteReader(CommandBehavior.CloseConnection);
        }
        catch
        {
            // Close the connection in case of error...
            cn.Close();
        }
        return dr;
    }
}
```

The *using* lines are defaults supplied by Visual Studio, except for the *using* line for *System.Data.SqlClient*. An integer parameter named *BlogEntryID* is declared and persisted into view state, as we've seen in earlier chapters.

The *Page_Load* event handler contains two *if* statements. The first is required, because to test the user control as a Web page, we must pass the *BlogEntryID* argument on the URL. This code will completely disappear when the page is converted to a user control. The second *if* statement binds the data to the labels in the user control and closes the *DataReader* object. This *if* statement also contains some code to properly display weather conditions in what should seem like normal English.

The *SelectBlogEntryDR* function is practically identical to the version used in Chapter 5 in the BetterEdit.aspx example. This version calls a different stored procedure, however, which adds descriptions of the weather columns in the BlogEntry table based on BlogEntryID. The stored procedure selects a single Blog Entry row as well as the descriptions of the weather columns from that row. The descriptions are stored in other tables and returned as a single returned result set.

The steps to convert a Web page to a user control are:

1. Remove all *<html>*, *<body>*, and *<form>* elements from the markup file.
2. Change the *@ Page* directive to an *@ Control* directive. Note that this could require changes to attributes supported on a page, but not in a control. For instance, the *Buffer* attribute is supported in the *@ Page* directive but not in the *@ Control* directive.
3. Include a *className* attribute in the *@ Control* directive. This allows the control to be strongly typed when it is added to a page or other server control programmatically.
4. Give the control a name that reflects how you plan to use it, and then change the extension of the markup file from .aspx to .ascx.
5. Rename the code file (change the name to match the markup file, and change .aspx.cs to .ascx.cs), and then change the class it is based on from *System.Web.UI.Page* to *System.Web.UI.UserControl*.

After I had DisplayBlogEntry.aspx working, the conversion was straightforward. First, I removed everything from DisplayBlogEntry.aspx except the markup inside the *div* tag. Then I changed the directive at the top of the page. Here is the original.

```
<%@ Page Language="C#" AutoEventWireup="true"
    CodeFile="DisplayBlogEntry.aspx.cs" Inherits="DisplayBlogEntry" %>
```

Here is the new directive.

```
<%@ Control Language="C#" AutoEventWireup="true"
    CodeFile="DisplayBlogEntryUC.ascx.cs" Inherits="DisplayBlogEntryUC" %>
```

Because I kept the original file in the solution, I renamed the file DisplayBlogEntryUC.ascx, and I changed the *Inherits* attribute and the name of the source file to reflect this change, so that the *Inherits* attribute matched the name of the class in the code-behind file. The rest of the markup remained the same.

The C# source code file, DisplayBlogEntryUC.ascx.cs, changed a little more than the markup did. The code is shown in Listing 6-7.

Listing 6-7 DisplayBlogEntryUC.ascx.cs

```
using System;
using System.Data;
using System.Data.SqlClient;
using System.Configuration;
using System.Web;
using System.Web.Security;
using System.Web.UI;
```

```
using System.Web.UI.WebControls;
using System.Web.UI.WebControls.WebParts;
using System.Web.UI.HtmlControls;

/// <summary>
/// Summary description for DisplayBlogEntryUC
/// </summary>
public partial class DisplayBlogEntryUC : System.Web.UI.UserControl
{
    public int BlogEntryID
    {
        get
        {
            return ViewState["BlogEntryID"] == null ? 0 :
                (int)ViewState["BlogEntryID"];
        }
        set
        {
            ViewState["BlogEntryID"] = value;
            SetData();
        }
    }
    public DisplayBlogEntryUC()
    {
        //
        // TODO: Add constructor logic here
        //
    }
    protected void Page_Load(object sender, EventArgs e)
    {
        // This code will be used in the final version of
        // the user control...
        if (this.IsPostBack == false)
        {
        }
    }

    private void SetData()
    {
        SqlDataReader dr = this.SelectBlogEntryDR(BlogEntryID);
        try
        {
            if (dr.Read())
            {
                string Weather = string.Empty;
                Weather = dr["WeatherCondition"].ToString() +
                           ", Wind " +
                    dr["WindStrength"].ToString();
                if (dr["WindStrength"].ToString().IndexOf("Still")
                           < 0)
                {
                    Weather += " Out of the " +
                        dr["WindDirection"].ToString();
                }
```

```
                this.lblWhen.Text =
                    ((DateTime)dr["DateEntered"]).ToString();
                this.lblSubject.Text =
                    dr["Subject"].ToString();
                this.lblMessage.Text =
                    dr["Message"].ToString();
                this.lblWeather.Text = Weather;
            }
        }
        finally
        {
            dr.Close();
        }
    }

    private SqlDataReader SelectBlogEntryDR(int BlogEntryID)
    {
        string spName = "spSelectBlogEntryAndWeather";
        SqlDataReader dr = null;
        SqlConnection cn = new SqlConnection(
            ConfigurationManager.ConnectionStrings[
            "BikeBlogConnectionString"].ConnectionString);
        cn.Open();
        try
        {
            SqlCommand cmd = new SqlCommand(spName, cn);
            cmd.CommandType = CommandType.StoredProcedure;

            cmd.Parameters.AddWithValue("@BlogEntryID", BlogEntryID);
            dr = cmd.ExecuteReader(CommandBehavior.CloseConnection);
        }
        catch
        {
            // Close the connection in case of error...
            cn.Close();
        }
        return dr;
    }
}
```

The first change to DisplayBlogEntryUC.ascx.cs was a change in the base class. Because the file was now a user control, it had to inherit from *System.Web.UI.UserControl* rather than *System.Web.UI.Page*. The next change required was to create a new way to set the BlogEntryID. When I created the page, the BlogEntryID was passed in on the URL. Because there could be many instances of the user control on a page, passing in the BlogEntryID on the URL is not an acceptable option. Fortunately, there is an easy alternative. Because the user control (like the page from which it is converted) has a property named *BlogEntryID*, the *BlogEntryID* property appears in the Properties window when an instance of the user control is dropped onto a form. Figure 6-8 shows the user control dropped onto a test

Web Form (TestUserControl.aspx) and the Properties window showing the *BlogEntryID* property set to 2.

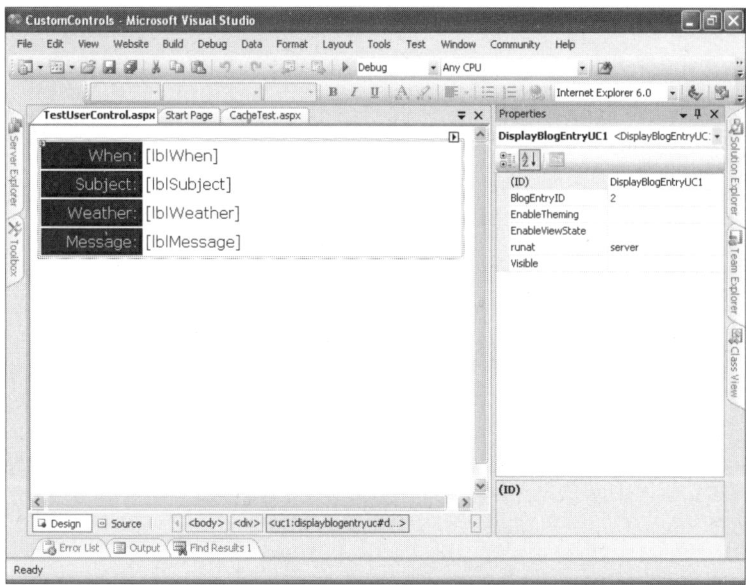

Figure 6-8 TestUserControl.aspx in Design view, showing the *BlogEntryID* property

A nice thing about user control properties is that, in addition to setting them in the Properties window, you can also set them in the markup. For instance, in TestUserControl.aspx, the markup for the user control is as shown here.

```
<uc1:DisplayBlogEntryUC ID="DisplayBlogEntryUC1" runat="server"
   BlogEntryID="2" />
```

Of course, property editing goes both ways. That is, if the *BlogEntryID* property is changed in the page markup, it is also changed in the Properties window.

Look back at Listing 6-6, showing DisplayBlogEntry.aspx.cs. The *BlogEntryID* property is set in the *Page_Load* event based on the value passed in on the URL. A much better solution for providing the BlogEntryID to possibly many controls on the page is to take the code from the section of the *Page_Load* event and create a new method, in this case named *SetData*. The *SetData* method is called in the *set* method of the BlogEntryID property. In this way, whenever the BlogEntryID property is set, the data associated with the ID is also retrieved from the database.

To show the user control in a more realistic setting, I created a new page in the Custom-Controls Web site named UserControlInRepeater.aspx. When run, the page appears as shown in Figure 6-9.

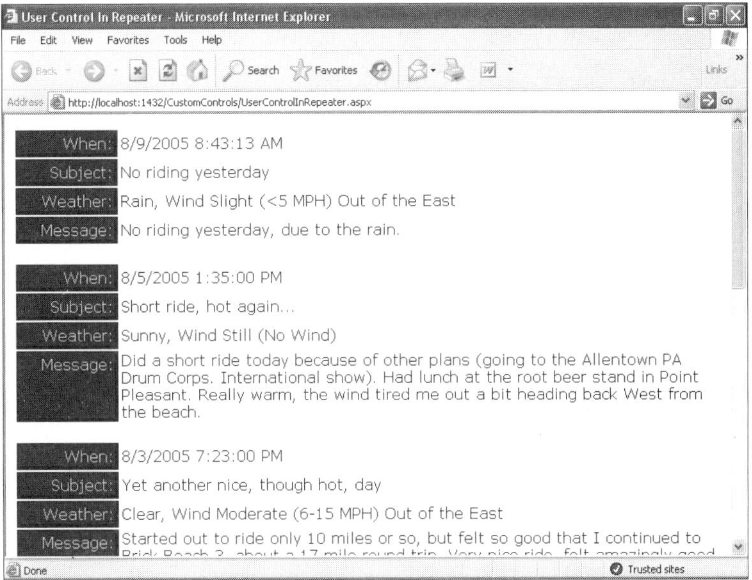

Figure 6-9 UserControlInRepeater.aspx running in the browser

UserControlInRepeater.aspx contains a single repeater and a single associated *SqlDataSource* control, as shown in Listing 6-8.

Listing 6-8 UserControlInRepeater.aspx.cs

```
<%@ Page Language="C#" AutoEventWireup="true"
    CodeFile="UserControlInRepeater.aspx.cs"
    Inherits="UserControlInRepeater" %>
<%@ Register Src="DisplayBlogEntryUC.ascx" TagName="DisplayBlogEntryUC"
    TagPrefix="uc1" %>

<!DOCTYPE html PUBLIC "-//W3C//DTD XHTML 1.1//EN"
    "http://www.w3.org/TR/xhtml11/DTD/xhtml11.dtd">

<html xmlns="http://www.w3.org/1999/xhtml" >
<head runat="server">
    <title>User Control In Repeater</title>
    <link href="StyleSheet.css" rel="stylesheet" type="text/css" />
</head>
<body>
    <form id="form1" runat="server">
    <div>
        <asp:Repeater ID="Repeater1" runat="server"
            DataSourceID="dsBlogEntryList">
            <ItemTemplate>
                <uc1:DisplayBlogEntryUC ID="DisplayBlogEntryUC1"
                     runat="server" BlogEntryID=
                     '<%# Bind("BlogEntryID")%>' /><br />
            </ItemTemplate>
        </asp:Repeater>
        <asp:SqlDataSource ID="dsBlogEntryList" runat="server"
```

```
                ConnectionString=
                "<%$ ConnectionStrings:BikeBlogConnectionString %>"
            ProviderName="System.Data.SqlClient"
                SelectCommand="SELECT [BlogEntryID] FROM [BlogEntry]
                ORDER BY [DateEntered] DESC">
        </asp:SqlDataSource>
    </div>
    </form>
</body>
</html>
```

In addition to the boilerplate text supplied by Visual Studio, I added the *@ Register* tag toward the top of the page. Next, I changed the title from the default supplied by Visual Studio. I dragged and dropped a repeater control from the Toolbox onto the form. I also dragged a *SqlDataSource* control onto the form and configured it. The SQL statement used selects only the *BlogEntryID* column from the *BlogEntry* table, and then it places the *BlogEntryID* values in descending order by *DateEntered*. To make the data source easily identifiable, I gave it a meaningful name–dsBlogEntryList.

> **Note** I could just as easily have used a stored procedure to retrieve the *BlogEntryID* column for each of the blog entries; however, retrieving a single column seemed to be one of the cases in which a simple SQL statement was reasonable.

After the *SqlDataSource* control was configured, I set the *DataSourceID* property of the repeater to *dsBlogEntryList* so that I could access all the columns from the data source in the repeater– in this case, just the BlogEntryID column. To add the user control, I switched to Source view and added the following item template.

```
<ItemTemplate>
    <uc1:DisplayBlogEntryUC ID="DisplayBlogEntryUC1"
        runat="server" BlogEntryID=
        '<%# Bind("BlogEntryID")%>' /><br />
</ItemTemplate>
```

Here's how the item template works. For each item in the data source, an instance of the *DisplayBlogEntryUC* user control will be instantiated, and the BlogEntryID will be set to the BlogEntryID in the data source. I could have added an alternate item template to alter the background on every other item to emphasize the transitions from one record to the next. However, I simply placed a break tag (*
*) at the end of the item template to add a line break between items.

User controls are often used for other, simpler uses. For instance, a menu, a header, or a footer might be made into a user control to be shared on many pages. Truthfully, with the advent of convenient Master Pages (described in Chapter 3, "Web Form Layout"), user controls are less likely to be used in such situations. There are still many reasons to use a user control.

Whenever you need to use some bit of markup or functionality on multiple pages, a user control is a possible solution.

Custom Server Controls

With the addition of the rich design-time support added in Visual Studio 2005, are there still reasons to use something other than a user control when you want to use the same bit of code and markup on multiple pages? Read on.

User controls can do almost anything you would like to do with a control. There are a few exceptions, however. For instance, if you are distributing a control beyond just a small group of developers, a user control, with multiple files required, might not be ideal. In addition, the developer experience is similar to that of the built-in controls, but not exactly the same. If your control must be located in the Toolbox rather than dragged from Solution Explorer, you need a custom server control.

Another significant issue with user controls is that some portion of the control is exposed to any developer who might be using it. Specifically, the .ascx file, which contains the markup for the user control, is usually available to a developer who is using the control for modification. This might not always be a good thing.

Note ASP.NET 2.0 can compile the markup in the .aspx and .ascx files, leaving behind only placeholder files.

A custom server control allows you to create controls that do not operate *almost* like the built-in controls, but *exactly* like them.

Building and Installing the Default *WebCustomControl* Control

It is best to create a separate project to contain all of your custom server controls so that they can easily be deployed to multiple Web sites. To contain the custom server controls for this chapter, I created another new project named CustomControlsLib, using the Class Library template, as shown in Figure 6-10. To create a project, rather than a Web site, point to New on the File menu, and then select Project, rather than Web Site.

After clicking OK, Class1.cs opens in the editor. This class is not required, so it can be deleted by opening Solution Explorer, right-clicking Class1.cs, and selecting Delete from the context menu.

To create a custom server control, right-click the project in Solution Explorer, select Add from the context menu, and then select New Item from the menu that appears. In the Add New Item dialog box, select Web Custom Control from the list of installed templates, as shown in Figure 6-11.

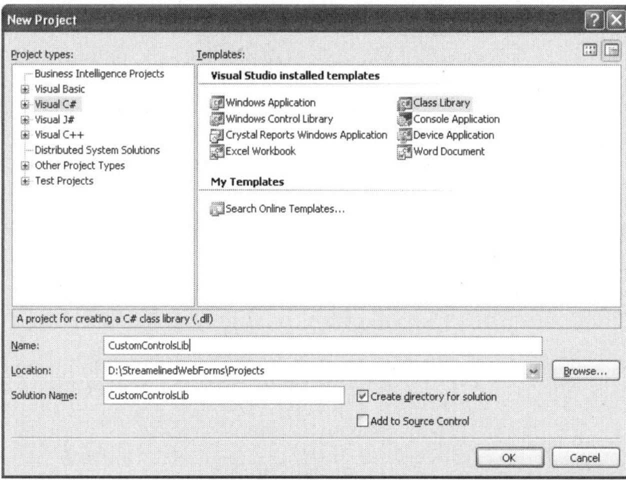

Figure 6-10 Creating a project in Visual Studio for custom server controls

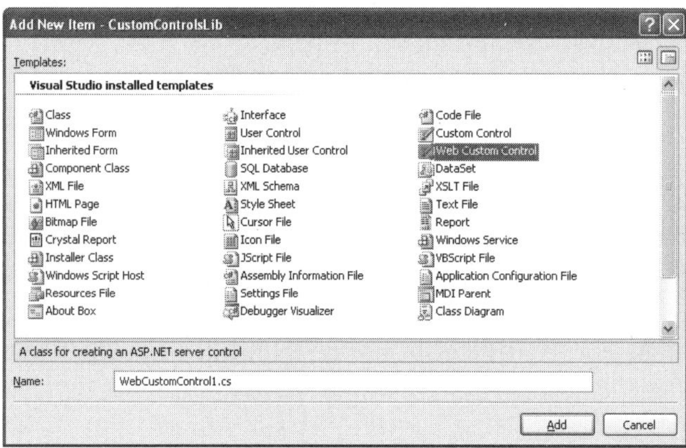

Figure 6-11 Creating a new Web custom control in Visual Studio

A default custom control is created, named *WebCustomControl1*. The simple default code for the control inherits from the *WebControl* class, as shown in Listing 6-9.

Listing 6-9 WebCustomControl1.cs, Created by Visual Studio

```
using System;
using System.Collections.Generic;
using System.ComponentModel;
using System.Text;
using System.Web.UI;
using System.Web.UI.WebControls;

namespace CustomControlsLib
{
    [DefaultProperty("Text")]
    [ToolboxData("<{0}:WebCustomControl1
```

```
    runat=server></{0}:WebCustomControl1>")]
    public class WebCustomControl1 : WebControl
    {
        private string text;

        [Bindable(true)]
        [Category("Appearance")]
        [DefaultValue("")]
        public string Text
        {
            get
            {
                return text;
            }

            set
            {
                text = value;
            }
        }

        protected override void Render(HtmlTextWriter output)
        {
            output.Write(Text);
        }
    }
}
```

After the standard *using* lines is a namespace declaration. A namespace is a way to ensure that names of classes are unique. After the namespace declaration and just above the class declaration are a few lines that set attributes for the class.

Note Attributes in .NET provide a declarative way to annotate or describe specific elements of code. Attributes can be relevant to classes, methods, or properties. At compile time, metadata describing the attributes specified are stored in the resulting executable code.

The *DefaultProperty* attribute specifies the default property for the component, which is the property that has focus when the Properties window is opened. The *ToolboxData* attribute describes how the control will be named when placed on a form.

After the attributes is the class declaration, where the code specifies that the *WebCustomControl1* class inherits from the *WebControl* class. In Chapter 2, "A Multitude of Controls," Table 2-6 described the important properties of the *WebControl* class.

The *WebCustomControl1* class contains a single private data member, named *text*. After *text* is declared, a property, somewhat confusingly named *Text* (note the uppercase *T*) is declared, which also has attributes. The first attribute is *Bindable*, and *true* is passed in as the argument, setting this attribute as bindable by default. The *Bindable* attribute is used at design time, and if it is set to *true*, two-way binding is supported. Two-way data binding in ASP.NET 2.0 allows changes to the underlying data to be pushed back. Two-way data binding uses the *Bind* method in places where one-way binding uses the *Eval* method. The *Bind* method can be used only in *GridView*, *DetailsView*, and *FormView* controls. Even if the *Bindable* attribute is set to *false*, the property can be used for data binding, although you should not rely on property change notifications being raised. The second attribute of the *Text* property is *Category*, which is used to place the property in a particular category when the properties of the control are viewed in category order. Finally, the *DefaultValue* attribute allows the developer of the control to supply a default value for the property. Visual Studio supplies an empty string ("") as the default value. The *get* and *set* methods of the *Text* property are very straightforward, simply returning or setting the *text* private data member.

The final member of the default *WebCustomControl1* class created by Visual Studio is an override of the *Render* method. The *Render* method has a single parameter, an *HtmlTextWriter* object. This object contains a large number of methods to emit markup for the control. In the example provided by Visual Studio, the *Write* method is used to write the contents of the *Text* property to an output stream to be sent to the client for rendering on the client browser.

After you build the CustomControlLib project, you can switch back to the CustomControl project and add the newly created control to the Toolbox. If you right-click the control in the Toolbox and click the *Choose Items* option, the Choose Toolbox Items dialog box appears, as shown in Figure 6-12.

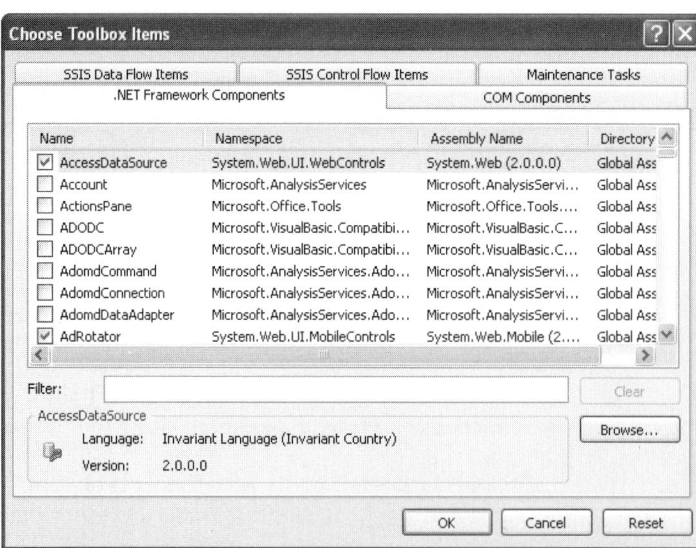

Figure 6-12 The Choose Toolbox Items dialog box in Visual Studio

To add the new control, click Browse, and then find the folder where the dynamic-link library (DLL) containing the control is located (in the bin\debug folder under the project folder).

Select the .dll file, and the Choose Toolbox Items dialog box appears as shown in Figure 6-13. The first of the controls found in the .dll file is highlighted and selected.

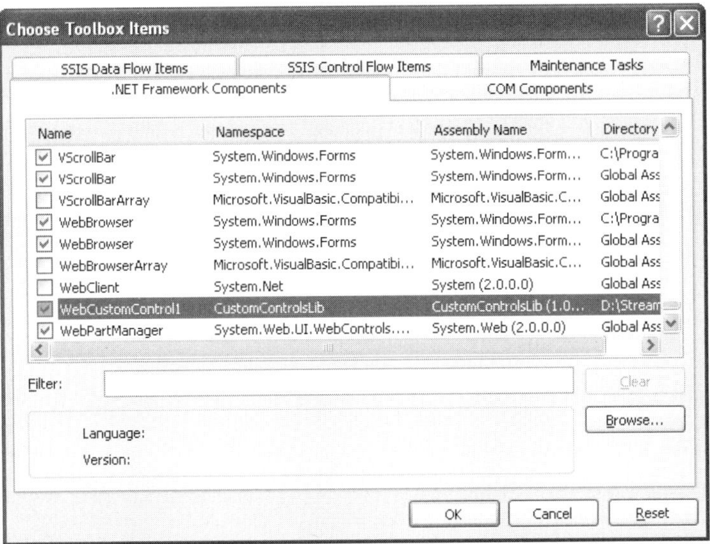

Figure 6-13 The Choose Toolbox Items dialog box in Visual Studio, with the new control selected

After you add the control to the Toolbox, it appears as shown in Figure 6-14.

Figure 6-14 The Toolbox with the new control added

To test the new control, I created a new Web Form in the CustomControl Web site named TestCustomControl.aspx. After changing the title of the page from the default, I switched to Design view and dragged an instance of the new *WebCustomControl1* control from the Toolbox onto the form. The control in Design view appeared as shown in Figure 6-15.

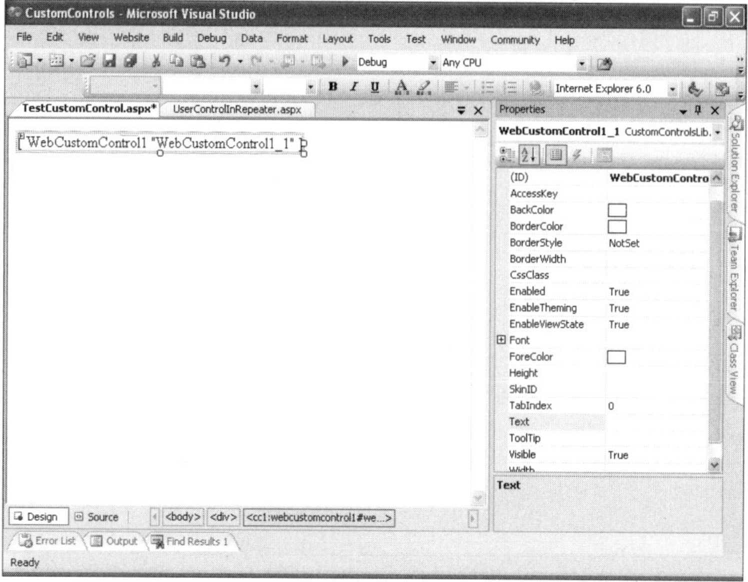

Figure 6-15 The *WebCustomControl1* control dropped onto TestCustomControl.aspx

The design-time support in Visual Studio is very powerful. If a property on your custom server control is changed, the design surface immediately changes. Setting the *Text* property in the Properties window, for example, immediately changes the appearance of the control in Design view. Figure 6-16 shows the control in Design view after the *Text* property was changed to "Hello World!"

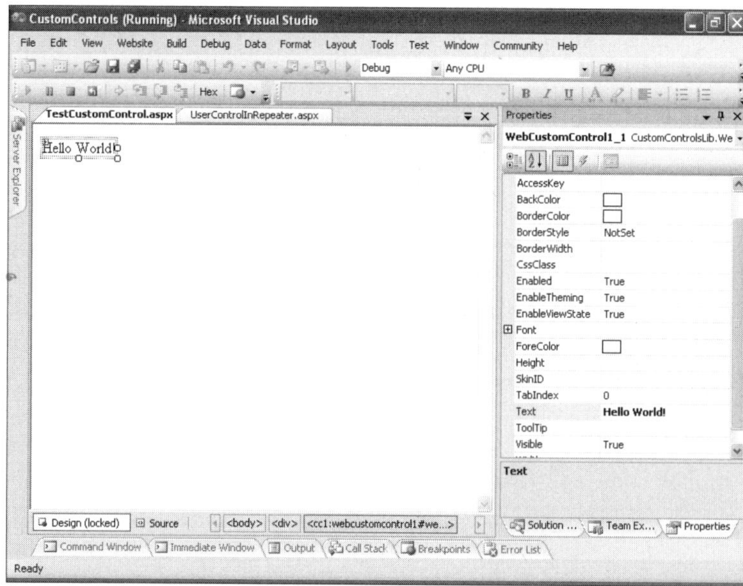

Figure 6-16 The *WebCustomControl1* control after changing the *Text* property in the Properties window

A more practical use for a custom control might be to create a label with some display attribute automatically applied. By changing the *Render* method, we could change the default appearance of the text rendered by the control. For instance, the control could be modified to display the text as an H1 header as follows.

```
protected override void Render(HtmlTextWriter output)
{
    output.Write(string.Format("<H1>{0}</H1>", Text));
}
```

After this change is made, the page looks like Figure 6-17 when run.

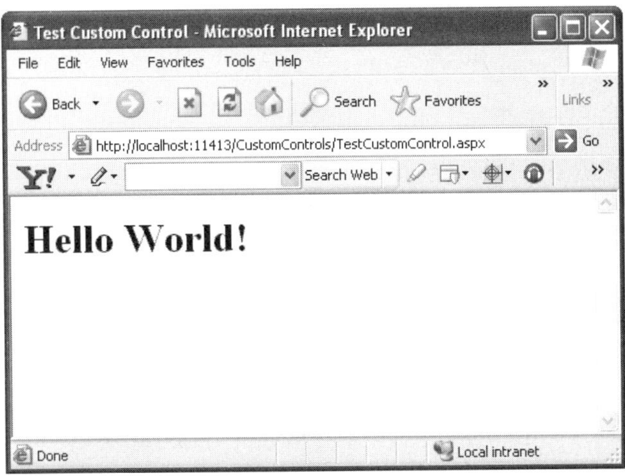

Figure 6-17 The *WebCustomControl1* control rendering the text as an H1 element

The example control here is very simple, but controls built by overriding the *Render* method can be as complex as you can imagine. You can provide HTML markup as simple or as intricate as you want. But there is yet another way to build custom server controls.

Building a Composite Control

Although creating very complex HTML is often a good way to create a custom server control, there is an alternative. For instance, imagine that you want to create a control that creates a drop-down list with a built-in required field validator. You could certainly do this by crafting JavaScript that allowed you to duplicate the functionality of a validator control, but a better solution would be to create a control that used the power of existing ASP.NET controls. Fortunately, a composite control is just that.

In addition to the *Render* method, the *CreateChildControls* method can also be overridden. By using this method, you can create the Web server controls that will, in the end, be rendered on the Web Form they are placed on, just as if the constituent controls had been placed on the form individually. I created a new file named RequiredTextBox.cs in the same way that I created

WebCustomControl.cs, and then I modified the code to use the *CreateChildControls* method and deleted the override provided for the *Render* method. Listing 6-10 shows the code for a control that uses composition to create a single component that acts as a required text box.

Listing 6-10 RequiredTextBox.cs

```
using System;
using System.Collections.Generic;
using System.ComponentModel;
using System.Text;
using System.Web.UI;
using System.Web.UI.WebControls;

namespace CustomControlsLib
{
    [DefaultProperty("Text")]
    [ToolboxData("<{0}:RequiredTextBox
       runat=server></{0}:RequiredTextBox>")]
    public class RequiredTextBox : WebControl, INamingContainer
    {
        private string text;
        private string errorMessage;
        private string validatorText;
        private string validationGroup;
        private System.Drawing.Color validatorColor;

        #region Properties
        [Bindable(true)]
        [Category("Appearance")]
        [DefaultValue("")]
        public string Text
        {
            get
            {
                return text;
            }

            set
            {
                text = value;
            }
        }
        [Bindable(false)]
        [Category("Validator")]
        public string ValidatorText
        {
            get
            {
                return validatorText;
            }

            set
            {
                validatorText = value;
```

```
        }
    }
    [Bindable(false)]
    [Category("Validator")]
    public System.Drawing.Color ValidatorColor
    {
        get
        {
            return validatorColor;
        }

        set
        {
            validatorColor = value;
        }
    }
    [Bindable(false)]
    [Category("Validator")]
    public string ErrorMessage
    {
        get
        {
            return errorMessage;
        }

        set
        {
            errorMessage = value;
        }
    }
    [Bindable(false)]
    [Category("Validator")]
    public string ValidationGroup
    {
        get
        {
            return validationGroup;
        }

        set
        {
            validationGroup = value;
        }
    }
    #endregion

    public RequiredTextBox()
    {
        this.ErrorMessage = "*";
        this.ValidatorText = "*";
        this.ValidatorColor = System.Drawing.Color.Red;
    }
```

```
        protected override void CreateChildControls()
        {
            System.Web.UI.WebControls.TextBox tb;
            System.Web.UI.WebControls.RequiredFieldValidator val;

            tb = new TextBox();
            tb.ID = this.UniqueID + "_TextBox";
            tb.Text = Text;

            val = new RequiredFieldValidator();
            val.ControlToValidate = tb.ID;
            val.ErrorMessage = this.ErrorMessage;
            val.Text = this.ValidatorText;
            val.ForeColor = this.ValidatorColor;
            val.ID = this.UniqueID + "_Validator";
            val.Display = ValidatorDisplay.Dynamic;
            val.ValidationGroup = this.ValidationGroup;

            Controls.Add(tb);
            Controls.Add(new LiteralControl(" "));
            Controls.Add(val);
        }
    }
}
```

This code contains the same *using* lines and namespaces that the code in Listing 6-9 contains. The class, *RequiredTextBox*, inherits from the *WebControl* class, but notice that it also implements the *INamingContainer* interface. *INamingContainer* is an interesting interface: it has no members, and it is used only as a marker interface. When a control implements the *INamingContainer* interface, a namespace is created to ensure that all of the IDs of all child controls are unique.

Note This code uses the *#region* and *#endregion* directives to enclose the properties. This allows you to easily collapse and hide the section of the source code that defines the properties in Visual Studio. When you are reviewing a section of the source, the ability to hide the sections of the code that you are not looking at often makes it easier to quickly scan large blocks of code.

The properties declared for the *RequiredTextBox* control are as follows:

- **Text** A string that is used as the default text for the *TextBox* control
- **ValidatorText** A string that is used as the *Text* property of the *RequiredFieldValidator* control
- **ValidatorColor** A *System.Drawing.Color* object that fills in the *ForeColor* property of the *RequiredFieldValidator* control
- **ErrorMessage** A string that is used as the *ErrorMessage* property of the *RequiredFieldValidator* control
- **ValidationGroup** A string that is used as the *ValidationGroup* property of the *RequiredFieldValidator* control

All properties are supported by private data members that have the same names (except that the first character of the private data members is lowercase (C# is case-sensitive). The constructor for the *RequiredTextBox* control then sets default values for some of the properties.

The *CreateChildControls* method is next in the code. This method first declares the two controls that make up the composite control, a *TextBox* control and a *RequiredFieldValidator* control. Next, properties of the control are set. The only properties set on the *TextBox* control are the *Text* property and the *ID* property. For the *ID* property, I used the *UniqueID* property of the underlying *WebControl* and appended "_TextBox". Similarly, I set the *ID* property of the *RequiredFieldValidator* control to the *UniqueID* property of the underlying *WebControl* and appended "_Validator". The rest of the properties of the *RequiredFieldValidator* control are self explanatory.

Finally, after the controls were created and their properties set, I had to actually add them to the control. By using the *Add* method of the *Controls* collection property of the *RequiredTextBox* control, I first added the *TextBox* control, then a dynamically created *Literal* control containing a single space to provide spacing between the two controls, and finally the *RequiredFieldValidator* control.

When the CustomControlsLib project was rebuilt and re-added to the Toolbox, the *RequiredTextBox* control was added to the Toolbox along with the *WebCustomControl1* control. To test the control, I created a new page named TestRequiredTextBox.aspx. When I dragged the *RequiredTextBox* control and a button onto the page, the page appeared as shown in Figure 6-18.

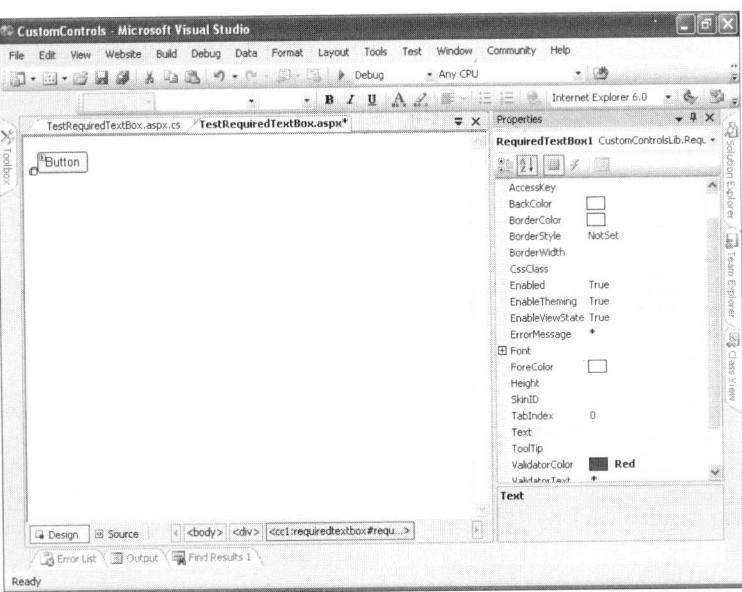

Figure 6-18 The *RequiredTextBox* control, placed on a form in Visual Studio

Notice the tiny box to the left of the button. That is the *RequiredTextBox* control–not exactly what we expected. The problem is that the control is not being rendered at design time. Fortunately, there is a solution.

The *System.Web.UI.Design* namespace contains a class called *ControlDesigner* that improves the appearance of controls at design time. To take advantage of this improved design-time appearance, we have to create a class that inherits from the *ControlDesigner* class and overrides one member method of the class, *GetDesignTimeHtml*.

To create a class that customizes the design-time appearance of the *RequiredTextBox* control, you must add a reference to the CustomControlsLib project. In Solution Explorer, right-click the project, and then select Add Reference. In the resulting dialog box, scroll down and select System.Design.

Tip Note that the namespace is *System.Web.UI.Design*, but the file that contains it is named System.Design.dll.

Several changes to the source are required to allow the new designer class to work. First, a few new *using* lines must be added.

```
using System.Web.UI.Design;
using System.IO;
using System.ComponentModel.Design;
```

Next, the class to handle the design-time appearance of the control must be added. This class is shown in Listing 6-11.

Listing 6-11 The *RequiredTextBoxDesigner* Class, to Be Added to RequiredTextBox.cs

```
class RequiredTextBoxDesigner : ControlDesigner
{
    public override string GetDesignTimeHtml()
    {
        RequiredTextBox rtb = (RequiredTextBox)Component;

        StringWriter sw = new StringWriter();
        HtmlTextWriter tw = new HtmlTextWriter(sw);

        Literal placeholder = new Literal();

        placeholder.Text = rtb.ID;
        placeholder.RenderControl(tw);

        return sw.ToString();
    }
}
```

The code writes a very simple bit of text, the ID of the control. The HTML can be as complex as you want it to be. Next, we'll add the *Designer* attribute to the *requiredTextBox* class, as shown here.

```
[Designer(typeof(RequiredTextBoxDesigner),typeof(IDesigner))]
```

The *Designer* attribute requires that you specify either the name of the designer and base type as a string or the exact types. Specifying the exact types seems a little cleaner. After these changes are made, the CustomControlsLib project should be recompiled, and the controls re-added to the Toolbox in the CustomControls Web site. Now, a *RequiredTextBox* control appears as shown in Figure 6-19 when added to the form.

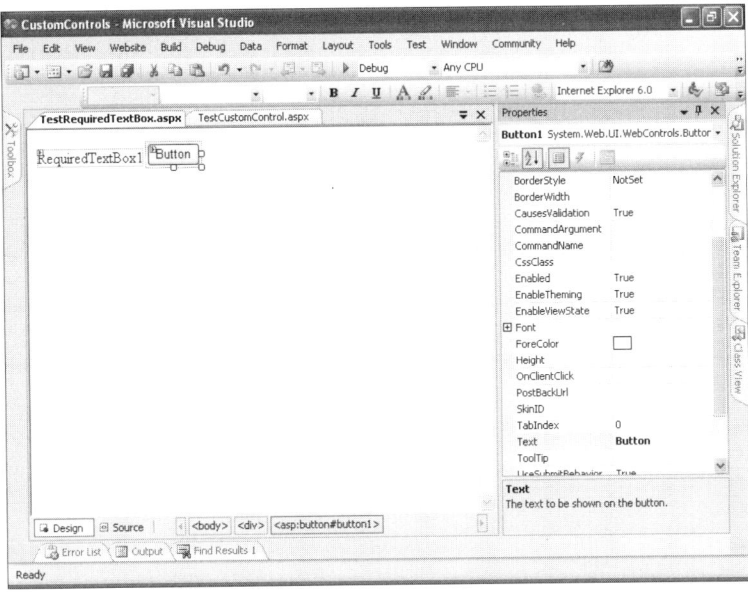

Figure 6-19 The *RequiredTextBox* control, placed on a form after adding a class descending from the *ControlDesigner* class

The difference is more than cosmetic. Before adding design-time support, selecting the control to adjust its properties was difficult at best. When the page is run, if you click the button without adding text to the text box, the page appears as shown in Figure 6-20.

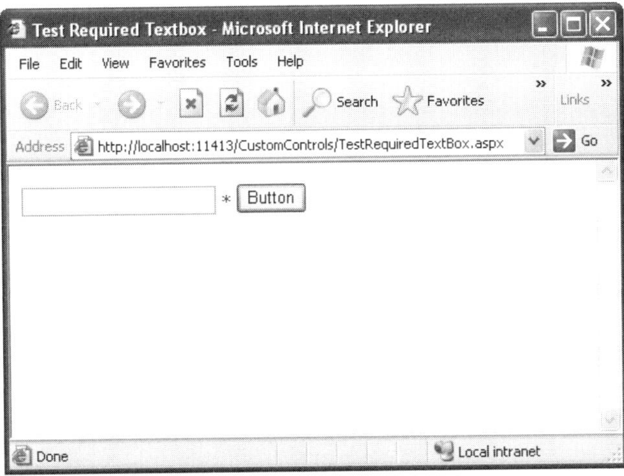

Figure 6-20 Testing the *RequiredTextBox* control

The *RequiredFieldValidator* control that is a part of this composite control is fired whenever the text box that is also part of the control is left empty and the user navigates away from the control or submits the form.

Creating a Control That Mixes Client and Server Code

Another common task involved with creating custom server controls is the addition of client-side code. Although you could add a control individually and then add the client script each time it is required, creating a control and standardizing the way that client script is added is a much cleaner solution.

Imagine that you have a system that must handle percentages. The users involved might enter a percentage as 0.35, meaning 35 percent, or they might enter 35, also meaning 35 percent. Handling this in a global way by using a control is much cleaner than adding the JavaScript code to each individual page that requires this processing. Using client-side script would ensure that the percentages would be visually corrected to fit a standard format as the user's cursor left the text box.

The best way to create a solution such as this is to create a new control that inherits from the *TextBox* control rather than the *WebControl* control. The advantage of inheriting from the *TextBox* control directly is that all the heavy lifting is already done. All of the properties of the *TextBox* control are available, as well as all of the data-handling capabilities. To create this control, I first added a new item to the CustomControlsLib project and, again, selected Web Custom Control from the list of templates. For this example, I changed the base control class from *WebControl* to *TextBox*. I removed most of the existing code that Visual Studio provided as a template.

To see how simple it is to create a client-enabled custom server control by using a class that already provides most of what you need (in this case, the *TextBox* control), take a look at Listing 6-12.

Listing 6-12 TextBoxFixPercent.cs

```
using System;
using System.Collections.Generic;
using System.ComponentModel;
using System.Text;
using System.Web.UI;
using System.Web.UI.WebControls;

namespace CustomControlsLib
{
    [DefaultProperty("Text")]
    [ToolboxData("<{0}:TextBoxFixPercent
        runat=server></{0}:TextBoxFixPercent>")]
    public class TextBoxFixPercent : System.Web.UI.WebControls.TextBox
    {
        protected override void Render(HtmlTextWriter output)
```

```
        {
            base.Render(output);
        }
        protected override void OnPreRender(EventArgs e)
        {
            StringBuilder script = new StringBuilder();
            script.Append(" <script language='Javascript'> ");
            script.Append("   function AdjustPercentages(sourceTextBox) ");
            script.Append("   {    ");
            script.Append(
                "     var inputtedNumber = sourceTextBox.value; ");
            script.Append("    if (!isNaN( parseFloat(inputtedNumber))) ");
            script.Append("    { ");
            script.Append(
                "      inputtedNumber = Number(inputtedNumber);    ");
            script.Append(
                 "     if (inputtedNumber < 1 && inputtedNumber != 0 " +
                 " && inputtedNumber > -1) ");
            script.Append("     { ");
            script.Append("      inputtedNumber = inputtedNumber * 100; ");
            script.Append(
                "      inputtedNumber = inputtedNumber.toFixed(2);     ");
            script.Append("     } ");
            script.Append("     else ");
            script.Append("     { ");
            script.Append(
                "      inputtedNumber = inputtedNumber.toFixed(2);    ");
            script.Append("     } ");
            script.Append("     sourceTextBox.value = inputtedNumber; ");
            script.Append("    }     ");
            script.Append("   }  </script> ");
            Page.ClientScript.RegisterClientScriptBlock(typeof(Page),
                "FixPercent", script.ToString());
            string func=
                string.Format("AdjustPercentages({0})",this.ClientID);
            this.Attributes.Add("OnBlur", func);        }
    }
}
```

The bulk of the code is involved in writing the client script to the browser. Rather than directly writing out the JavaScript to a literal control or any similar operation, the *Page* class has a *ClientScript* member that is of type *ClientScriptManager*. This *ClientScriptManager* class has several methods that write out client script, including the *RegisterClientScriptBlock* method, which is used in this code. Other methods in the *ClientScriptManager* class that register script can be used to register an include for a script file or for use in a particular event, such as the form's submission. Using the *ClientScriptManager* class ensures that a script is sent to the browser only once.

When you create a control, knowing exactly when the client script is written is critical. You might think that the *Render* method would be a logical place to have the script written to the client browser. This, however, does not work, because the *Render* method takes place too late in the cycle. Fortunately, the *OnPreRender* event is available. The script block is built up in a *StringBuilder* object called *script*.

Note Using the *StringBuilder* class is much more efficient than just concatenating strings by using the plus operator. Each time a string is concatenated, a new string is created in memory. All these strings can cause surprisingly large amounts of memory use. When you use a *StringBuilder* object, the *Append* method allows you to append the supplied string to an internal buffer in the *StringBuilder* class, so the number of strings created is greatly reduced. In production code, I'd use a separate .js file and load that, but, for example purposes, embedding the JavaScript in code makes for a somewhat easier to understand example.

After I called the *RegisterClientScriptBlock* method, I created a string named *func* that contained the code to call the method in the script block (named *AdjustPercentages*) and pass in the current control by *ClientID*. Note that I also had to ensure that the JavaScript function was called at an appropriate time. The best client-side event to use is the *OnBlur* event, which fires as the user leaves the edit control. I added an *OnBlur* attribute by calling the *Add* method of the *Attributes* collection. *Attributes* is a property of the underlying *TextBox* class from which *TextBoxFixPercent* is derived.

In the CustomControls project, I added a new page, named TestTextBoxFixPercent.aspx. I re-added the file created in CustomControlsLib to the Toolbox in the CustomControls Web site. Then I added a *Button* control to the page. When I ran the page, I entered a number (0.35) into the *TextBoxFixPercent* control. Figure 6-21 shows what the page looked like before I pressed the Tab key.

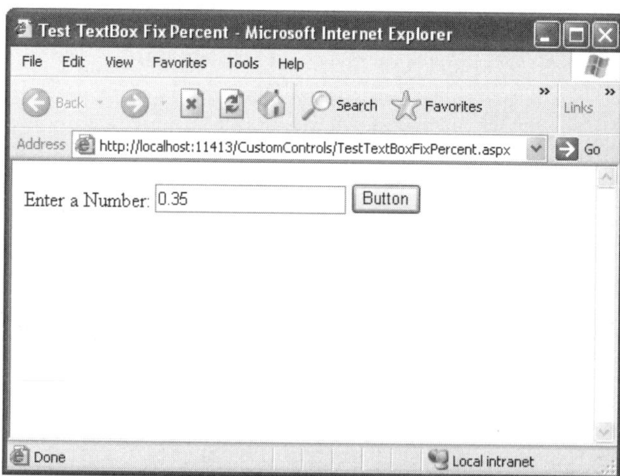

Figure 6-21 The *TextBoxFixPercent* control before pressing the Tab key

When the cursor exited the control, the number was reformatted, as shown in Figure 6-22.

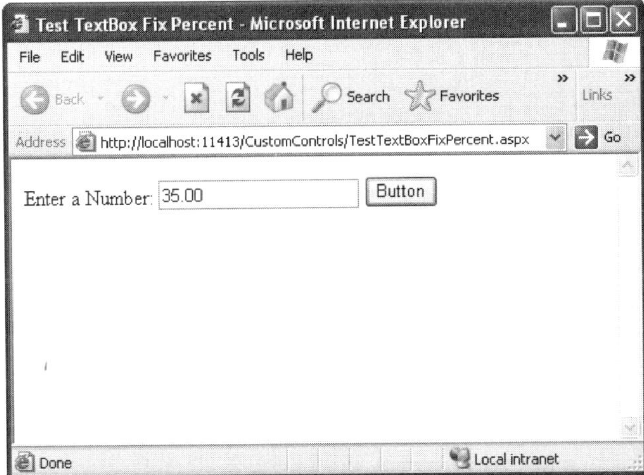

Figure 6-22 The *TextBoxFixPercent* control after exiting the control

When TestTextBoxFixPercent.aspx is run and you view the source of the page, the following markup is emitted for the *TextBoxFixPercent* control.

```
<input name="TextBoxFixPercent1" type="text" id="TextBoxFixPercent1"
    OnBlur="AdjustPercentages(TextBoxFixPercent1)" />
```

Again, this example is a relatively simple control. This technique, however, should allow you to create controls that inherit from existing controls as well as to add client-side scripting support as required.

Custom Web Parts

Recall from Chapter 4 that Web Parts are a new feature of ASP.NET 2.0. Standard server controls can be added to Web Part zones, but you can also add user controls; or perhaps even better, a developer can create custom Web Parts to take fuller advantage of the Web Parts environment. Custom Web Parts all derive from the *System.Web.UI.WebParts.WebPart* class.

Deriving from the *System.Web.UI.WebParts.WebPart* class allows you to control the appearance and behavior of a control displayed in a Web Part–enabled page. First, let's look at a very simple example Web Part, shown in Listing 6-13.

Listing 6-13 SimpleWebPart.cs

```
using System;
using System.Data;
using System.Configuration;
using System.Web;
using System.Web.Security;
using System.Web.UI;
using System.Web.UI.WebControls;
```

```
using System.Web.UI.WebControls.WebParts;
using System.Web.UI.HtmlControls;

/// <summary>
/// Summary description for SimpleWebPart
/// </summary>
public class SimpleWebPart : System.Web.UI.WebControls.WebParts.WebPart
{
    private string text;
    private bool allowClose;

    public string Text
    {
        get
        {
            return text;
        }

        set
        {
            text = value;
        }
    }

    public override bool AllowClose
    {
        get
        {
            return false;
        }
        set
        {
            // Ignore...
        }
    }

    public SimpleWebPart()
    {
        this.Title = "Simple Web Part";
        text = "This is a Simple Web Part.";
    }

    protected override void RenderContents(HtmlTextWriter writer)
    {
        writer.Write(Text);
    }

}
```

I started from a new Class file in the CustomControlsLib project site, which I named SimpleWebPart.cs.

Note Much of this chapter has covered creating user controls and the power possible with those controls. The designer support for user controls in Visual Studio 2005 is quite good, and the ability to create the markup declaratively rather than programmatically is hard to beat. However, there is no designer support for Web Part–derived controls in Visual Studio, and any user interface created for a *WebPart*-derived class must be created programmatically.

I changed the declaration for the class so that it would inherit from the *System.Web.UI.WebParts.WebPart* class. In addition to the *Text* property used in previous examples in this chapter, I also provided an override for the *AllowClose* property. By always returning *false*, I prevented the Web Part from being closed. There is no particular reason in this case for not allowing the Web Part to be closed, but it demonstrates some of the power of creating your own Web Part. The constructor for the Web Part sets some properties, including *Title*, which identifies the Web Part when displayed. Other properties can be modified as well, including *TitleIconImageUrl*, which customizes the title icon image. Finally, I provided an override for the *RenderContents* method that simply writes out the *Text* property.

Tip If you don't have SQL Server 2005 Express Edition installed, you might receive a timeout error message the first time you run the application. If you are running the full version of SQL Server 2005 rather than SQL Express, you can resolve the problem the same way we resolved it in Chapter 4: Simply copy the following lines from the Web.config file from the WebParts Web site to the CustomControls Web site.

```
<remove name="LocalSqlServer"/>
<add name="LocalSqlServer" connectionString="data
   source=.;Integrated Security=SSPI;Initial Catalog=aspnetdb"
   providerName="System.Data.SqlClient"/>
```

To test this simple Web Part, I created a new Web Form in the CustomControls Web site named TestSimpleWebPart.aspx. To that new page, I added several components:

- A *WebPartManager* control, a non-visual control that must be added to enable the page to handle Web Parts.
- A *DropDownList* control, to allow the user to control the mode of the page. I added three items to the control ("Browse," "Edit," and "Design"), and then I set the *AutoPostback* property to true, so that the page is notified of changes immediately.
- Two *WebPartZone* controls.
- A *CatalogZone* control.
- A *PageCatalogZone* control, which must be added to the *CatalogZone* control.

For all of the controls with a Tasks menu (accessed from the smart tag), I selected the Professional scheme from the Auto Format dialog box. When completed, the TestSimpleWebPart.aspx page looked like Figure 6-23 in Design view.

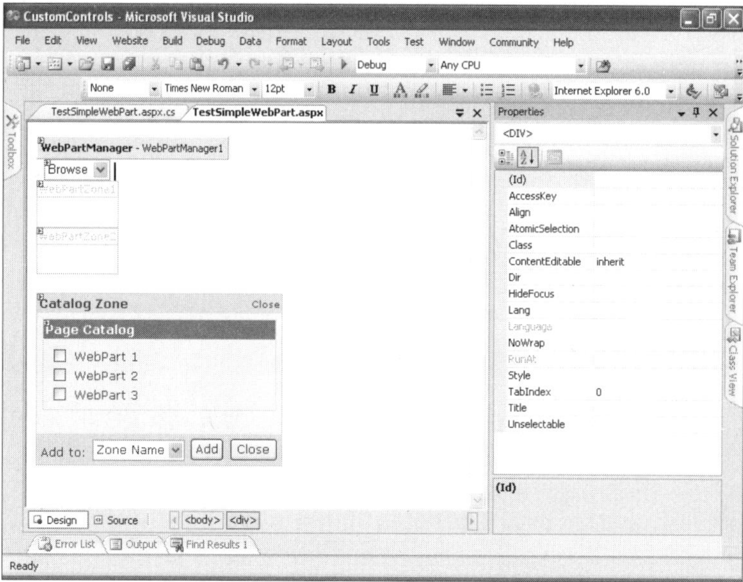

Figure 6-23 TestSimpleWebPart.aspx in Design view

In Browse mode, the screen appeared as shown in Figure 6-24.

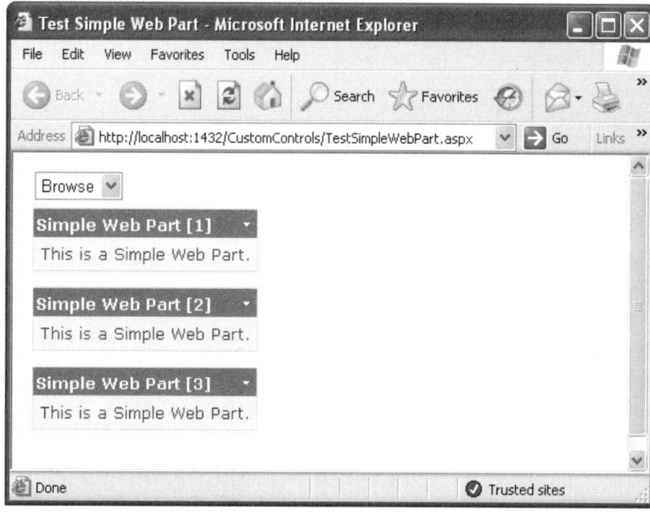

Figure 6-24 TestSimpleWebPart.aspx in Browse mode

In addition to the code that handles the change of display mode (which was covered in Chapter 4), TestSimpleWebPart.aspx also has a bit of code in the *Page_Load* event handler to ensure that there are always at least three instances of the *SimpleWebPart* control on the page. The code from the *Page_Load* event handler is shown here.

```
protected void Page_Load(object sender, EventArgs e)
{
```

```
    if (this.IsPostBack==false)
    {
        // Ensure there are at least three instances of the Web Part
        while (WebPartManager1.WebParts.Count < 3)
        {
            WebPart wp = new SimpleWebPart();
            WebPartManager1.AddWebPart(wp, this.WebPartZone1,
                WebPartManager1.WebParts.Count);
        }
    }
}
```

If fewer than three of our custom Web Parts are registered, the code creates a new instance of the *SimpleWebPart* class and adds the Web Part to the *WebPartZone1* control.

Wrapping Standard Controls for Use in Web Parts

Web Part controls can be a good solution, especially when you are creating a control from scratch. However, you might often have an existing control that would make a great Web Part. What problems might you face when using your existing user controls or custom controls?

Looking back at the examples in Chapter 4, notice that all of the native controls not derived from the *WebPart* class dropped into a *WebPartZone* control have "Untitled" as their title; of course, customizing the icon is not possible. The same is also true of adding user controls as Web Parts.

So, do you have to give up custom titles or icons to get the advantages of user controls? Thankfully, the answer is no. Recall the code used in Chapter 4 to programmatically add a *TextBox* control as a Web Part.

```
GenericWebPart gwp = this.WebPartManager1.CreateWebPart(tb);
this.WebPartManager1.AddWebPart(gwp, this.WebPartZone1, 0);
```

The *GenericWebPart* class acts as a wrapper for the class when you create a Web Part. If you wanted to, you could set properties of the *GenericWebPart* control in the *Page_Init* event handler of the user control, as shown here.

```
void Page_Init(object sender,EventArgs e)
{
    GenericWebPart gwp = Parent as GenericWebPart;
    if ( gwp != null )
    {
        gwp.Title="New User Control/Web Part Title";
    }
}
```

Another alternative is to implement the *IWebPart* interface in a user control. The *IWebPart* interface consists of several properties. These properties are the values that you would probably want to change, such as *Title* and *TitleIconImageUrl*.

To demonstrate how implementing the *IWebPart* interface works in a user control, I created a copy of DisplayBlogEntryUC.aspx, naming it DisplayBlogEntryUCasWP.ascx. In the class declaration, I added the *IWebPart* interface after *UserControl* in the class declaration, to indicate that the class implements the *IWebPart* interface, as shown here.

```
public partial class DisplayBlogEntryUCasWP :
    System.Web.UI.UserControl,IWebPart
```

Visual Studio 2005 includes several new refactoring tools. One of the most useful of these tools offers the ability to right-click an interface name in code and select Implement Interface from the resulting context menu. Doing this creates default implementations for all members of the interface. These default implementations simply throw an *Exception* object, with a message that the method or operation is not implemented. I did this and modified the generated code to provide the correct functionality. Listing 6-14 shows the resulting implementation of the *IWebPart* interface in DisplayBlogEntryUCasWP.ascx.cs.

Listing 6-14 The Implementation of the *IWebPart* Interface in DisplayBlogEntryUCasWP.ascx.cs

```
#region IWebPart Members

private string catalogIconImageUrl;
private string description;
private string subTitle;
private string title;
private string titleIconImageUrl;
private string titleUrl;


public string CatalogIconImageUrl
{
    get
    {
        return catalogIconImageUrl;
    }
    set
    {
        catalogIconImageUrl=value;
    }
}

public string Description
{
    get
    {
        return description;
    }
    set
    {
        description=value;
    }
}
```

```
public string Subtitle
{
    get { return subTitle; }
}

public string Title
{
    get
    {
        return title;
    }
    set
    {
        title=value;
    }
}

public string TitleIconImageUrl
{
    get
    {
        return titleIconImageUrl;
    }
    set
    {
        titleIconImageUrl = value;
    }
}

public string TitleUrl
{
    get
    {
        return titleUrl;
    }
    set
    {
        titleUrl=value;
    }
}

#endregion
```

Visual Studio conveniently wraps the implementation of the interface inside a set of *#region and #endregion* directives. The constructor and *Page_Load* event handler are also different, as shown here.

```
public DisplayBlogEntryUCasWP()
{
    catalogIconImageUrl=string.Empty;
    description = string.Empty;
    subTitle = string.Empty;
    title = "Bike Blog";
```

```
        titleIconImageUrl = string.Empty;
        titleUrl = string.Empty;
    }
    protected void Page_Load(object sender, EventArgs e)
    {
        // Should really get most recent entry...
        this.BlogEntryID = 7;
    }
```

The constructor for *DisplayBlogEntryUCasWP* sets some of the supporting private data members for the *IWebPart* properties. Finally, the *Page_Load* event handler sets the *BlogEntryID* property of the user control. In the real world, rather than hard coding the *BlogEntryID* property, the code would find the most recent blog entry and display that (we would use data retrieval code similar to the previous examples in the chapter).

Like I did with TestSimpleWebPart.aspx, I set up a new page in the CustomControls Web site, named TestUCasWP.aspx. I added the same *DropDownList* control and Web Part–related controls, and I set the schemes of all the Web Part–related controls to Professional.

The *Page_Load* event handler for TestUCasWP.aspx contains the code required to load the user control, assuming there is not already a Web Part on the page. The code to do that is shown here.

```
protected void Page_Load(object sender, EventArgs e)
{
    if (this.WebPartManager1.WebParts.Count == 0)
    {
        Control uc = this.LoadControl("~/DisplayBlogEntryUCasWP.ascx");
        uc.ID = "UCasWP1";
        GenericWebPart gwp = WebPartManager1.CreateWebPart(uc);
        this.WebPartManager1.AddWebPart(gwp, this.WebPartZone1, 0);
    }
}
```

The *LoadControl* method of the *Page* class takes the URL of the user control and loads an instance of the control. The *LoadControl* method is often used to dynamically load a user control. The code that follows is identical to the code in *TestSimpleWebPart.aspx* that dynamically loaded controls as Web Parts.

When run, TestUCasWP.aspx looks like Figure 6-25.

The look of the blog entry shown in Figure 6-25 is very different from the version shown in Figure 6-7. Without the style sheet used in Figure 6-7, the blog entry takes on the appearance specified by the Auto Format scheme. Also noteworthy is that, rather than "Untitled," the user control shown in Figure 6-25 is titled "Bike Blog."

When you switch to Design mode, you can drag the user control, which is masquerading as a Web Part, from one Web Part zone to another, as shown in Figure 6-26.

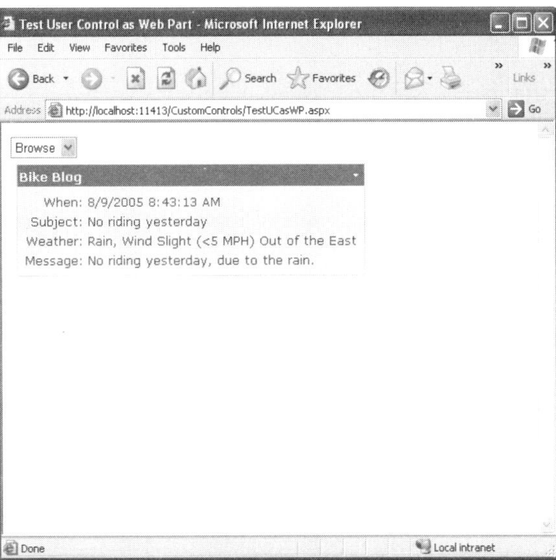

Figure 6-25 TestUCasWP.aspx in Browse mode

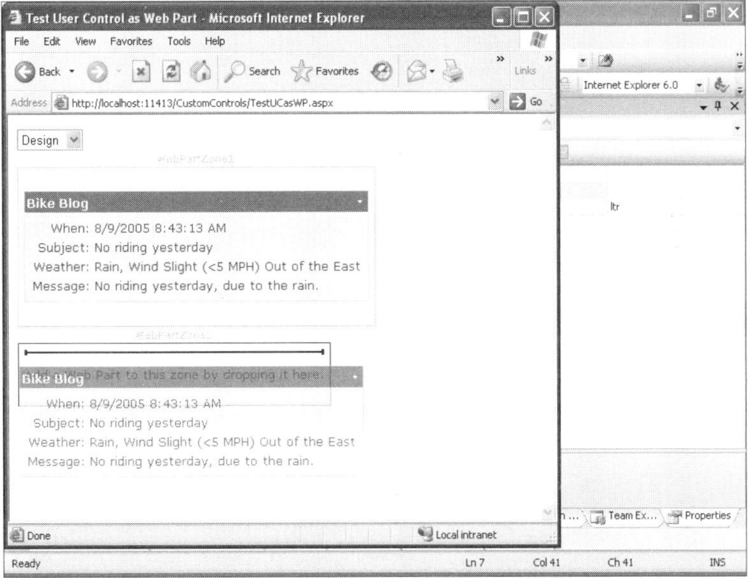

Figure 6-26 TestUCasWP.aspx in Design mode, dragging a user control–based Web Part

Conclusion

Now you know enough to start taking full advantage of the extensibility that creating controls, of all sorts, adds to Web Forms development with ASP.NET 2.0. As with most development decisions, the choice between user controls, custom server controls, and Web Parts is not always clear-cut. ASP.NET 2.0 eliminates many of the reasons that user controls were not as convenient as custom server controls. The less-than-ideal design-time experience for consumers of user controls in Visual Studio .NET and ASP.NET 1.x has been replaced by first-class support for user controls in design time.

In the next chapter, we will look at the administrative side of ASP.NET 2.0. This discussion would be quite short if it covered administrative tools included with previous versions of ASP.NET only–there were none! Not so with ASP.NET 2.0 and Visual Studio 2005. Also in the next chapter, I will cover the ASP.NET controls that help you provide nearly codeless user security for your Web Forms applications.

Chapter 7

Web Forms User Security and Administration

In this chapter:

One of the areas of Microsoft ASP.NET that I have a special interest in is application security, especially with respect to user security and administration. I do a great deal of work in the health care industry, so in addition to the normal Web site security concerns, I must also be aware of any legal requirements. For me, this is simply a matter of doing the right thing. As a patient, I expect that my personal medical information will be kept secure and that it will remain between my healthcare providers and me.

Even if your site itself does not contain data of high value, properly managing users credentials is a very important security issue. Here's an example. I recently worked on a secure site for a manufacturer. The user names and passwords required for the site were merely intended for user personalization, rather than for protection of user data. Nevertheless, I insisted that the security system use one-way hashing on the passwords supplied by the users. Using a one-way hash meant that even I would not be able to decrypt the passwords. To be verified, a password supplied by a user would be hashed and then compared to the hash stored in the database. However, if a user forgot his or her password, recovering it would be a bit more complex than just e-mailing the password to the user.

Management objected to the minor amount of extra development time and possible user inconvenience this might cause. I reminded them that users often use a single password for many sites; any compromise to their site, regardless of the value of the site's contents, could help the bad guys compromise other sites of higher value. To illustrate this point, I visited one of the company's existing public Web sites and used its terribly designed password recovery option. By entering the e-mail address of one of the company's managers, I was able to retrieve the manager's password for the site, which, to the horror of all involved, was the same password that the manager used as his Microsoft Windows domain password. After that, I encountered no more resistance to using best practices to handle user names and passwords.

Implementing user management correctly is not necessarily hard. But it does involve some work, and doing it right often involves a little more work than doing it wrong. After you have built several sites, you discover that virtually all of the code used to log in and manage users is the same from project to project. Realizing this, the developers of ASP.NET 2.0 added a complete set of components for managing user login, registration, and administration. The controls, and the underlying security providers, use best practices to help keep users' information secure. Even better, a Web-based interface allows you to manage many administrative aspects of your Web site.

This chapter will cover all aspects of managing users of your ASP.NET 2.0 Web Forms applications. First, I will discuss the new Web site administration user interface. This tool allows you to perform much of the site configuration that previously required manual editing of the Web.config file. Next, I will cover the login controls that are new to ASP.NET 2.0, which you can use to add user security to your Web Forms applications. The login controls allow your applications to log users in, allow you to add new users, and allow users to manage their passwords.

Finally, I will apply what we have learned in this chapter to the bike blog application. With the addition of user security, the site can track who is logged in, allow entry of information that can be attributed to a particular user, and limit what a particular user can do on the site.

Administering an ASP.NET 2.0 Site

As I mentioned in the conclusion of the last chapter, a chapter based only on ASP.NET 1.x administration support would be short. There is no real user interface for administration in ASP.NET 1.1. Any changes require manual modifications to the Web.config or Machine.config file or the Internet Information Services (IIS) Manager. Although the error messages improved over the years as ASP.NET 1.0 became ASP.NET 1.1, the messages resulting from an errant setting in one of the configuration files could result in an error message that was very difficult to associate with the actual problem setting. In no area was this more true than in setting up user security.

Fortunately, all that has changed in ASP.NET 2.0. In addition to the basics, such as setting up the type of authentication, the new ASP.NET Web Site Administration Tool allows you to create users, roles, and access rules. The result is that you can create users for a site by using the ASP.NET Web Site Administration Tool, enabling user authentication even before you create the interface that allows users to register on the site. The icing on the cake is that creating the user registration interface is easy, requiring no code at all if the standard implementation satisfies your requirements. In many cases, the standard implementation will be just fine. If you need something a little different, modifying the default implementation of all security settings is not very difficult.

For this chapter, I created a Web site called BikeBlogSecured, which is similar to the versions of the bike blog in previous chapters.

Tip In earlier versions of the bike blog that allowed editing of blog entries, the listing of all entries and the editing screen were both on the same page. An unintended consequence of that structure was that there was no way, using a URL with command-line arguments, to jump to a particular entry for editing or display. Blogs almost always provide a way to jump to a particular entry by using a URL known as a *permalink*. Having the listing and the editing on a single page would also require code to ensure that only authorized users added entries. As you will see later in this chapter, creating a new page for editing existing entries and adding new entries, and placing it in a subfolder, allows for easy configuration of security with very little code.

A common pattern used by ASP.NET developers to secure portions of an application is to create a folder for Web Forms that should be accessed only by certain users or certain groups. This pattern is quite reasonable, and I will use it in the BikeBlogSecured Web site. To create a new folder in a Web site within Microsoft Visual Studio, right-click the Web site in Solution Explorer, and then select New Folder from the context menu. Name the folder Admin.

More Info In addition to securing folders, as I will do in this Web site, you can secure individual files in any folder that is part of an ASP.NET Web Forms application. It is easier to apply security to one folder at a time rather than to one file at a time, and the ASP.NET Web Site Administration Tool supports only folder-level restrictions. (Single-file restrictions can be added manually to the Web.config file.) Complete details on how this is done can be found in the MSDN documentation.

To configure a new site, click ASP.NET Configuration on the Website menu in Visual Studio. You should see a page similar to Figure 7-1.

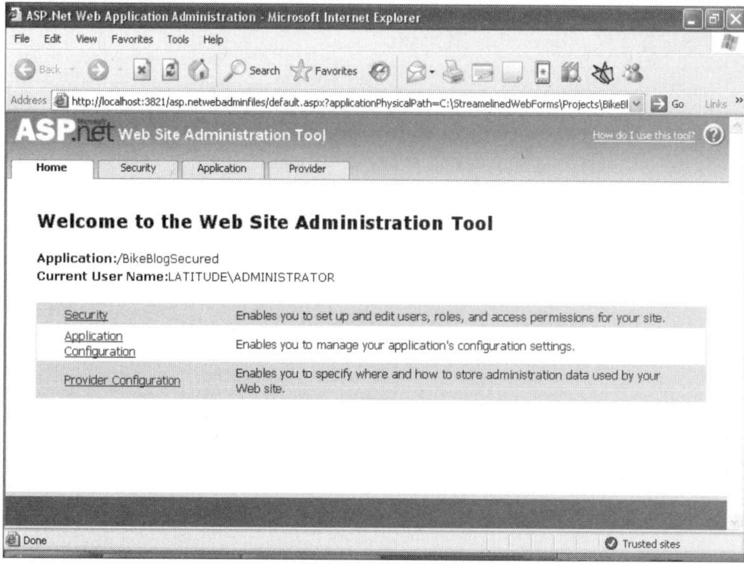

Figure 7-1 The ASP.NET Web Site Administration Tool

Provider Configuration

My first task using the ASP.NET Web Site Administration Tool was to set up the provider configuration. Figure 7-2 shows the Provider page.

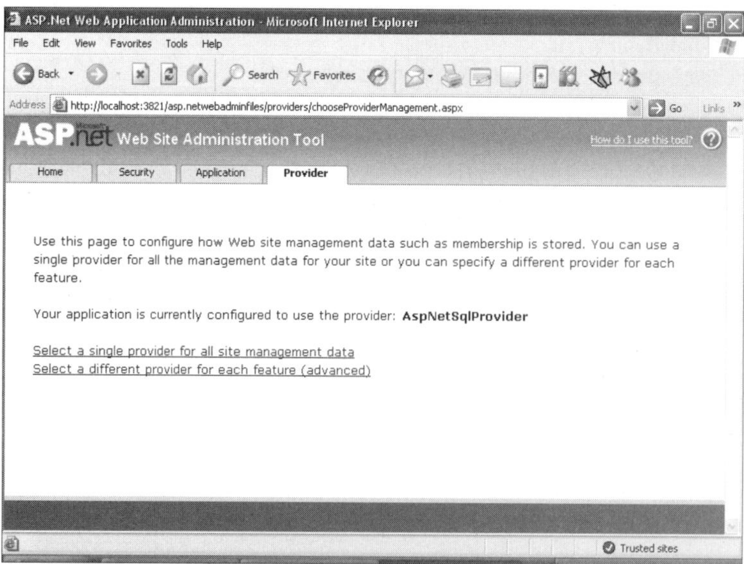

Figure 7-2 The Provider page in the ASP.NET Web Site Administration Tool

Note If you have the Web.config file open in Visual Studio while you make changes with the ASP.NET Web Site Administration Tool, you might get a message when you return to Visual Studio telling you that the Web.config file has been changed outside of Visual Studio. You should accept the changes.

Of the two options, the first is the most commonly selected and easiest to use. Click Select A Single Provider For All Site Management Data, and the page appears as shown in Figure 7-3.

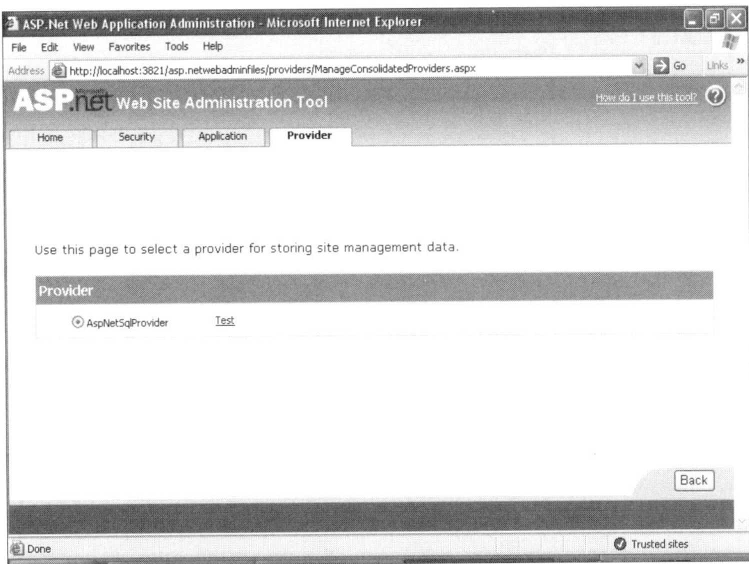

Figure 7-3 Selecting a provider in the ASP.NET Web Site Administration Tool

Generally, a single provider is listed. You should click Test to ensure that the provider is properly configured. If it is not properly configured, you are instructed to run Aspnet_regsql.exe, as described in Chapter 5, "Data Binding."

Security

My next step was to configure the security on the Web site. A major goal of the BikeBlog-Secured Web site was to allow authorized users to enter information while allowing read-only access for all others. Classic ASP had absolutely no support for security, so pages had to be secured manually in code. With ASP.NET, developers could declaratively configure security by adding tags in the Web.config file that would allow or deny access to specific users or groups of users. This was a huge step in the right direction, but a great deal of manual work was still required to get security working correctly. Fortunately, ASP.NET 2.0 offers excellent support for developers who need to secure their applications.

Users of ASP.NET applications (and in fact, users of any application that uses IIS) can be authenticated in one of two ways. The default authentication method is Windows Authentication.

When Windows Authentication is selected, the user of the Web Forms application is determined by the identity of the user in some Windows domain. For an intranet application, this can be convenient. As the developer of the application, you have to do very little to maintain a user list. The user list, by default, is the list of users in the domain. You can restrict that list by using some other means, (for instance, by checking the user's domain name against a database of domain users, such as Active Directory directory service, that you want to allow into your application), but precautions such as login Web Forms are generally not required, because users will either be automatically recognized or prompted for credentials before they reach the site.

Windows Authentication is not always the perfect solution, however, especially for Internet applications. You cannot expect any user who needs to be identified in your Internet application to have domain credentials on your Windows domain. Fortunately, forms authentication is a good alternative. By using forms authentication, you as the developer are responsible for providing a page that allows users to enter their credentials. More importantly, the storage of those credentials and the management of user information is also up to you. Sadly, most users get the details of storing user credentials wrong. As we will see later in this chapter, this potentially daunting task is made much easier in ASP.NET 2.0 by several controls designed to assist you in identifying and registering users.

From the main page of the ASP.NET Web Site Administration Tool, click the Security tab to see a page like the one shown in Figure 7-4.

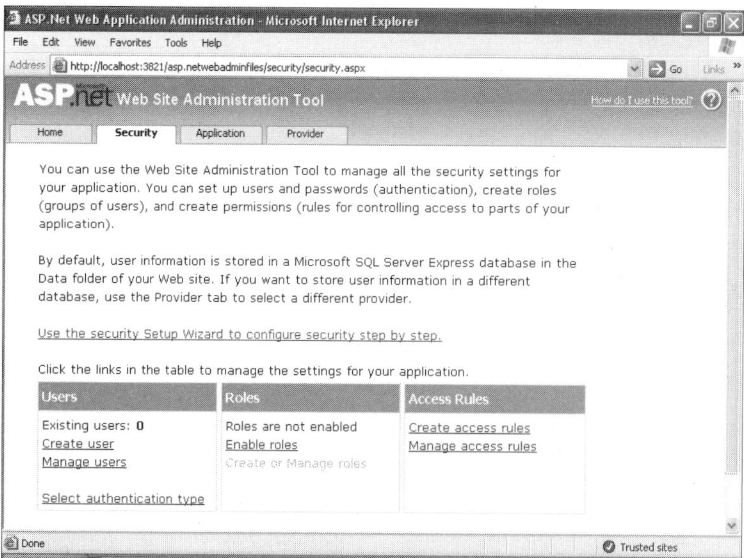

Figure 7-4 The Security page in the ASP.NET Web Site Administration Tool

The easiest way to configure security is to click Use The Security Setup Wizard To Configure Security Step By Step. The first step of the Security Setup Wizard is a welcome page, as shown in Figure 7-5.

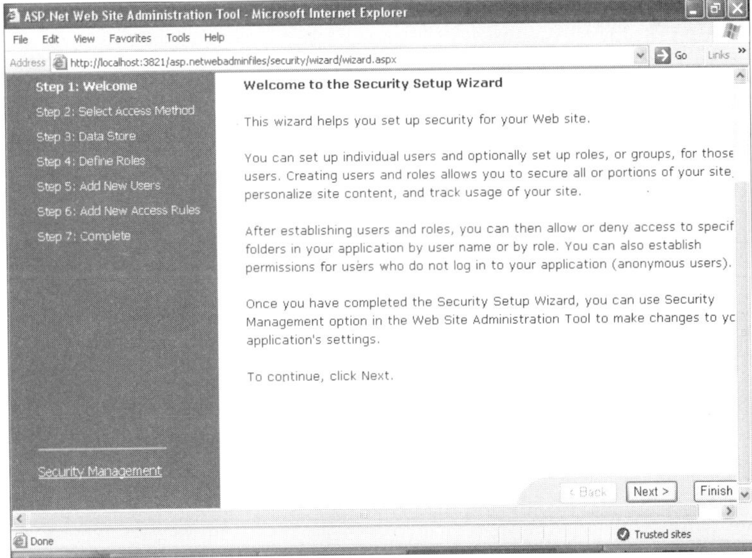

Figure 7-5 The Security Setup Wizard welcome page

Click Next to proceed to step 2, Select Access Method, shown in Figure 7-6.

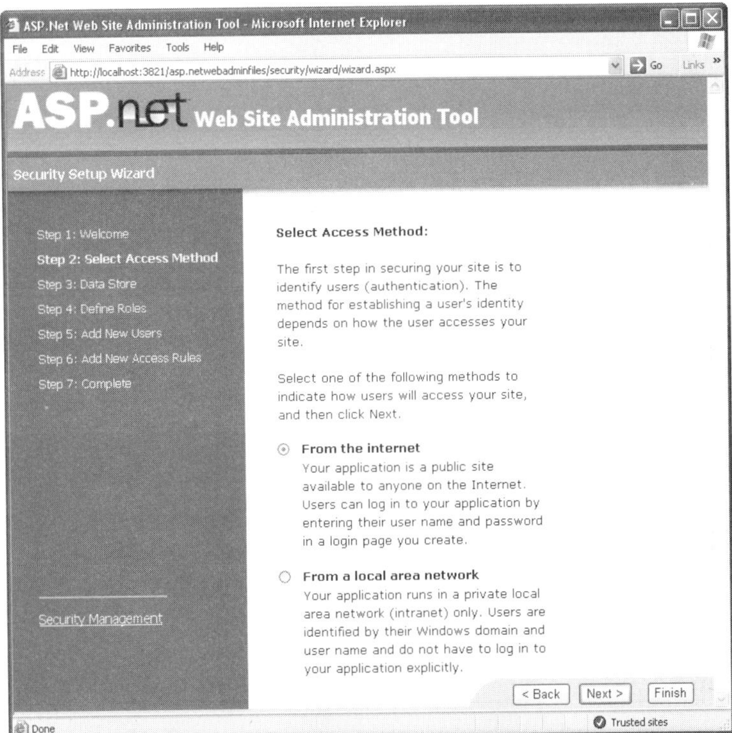

Figure 7-6 The Security Setup Wizard Select Access Method step

Although the wizard page shown in Figure 7-6 does not refer to the authentication methods by name, the first option, From The Internet, refers to forms authentication, and the second option, From A Local Area Network, refers to Windows Authentication. For the BikeBlog-Secured Web site, I selected From The Internet and clicked Next. The third step, Data Store, simply reminds me that the provider settings that I configured in the previous section are established outside of this wizard. Any changes that I might like to make at this point must be made from the administration tool's Provider page (see Figure 7-2). The Data Store step is shown in Figure 7-7.

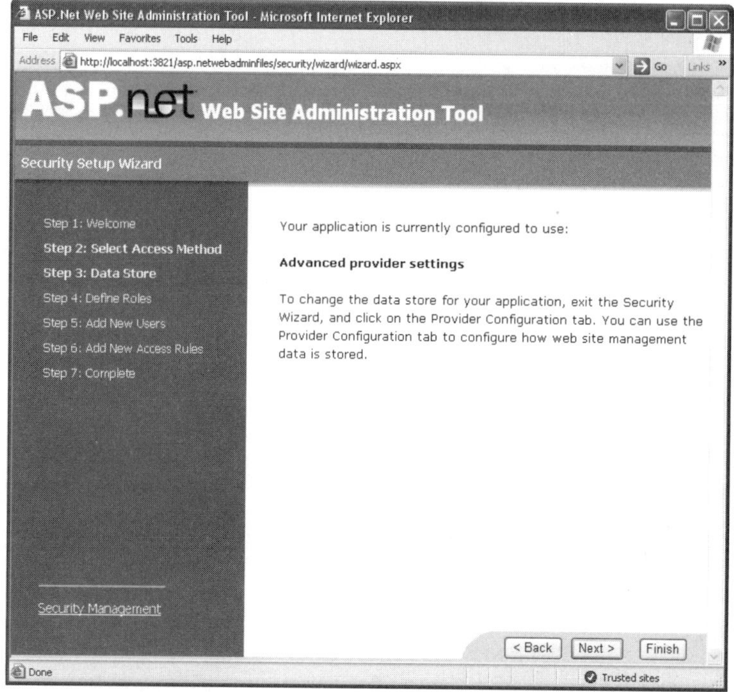

Figure 7-7 The Security Setup Wizard Data Store step

Click Next to proceed to the next step, Define Roles, as shown in Figure 7-8.

Roles are a convenient way to group together users who need the same set of rights to the application. Even when only one user will need to perform a given task, assigning that task to a role and adding the single user to the role is cleaner than assigning the task to each user individually, and it allows for flexibility in the future. For the BikeBlogSecured Web site, I enabled roles by selecting the Enable Roles For This Web Site check box and clicking Next, which opened the page shown in Figure 7-9.

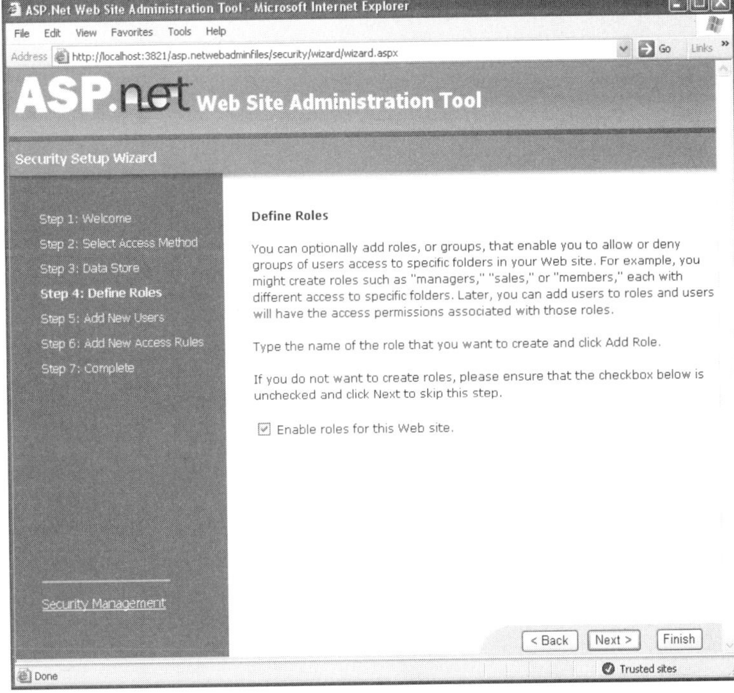

Figure 7-8 The Security Setup Wizard Define Roles step

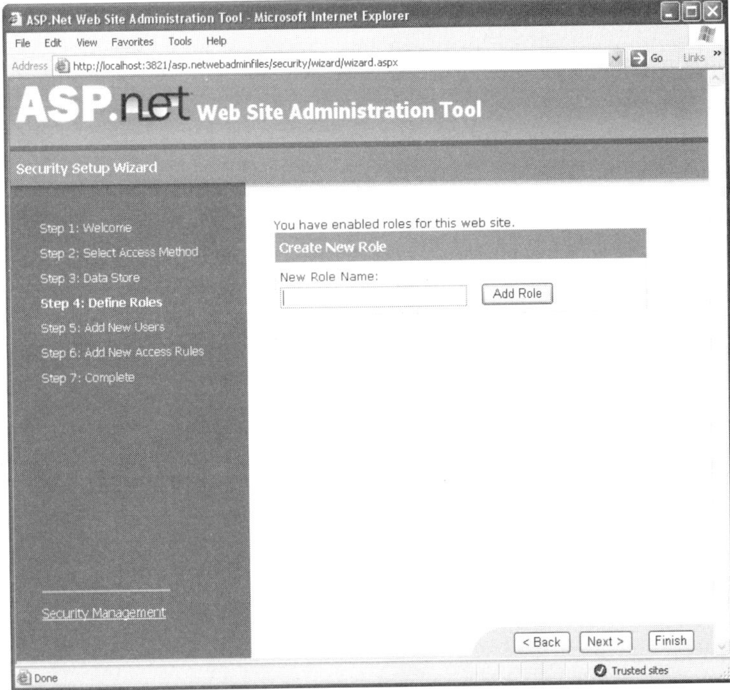

Figure 7-9 The Security Setup Wizard Create New Role page

I created a new role named admins and clicked Add Role, which resulted in the page shown in Figure 7-10.

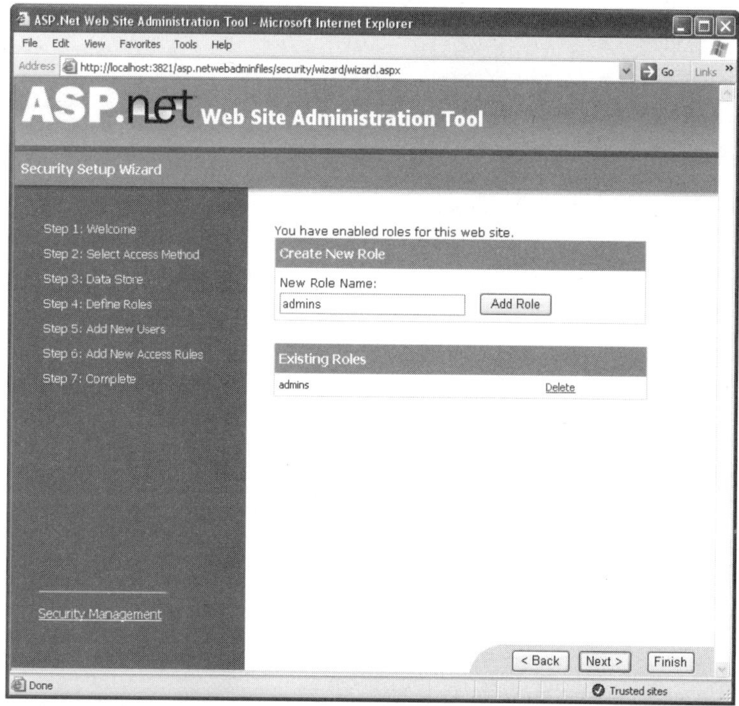

Figure 7-10 The Security Setup Wizard Create New Role page, after creating the admins role

After I clicked Next, step 5, Add New Users, appeared. I entered a new user, filling in the fields as shown in Figure 7-11.

When I clicked Create User, the user was created and a page appeared confirming this and offering me the opportunity to continue. After I clicked Continue, an empty Create User page appeared. I clicked Next again, and the Add New Access Rules step appeared, as shown in Figure 7-12.

The page shown in Figure 7-12 allows you to create rules to allow and deny users at the directory level. By selecting Admin in the list of folders, clicking Admins in the list of roles, and clicking Allow in the Permission section, you can add a rule that allows members of the admins group to access the Admin folder. Next, add another rule: Select Admin in the list of folders, click All Users in the list of roles, and click Deny in the Permission section. When you have added the two rules, to allow admins and deny all users to the Admin folder, a list of rules is displayed, as shown in Figure 7-13.

After access rules have been set, the Security Setup Wizard is complete. Click Finish, and you are almost done. On the Security page of the ASP.NET Web Site Administration Tool, click Create Or Manage Roles. The page shown in Figure 7-14 appears.

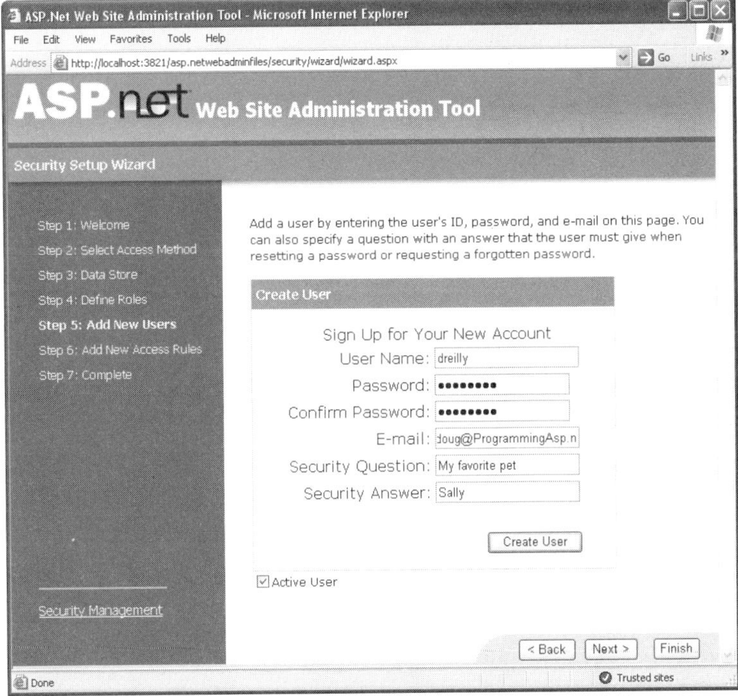

Figure 7-11 The Security Setup Wizard Add New Users step

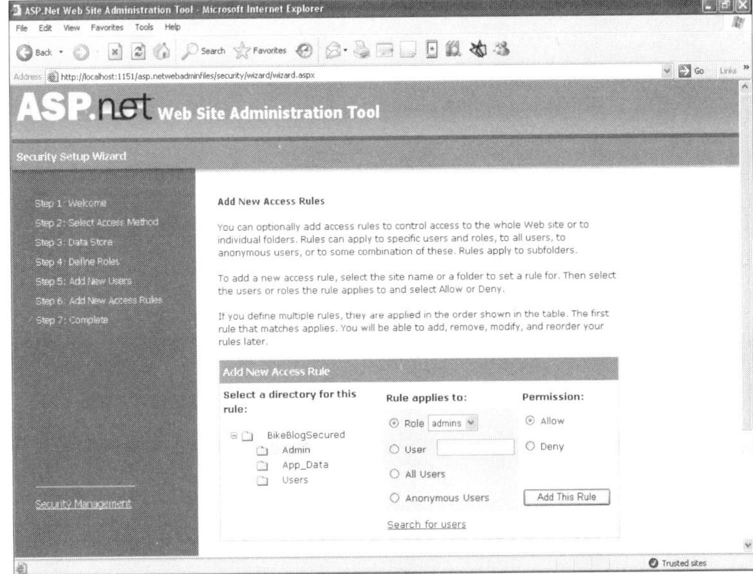

Figure 7-12 The Security Setup Wizard Add New Access Rules step

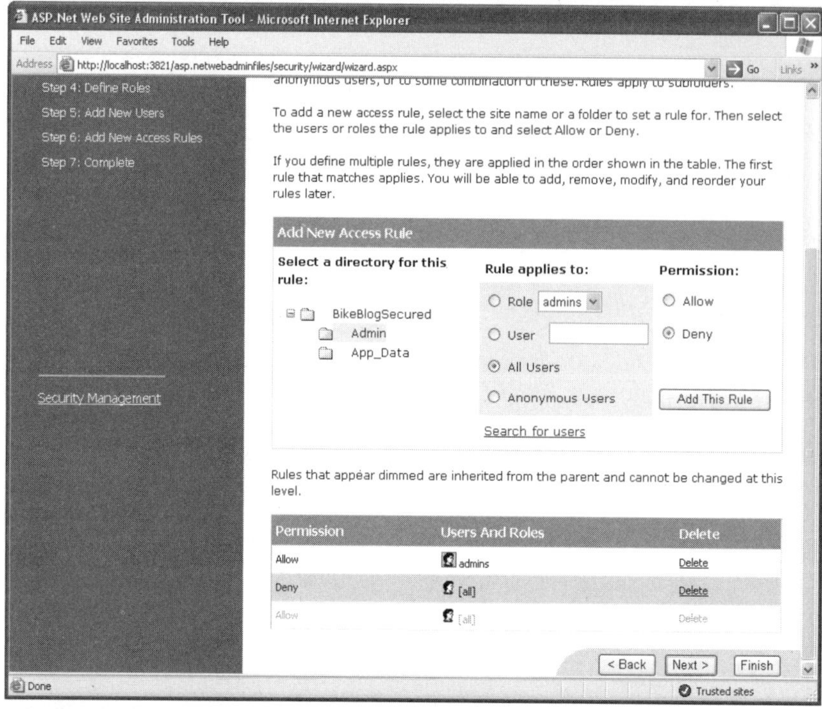

Figure 7-13 The Security Setup Wizard Add New Access Rules step, after adding two rules

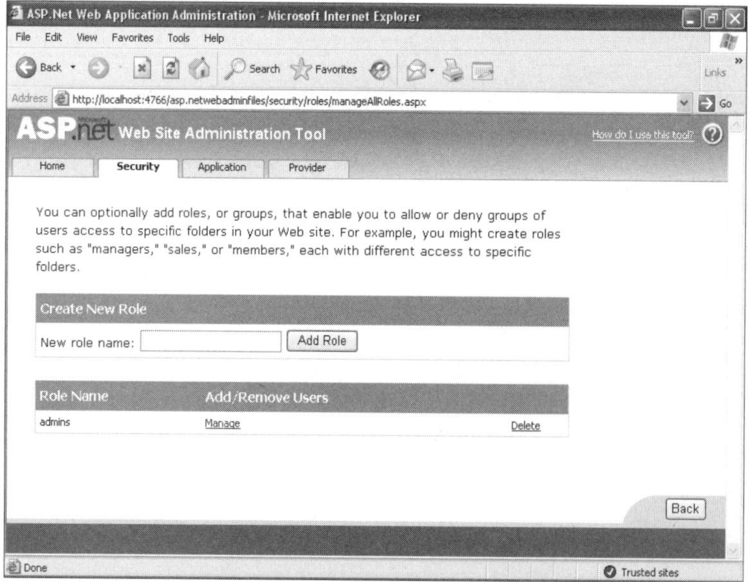

Figure 7-14 The Manage Roles page in the ASP.NET Web Site Administration Tool

Click the Manage link next to the admins group, and a page appears that allows you to search for a user. In my case, I added user "dreilly." By clicking the D link, I saw that the single user had been added, and I could select a check box entitled User Is In Role, which, when selected, indicates that the user is a member of the role, as shown in Figure 7-15.

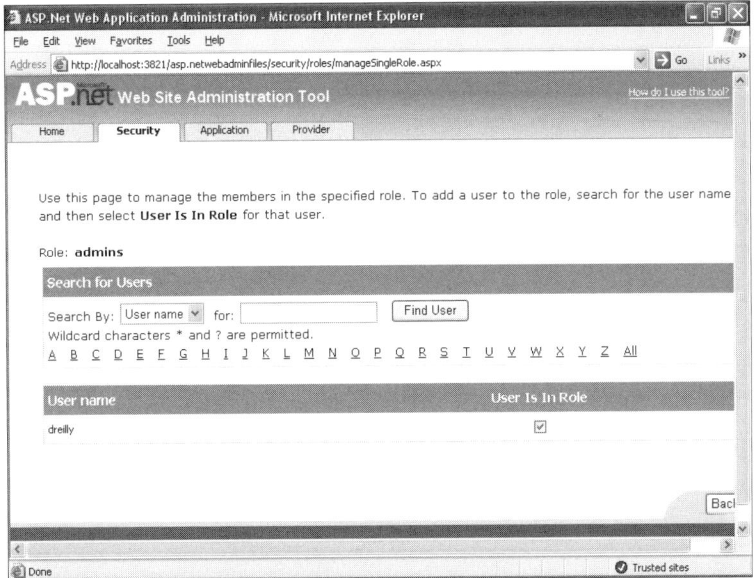

Figure 7-15 Adding the user dreilly to the admins role in the ASP.NET Web Site Administration Tool

Clicking Back twice returns you to the main Security page of the ASP.NET Web Site Administration Tool.

Behind the new administrative interface, ASP.NET 2.0 continues to store information about user rights inside the Web.config file. For instance, after I set the rules for the admin folder, a Web.config file was stored in the admin folder with the rules spelled out, as shown here.

```
<?xml version="1.0" encoding="utf-8"?>
<configuration xmlns="http://schemas.microsoft.com/.NetConfiguration/v2.0">
    <system.web>
        <authorization>
            <allow roles="admins" />
            <deny users="*" />
        </authorization>
    </system.web>
</configuration>
```

The *</authorization>* section tells ASP.NET that admins are allowed in the folder and all other users are denied.

Application

One page remains in the administration tool. Click the Application tab to see a page similar to the one shown in Figure 7-16.

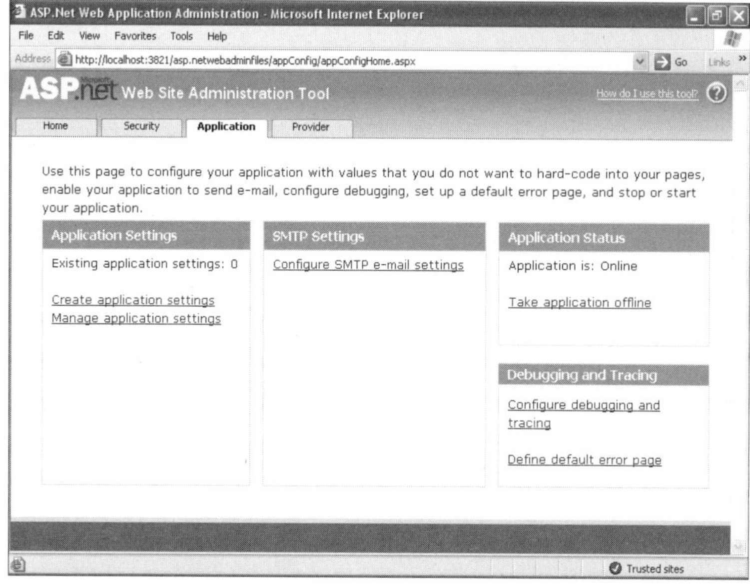

Figure 7-16 The Application page in the ASP.NET Web Site Administration Tool

The Application Settings section allows you to create and mangage application settings. Application settings consist of a key and value pair. For instance, you might have a setting that lists the number of blog entries to show on a page, for which the key would be "NumberOfBlogEntries" and the value would be "4". Application settings are stored in the Web.config file and can be accessed by using the *ConfigurationSettings* class, as shown here.

```
int32 PageSize=0;
int32.TryParse(ConfigurationSettings.AppSettings["NumberOfBlogEntries"],
      out PageSize);
```

Tip Here I am using the new *TryParse* method of the *int32* class. In earlier versions of the Microsoft .NET Framework, you had to attempt the parse of a string containing an integer inside a *try/catch* block. The *TryParse* method, which was available for doubles and *DateTime* objects (and a few other classes) in earlier versions of .NET, is now available for integer classes in .NET 2.0. Note that the *PageSize* parameter is passed as an *out* parameter, and the *TryParse* method returns not the number, but a *bool* value that indicates whether the string can be parsed as an integer.

A feature of the login and registration controls that will be covered in the next section is the ability to e-mail users when they have forgotten their passwords. Clicking the Configure SMTP E-Mail Settings link opens the page shown in Figure 7-17, which allows you to set up a Simple Mail Transfer Protocol (SMTP) server.

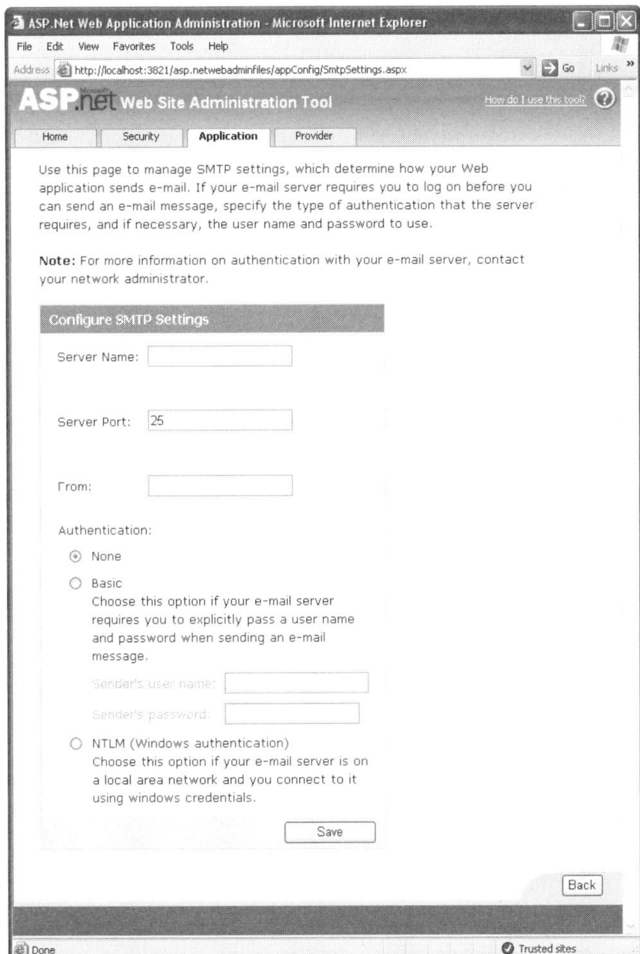

Figure 7-17 Setting the SMTP server in the ASP.NET Web Site Administration Tool

Other options on the Application page allow you to configure debugging and tracing, as well as take the application offline.

The Login Controls

In earlier versions of ASP.NET, the developer was responsible for creating the user interface for all aspects of user administration. Fortunately, ASP.NET 2.0 has several new login-related controls. Figure 7-18 shows the controls in the Login section of the Visual Studio Toolbox.

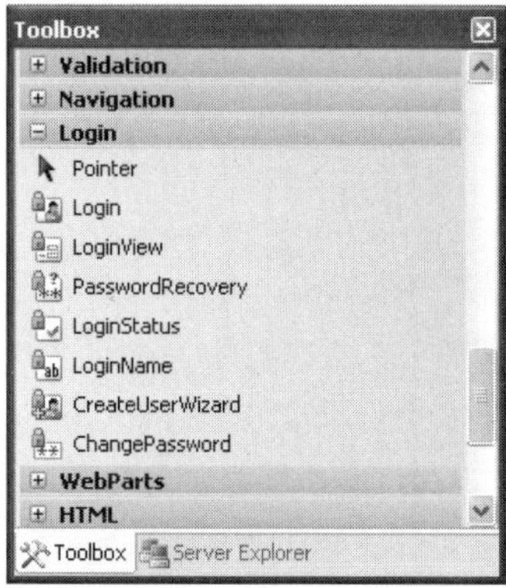

Figure 7-18 The Login controls in the Visual Studio Toolbox

In the following sections, I will provide a brief overview of each of these controls. Virtually all text used in all of these controls can be configured by using properties of the controls. The first item in Figure 7-18 is the Pointer, which merely deselects a currently selected toolbar control.

Login

The *Login* control presents a user interface in which the user can enter a user name and password. Users can choose to have the Web site remember who they are, so that they do not need to log in each time they visit the site. As with almost all of the login-related controls, you can use the Auto Format dialog box to apply several styles all at once, or you can apply styles individually. The appearance of the *Login* control can be modified in a variety of ways, and you can even convert the control to a templated version and then modify the template to more closely match the rest of your site.

LoginView

The *LoginView* control detects the login status of the user and displays different text based on that status. Anonymous users will see different text than users who are logged in, and different information can also be displayed to users in different roles.

PasswordRecovery

The *PasswordRecovery* control allows a user to retrieve his or her password if it has been lost. The *PasswordRecovery* control does not display the user's password on the Web page, which would be a terrible security breach. Depending on several other settings, some passwords may not be recoverable. If you are using a one-way hash (a hash that cannot be converted back to clear text), the password cannot be recovered, but it can be reset and e-mailed to the user. For example, when I reset my password, I received an e-mail with the following text:

> *Please return to the site and log in using the following information.*

User Name: dreilly

Password: wAdW]+MH{!K[kG

LoginStatus

The *LoginStatus* control is rendered as a link that either sends the anonymous user to the specified login page (Login.aspx by default) or logs out the currently logged in user. Again, almost all text in this control can be modified.

LoginName

The *LoginName* control renders the user's name for logged in users and nothing for anonymous users.

CreateUserWizard

One task that is required in most sites is the creation of new users. The *CreateUserWizard* control is one of the more complex login-related controls. By default, the *CreateUserWizard* control has only two steps, although you can add custom steps, customize individual steps, or template the control in several ways. In the first step, the user enters the required information (e-mail address, user name, password, and so on), and the second and final step provides confirmation. You can set the *PasswordRegularExpression* property to validate passwords against a custom rule defined by a regular expression.

ChangePassword

The *ChangePassword* control is another fairly complex control that also allows significant customization. The control, by default, has the standard three text boxes, one for the current password, one for the new password, and a third to re-enter the new password–to ensure that the password, which is masked, is entered correctly.

The BikeBlogSecured Application

An application such as a Web log must often know who is accessing the application. As in most applications, certain tasks such as entering blog entries should only be performed by certain users. The complete source for the BikeBlogSecured Web site is included with the content available for download. (For more information about the downloadable code, see the Introduction.)

While working through the Security Setup Wizard in the ASP.NET Web Site Administration Tool, I entered a single user, named dreilly. After that, I added that user to the admins role. Finally, I set up rules to allow only users in the admins role to access pages in the Admin folder.

By now you might be thinking, "How would a user know to type in the complete URL for a page in my admin folder? I never show the administrator links to non-administrator users. Why do I have to secure the administrator pages?" There are a couple of responses to this. First, never underestimate what users of your system might do, intentionally or unintentionally. Users can often stumble into unsecured portions of the system that you do not intend to expose to them. Second, imagine a scenario in which a user has rights to use the administrative interface on your Web site; then that user leaves the company. If the user has the URL for the administrative interface of your Web site saved in his or her favorites, even if you never directly link to the page, the user might be able to return to the page. Never rely on "security by obscurity."

After I ran the ASP.NET Web Site Administration Tool and created an initial user, I needed to test the ability to log in to the site. The Web site was created with a Master Page used for all pages except *Login.aspx*. On the Master Page, I added two of the login-related controls, a *LoginStatus* control and a *LoginName* control. When the Web site is run, the page looks like Figure 7-19.

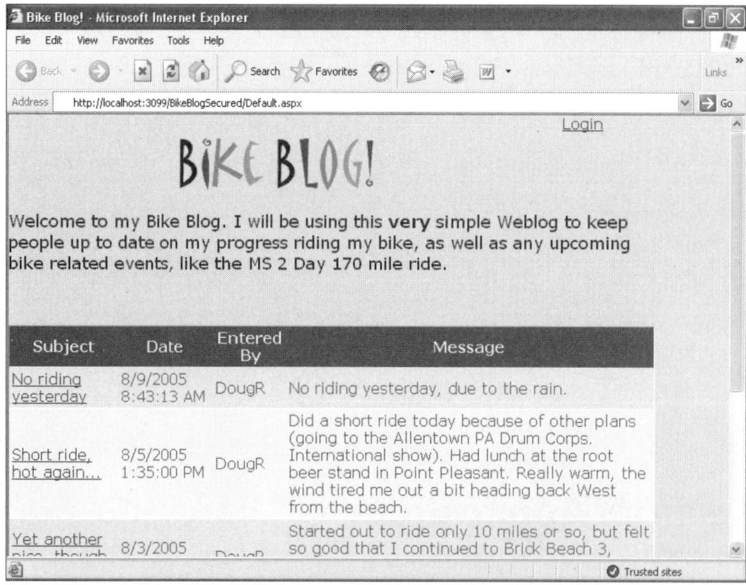

Figure 7-19 The main page of the BikeBlogSecured Web site

Much of this page is the same as previous versions, displaying blog entries in a *GridView* control. In the upper-right, the *LoginStatus* control is visible, rendered as the Login link. Clicking the link opens the Login.aspx page, shown in Figure 7-20.

Note that the *Login.aspx* page does not use the Master Page that all the other pages in the Web site use. I did this to ensure that the Login link does not appear on the login page. The login page contains two of the login-related controls, a *Login* control and a *PasswordRecovery* control. It is worth noting that there is no code at all in the code file for *Login.aspx*.

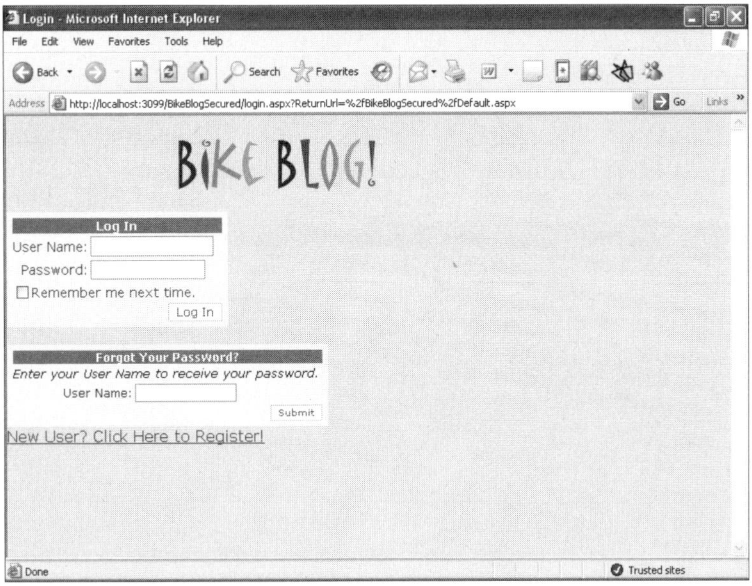

Figure 7-20 The Login.aspx page of the BikeBlogSecured Web site

Look at Figure 7-20 again. The URL in the Address bar has an argument tacked onto it, the *ReturnUrl*. The value is somewhat obscured by the fact that several special characters in the URL are escaped, or replaced with a substituted value (for example, "/" is replaced by "%2f"), but the argument indicates that when users log in, they will be returned to /BikeBlogSecured/Default.aspx, the page they came from. When users are successfully logged in and returned to Default.aspx, a Logout link is displayed instead of a Login link, and the user name is displayed in the upper-right corner of the page, as shown in Figure 7-21.

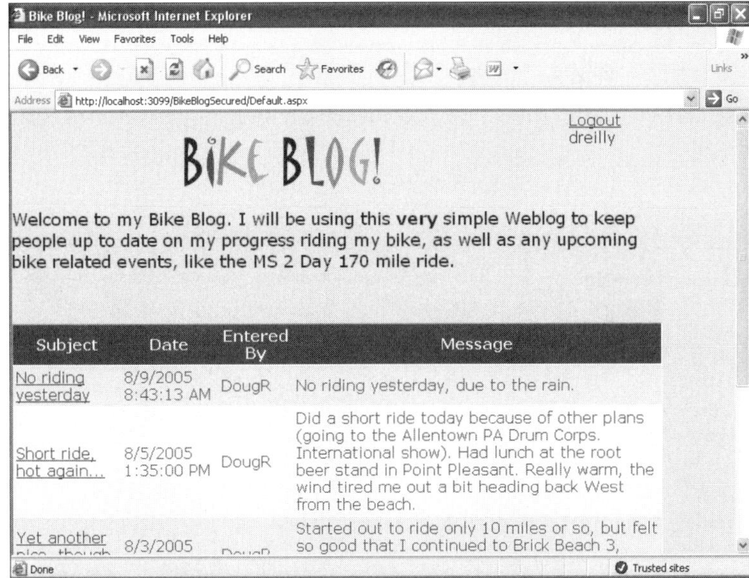

Figure 7-21 Default.aspx when a user is logged in

If I click the Logout link, I am immediately logged out of the application, and the screen appears as shown in Figure 7-19.

After I am logged in, I might want to add a comment to an entry. To do so, I click the subject link in the *GridView* control; a details page displays current comments and allows me to add additional comments. Figure 7-22 shows the BlogEntryDetails.aspx page.

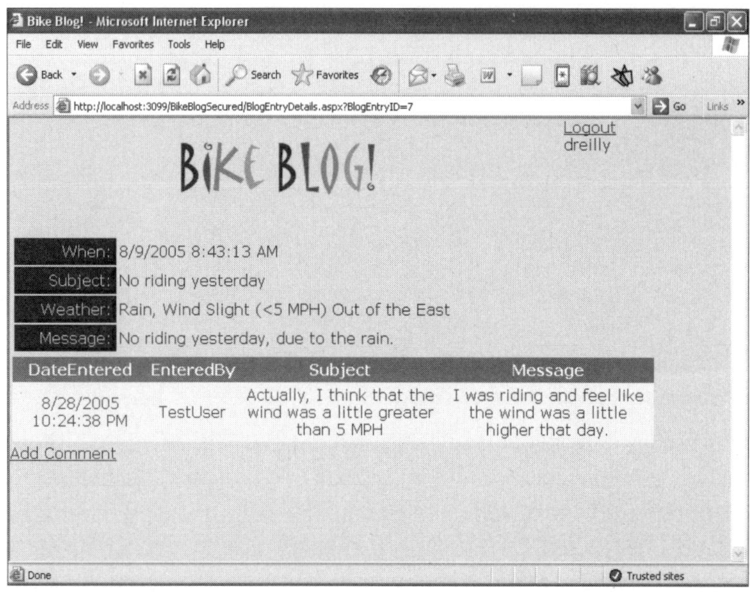

Figure 7-22 BlogEntryDetails.aspx showing a comment and the Add Comment link

BlogEntryDetails.aspx contains a copy of the DisplayBlogEntryUC.ascx user control built in the last chapter and a *GridView* control to show comments on the current entry. A *SqlDataSource* control also points to a stored procedure that selects comments for a specified BlogEntryID and returns them sorted in order of DateEntered. The BlogEntry-Details.aspx page takes advantage of a useful feature of the *GridView* control, the *EmptyDataText* property that sets text to be displayed when no results are returned. Figure 7-23 shows BlogEntryDetails.aspx when no comments have been entered.

The Add Comment link is visible in Figure 7-22 and Figure 7-23. This link does not appear for anonymous users. This could have been done in several ways. For example, I could have used a *LoginView* control with nothing in the "logged out" user template and the Add Comment link in the "logged in" user template. Instead, I opted to control the visibility of the link by using code, so that I could demonstrate the programmatic interface to the authentication system. Listing 7-1 shows the code in BlogEntryDetails.aspx.cs.

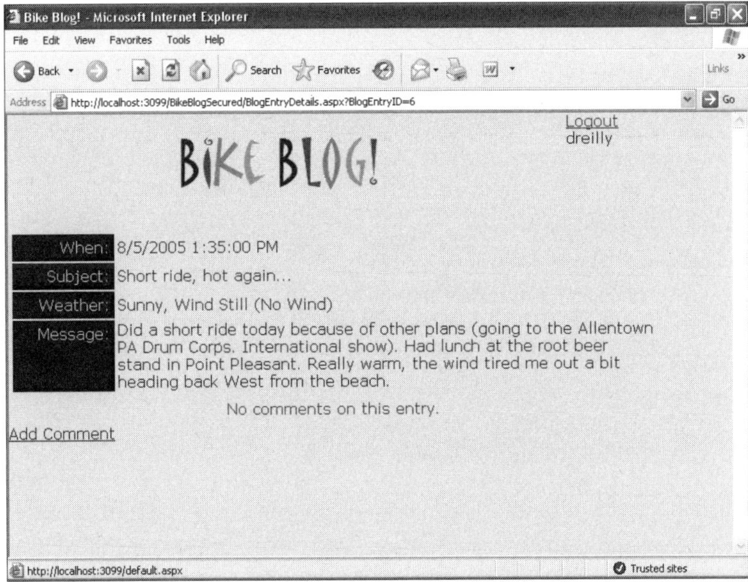

Figure 7-23 BlogEntryDetails.aspx showing no comments

Listing 7-1 BlogEntryDetails.aspx.cs

```
using System;
using System.Data;
using System.Data.SqlClient;
using System.Configuration;
using System.Collections;
using System.Web;
using System.Web.Security;
using System.Web.UI;
using System.Web.UI.WebControls;
using System.Web.UI.WebControls.WebParts;
using System.Web.UI.HtmlControls;

public partial class BlogEntryDetails : System.Web.UI.Page
{
    public int BlogEntryID
    {
        get
        {
            return ViewState["BlogEntryID"] == null ? 0 :
                (int)ViewState["BlogEntryID"];
        }
        set
        {
            ViewState["BlogEntryID"] = value;
        }
    }
    protected void Page_Load(object sender, EventArgs e)
    {
```

```
        if (this.IsPostBack == false)
        {
            int blogEntryID;
            int.TryParse(Request["BlogEntryID"],
                out blogEntryID);
            BlogEntryID = blogEntryID;
            this.DisplayBlogEntryUC1.BlogEntryID = BlogEntryID;
            if (User.Identity.IsAuthenticated)
            {
                this.hlAddComment.Visible = true;
                this.hlAddComment.NavigateUrl =
                    "~/users/addcomment.aspx?BlogEntryID=" +
                    BlogEntryID.ToString();
            }
            else
            {
                this.hlAddComment.Visible = false;
            }
        }
    }

}
```

First, I added a property to hold the BlogEntryID, using a pattern that should be familiar by now, storing the value in view state. In the *Page_Load* event handler, all code is inside an *if* block and is only executed when the *IsPostBack* property is *false*. I declared an *int* variable, *blogEntryID*, the same as the property but with a lowercase character as the first character. I used the *blogEntryID* variable in the call to the *TryParse* method because as a property, *BlogEntryID* cannot be passed directly as the second parameter to *TryParse*; the second parameter is an *out* parameter, meaning that the value is modified by the method being called. I set the *BlogEntryID* property and used that to set the *BlogEntryID* property of the user control that displays blog entry details.

After I set the *BlogEntryID* property, I checked to see whether the user is an authenticated user. *User.Identity.IsAuthenticated* is a *bool* property that is *true* if the user has been authenticated and *false* if not. Remember that simply not exposing a link is not enough to ensure that the link is secured. To ensure that an unauthenticated user does not bypass the login page and simply enter the URL to add a comment, I added a new folder to the application named Users, and then I added the AddComment.aspx page to that folder. I added a rule in the ASP.NET Web Site Administration Tool that denies access to anonymous users, as shown in Figure 7-24.

With this rule in place, even if a user knows the URL for the AddComment.aspx page, he or she can access the Web Form only if authenticated.

When a user is logged in and clicks the Add Comment link, the AddComment.aspx Web Form appears, as shown in Figure 7-25.

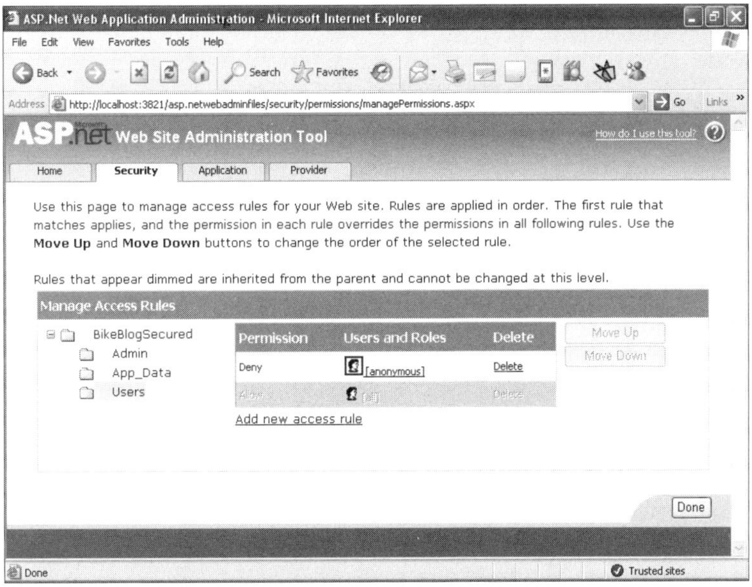

Figure 7-24 Setting permissions for the Users folder

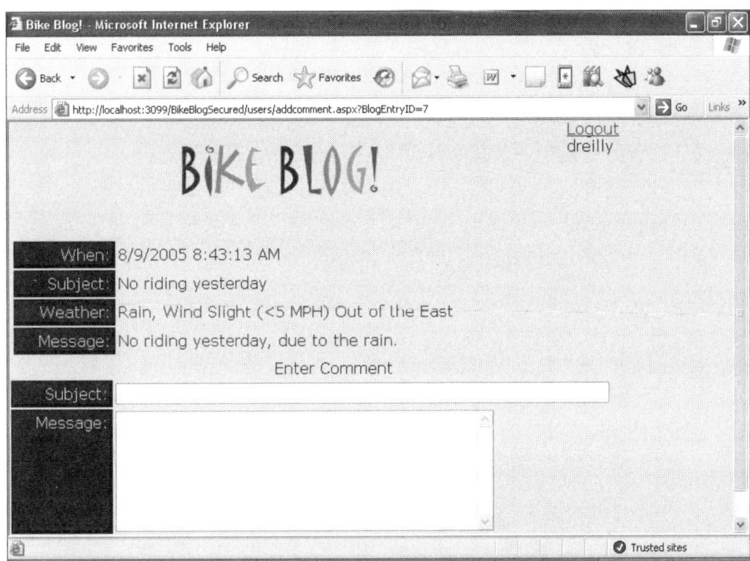

Figure 7-25 AddComment.aspx

AddComment.aspx uses the Master Page, and it has a copy of the DisplayBlogEntryUC.ascx control, as well as subject labels and message text boxes. Most of the code on the AddComment.aspx page is similar to code shown in previous examples. However, one method, *btnSave_Click*, is entirely new, as shown here.

```
protected void btnSave_Click(object sender, EventArgs e)
{
    SqlConnection cn =
```

```
            new SqlConnection(
                ConfigurationManager.
                    ConnectionStrings[
                    "BikeBlogConnectionString"].ConnectionString);
        cn.Open();
        try
        {
            SqlCommand cmd = new SqlCommand("spInsertComment", cn);
            cmd.CommandType = CommandType.StoredProcedure;

            cmd.Parameters.AddWithValue("@BlogEntryID", BlogEntryID);
            cmd.Parameters.AddWithValue("@Subject", this.edSubject.Text);
            cmd.Parameters.AddWithValue("@Message", this.edMessage.Text);
            cmd.Parameters.AddWithValue("@EnteredBy", User.Identity.Name);

            cmd.ExecuteNonQuery();

            Response.Redirect("~/BlogEntryDetails.aspx?BLogEntryID=" +
                BlogEntryID.ToString(),false);
        }
        finally
        {
            cn.Close();
        }
    }
```

This code uses the objects in the *System.Data.SqlClient* namespace to insert a comment into the database. The Comment table (and most other tables in the BikeBlog database) has a column named EnteredBy that keeps track of the user who entered the information. To supply the user name, I used another property of *User.Identity* object, in this case *Name*.

Note When you use Windows Authentication, the user name will be the domain name and the user name, something like *DOMAIN\User*.

One more feature should be added to this example. As an administrator of the site, I should be able to add a new blog entry. A page in the Admin folder named AddEditBlog-Entry.aspx allows addition or editing of a blog entry. Most of this code is copied from the BetterEdit.aspx example from Chapter 5. To ensure that the link appears when, and only when, an administrator is logged in, I used the *User.IsInRole* method. I added a hyperlink control to the Default.aspx page and name it *hlAddEntry*. I set the *NavigateUrl* property to point to AddEditBlogEntry.aspx and pass in a *BlogEntryID* of 0, because I am creating a new entry.

Even if I had stopped here, the site should be adequately secure. If a user who was not a member of the admins role had access to the link, he or she would be unable to access the page. However, this would be confusing to the user, so the link should be hidden if it is not applicable to the user. Default.aspx previously contained no code that was not part of the Visual Studio template for a code file. To hide or show the hyperlink used to add a new entry, I added the following code to Default.aspx.

```
protected void Page_Load(object sender, EventArgs e)
{
    if (User.IsInRole("admins"))
    {
        this.hlAddEntry.Visible = true;
    }
    else
    {
        this.hlAddEntry.Visible = false;
    }
}
```

The code uses the *Users.IsInRole* method to determine whether the user is in the admins role. If the user is in the admins role, the hyperlink is shown; otherwise, the hyperlink is invisible.

Many more enhancements could certainly be made to the BikeBlogSecured site as presented here. For example, there is no way for the user to directly edit an entry, although an administrator could easily do so by entering the URL. You could solve this problem by having the BlogEntryDetails.aspx page determine at runtime whether the user is a member of the admins role, and if so, redirect the user to AddEditBlogEntry.aspx. Another possible solution would be to add a column to the *GridView* control on the main page that allowed members of the admins role to jump directly to the AddEditBlogEntry.aspx page.

As another improvement, the login-related controls that expose a user interface could be templated to blend into the site better than they currently do. Nonetheless, the login-related controls as presented in this chapter allowed me to create a reasonably complete user management system without having to write much code.

Conclusion

The examples presented in this chapter, using the new Web site administration tool and login controls, clearly demonstrate that the ASP.NET 2.0 team reached its goal of a 70 percent reduction in code in some cases. I have not done any detailed analysis, but the number of lines of code directly related to user security in the BikeBlogSecured application is minimal, certainly 70 percent less than I would have expected were this an ASP.NET 1.x application.

In the next chapter, I will offer a brief overview of integrating a Web site into a Windows Forms application. Microsoft .NET Framework 2.0 also includes *HtmlDocument* and *WebBrowser* classes for Windows Forms applications. By using these classes, you can quickly create a Web browser of your own. In addition, I will take a quick look at other ways to integrate Windows Forms and Web Forms applications.

Chapter 8

Integrating with Windows Forms Applications

In this chapter:

After writing seven chapters about the wonders of Web Forms applications, I must acknowledge that Web Forms applications are not the complete solution to every problem. As the Microsoft ASP.NET team worked on improvements and enhancements, the team supporting Microsoft Windows Forms applications was not standing still.

Improvements to Windows Forms applications have not taken place in isolation from the Internet and Web Forms applications. For example, ClickOnce deployment of Windows Forms applications is a new feature of Windows Forms applications in .NET 2.0 that leverages the Internet. Traditionally, Windows Forms applications required a multi-step installation process on each workstation running the application. ClickOnce deployment uses the Internet or an intranet for both initial deployment and updates of a Windows Forms application.

A less-heralded improvement, but one that is significant for Web Forms developers, is the inclusion of the *WebBrowser* control. The *WebBrowser* control is a managed wrapper around the Microsoft ActiveX control that Microsoft Internet Explorer uses to display Web pages. Strictly speaking, developers always could use the ActiveX Web browser control in their applications; however, the *WebBrowser* control makes it a great deal easier. The *WebBrowser* control is the focus of this chapter. Details will follow, but first, let's take a brief look at what the control can do.

WebBrowser Control Example

To test out the new *WebBrowser* control, we first need to create a new Windows Forms application. In Microsoft Visual Studio 2005, select New on the File menu, and then select Project. The New Project dialog box appears, as shown in Figure 8-1.

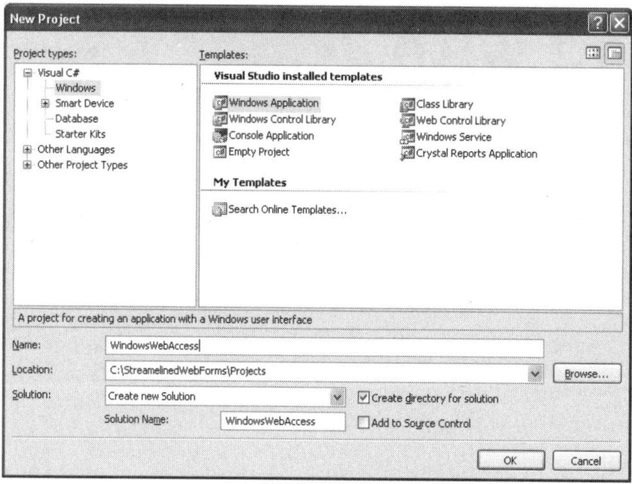

Figure 8-1 The New Project dialog box in Visual Studio, set to add a new Windows Forms application

In the Project Types list on the left, expand Visual C#, and then select Windows. Select Windows Application from the list of installed templates on the right. Name the project WindowsWebAccess. Click OK, and you will see a screen like the one shown in Figure 8-2.

From the Common Controls group of the Toolbox, drag and drop a *WebBrowser* control onto the form. The control is automatically sized to take up the entire form. In the Properties window, you can set properties just as you can for Web Forms controls. One of the properties of the *WebBrowser* control is the *Url* property. Set this property to *www.microsoft.com/learning/books/*. On the Debug menu, select Start Debugging (or press F5) to run the application. Maximize the form, and you will see the Microsoft Press home page, similar to the page shown in Figure 8-3.

With no code, and a single property setting, we have a very simple, serviceable Web browser. If you right-click the *WebBrowser* control, the menu that appears is the same menu that appears when you right-click a Web page in Internet Explorer, allowing you to go back and forward, view the source of the page, and so on.

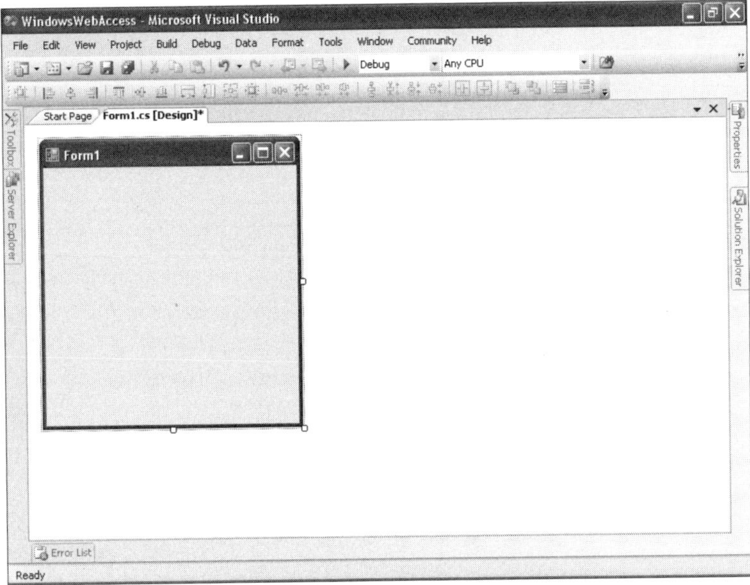

Figure 8-2 New Windows Forms application in Design view

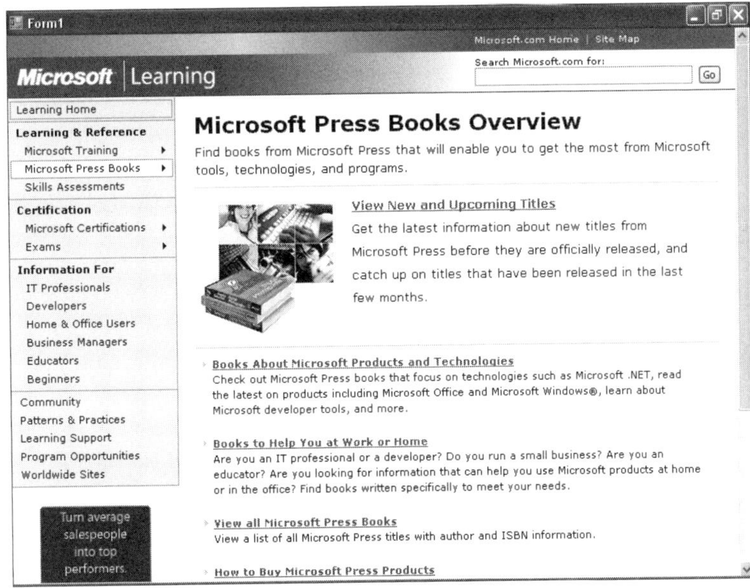

Figure 8-3 Windows Forms application displaying the Microsoft Press home page in a *WebBrowser* control

WebBrowser Control Details

In addition to the one property of the *WebBrowser* control that we have already seen, the *Url* property, the *WebBrowser* control exposes a variety of other properties, events, and methods. The most important of these are shown in Table 8-1.

Table 8-1 *WebBrowser* Class Members

Member Name	Description
AllowNavigation	A property that gets or sets a value indicating whether the control can navigate to a different page after its initial page is loaded.
AllowWebBrowserDrop	A property that gets or sets a value indicating whether the *WebBrowser* control navigates to documents dropped onto it.
CanGoBack, CanGoForward	Properties that get values indicating whether the *WebBrowser* control can go back or forward.
Document	A property that gets a *System.Windows.Forms.HtmlDocument* object representing the Web page currently displayed in the *WebBrowser* control. The *HtmlDocument* object gives the developer access to the Document Object Model (DOM) of the page currently loaded in the *WebBrowser* control.
DocumentText	A property that gets or sets the HTML text of the *WebBrowser* control. By using this property, you can completely examine the text retrieved from a Web site. By using a *WebBrowser* control with the *Visible* property set to false, a developer can use the *DocumentText* property to do what is commonly known as *screen scraping*, or retrieving values from a Web page.
IsBusy	A property that gets a value indicating whether the *WebBrowser* control is currently loading a new document.
IsOffline	A property that gets or sets a value indicating whether the *WebBrowser* control is in offline mode.
ScriptErrorsSuppressed	A property that gets or sets a value indicating whether script errors display a dialog box that indicates the error.
Url	A property that gets or sets the value of the URL of the current document.
DocumentCompleted	An event that occurs when the *WebBrowser* control completes the loading of a document.
FileDownload	An event that occurs before the *WebBrowser* control downloads a file. This event can be used to disable file downloads by canceling them.
Navigated	An event that occurs when the *WebBrowser* control has navigated to a new page and has begun downloading it.
Navigating	An event that occurs before the *WebBrowser* control navigates to a new page.

Table 8-1 *WebBrowser* Class Members

Member Name	Description
NewWindow	An event that occurs before a new browser window is opened. Note that new windows opened by right-clicking a link in the *WebBrowser* control and selecting Open In A New Window will open in a new Internet Explorer window. Intercepting this event can allow you to handle the new page in some other way.
ProgressChanged	An event that occurs when the control has updated information about the progress of the document being loaded. This event can be used to provide a progress bar for page loads.
GoBack, GoForward	Methods that navigate to the previous or next page in the navigation history, if one exists.
Navigate	A method that loads a document specified by a parameter to this method.
Print	A method that prints the document currently displayed in the *WebBrowser* control using the default settings.
Refresh	A method that reloads the current document in the *WebBrowser* control.
ShowPrintDialog	A method that opens the Internet Explorer Print dialog box.
ShowPrintPreviewDialog	A method that opens the Internet Explorer Print Preview dialog box.
ShowSaveAsDialog	A method that opens the Internet Explorer Save As dialog box.
Stop	A method that cancels the loading of any pending document.

Note The *WebBrowser* control also exposes a large number of other properties, methods, and events that are common to all Windows controls. The members shown in Table 8-1 are properties specific to the *WebBrowser* class.

A Tabbed Interface Web Browser

One of the most anticipated new features of Internet Explorer 7 is the new tabbed interface. Rather than opening a new window for each new page that you want to look at, Internet Explorer 7 allows multiple tabbed pages to exist in a single browsing window; switching from page to page is easy, and it's much easier to see which pages are loaded. As I write this, Internet Explorer 7 is in an early beta.

Even though at this time Internet Explorer 7 isn't available, I still like the concept of tabbed pages. Therefore, by using the members of the *WebBrowser* control, in addition to several other Windows Forms controls, I was able to create a simple form that does exactly what Internet Explorer 7 does. Figure 8-4 shows the form in action, with the Microsoft home page, the Microsoft Learning home page, and the MSN home page loaded on separate tabs.

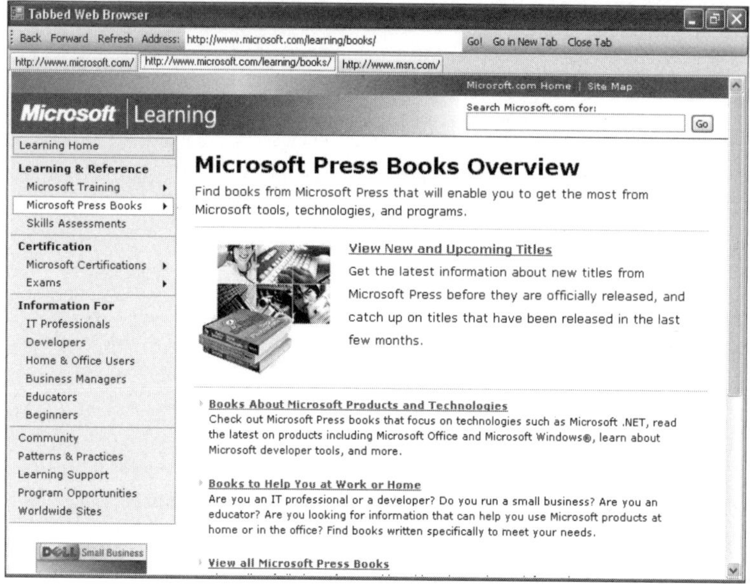

Figure 8-4 The tabbed Web browser example

Across the top of the form in Figure 8-4, notice the *ToolStrip* control. The *ToolStrip* control can contain any number of other controls. I added the following controls to the *ToolStrip* control:

- **Back** A button used to move the *WebBrowser* control in the current tab to the previous page in the browser history, if there is one.
- **Forward** A button used to move the *WebBrowser* control in the current tab to the next page in the browser history, if there is one.
- **Refresh** A button used to reload the current page in the *WebBrowser* control on the current tab.
- **Address** A text box used to enter the address of a new Web page.
- **Go!** A button used to load the address entered in the Address text box into the *WebBrowser* control on the current tab.
- **Go in New Tab** A button used to load the address entered in the Address text box into a new *WebBrowser* control on a new tab.
- **Close Tab** A button used to close the current tab.

Just under the *ToolStrip* control, I dropped a *TabControl* onto the page. A *TabControl* creates a tabbed user interface, which is just what we need to simulate Internet Explorer 7. I set the *Dock* property of the *TabControl* to *Fill*, so that the *TabControl* fills the rest of the form. By default, the *TabControl* has two tabs when dropped on a form. I deleted one of those tabs, and I changed the *Text* property of the remaining tab to "Default." With the *TabControl* selected in Design view, I dropped a *WebBrowser* control onto the *TabControl*. This is the initial *WebBrowser* control used when the page is first loaded.

A reasonable amount of code is required to get this form up and running as described. The code is shown in Listing 8-1.

Listing 8-1 Code Used for the Tabbed Web Browser

```
using System;
using System.Collections.Generic;
using System.ComponentModel;
using System.Data;
using System.Drawing;
using System.Text;
using System.Windows.Forms;

namespace WindowsWebAccess
{
    public partial class Form1 : Form
    {
        public Form1()
        {
            InitializeComponent();
        }

        private void btnGo_Click(object sender, EventArgs e)
        {
            WebBrowser wb =
                (WebBrowser)this.tabControl1.SelectedTab.Controls[0];
            wb.Navigate(this.edAddress.Text);
        }

        private void webBrowser1_Navigated(object sender,
                WebBrowserNavigatedEventArgs e)
        {
            this.edAddress.Text = ((WebBrowser)sender).Url.ToString();
            this.tabControl1.SelectedTab.Text = this.edAddress.Text;
        }

        private void btnGoNewTab_Click(object sender, EventArgs e)
        {
            WebBrowser wb = new WebBrowser();
            string key = Guid.NewGuid().ToString();
            wb.Dock = DockStyle.Fill;
            wb.Name = key;
            wb.Navigated +=
                new System.Windows.Forms.WebBrowserNavigatedEventHandler(
                this.webBrowser1_Navigated);
            this.tabControl1.TabPages.Add(key, this.edAddress.Text);
            this.tabControl1.TabPages[key].Controls.Add(wb);
            ((WebBrowser)this.tabControl1.TabPages[key].Controls[0])
                .Navigate(this.edAddress.Text);
            this.tabControl1.SelectTab(key);
        }
```

```
        private void btnCloseTab_Click(object sender, EventArgs e)
        {
            this.tabControl1.TabPages.Remove(this.tabControl1.SelectedTab);
        }

        private void btnBack_Click(object sender, EventArgs e)
        {
            WebBrowser wb =
                this.tabControl1.SelectedTab.Controls[0] as WebBrowser;
            if (wb != null)
            {
                wb.GoBack();
            }
        }

        private void btnForward_Click(object sender, EventArgs e)
        {
            WebBrowser wb =
                this.tabControl1.SelectedTab.Controls[0] as WebBrowser;
            if (wb != null)
            {
                wb.GoForward();
            }
        }

        private void btnRefresh_Click(object sender, EventArgs e)
        {
            WebBrowser wb =
                this.tabControl1.SelectedTab.Controls[0] as WebBrowser;
            if (wb != null)
            {
                wb.Refresh();
            }
        }
    }
}
```

The *btnGo_Click* event handler has two lines of code that retrieve the correct *WebBrowser* object, and another that sets the new URL.

```
WebBrowser wb =
    (WebBrowser)this.tabControl1.SelectedTab.Controls[0];
wb.Navigate(this.edAddress.Text);
```

This event handler replaces the current Web page in the currently selected tab with the URL entered in the Address text box. To get the correct *WebBrowser* control, I examined the *Controls* collection of the *SelectedTab* property of the *TabControl* object, and I selected the first and only element of the *Controls* collection of that tab. Because the *Controls* collection is a collection of *Control* objects, it must be cast to the correct type. After the correct *WebBrowser* control is found, the *Navigate* method is called, passing in the string entered in the Address text box.

The *btnGoNewTab_Click* event is a bit more complex. The code is shown here.

```
WebBrowser wb = new WebBrowser();
string key = Guid.NewGuid().ToString();
wb.Dock = DockStyle.Fill;
wb.Name = key;
wb.Navigated +=
    new System.Windows.Forms.WebBrowserNavigatedEventHandler(
    this.webBrowser1_Navigated);
this.tabControl1.TabPages.Add(key, this.edAddress.Text);
this.tabControl1.TabPages[key].Controls.Add(wb);
((WebBrowser)this.tabControl1.TabPages[key].Controls[0])
    .Navigate(this.edAddress.Text);
this.tabControl1.SelectTab(key);
```

In this code, I created a new *WebBrowser* object. I also created a new *Guid* object, using the *NewGuid* method of the *Guid* class. A *Guid* object represents a globally unique identifier (GUID), a 128-bit number generated in a way that ensures that the identifier will be unique. I called the *ToString* method on the newly created *Guid* object and set a local variable, *key*, to the return from *ToString*. This provides a string that is guaranteed to be unique. I set the *Dock* property of the new *WebBrowser* object to *DockStyle.Fill*. When you drag a *WebBrowser* control onto a form in Visual Studio, this happens automatically. I added a *Navigated* event handler to the new *WebBrowser* control, using the same event handler that I used for the initial *WebBrowser* control.

Next, I set the *Name* property of the *WebBrowser* control to the *key* variable, the string variable containing the string representation of the new GUID I generated. I then added a new page to the *TabPages* collection of the *TabControl* object, giving it a key and the text to be used as the text on the tab. Several overloads of *Add* allow you to add a tab; I used the one that accepts a key and the text for the tab so that I could identify the tab in the following steps by the tab's key value. The GUID used as the key ensures that I can later access the specific tab, and there is no chance of tabs using the same key.

After adding the tab, I added the *WebControl* object to the *Controls* collection of the newly created tab. I navigated to the address specified in the Address text box, and I used the *SelectTab* method of the *TabControl* to ensure that the newly created tab was the currently selected tab.

The *btnCloseTab_Click* event handler has a single line of code.

```
this.tabControl1.TabPages.Remove(this.tabControl1.SelectedTab);
```

This line of code removes the currently selected tab, ensuring that your collection of tabs will not just continue growing.

The other event handlers, for the Back, Forward, and Refresh buttons, are self explanatory, calling a single method of the *WebControl* object after obtaining the correct control from the *Controls* collection of the currently selected tab of the *TabControl*.

Accessing Content from a *WebBrowser* Control

The previous example showed that you could do a lot with the *WebBrowser* control. However, it did not allow you to access the contents of the documents that are loaded. To give a simple demonstration of what is possible, I created a new form in the WindowsWebAccess project named DocumentTest. I added two *Panel* controls. I docked one to the bottom, and I docked the other using *DockStyle.Fill* as the value for the *Dock* property. I sized them so that the bottom panel takes up a very small slice at the bottom of the screen. I added a *WebBrowser* control to the top panel and a button to the bottom panel named *btnSubmit*. In Design view, the form looked like Figure 8-5.

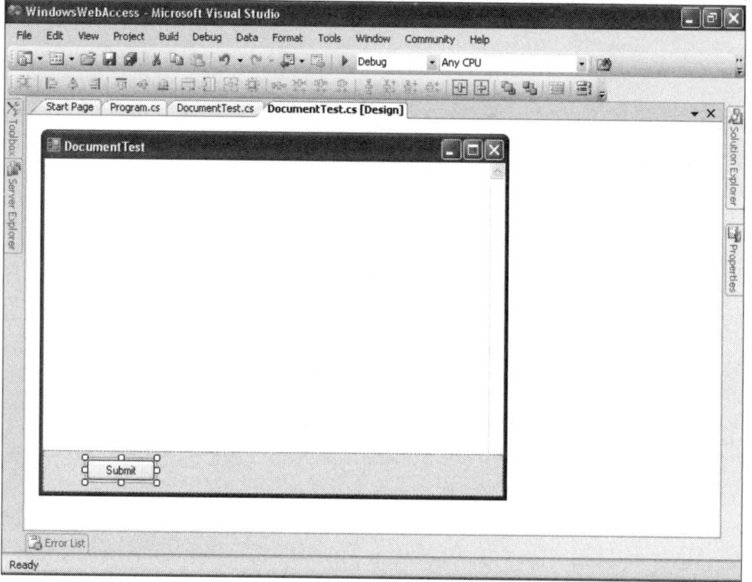

Figure 8-5 The DocumentTest form in Design view

I added some code to the *Activated* event of the form and the *Click* event handler on the button control, as shown in Listing 8-2.

Listing 8-2 Code for the DocumentTest Form

```
using System;
using System.Collections.Generic;
using System.ComponentModel;
using System.Data;
using System.Drawing;
using System.Text;
using System.Windows.Forms;

namespace WindowsWebAccess
{
```

```
    public partial class DocumentTest : Form
    {
        public DocumentTest()
        {
            InitializeComponent();
        }

        private void DocumentTest_Activated(object sender, EventArgs e)
        {
            string theDoc = "<html><body><form id='myForm'>" +
                "Enter Name: <input id='name' /></form></body></html>";
            this.webBrowser1.DocumentText = theDoc;
        }

        private void btnSubmit_Click(object sender, EventArgs e)
        {
            System.Windows.Forms.HtmlDocument doc =
                this.webBrowser1.Document;
            if (doc != null && doc.All["name"] != null &&
                doc.All["name"].GetAttribute("value").Length == 0)
            {
                System.Windows.Forms.MessageBox.Show(
                    "Please enter a name!");
            }
            else
            {
                System.Windows.Forms.MessageBox.Show("You entered: " +
                    doc.All["name"].GetAttribute("value"));
            }
        }
    }
}
```

The *DocumentTest_Activated* event handler sets the *DocumentText* property of the *WebBrowser* control. The text is a very simple HTML page that contains a form with some literal text and an input control. The input control is named *name.*

The *btnSubmit_Click* event handler gets the *Document* property of the *WebBrowser* control, which it uses to determine whether anything was entered in the *name* input control. If nothing was entered, the screen displays the message box shown in Figure 8-6.

If you enter something in the input control, the message shown in Figure 8-7 appears.

The *All* property of the *HtmlDocument* class is a collection of all *HtmlElement* objects for the document. You can also access the elements of a single form, by using the *Forms* property of the *HtmlDocument* object, which is a collection of all the forms in the document.

The *DocumentTest* example is a simple one; however, the ability to access the properties of a Web Form, as well as the actual HTML, allows you to control the Web Form in new and different ways.

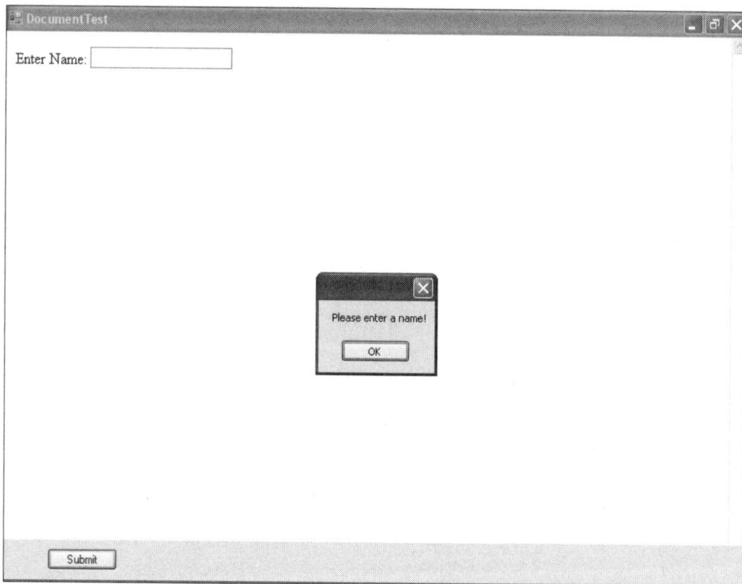

Figure 8-6 DocumentTest form showing the message box that appears when no name is entered

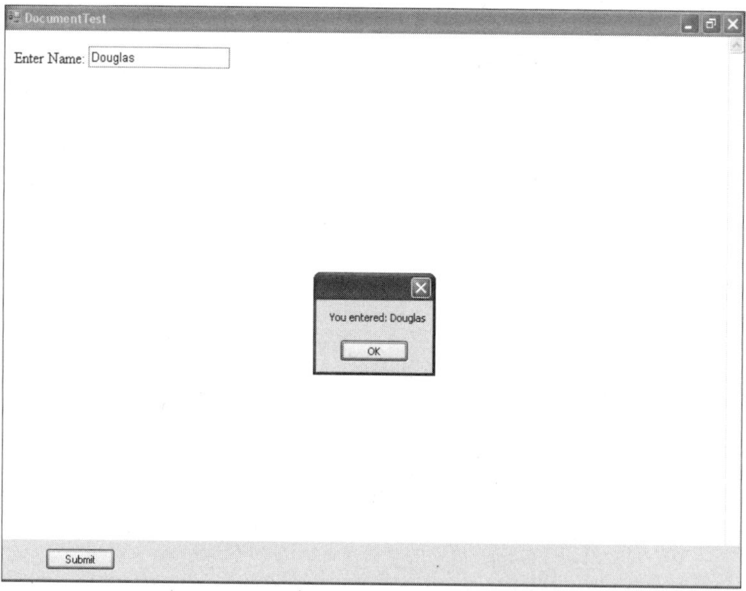

Figure 8-7 DocumentTest form showing the message box that appears when a name is entered

Other Ways to Work with Web Data

Earlier, I mentioned that you could use a *WebBrowser* control for screen scraping, a practice in which you gather the text of a Web Form and parse through it to retrieve a single value. For instance, you might use screen scraping on a search engine page to leverage the power of a search engine within the application.

In practice, there are problems with this approach. First, your code often relies on the exact layout of the page you are scraping. If the page design changes, it is possible that your code will be unable to find what it is looking for. A bigger issue is that, to retrieve a single fact from a page, the entire page must be downloaded. For example, I know of authors who have developed applications to access a Web page on a book seller's site to get the current sales rank of their book. This code retrieves a rather large page for one bit of information.

Some Web site developers recognize the value of other developers accessing their content. In some cases, Web site developers see a way to gather additional revenue, and in other cases, they expect that the increase in "mind share" among developers will help them in other areas. Seeing this, many Web sites have developed new APIs that use Web services to provide information that other developers can use within their applications. In addition to supporting Web services supplied by other vendors, ASP.NET provides good support for creating custom Web services. Web services provide a standard way for sending information from a Web server to your application. By using ASP.NET Web services, you could easily send a *DataSet* object from a Web service to your Windows Forms application.

Tip As mentioned in Chapter 5, "Data Binding", using a *DataSet* object to a Web service, or retrieving one from a Web service, may not be a practical idea. First, the overhead associated with a *DataSet* object degrades performance significantly. Also, transferring a *DataSet* ties you to .NET for both the client and for the Web service, sacrificing interoperability (a key goal when developing Web services).

Web services is a topic beyond the scope of this book. However, it is covered in the book *Building XML Web Services for the Microsoft .NET Platform*, by Scott Short (Microsoft Press, 2002).

Conclusion

The power of the Internet combined with the power of a Windows Forms application is a combination that cannot be beat. For situations that require a richer user interface than the browser can alone provide, but that still require access to information available only on the Web, using the *WebBrowser* control from a Windows Forms application can be ideal.

Appendix A

Creating and Deploying Applications in IIS

In this appendix:

Unlike earlier generations of applications, deploying Web applications in general, and ASP.NET applications specifically, does not require modifying the registry or installing Component Object Model (COM) components. However, you must still perform some administrative tasks to prepare your application to work on another machine.

Creating an Application in IIS

To process ASP.NET Web pages on the Web server through Internet Information Services (IIS), you must first create an *application* in IIS. To IIS, an application isn't just your Web code. It's a specific setting used to bring IIS internal operations into play over and above what would be required to serve simple HTML pages. To create an application in IIS, open Administrative Tools from Control Panel. From the list of administrative tools, open Internet Information Services Manager.

Note If you are using Microsoft Windows XP Professional, you might need to click Switch To Classic View in Control Panel to see the Administrative Tools option.

The dialog box should look as shown in Figure A-1.

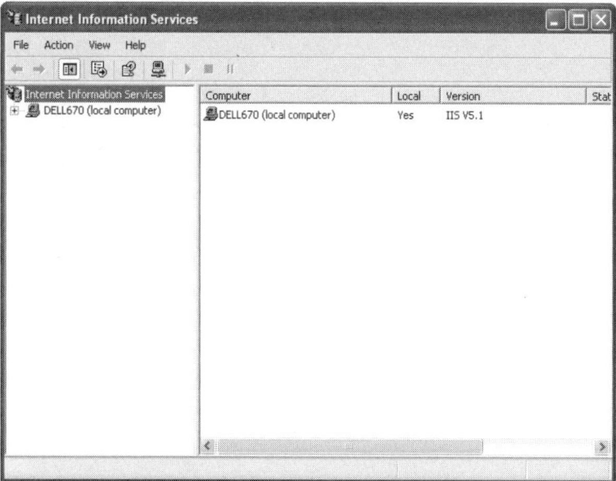

Figure A-1 The IIS Manager dialog box

In the console tree on the left, click the + sign next to the name of your computer to expand the information related to the computer. Next, expand Web Sites, and then expand Default Web Site. The resulting view will look like Figure A-2, although you might have some additional branches in your file structure.

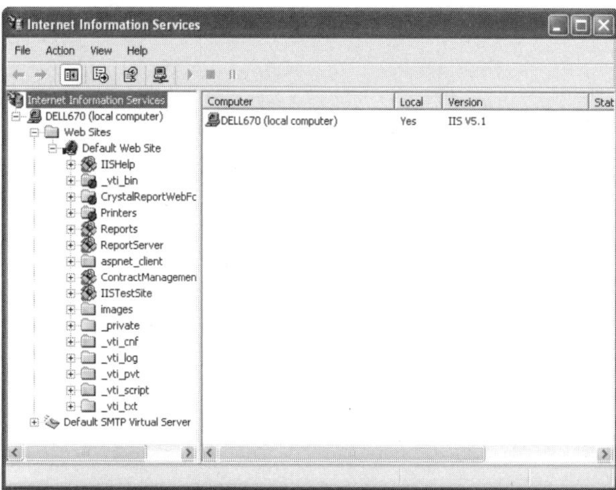

Figure A-2 The IIS Manager console tree with expanded file structure

The icons next to the folder names will vary from one operating system to another. However, any folder with a simple file folder icon is *not* set up as an application in IIS.

There is one minor problem with using IIS Manager. While you can easily convert an existing folder to an IIS application folder, there is not an obvious or convenient way to create a new folder in IIS Manager. By convention, folders in c:\inetpub\wwwroot (presuming c: is the system drive) appear in the tree view in IIS Manager. IIS applications can be placed anywhere in the file system, but it is generally easier to just create new applications in c:\inetpub\wwwroot.

To create a totally new application (folder and all) in IIS Manager, begin by right-clicking Default Web Site. On the menu that appears, click New, and then click New Virtual Folder. A wizard appears, and the first page should look like Figure A-3.

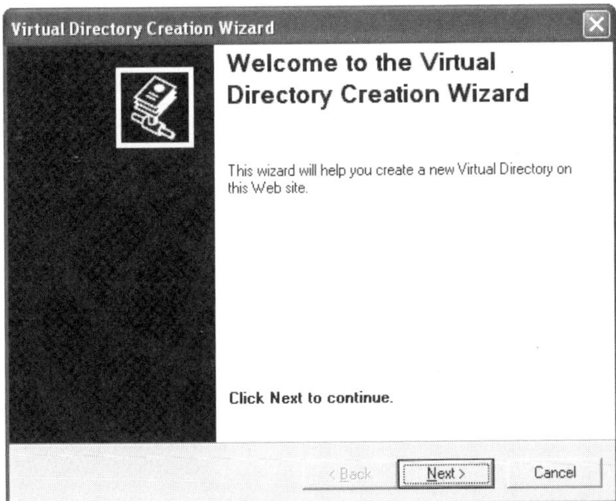

Figure A-3 The Virtual Directory Creation Wizard in IIS Manager

Click Next to see a page similar to Figure A-4.

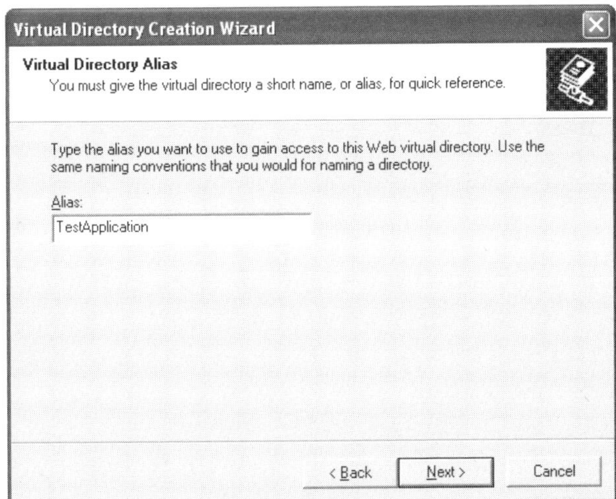

Figure A-4 The Virtual Directory Alias page

This page of the wizard asks you to name the virtual folder. The name of the folder must follow the same naming conventions as directory names. When you enter a name, make sure you can remember it. In the next step, the wizard asks for the physical directory name for the virtual folder. Keep in mind that the virtual folder name ultimately forms part of the URL for your Web pages, so choose wisely. Click Next to see a page similar to Figure A-5.

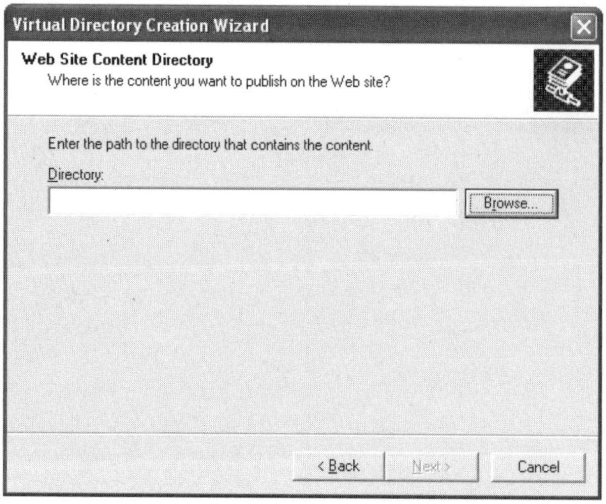

Figure A-5 The Web Site Content Directory page

On this page, you can enter the folder name directly. If you are a terrible typist like me, or if you want to create a new folder, click Browse. The resulting dialog box is a standard folder selection dialog box. Locate the wwwroot folder (remember, it will be c:\inetpub\wwwroot if Windows is installed on the c: drive). The dialog box should look like Figure A-6.

Figure A-6 The Browse For Folder dialog box

Click Make New Folder, and a new folder is created for you to rename, as shown in Figure A-7.

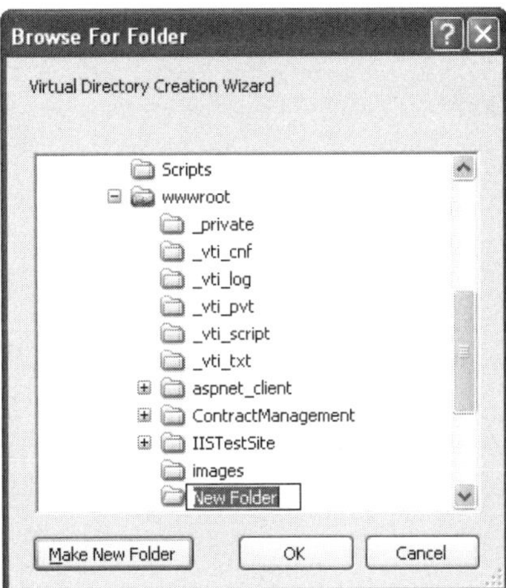

Figure A-7 Creating a new folder in the wizard

Enter the same name that you used for the virtual folder. Click OK, and then click Next. The next page is the Access Permissions page, as shown in Figure A-8.

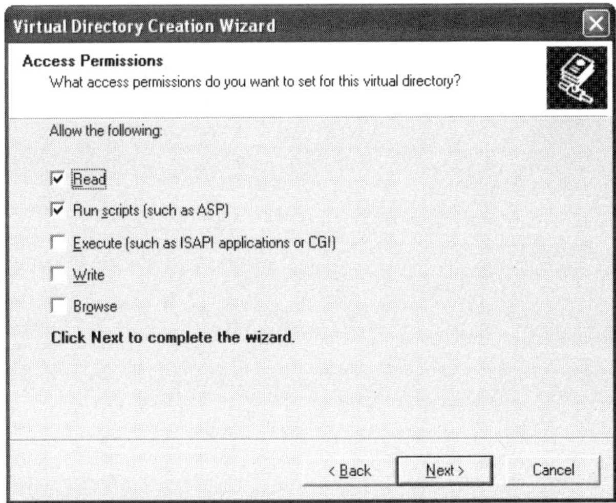

Figure A-8 The Access Permissions page

The default selection on this page is almost always adequate. The Run Scripts (such as ASP) option refers to classic ASP files, not ASP.NET. Because ASP.NET provides for compiled applications, you might think that you should select the Execute (such as ISAPI Applications Or CGI) check box, but you should not. ASP.NET is internally quite different from these technologies, so the default security should be adequate. Click Next. On the final page of the wizard, click Finish.

You should see the folder you created in the IIS Manager console tree, as shown in Figure A-9.

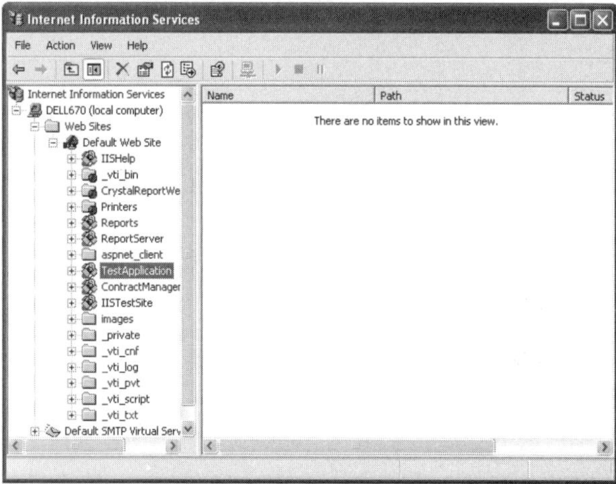

Figure A-9 IIS Manager with the new virtual application

The wizard allows you to set most of the options for the virtual folder, but not all of them. When you right-click the new folder and select Properties, the properties folder for the application appears as shown in Figure A-10.

Figure A-10 The IIS Manager virtual folder properties dialog box

It is here that you configure your virtual folder to become an IIS application if it's not already configured. If the Application Name text box is empty or disabled, the virtual directory is not configured as an IIS application. Simply click Create, and the application will be named and configured for you. If you were to close the properties dialog box now, you would see that the folder icon representing your virtual folder wasn't the typical yellow Windows folder icon, but rather a dark ball with a yellow "x" in an open box. This icon tells you that IIS has identified your virtual folder as an IIS application folder.

Before you close the properties dialog box, you might want to check some other things. For example, click Configuration on the Virtual Directory tab to open the Application Configuration dialog box, as shown in Figure A-11.

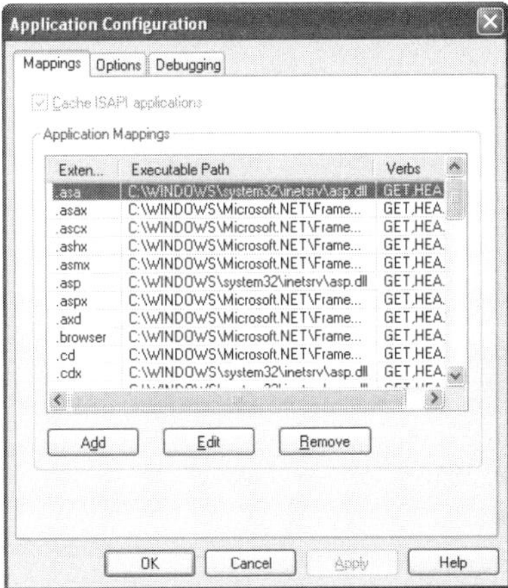

Figure A-11 The Application Configuration dialog box

The Mappings tab provides a list of file extensions, along with paths to the executables that will process files with each extension in the folder. Highlighting the .aspx extension and clicking Edit, for instance, allows you to see which executable will handle the .aspx extension. In user newsgroups, a common problem new users report is that none of their ASP.NET Web controls are rendered. If Web controls are not being rendered, a likely cause is that ASP.NET has not been installed, or the configuration for the folder is incorrect. You can explore the other tabs, and then click Cancel to exit the Application Configuration dialog box.

The ASP.NET tab allows you to control, among other things, which version of ASP.NET is used for the folder. In Figure A-12, I am using version 2.0.50215.0. If you have multiple versions of ASP.NET installed, you can select a version from the ASP.NET Version list.

Figure A-12 The ASP.NET tab in the virtual folder properties dialog box

On the Directory Security tab, click the first Edit button, and the dialog box shown in Figure A-13 appears.

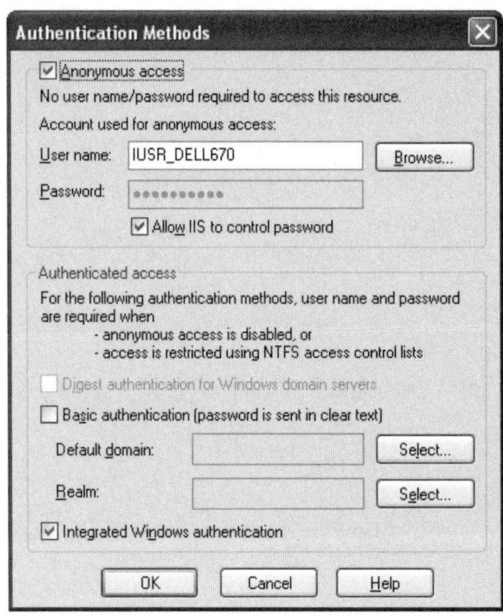

Figure A-13 The Authentication Methods dialog box

The top section of the Authentication Methods dialog box allows you to determine whether anonymous access to the virtual directory is allowed. That is, if a user tries to enter the site, and the user is not logged in to a user account recognized by the Web server, should the user be allowed in? If you select the Anonymous Access check box, users who are not recognized will be allowed into the site and will take on the identity of the user specified, generally IUSR_<*MachineName*> (in this example, IUSR_DELL670). In Classic ASP, this user had to have rights to whatever resources your ASP application needed to access. In ASP.NET, things are a little more complicated, and authentication and authorization involve a mixture of settings in IIS and in the Web.config file. Anonymous access is almost always enabled for Internet Web Forms applications. In most cases, even intranet applications are configured to allow anonymous access.

> **Note** The issue of identifying users who want to use your Web Forms application is covered in Chapter 7, along with login controls.

Deploying a Web Forms Application

After you create a Web Forms application and configure IIS, the next step is to deploy your application. You do this in one of three ways. The first option is to just copy the files from the development machine to the deployment machine. This is often called *XCopy deployment*, because the command-line XCopy utility is sometimes used for this kind of deployment. The other options are to use Microsoft Visual Studio to copy the Web site, or to create a setup program that installs the application.

Each of the following explanations assumes that your Web site will be deployed on a machine that is running IIS. I will be using the World Wide Web service for these examples.

Deploying an Application Using XCopy Deployment

When you want to deploy an application to a new server, you can often just copy the entire folder to the new server, and then create the virtual application using the methods described in the previous section. When you look at a Web application folder from your development machine, you will likely see files with .aspx, .aspx.cs, and .config file extensions. For example, Figure A-14 shows the folder with some of the sample applications used in this book.

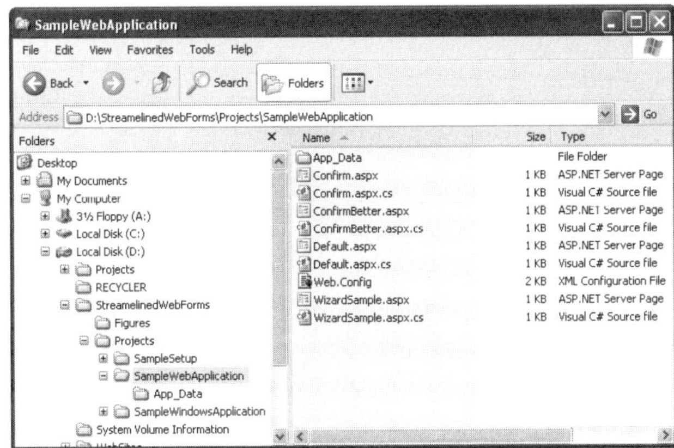

Figure A-14 The SampleWebApplication folder in Windows Explorer

Copying all files is often the simplest solution, especially after IIS is configured. The copying can take place literally using *xcopy* from the command prompt, or (more commonly) using Windows Explorer or a tool that allows File Transfer Protocol (FTP) transfers.

If you are moving the application to a server on which you do not want to deploy source code, you can precompile the application, and then deploy only placeholder files (described in a moment) and a .dll file with the compiled code. For instance, using the following line from a command prompt running on the Web server creates a compiled version of the application in the server's c:\projects\test folder.

```
ASPNET_Compiler.exe -v /SampleWebApplication c:\projects\test
```

The folder will be created if it does not already exist, with the files shown in Figure A-15. This folder need not be configured in IIS.

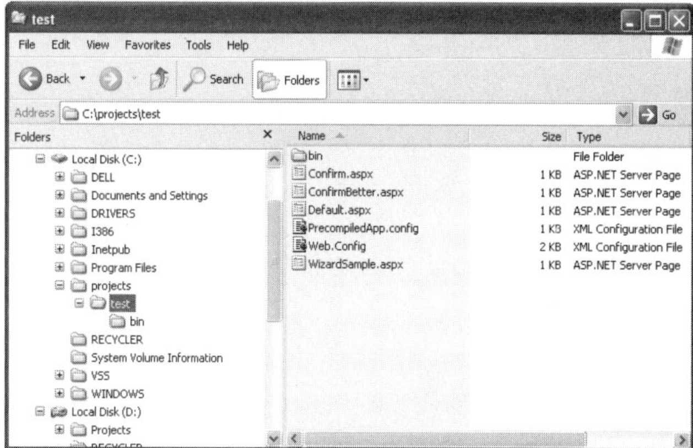

Figure A-15 The compiled version of the SampleWebApplication folder in Windows Explorer

Note that the .aspx files shown in Figure A-15 do not contain the actual markup code from our original application; they are simply placeholders so that ASP.NET knows which pages the application makes available to your users. They don't contain any markup, as you might have gathered by examining the file sizes shown in Figure A-15, which are abnormally small. The markup that was originally in the .aspx files is compiled, and files with an extension of .compiled are placed in the bin folder.

ASPNET_Compiler.exe is a program included with the .NET Framework that precompiles all files that are part of an ASP.NET application. In addition to allowing deployment of an application without source code and markup to protect your code, precompiling the application eliminates the delay that can be present when an application is accessed for the first time. An implication of compiling the pages using ASPNET_Compiler.exe is that you cannot change the markup on an .aspx file without going back to the original version of the site, editing the .aspx file, and then recompiling the site. But perhaps more importantly, the .aspx.cs files are not in the target folder specified on the command line. The bin folder contains a .dll file for the site, as well as files with an extension of .compiled for each of the .aspx files in the application. For more information, search the MSDN documentation for ASPNET_Compiler.exe.

Deploying an Application Using Visual Studio

Another option for copying an application from the development machine to another server for deployment is to use the Copy Web Site option in Visual Studio. Click Copy Web Site on the Website menu in Visual Studio to open a screen similar to the one shown in Figure A-16.

Figure A-16 shows all the files and folders in the local project on the left side of the screen. The right side is blank. To select the destination for the copy of the Web site, click Connect. You should see a dialog box similar to the one shown in Figure A-17.

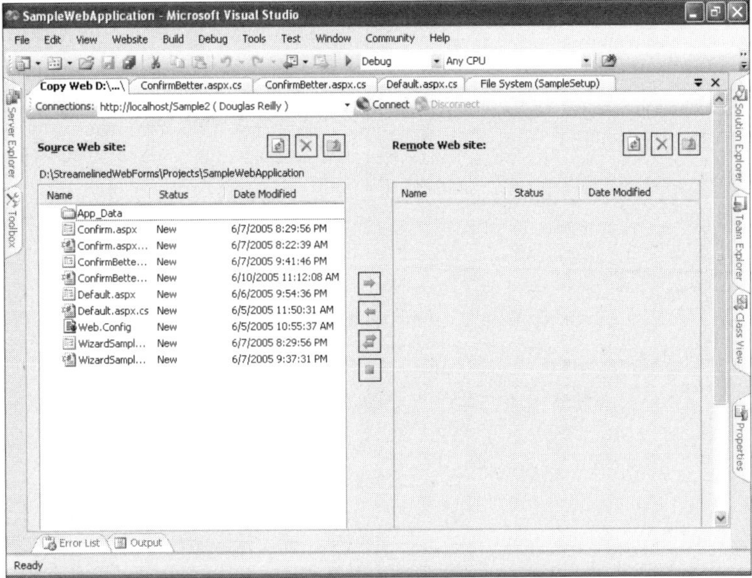

Figure A-16 The Copy Web site screen in Visual Studio

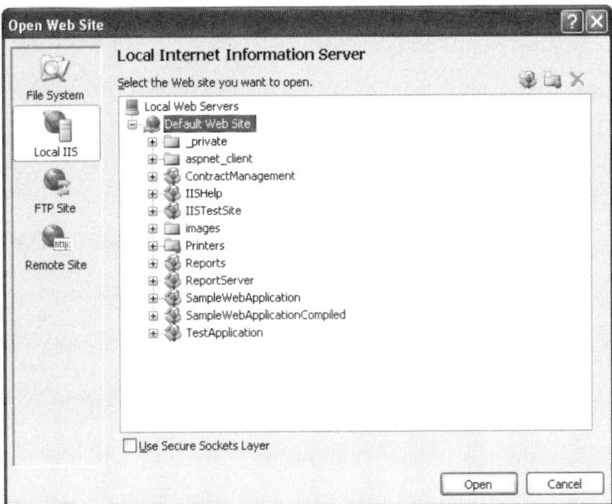

Figure A-17 The Open Web Site dialog box

The left pane of the Open Web Site dialog box allows you to copy to one of four types of destinations. The first is File System. Click File System, and you will be able to navigate to a folder on the local file system or a networked drive.

The second type of destination (and the default, presuming IIS is running on your machine) is Local IIS. Although it is not initially obvious (it was not to me), in the upper-right section of the dialog box, the left-most of the three icons allows you to create a new Web site. Click the Create New Web Application icon, and a new Web site folder appears in the tree view of the local IIS system, as shown in Figure A-18.

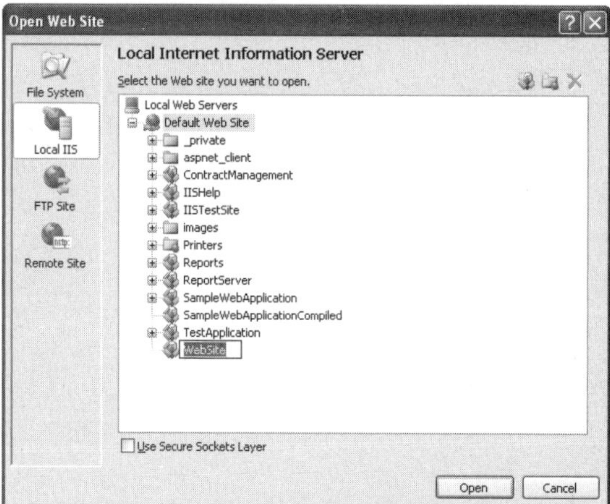

Figure A-18 Creating a new Web application in the Local IIS

This feature works like the New Folder option in Windows Explorer. Figure A-19 shows the screen that results after I change the name of the folder to Destination and click Open.

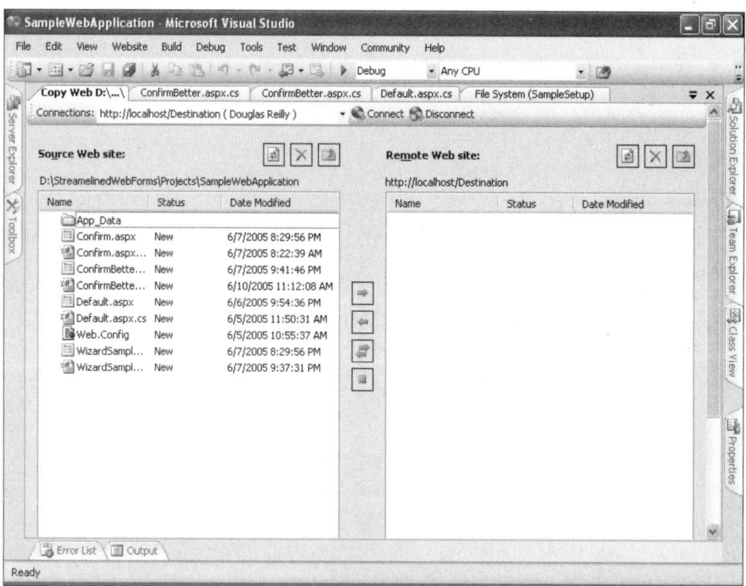

Figure A-19 Files in the Destination folder that can be copied form the source site to a remote site

Selecting all files and then clicking the right arrow button moves all selected files to the newly created virtual application on your local IIS.

If you look back at Figure A-17, you will see that below the Local IIS destination option is the FTP Site option. The FTP Site option allows you to use FTP to send files from the local machine to any server with a running FTP server that is accessible to your current machine. The final option, Remote Site, is similar to the Local IIS option, but the destination server must be running Microsoft FrontPage Server Extensions.

Deploying an Application Using a Web Setup Project

The final option for deploying a Web application is to create a setup application. On the File menu in Visual Studio, click New, and then click Project. In the dialog box that appears, expand Other Project Types, and then expand Setup And Deployment. Click the Web Setup Project template (presuming it is available to you; it may not be available in all versions of Visual Studio), and the dialog box that appears should be similar to the one shown in Figure A-20.

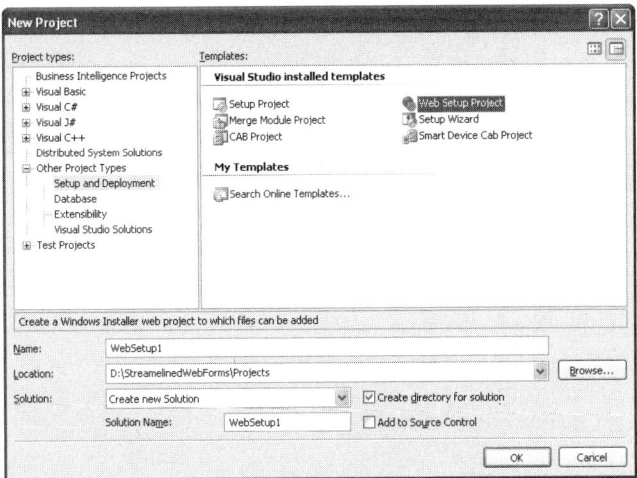

Figure A-20 The New Project dialog box, with Web Setup Project selected

In the Solution list, select Add To Solution, and then click OK. On the screen that appears (shown in Figure A-21), right-click Web Application Folder, click Add on the menu that appears, and then click Project Output.

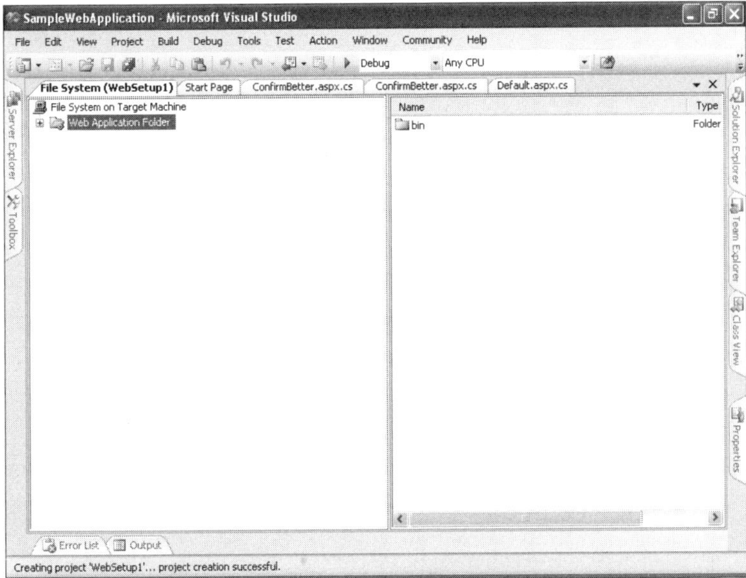

Figure A-21 The newly created Web Setup Project in Visual Studio

If the solution contains only a single Web application (as the SampleWebApplication solution does), a dialog box similar to Figure A-22 appears.

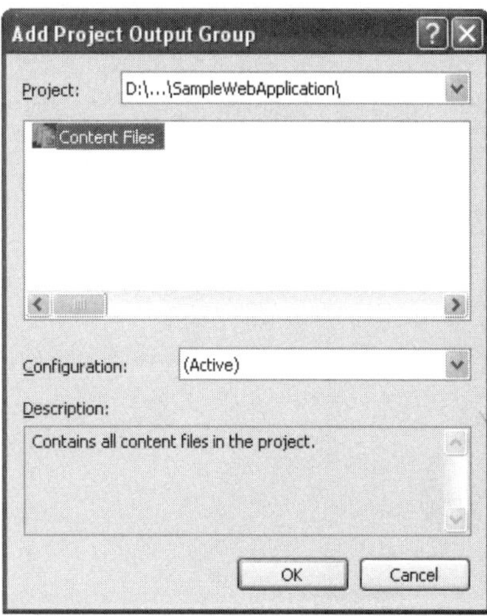

Figure A-22 Selecting project output in Web Setup Project

Click OK to add the project output to the Web setup output. On the Build menu in Visual Studio, click Build WebSetup1. The Web setup project is built, containing the output from the Web application. When you navigate to the Debug folder under the project folder, you should see the Setup.exe and WebSetup1.msi files, as shown in Figure A-23.

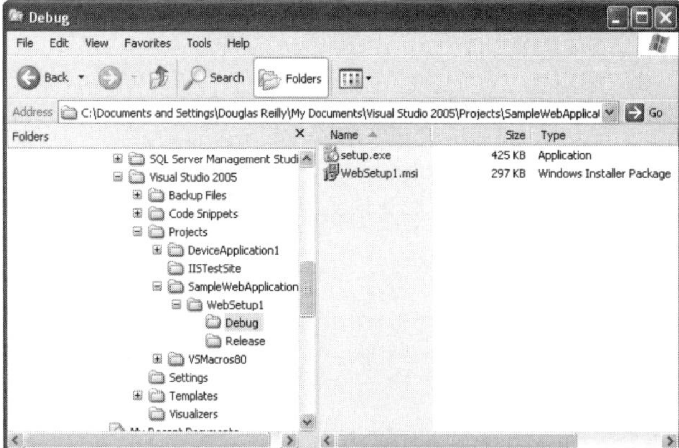

Figure A-23 The output from a Visual Studio Setup project

If you run Setup.exe, the setup program walks you through installation of the Web application. One of the screens allows you to specify the name of the virtual folder in which the Web application should be installed. The setup program creates the virtual directory in IIS. By right-clicking Web Application Folder (shown in Figure A-21) and then selecting Properties, you can specify options for the setup project, including the default name of the virtual folder used by the setup program.

Which Deployment Option Is Right for You?

Which deployment option you should use depends on a variety of factors. If you must deploy to a remote server, and the only access to that remote server is via FTP (a situation that is common when you are paying for a site on a shared server), you must either use an FTP program outside of Visual Studio or use the Copy Web Site option in Visual Studio. If the destination server has FrontPage Server Extensions installed, using the Remote Site destination in the Copy Web Site option in Visual Studio is a reasonable option. If the application must be installed by another user, who might not be familiar with ASP.NET applications, creating a Web setup program should allow a user unfamiliar with IIS to install the application. Just as important, if your application has any unusual requirements and must be installed on many different servers, the Web setup program should allow repeated installs to be performed in a consistent manner.

In many cases, becoming familiar with IIS and manually deploying the Web application might be the easiest option, in the long run.

Index

N

O

P

R

S

T

U

V

X-Z

About the Author

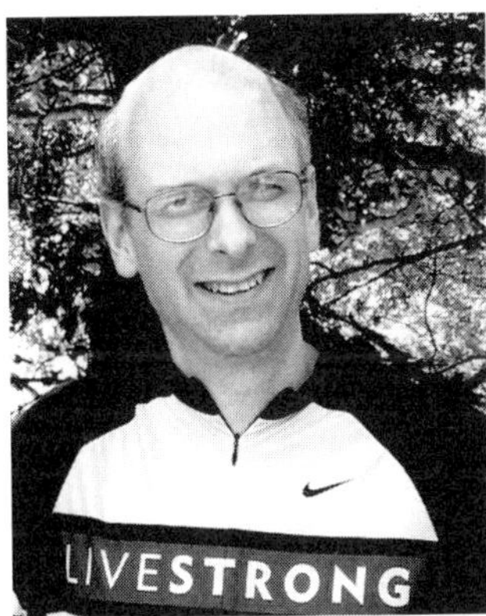

Ever since he convinced his wife to spend what seemed like far too much money on an Atari 800, Douglas J. Reilly has loved playing with computers. For many years before that, he made a living repairing photocopiers and early personal computers. After a while, the software seemed more fun to him than the hardware.

Doug is the owner of Access Microsystems Inc., a small consulting firm that develops software using Microsoft Visual C++, Borland Delphi, and of course, the Microsoft .NET Framework with C# and Microsoft Visual Basic .NET. He has created applications to test job applicants electronically, track retailers' inventory, and repair damaged databases. Currently, he is working on a variety of applications for the health care industry and for other organizations. In addition to developing software, Doug has written articles published in *Dr. Dobb's Journal* and *Software Development*. He writes a weblog for *Mobilized Software* (*http://MobilizedSoftware.com*), and he writes the *Database Geek of the Week* series of articles for *Simple Talk* (*http://www.Simple-Talk.com*). Doug also wrote the book *Designing Microsoft ASP.NET Applications* (Microsoft Press, 2002).

Doug lives with his wife, Jean, and one of his two children, Erin. His son, Tim, is a pharmacist out on his own. When not programming, Doug enjoys music, reading, and bicycle riding. Even while writing this book, he managed to get in almost 1,400 miles of bike riding during the summer of 2005.

Doug can be reached by e-mail at *doug@ProgrammingASP.NET*.

Additional Resources for Database Developers

Published and Forthcoming Titles from Microsoft Press

Microsoft® SQL Server™ 2005 Express Edition *Step by Step*

Jackie Goldstein • ISBN 0-7356-2184-5

Teach yourself how to get database projects up and running quickly with SQL Server Express Edition—one step at a time! SQL Server Express is a free, easy-to-use database product that is based on SQL Server 2005 technology. It's designed for building simple, dynamic applications, with all the rich functionality of the SQL Server database engine and using the same data access APIs such as Microsoft ADO.NET, SQL Native Client, and T-SQL. With *Step by Step*, you work at your own pace through hands-on, learn-by-doing exercises. Whether you're new to database programming or new to SQL Server, you'll learn how, when, and why to use specific features of this simple but powerful database development environment. Each chapter puts you to work, building your knowledge of core capabilities and guiding you as you create actual components and working applications. You'll also discover how SQL Server Express works seamlessly with the Microsoft Visual Studio® 2005 environment, simplifying the design, development, and deployment of your applications.

Programming Microsoft ADO.NET 2.0 Applications: *Advanced Topics*

Glenn Johnson • ISBN 0-7356-2141-1

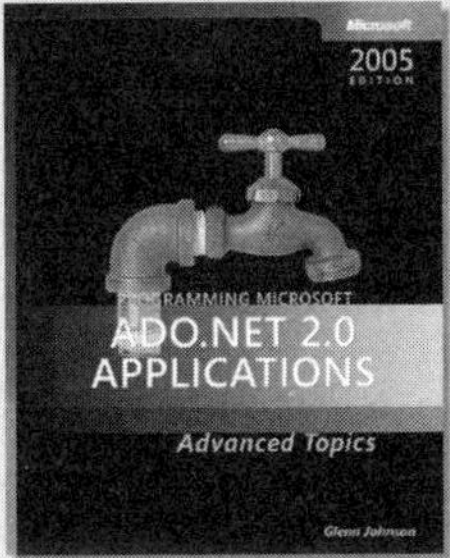

Get in-depth coverage and expert insights on advanced ADO.NET programming topics such as optimization, DataView, and large objects (BLOBs and CLOBs). Targeting experienced, professional software developers who design and develop enterprise applications, this book assumes that the reader knows and understands the basic functionality and concepts of ADO.NET 2.0 and that he or she is ready to move to mastering data-manipulation skills in Microsoft Windows. The book, complete with pragmatic and instructive code examples, is structured so that readers can jump in for reference on each topic as needed.

Microsoft ADO.NET 2.0 *Step by Step*

Rebecca Riordan • ISBN 0-7356-2164-0

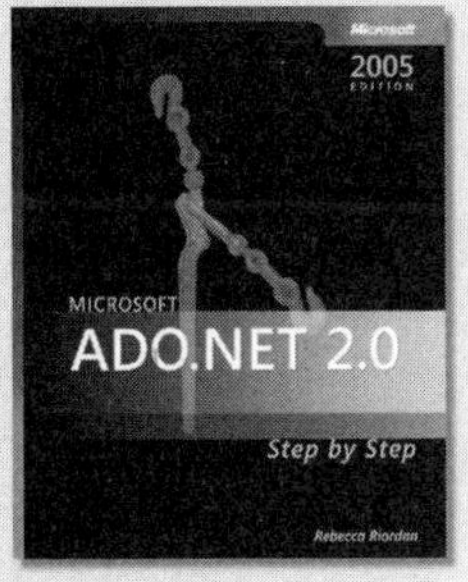

In Microsoft .NET Framework 2.0, data access is enhanced not only through the addition of new data access controls, services, and the ability to integrate more seamlessly with SQL Server 2005, but also through improvements to the ADO.NET class libraries themselves. Now you can teach yourself the essentials of working with ADO.NET 2.0 in the Visual Studio environment—one step at a time. With *Step by Step*, you work at your own pace through hands-on, learn-by-doing exercises. Whether you're a beginning programmer or new to this version of the technology, you'll understand the core capabilities and fundamental techniques for ADO.NET 2.0. Each chapter puts you to work, showing you how, when, and why to use specific features of the ADO.NET 2.0 rapid application development environment and guiding as you create actual components and working applications for Microsoft Windows®.

Programming Microsoft ADO.NET 2.0 *Core Reference*

David Sceppa • ISBN 0-7356-2206-X

This *Core Reference* demonstrates how to use ADO.NET 2.0, a technology within Visual Studio 2005, to access, sort, and manipulate data in standalone, enterprise, and Web-enabled applications. Discover best practices for writing, testing, and debugging database application code using the new tools and wizards in Visual Studio 2005, and put them to work with extensive code samples, tutorials, and insider tips. The book describes the ADO.NET object model, its XML features for Web extensibility, integration with Microsoft SQL Server 2000 and SQL Server 2005, and other core topics.

Programming Microsoft Windows Forms
Charles Petzold • ISBN 0-7356-2153-5

Programming Microsoft Web Forms
Douglas J. Reilly • ISBN 0-7356-2179-9

Inside Microsoft SQL Server 2005: The Storage Engine (Volume 1)
Kalen Delaney • ISBN 0-7356-2105-5

Debugging, Tuning, and Testing Microsoft .NET 2.0 Applications
John Robbins • ISBN 0-7356-2202-7

Microsoft SQL Server 2005 Programming *Step by Step*
Fernando Guerrero • ISBN 0-7356-2207-8

Programming Microsoft SQL Server 2005
Andrew J. Brust, Stephen Forte, and William H. Zack
ISBN 0-7356-1923-9

For more information about Microsoft Press® books and other learning products, visit: **www.microsoft.com/books** *and* **www.microsoft.com/learning**

Microsoft® Press

Microsoft Press products are available worldwide wherever quality computer books are sold. For more information, contact your book or computer retailer, software reseller, or local Microsoft Sales Office, or visit our Web site at **www.microsoft.com/mspress**. To locate your nearest source for Microsoft Press products, or to order directly, call 1-800-MSPRESS in the United States. (In Canada, call **1-800-268-2222**.)

Additional Resources for C# Developers

Published and Forthcoming Titles from Microsoft Press

Microsoft® Visual C#® 2005 Express Edition: Build a Program Now!

Patrice Pelland • ISBN 0-7356-2229-9

In this lively, eye-opening, and hands-on book, all you need is a computer and the desire to learn how to program with Visual C# 2005 Express Edition. Featuring a full working edition of the software, this fun and highly visual guide walks you through a complete programming project—a desktop weather-reporting application—from start to finish. You'll get an unintimidating introduction to the Microsoft Visual Studio® development environment and learn how to put the lightweight, easy-to-use tools in Visual C# Express to work right away—creating, compiling, testing, and delivering your first, ready-to-use program. You'll get expert tips, coaching, and visual examples at each step of the way, along with pointers to additional learning resources.

Microsoft Visual C# 2005 *Step by Step*

John Sharp • ISBN 0-7356-2129-2

Visual C#, a feature of Visual Studio 2005, is a modern programming language designed to deliver a productive environment for creating business frameworks and reusable object-oriented components. Now you can teach yourself essential techniques with Visual C#—and start building components and Microsoft Windows®-based applications—one step at a time. With *Step by Step*, you work at your own pace through hands-on, learn-by-doing exercises. Whether you're a beginning programmer or new to this particular language, you'll learn how, when, and why to use specific features of Visual C# 2005. Each chapter puts you to work, building your knowledge of core capabilities and guiding you as you create your first C#-based applications for Windows, data management, and the Web.

Programming Microsoft Visual C# 2005 Framework Reference

Francesco Balena • ISBN 0-7356-2182-9

Complementing *Programming Microsoft Visual C# 2005 Core Reference*, this book covers a wide range of additional topics and information critical to Visual C# developers, including Windows Forms, working with Microsoft ADO.NET 2.0 and Microsoft ASP.NET 2.0, Web services, security, remoting, and much more. Packed with sample code and real-world examples, this book will help developers move from understanding to mastery.

Programming Microsoft Visual C# 2005 *Core Reference*

Donis Marshall • ISBN 0-7356-2181-0

Get the in-depth reference and pragmatic, real-world insights you need to exploit the enhanced language features and core capabilities in Visual C# 2005. Programming expert Donis Marshall deftly builds your proficiency with classes, structs, and other fundamentals, and advances your expertise with more advanced topics such as debugging, threading, and memory management. Combining incisive reference with hands-on coding examples and best practices, this *Core Reference* focuses on mastering the C# skills you need to build innovative solutions for smart clients and the Web.

CLR via C#, Second Edition

Jeffrey Richter • ISBN 0-7356-2163-2

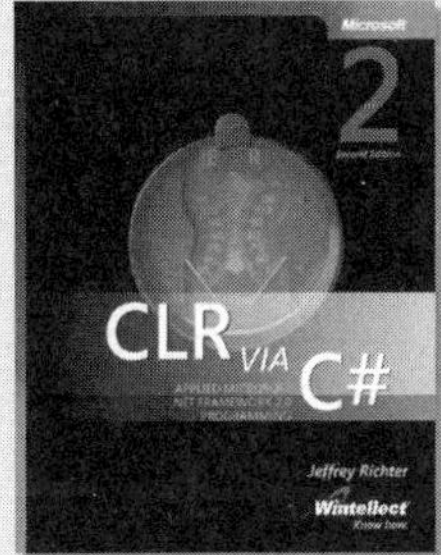

In this new edition of Jeffrey Richter's popular book, you get focused, pragmatic guidance on how to exploit the common language runtime (CLR) functionality in Microsoft .NET Framework 2.0 for applications of all types—from Web Forms, Windows Forms, and Web services to solutions for Microsoft SQL Server™, Microsoft code names "Avalon" and "Indigo," consoles, Microsoft Windows NT® Service, and more. Targeted to advanced developers and software designers, this book takes you under the covers of .NET for an in-depth understanding of its structure, functions, and operational components, demonstrating the most practical ways to apply this knowledge to your own development efforts. You'll master fundamental design tenets for .NET and get hands-on insights for creating high-performance applications more easily and efficiently. The book features extensive code examples in Visual C# 2005.

Programming Microsoft Windows Forms
Charles Petzold • ISBN 0-7356-2153-5

CLR via C++
Jeffrey Richter with Stanley B. Lippman
ISBN 0-7356-2248-5

Programming Microsoft Web Forms
Douglas J. Reilly • ISBN 0-7356-2179-9

Debugging, Tuning, and Testing Microsoft .NET 2.0 Applications
John Robbins • ISBN 0-7356-2202-7

For more information about Microsoft Press® books and other learning products, visit: **www.microsoft.com/books** *and* **www.microsoft.com/learning**

Microsoft Press products are available worldwide wherever quality computer books are sold. For more information, contact your book or computer retailer, software reseller, or local Microsoft Sales Office, or visit our Web site at **www.microsoft.com/mspress**. To locate your nearest source for Microsoft Press products, or to order directly, call 1-800-MSPRESS in the United States. (In Canada, call **1-800-268-2222**.)

What do you think of this book? We want to hear from you!

Do you have a few minutes to participate in a brief online survey? Microsoft is interested in hearing your feedback about this publication so that we can continually improve our books and learning resources for you.

To participate in our survey, please visit:
www.microsoft.com/learning/booksurvey

And enter this book's ISBN, 0-7356-2179-9. As a thank-you to survey participants in the United States and Canada, each month we'll randomly select five respondents to win one of five $100 gift certificates from a leading online merchant.* At the conclusion of the survey, you can enter the drawing by providing your e-mail address, which will be used for prize notification *only*.

Thanks in advance for your input. Your opinion counts!

Sincerely,

Microsoft Learning

Learn More. Go Further.

To see special offers on Microsoft Learning products for developers, IT professionals, and home and office users, visit: *www.microsoft.com/learning/booksurvey*

* No purchase necessary. Void where prohibited. Open only to residents of the 50 United States (includes District of Columbia) and Canada (void in Quebec). Sweepstakes ends 6/30/2006. For official rules, see: *www.microsoft.com/learning/booksurvey*